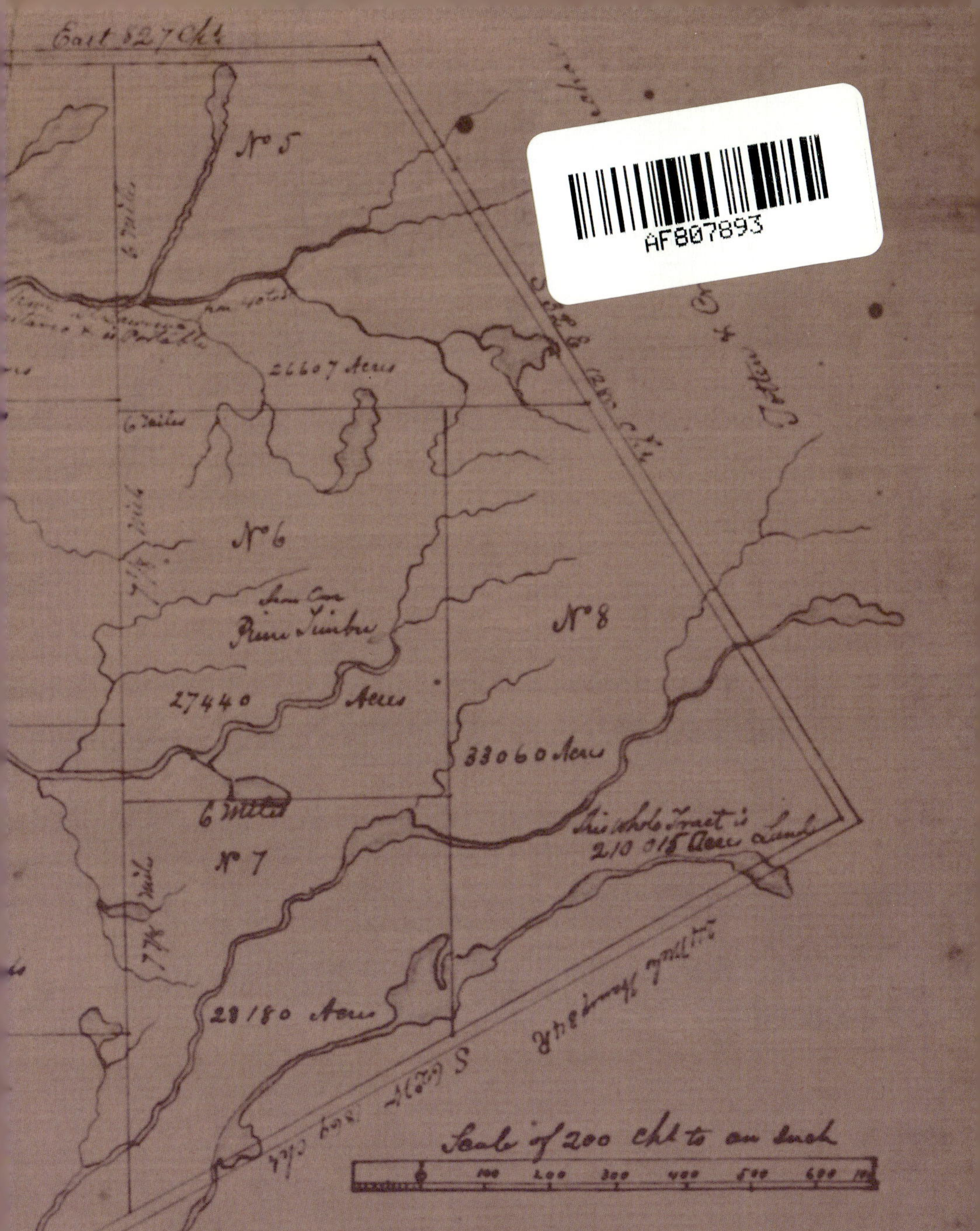

This Delineation exhibits the true Contents into which John Julius Augustine's Tract is divided as taken by actual Survey July 1796 pr Nathl Smith Surveyr

True Copy of a true Copy taken by Osgood Carleton

Danl Bell

John Brown's Tract

John Brown's Tract:

Lost Adirondack Empire

by
Henry A. L. Brown
and
Richard J. Walton
with an introduction by William G. McLoughlin

Published for
The Rhode Island Historical Society
by
Phoenix Publishing
Canaan, New Hampshire

Library of Congress Cataloging-in-Publication Data

Brown, Henry, A. L., 1931-
John Brown's tract.

Bibliography: p. 344
Includes index.
1. Adirondack Mountains (N.Y.)—History. 2. Brown, John, 1736-1803. I. Walton, Richard J. II. Rhode Island Historical Society, III. Title.
F127.A2B67 1988 974.7'5303'0924 88-9962
ISBN 0-914659-34-0

Printed in the United States of America

To my beloved parents

Francis and Susanne Brown

H. A. L. B.

For my niece

Sarah Walton

R. J. W.

Contents

Introduction

THE BROWNS of Providence cut a broad swath through early American history. They and their relatives have continued to play important roles in the history of Rhode Island and the nation. From the 1750s the Browns were a major commercial force in New England and their business connections extended to New York, Philadelphia, the West Indies, London, Africa, China in a worldwide trading system; Brown University still bears their family name as philanthropist. Perhaps the most notable, if not notorious, of the early family entrepreneurs was John Brown (1736-1803) whose chief claim to local fame was his part in the burning of the British revenue cutter, the *Gaspee*, on June 9, 1772 – a melodramatic though unlawful incident which Rhode Islanders still celebrate as the opening shot of the American Revolution. This book is about one of John Brown's best known, but less successful, efforts in business speculation. But in contains much more than the story of his famous "tract" in what we now call "the Adirondacks."

By utilizing a hitherto untapped trove of family letters, Henry A. L. Brown (a collateral descendant) and Richard Walton (a Rhode Island author who lives near Henry Brown in Pawtuxet) provide us with a fascinating portrait not only of John Brown but of some of his less well-known descendants. The book covers the period 1770 to 1850 and centers upon John Brown's effort to make money by opening up the frontier to settlement – the frontier for most New Englanders in that day being central and western New York. This was not one of the Brown family's more successful ventures. In fact, it was a serious financial failure, but that does not make it any less fascinating. Not everything the Brown family touched turned to gold. Even the rich and famous sometimes come a cropper.

The poignant and often heart-rending letters which form the basis for this story, demonstrate that the failure to develop "John Brown's Tract" did not result from lack of hard work by the descendents who inherited the 210,000 acres stretching across what are now Herkimer, Lewis and Hamilton counties, seventy-five miles northwest of Albany. From 1803 to 1850 two sons-in-law and two grandsons of John Brown strove mightily to attract settlers to an area which today is one of the great park regions of the United States — the Adirondack State Park — scene of two winter Olympics (at Lake Placid), of Theodore Roosevelt's family vacation at the Tahawus Club, and of the notorious murder at Big Moose Lake which Theodore Dreiser made famous in his novel, *An American Tragedy*. Millions of Americans visit the Adirondacks every year. It is one of the great playgrounds of the east; to have a family camp on a lake in these gorgeous mountains is to own a virtual gold mine. But John Brown and his descendants hoped to mine the region for iron ore and to cut its timber to make way for farmers who would grow "cereals" (as John Brown put it) — i.e., wheat, corn, oats, and barley. Had the family been able to keep this immense tract in its hands for another fifty years, it would have paid handsome dividends; but as these family letters indicate, those who inherited the eight townships were "land poor." They paid taxes year after year but could not persuade westward moving families to purchase, clear, and farm the land. The efforts to develop an iron manufactury at Old Forge proved most tragic of all, for the despairing son-in-law who started the forge lost his shirt and took his life.

The epistolary center of this volume is essentially the papers of John Francis, his brother Thomas Willing Francis, and their descendants. Hundreds of these family letters, diaries, account books, and business papers have been stored undisturbed for generations at Spring Green Farm in Warwick, Rhode Island. John Francis married John Brown's daughter Abby, and thus became closely connected with the men who married John Brown's other daughters — Charles Frederick Herreshoff (who married Sally Brown) and James Mason (who married Alice Brown). Some of the most interesting letters concern the courtship of these three Brown women; students of family history as well as feminist history, will find much of interest in the spritely letters of the women in the family which fill these pages. John Francis was related to Thomas Willing of Philadelphia, the president of the First Bank of the United States and one of the great financiers of the Revolutionary Era. The Browns and their in-laws knew and wrote about many of the leading figures of their day — Lafayette, Washington, Alexander Hamilton, Aaron Burr, Robert Morris, Abigail Adams, Charles Wilson Peale, Philip Livingston, the Biddles, the Lenoxes, the Byrds of Virginia. Some of the most striking letters describe scenes in Paris and London when John Francis visited Europe during the French Revolution. Though a "republican," young Francis was horrified by the crimes committed during "The Reign of Terror" in the name of "liberty, equality, and fraternity."

John Francis led his father-in-law into the purchase of the famous

Adirondack tract during a business transaction in New York in 1795, when he accepted the 210,000 acres as collateral for a purchase of China tea by a partner of Robert Morris named James Greenleaf. When Morris and Greenleaf went bankrupt two years later, ending in debtors' prison, John Brown was delighted to find himself the owner of this land which he believed to be a most valuable addition to his family fortune. He visited the tract twice before he died, had it surveyed into townships, ordered extensive road-building, made plans to sell plots to farmers, and started the search for iron and other natural resources which he was sure lay hidden in those mountains. But he died in 1803 before much headway had been made on these plans. In his will, he divided the land among his three daughters and their husbands. The letters in this volume trace the efforts of Charles Frederick Herreshoff, his son, John Brown Herreshoff, James Mason, and John Brown Francis (son of John Francis) to carry out the plans of John Brown. In essence, the book reveals the trials and tribulations of land developing during the first half of the nineteenth century – an era when speculation in western land was the very essence of American expansionism, manifest destiny, and the heroics of "Westward ho" to the shores of the Pacific. Those atttached to the positive side of "the American success myth," may not want to hear about this other side of the coin, but it is as essential to an understanding of "free enterprise" and "entrepreneurship" as the brighter side.

Those less interested in business history will find other rewards in this volume. First of all, it is an intensely personal history, for it is told in terms of the letters between husbands and wives, fathers and son, brothers and sisters who share week-by-week in the vicissitudes of the struggle to settle the eastern "West," as it were. Hopes soar, and expectations flounder; sickness, loneliness, tragedy and heartbreak are mingled with the details of land development. The dogged perserverance of the scions of John Brown is quietly heroic, and so is the patience of their long-suffering wives and children. We have these letters only because the husbands who went to the Adirondacks to tame it, left their wives and children in more comfortable homes in Rhode Island. Love and loyalty are the themes of the long, forced separations in the struggle for success against mounting odds.

Second, readers will be enlightened by new insights into the early career of John Brown and the history of the Adirondacks. Despite the magnificent research of James B. Hedges in his two-volume family history, *The Browns of Providence Plantations*, and despite the magisterial volumes of Alfred L. Donaldson, *The History of the Adirondacks*, neither of these professional historians had access to the hundreds of letters and business papers which this volume makes public for the first time. As any historian knows, there is nothing like firsthand, primary sources to alter an interpretation of historical events. Even those most familiar with the story of the Brown family and the Adirondacks are in for surprises as they read these letters and benefit from the exhaustive research by the authors.

Finally, readers will see what the actors in this story could not see. Their sense of the struggle to subdue the intractable wilderness will be heightened by the realization that the efforts of the Francises, Herreshoffs, and Masons, were doomed from the start. Most of John Brown's enormous tract was simply not viable for farming and none of it contained the rich mineral deposits expected. In fact, the land looks pretty much the same today as it did in 1795 — rugged, awesome, beautiful in summer and winter, but beyond the limits of human agriculture. The soil was too rocky and sparse, the growing seasons too short, the winters too harsh, the roads and bridges unmaintainable (there are still almost no roads through the area). Most important, there are better farming lands to the west of the tract which encouraged frontier settlers to move through and around it rather than to settle in it.

Best of all, this family story, which epitomizes so much of American history, is told in a lively, readable style which pulls the reader into the very human center of the struggle. Brown and Walton mix their own historical research with long and compelling excerpts from the letters; like a movie epic, their vision moves dexterously from the wide-angle shot to the close up, from the sweeping horizon to the tear-stained face. This is history on a very human scale. We come to know and care about those who play the major roles because they reveal so much about themselves in their letters.

For those acquainted with Rhode Island and the Brown family, this is double fascinating, but for those who simply want an emotional chunk of American history told in the words of the participants, this is equally gripping. We know how it will end, as the taxes mount and the hopes of settlement and iron manufacturing fade, but we continue to feel with the participants, that somehow, hard work, perseverance, and luck may turn the tide. This is history to be savored because it is by and about the people who made it.

William G. McLoughlin

Providence, Rhode Island
February 14, 1988

Foreword

AS A YOUNG BOY I remember my grandfather enthusiastically showing John Brown's chariot, c. 1782, to friends, neighbors, sightseers, and even my entire fifth grade class, which visited the farm on a class outing. Once the chariot was teamed up to our farm horses and driven up and down the grassy border of the lane leading to Spring Green, thus giving all the children of the family, including myself, an opportunity to ride in and enjoy their ancestor's ancient relick! Little did we realize that shortly this same carriage would be painstakingly restored and returned to the John Brown mansion in Providence by the end of the fifties.

How vividly I recall my grandfather sharing with the family the many leather bound letter books belonging to our ancestors. One of particular interest told of John Francis' trip to France in 1792, which my grandfather had transcribed and typed, making it easily read. On Sunday afternoons we could read John Francis' travel journals or his letters of endearment to his betrothed Abby, the eldest daughter of John and Sarah Brown.

My parents were also extremely fascinated with the old family accounts. Once father was asked to speak about Francis' eyewitness account of the bloody French Revolution. He related the young American's intense descriptions of the mob storming and burning the Tuilleries, and the massacre of the Swiss Guard. Francis viewed with horror lifeless corpses heaped at the feet of the Virgin Mary at the Royal Chapel, where only three days before he witnessed the King and Queen at prayer.

These true-to-life stories and adventures, etched into my mind at such an early age, made me grow very fond of my ancestor, John Francis. Years later, I heard stories about Francis betraying John Brown, now his business partner and father-in-law, by gambling away a valuable cargo for a 210,000 acre tract of land with an imperfect title located in the wilderness of northern New York. It was very difficult for me to believe this, so I searched for and found no satisfactory account of John Francis' life. One publication entitled "In Search of Cahoone, The Diary of John Francis," printed in 1969, added new dimension but did not fully tell the story. I then decided to attempt the task myself! I started with the material of his devoted mother, Anne Willing Francis, first compiling it chronologically, then transcribing and finally having it reviewed for accuracy by my mother.

In the summer of 1970 Susanne, my mother, invited our cousins, Clarence Herreshoff and Louise D'Wolf of Bristol, for tea. Here was an opportunity for me to explain my quest, and share my discoveries. Clarence was extremely interested in the project and added that his ancestor, Charles Frederick Herreshoff, also a son-in-law of John Brown, had been unfairly pictured by earlier writers! I gladly volunteered to undertake the task of vindicating his ancestor as well as mine. Soon after our visit, Clarence forwarded copies of engineering drawings of forge parts, hammer, anvil and trip, which he compiled on a trip to our ancestral land at Old Forge, New York.

That summer we were invited to visit a cousin, Jean Kane Foulke Dupont, on Block Island. I discussed my project with her and discovered that she was the great, great granddaughter of Thomas Willing Francis, the brother of John Francis. She supplied me with early documents relating to the Francis genealogy.

Albert Klyberg, then the newly appointed director of the Rhode Island Historical Society, produced copies of John Brown's correspondence covering more than thirty years. This, however, was only the beginning, for slowly over the next decade he led me to untapped sources of historical data.

By 1983 I had amassed a significant amount of historical documentation, enough so that I felt it was time to move forward! Fortuitously, living in nearby Pawtuxet Village, was a friend and neighbor, Richard J. Walton, a very talented and experienced writer, whom I enlisted to review my research. His reaction was extremely positive and we enthusiastically started writing this book. Over the eighteen months we worked together, producing a manuscript in June of 1985.

I am glad to acknowledge and record my indebtedness to the following while apologizing to any whose names I may have inadvertently omitted: Gordon H. Allen; Mrs. Clarence Benedict; Eleanor Fair Brown; Francis H. Brown Jr.; John Francis Brown Jr.; Susanne R. L. Brown; George R. Cataldo; the late Mrs. E. Paul Dupont of Montchain, Delaware; Arthur Einhorn; Paul S. Eno; Thelma M. Erbin; Craig A. Gilborn; Joan L. Gordon; Arlene S. Hall; Halsey C. Herreshoff; Anne Hintenlang; Marion Holmes; Elizabeth F. Brown Holton; Samuel Hough; Ilse E. Kramer; Marc D. Klimek; Livingston Lansing; Mildred S. Longo; Judge Robert J. Lynch; Irene M. Marks; Marie G. McCue; Judy Meekins; Dorothy O'Brien; Judge

John S. Parker; Hazel C. Patrick; Jerold Pepper; James S. Pitcher; Douglas M. Preston; Toni Risoli; Kit Rodman; F. O. Rose 3rd; Nancy S. Rose; Charles B. Round, M. D.; Nancy Sepi; the late Evelyn Scott; Brenda H. Shaw; Nathaniel Shipton; Jane Spellman; Sally Szijarto; Mary Teal; Louise Francis Terrett; Alfred Ward.

I have received much generous assistance from many societies, libraries and institutions, particularly the following: The Rhode Island Historical Society and Library; Oneida Historical Society; John Carter Brown Library; John Hay Library; Adirondack Museum; Herkimer County Historical Society; Herkimer County Clerk's Office; New York State Library; Historical Society of Pennsylvania; Webb Historical Society; Lewis County Historical Society; Lewis County Surrogate; Lewis County Clerk's Office; Lowville Free Library; *Journal and Republican* of Lowville; *Boonville Herald & Adirondack Tourist*; Burke Library of Hamilton College.

My final debt remains to be recorded to very special assistance from my mother Susanne R. L. Brown, Albert T. Klyberg, Norman Herreshoff, Ted Comstock, Sarah C. Comstock, and A. Richard Cohen.

To my wife Ann, and to my sons William and Daniel, I have to say that this book depended upon them far more than they imagined, and not least their calm assumption that it would actually get written.

Henry A. L. Brown

Warwick, Rhode Island
March 25, 1988

John Brown's Tract

I

The Background

1

In the Beginning

This tract is still almost an unbroken wilderness, and in common parlance, the term "Brown's Tract" has come to be used as a general designation of the whole of the great wilderness of Northern New York.

Franklin B. Hough, 1872[1]

LONG AFTER the vast expanse of the American West had been explored, the great northern wilderness of New York State was largely unknown even though its southern reaches were less than fifty miles north and northwest of Albany which, at the head of navigation on the Hudson River, was from earliest colonial times one of the most important commercial and transportation centers in the new nation.

Why this immense wilderness—"wild lands" they called them in early days—took on the name "John Brown's Tract" no one now can say for sure. The name "Adirondacks," now so familiar, was not even suggested until after 1837 and took decades to reach common acceptance. Probably it was because John Brown, with two generations of his descendants, was the first to try to tame this cold, stubborn land. It was and is a stubborn land but so too were John Brown and those of his family who followed him onto the tract: his German immigrant son-in-law, Charles Frederick Herreshoff, whose name became famous when later generations became America's greatest sailboat builders; his grandson, John Brown Francis, later Governor of Rhode Island and United States Senator; and another grandson, John Brown Herreshoff.

This is in one sense a tragic story, for the Brown family failed utterly and with great human cost. Yet had John Brown succeeded, later genera-

John Brown (1736-1803). This miniature by Edward Greene Malbone is the only likeness known to exist.

tions might never have had the Adirondack Forest Preserve, an immense tract larger than the State of Massachusetts that, by mandate of the New York State Constitution, remains "forever wild." In those early days conservation was unknown, for everyone assumed that the nation's resources were limitless and could be freely used to meet man's immediate wants. There was, so it seemed, always plenty. But the failure of John Brown and his family, who paid in human as well as financial terms, preserved for future generations an area to fish and hunt in and, most importantly, in which they can immerse themselves in a natural setting as it has existed since the great glaciers moved inexorably across North America, an experience that in urban and technological America is beyond price.

The failure of John Brown's labors served to discourage other efforts at development. Although there was some rapacious lumbering later, the great wilderness survived until it could be saved by the conservationist movement nearly a century later.

The John Brown who tried to tame this inhospitable land was not, as is often thought, the John Brown whose "body lies a moulderin' in the grave." That John Brown's grave is in the lovely Adirondack town of North Elba, where he lived for a time trying to help a group of runaway slaves make a go of their settlement on land donated by a wealthy abolitionist, Gerrit Smith. Well-meaning Smith certainly was, but the grudging land and bitter winters hardly constituted the best place to settle blacks from the South. When the settlement inevitably failed, that John Brown left for Kansas where, with his sons and some others, he made the fiery raids on slaveholders' property that made him an imperishable figure in American history.

The John Brown of our story was one of the famous four brothers of Providence, Rhode Island: Nicholas, Moses, John and Joseph—"Nick, Moe, John and Joe." They, singly and collectively, constituted one of the great merchant families of the colonial and federal periods. Nicholas was a prudent merchant and manufacturer. Moses, a passionate abolitionist, was largely instrumental in the establishment of the textile industry in Rhode Island, and thus New England and the United States. A well-known preparatory school in Providence bears his name. Joseph, the least commercial-minded of the four, was also a man of science and a gifted architect, Among his many fine buildings are the John Brown house, his brother's "most magnificent mansion," and the First Baptist Church of America (1774) whose slender, graceful spire has been admired by students of architecture for more than two centuries. He also taught at Rhode Island

College which later, because of the four brothers' benefactions, took the name Brown University, one of the oldest and most highly regarded universities in the United States.

John Brown was an impulsive man given to direct action. He was one of the men (some historians say he was the leading spirit) who organized and carried out what was probably the first blow struck in the American Revolution. In June 1772, a year and a half before the more famous Boston Tea Party, a British revenue schooner, the *Gaspee,* was pursuing an American vessel suspected of trying to avoid His Majesty's taxes. The American captain, who knew the waters of Narragansett Bay, lured the British ship onto a sandbar off what is now known as Gaspee Point. That evening patriots, tax evaders the British called them, gathered in Providence coffee houses and decided to take action. Later that night (on June 9/10) the Rhode Islanders, John Brown among them, rowed out to the *Gaspee* with their oarlocks muffled and burned the ship to the waterline. This book was written on the Spring Green Farm that John Brown bought eleven years later, overlooking the bay only a few hundred yards from where the *Gaspee* was set afire.

If their willingness to take direct, even violent, action constituted a similarity between the two John Browns, there was an even greater difference. Our John Brown, one of the most venturesome shipowners of the period, took part in the slave trade well after most New England shipowners had abandoned it. He eventually abandoned it more because it was unprofitable than because of moral scruples and the constant lecturing of his brother Moses on the subject of "that unrighteous traffic." Moses was a Quaker and was one of New England's most dedicated abolitionists. Indeed, when John Brown served in Congress in 1800, he defended the slave trade in the House of Representatives.[2]

To tell the story of John Brown's Tract, we must look briefly at the land itself and its history before he, by a characteristic persistence, obtained title to the land, an act against which he was cautioned and which his heirs must often have rued.

If, for man, character is fate, for land it is geography. Man, for all his skill at exploiting, even despoiling, the land can do only so much. For a century man presumed to make of Brown's Tract, and of the entire Adirondacks region, something it was not – a land to be exploited. There was timber and much of it was cut ruthlessly. Enormous areas were laid waste with total disregard for the future. But even the insatiable appetite for lumber and for charcoal to process iron ore could not consume the

The burning of the British revenue cutter "Gaspee" as painted in 1892 by Charles DeWolf Brownell.

trackless forests as, gradually, the conservation movement of the later 1800's saved the Adirondacks as a place where man could refresh his soul, as a watershed for the growing populations to the south and, through biological processes, as a provider of pure air.

The plow, however, was a greater threat to the forests than the axe and here nature was adamant. To be sure, trees could be cut and the stumps laboriously wrenched out by teams of oxen. But the soil was sparse and only grudgingly gave nourishment to crops. Nor was that the only handicap. The Adirondacks region is almost entirely mountain and plateau. Even the plateaus have short growing seasons and frost is possible even in summer. In living memory, only August has not recorded snow and winter is long and bitter. In the early days only the hardy, or the foolhardy, would even try to survive, for one was trapped in the winter. Food was scanty and monotonous. Before electricity, it was difficult to read because of the long winter nights even if one had more than the Bible and a few other books. Travel was difficult and the outside air cruelly cold. Neighbors were few and even those were likely to be many miles away. Boredom and depression were surely the common lot of those few who dared the winters.[3] And the "inexhaustible" veins of iron ore that many thought would bring them riches turned out to be inferior and very few manufacturing ventures succeeded.

For centuries the land was unoccupied. The Indians, Iroquois and Adirondacks, fished and hunted and travelled through the beautiful silent forests by canoe on lakes numerous beyond counting. They fought over it but no traces of permanent Indian settlements have been found in the Adirondacks, leading one to conclude that they, unlike the European settlers, quickly recognized that it was a fine place to visit but not to live. They used the area as a resort for hunting and fishing, a sensible use that was not adopted by the white man until the time of the Civil War.

About the only permanent thing left behind by the Indians was the name for, since they did not despoil the land, little marked their passage. An early (1616) Dutch map of the area called it Ir-o-coi-sia, an obvious reference to the Iroquois who were the dominant tribe in the region. But the name that stuck, although not used for more than two centuries, was the derisive name "Ha-de-ron-dah," which in the guttural accents of the Iroquois sounded to white traders like "Adirondack." The powerful Iroquois applied the name, which means "eater of trees," to the Montagnais branch of the Algonquins, a traditional foe. The Montagnais were not agriculturists, supporting themselves entirely by hunting and fishing. When fortune was bad, they resorted to gnawing on twigs and roots until a better day arrived.

For decades the entire region was known as Brown's Tract, or the Wilderness, or the Northwoods. The name Adirondacks was introduced by a New England geologist, Professor Ebenezer Emmons, who was doing a geological survey of the region authorized by the New York State legislature. In 1837 he scaled the highest mountain in the region, which he tactfully called Mt. Marcy for William L. Marcy, then serving his third term as governor. The following year he submitted a report to the legislature calling the entire region the "Adirondacks Range" after the Montagnais. It was one of the rare times when the losers were remembered and the victors forgotten. Who but a few scholars know, or care, that the Iroquois name was "Couchsachrage." It took decades, until about 1875, for the term Adirondack to become the accepted name.[4]

No one knows who was the first white man to see the Adirondacks. Perhaps it was the great French explorer Jacques Cartier who entered and named the St. Lawrence on August 10, 1535, the saint's feast day. More than a year later he journeyed west to the Indian village that one day would be the great city of Montreal. Surely he would have climbed the hill later named Mount Royal and gazed in all directions. To the south, across the great St. Lawrence River, if it were a clear autumn day, he could have seen 70 miles distant and blue against the horizon, the mountains that

Professor Emmons named 300 years later. But one cannot even speculate who might have been the first white man to set foot in the region. Whoever it was, there's a good chance he was one of the intrepid *coureurs de bois,* the French-Canadians who penetrated the forests in search of the furs on which France based its American empire.[5]

The next European account we have is three-quarters of a century later when another French explorer was establishing what was called New France, of which he became the Governor-General. On his third voyage to American in 1608, Samuel de Champlain founded the City of Quebec. At Quebec, while sitting around the campfires with his Indian allies, he heard wonderful stories of an inland sea to the south in the land of the dreaded Iroquois. As soon as the melting snows of spring permitted, Champlain ventured south with only two French companions and 60 Indians – Hurons, Algonquins, and Montagnais – hereditary enemies of the Iroquois. In July they reached "the wilderness sea of the Iroquois" and within a few days the inevitable happened. The Iroquois and their enemies confronted each other in battle. Champlain, who had been concealed, suddenly appeared in the front lines clad in armor and bearing an arquebuse, an early firearm. The Iroquois were astonished by this glittering apparition and before they could overwhem Champlain and his Indian allies by the weight of numbers, he opened fire as did the other Frenchmen. Their weapons spat fire and smoke, made thunderous noise, and felled the Iroquois with leaden balls. Brave as they were, the Iroquois were terrified by these strange and deadly weapons. They turned and fled and from that day on became the sworn enemies of the French. They became allies of the British in the French and Indian Wars that for decades brought death and savagery to the silent forests of the North. The lake, of course, was what became known as Lake Champlain, an eastern boundary of the Adirondacks.[6]

In 1609, the same year that Champlain forever alienated the Iroquois, Henry Hudson discovered the great river that bears his name. Explorers pushed north along the river from the great natural harbor of New Amsterdam (New York) and thus a trading post was established at the head of navigation, stockaded against surprise attacks by Indians. This was about 1614 and it was called Fort Orange.

For more than a century and a half this beautiful, silent and largely unoccupied land was the scene of sporadic but bloody battles between the tribes of the Iroquois confederation and the tribes in French Canada, often at the instigation of the white man. All during these years Catholic missionaries endeavored to make peace among the Indians, but often they were victims of the Indians on one side or the other. Now these lands had a value to English and French, greater even than the territorial claims of empire—the beaver. Beaver hats became the rage in Europe and these gentle builders of dams were ruthlessly pursued. In 1635 alone, 14,891 beaver skins were shipped from Albany. White trappers, many of whom must have perished alone in the forests, sought the beaver and so too did the Indian, for the forests were his home. Beaver skins could be traded to the French at Montreal or the English at Albany. In 1689 three beaver skins fetched a gun, four skins brought eight pounds of powder or forty pounds of lead for bullets. And each beaver skin was worth a quart of rum.[7] So valuable were the beavers that they were trapped almost to extinction. By the time of the Civil War the population of many thousands had dwindled to an estimated one hundred or so. By 1895 the figure was put at only ten. The species seemed doomed. But then a public outcry was raised and, early in this century at Old Forge, which occupies a central place in our story, the state released some beavers imported from Yellowstone National Park. Private persons also released some, a total of forty or so. By 1915 the number of beavers was conservatively put at 15,000 to 20,000. Obviously beavers did not spend all their time building dams.

The threads of the story of John Brown's Tract start to come together very early in the 18th century. In 1710 Tench Francis, the young son of The Very Rev. John Francis, Dean of the Anglican Cathedral of Linsmore, Ireland, was notified that, for whatever reason, he could not have a summer vacation but must remain at school. His response was to slip away and ship on a vessel bound for the Choptank River in eastern Maryland. The day after his arrival, according to a family account, he obtained a small boat and was fishing for crabs on what turned out to be the estate of Benjamin Peck, a leading lawyer in Talbot County. Peck noticed the boy and went out to talk to him. Quickly he discerned from Francis' speech and manner that he was not an ordinary seaman. He instructed the boy to go to his house and said he would arrange his discharge from the ship, for he knew the captain well.

Indeed, much of our story resembles a costume soap opera, for all three of John Brown's daughters had, as we shall see, unfortunate marriages of a kind that would make likely grist for the mills of present-day afternoon television. The rest reads like one of those romantic novels so popular these days. Young Francis, who by letter notified his family in Ireland of his fate, studied law with Peck and wooed and won Elizabeth Turbutt, a belle of Talbot County who had many admirers:

. . . . it is related that at the wedding when the clergyman read the portion of the service where it says, "If anyone knows just cause or impediment why these two should not be lawfully joined together, let him now speak or else hereafter hold his peace," the bridegroom . . . turned round and glared at the congregation with his hand on his sword, ready to draw it, if anyone should so far presume.[8]

Tench Francis and his family moved to Philadelphia, where he became a leading attorney and eventually Attorney-General of Pennsylvania. He established a family that has remained prominent in Pennsylvania and Maryland to this day. Among his grandchildren were Tench Tilghman, a colonel in the Revolutionary army who was an aidé-de-camp to George Washington; William Tilghman, Chief Justice of Pennsylvania; Elizabeth Lawrence, whose daughter Elizabeth married James Allen, son of the famous Chief Justice William Allen, one of the most prominent men in Pennsylvania history (their daughter Ann Penn, in an extraordinary irony that will become apparent later, married James Greenleaf.) Another of Tench Francis' daughters, Margaret, married Chief Justice Edward Shippen, a member of perhaps the most prominent Philadelphia family of that era. But most important to our history is the birth in 1730 of Tench Francis the Younger. Not only as a prominent merchant did Tench the Younger establish close financial and personal ties with the Brown Brothers of Providence, but he was the father of John Francis, who as son-in-law and business partner of John Brown, obtained a mortgage on what became the legendary John Brown's Tract. Another son of Tench the Younger was Thomas Willing Francis, a prominent merchant who also plays a leading role in the middle stages of the narrative. Thus it is that a prominent Philadelphia family joins a prominent Providence family in a drama that is played out in the remote wilderness of northern New York State.[9]

But while Tench Francis' family was providing the material that has interested genealogists for decades, events were unfolding in the North Country that would significantly influence our story. In 1724 Cadwallader Colden, surveyor general of New York, said that the north provided "such a scene of inland Navigation as cannot be paralleled . . . " and others were discussing a link between the Great Lakes and the Hudson River and thus the Atlantic. The goal was to divert the trade, actual and potential, of what was then considered the West, through Albany and New York rather than through the French cities of Montreal and Quebec via the St. Lawrence River.[10] It became an article of faith that canals would be the economic solution for the Brown's Tract.

During these same decades the mighty struggle between Britain and France was being waged not only in Europe but, with fierce Indian allies, in the forests and fields between the Mohawk and St. Lawrence rivers. The struggle swung back and forth between the French based at Montreal and the British at Fort Orange (Albany), which they had seized from the Dutch in 1644. The prize: the rich fur trade and the water route along Lake Champlain and Lake George. For a while it seemed as if the eastern Adirondacks would become French, for they built a fort at a strategic point — Ticonderoga. But in 1759 the British under Lord Geoffrey Amherst ended two years of conflict in which Indian massacres were common. To the martial skirl of bagpipes, the Scots of the Black Watch Regiment five times threw themselves against the ramparts of Fort Ticonderoga and five times were thrown back by the French. Then Amherst turned his artillery on the fort. It took a terrible toll, causing the French to blow up their powder magazine and flee north. That same year saw one of the pivotal battles of history, that on the Plains of Abraham just outside Quebec City, in which the British wrested from the French the great North American empire that stretched from Canada down the Mississippi all the way to New Orleans.

With peace the royal governor at Albany wanted to attract people to a frontier that for the first time in decades seemed open to settlement. Veterans were offered land grants — 5,000 acres for officers, only 100 for privates. A few New Englanders came to clear land but many others sold their warrants to speculators in Boston and New York. Already, speculation in wild lands, which enriched a few and ruined many, was beginning to reach fever pitch.[11] But there was insufficient time between the end of the war between the British and the French and the beginning of the American Revolution for land speculation to reach the ruinous fever that would characterize the years immediately after the Revolution.

While the course of empire was being decided in the North Country, other threads of our story were beginning to gather. In 1736, John Brown was born, a great-grandson of Chad Browne, the preacher-surveyor who had joined the colony at Providence soon after it was established by Roger William a century before the child's birth. John, along with his brothers Nicholas, Moses and Joseph (their father James had died on a voyage to Chespeake Bay) came under the commercial tutelage of their Uncle

Obadiah Brown. He was one of the leading merchants in the then small town of Providence which had not yet reached the commerical stature of its rival Newport. He trained them well and the four Brown brothers became one of the great merchant families of the colonial and post-revolutionary periods. They were engaged in just about everything—shipping to the West Indies and later the Orient, the manufacture of spermaceti candles, the manufacture of iron and rope, the distilling of rum and gin, the slave trade, the import/export of molasses, rum, foodstuffs, cider, potatoes, even cannons and surgical instruments. Like all Rhode Island merchants, they had to be imaginative, for the tiny state had very little in the way of resources and had to import almost everything it exported, rather like Japan in the modern world.

Successful they were but the Browns were chronically short of hard cash and some essential products (like spermaceti oil necessary for their profitable candle business) could not be obtained by barter. The Nantucket whalers demanded cash and got it. Thus the Brown family needed correspondents who would sell their goods and advance the cash. Boston was nearby, but its business was much the same as Rhode Island's so it was not a good market. The Brown family turned for a "settled correspondent" to Philadelphia, a good market. In 1756 Obadiah Brown chose Tench Francis the Younger. During the Revolution, Francis was a colonel of a Pennsylvania militia unit and one of twenty-seven Friendly Sons of St. Patrick in June 1780 to subscribe money to support Washington's impoverished army. The Browns sent the sloop *Charming Molly* back and forth between Providence and Philadelphia. On all goods he sold, Francis received the standard 5 percent commission, and on all money he advanced in anticipation of sales he received 6 percent interest. In effect, Francis was their banker as well as their sales agent. He was also their friend and advisor, keeping them informed as to business conditions, arranging for their insurance, even handling their litigation in the courts of Pennsylvania and England.

> *Over and above his strictly business functions for which he exacted business fees, the faithful correspondent in his capacity as friend and advisor, performed many acts of kindness for his principal, for which he expected no compensation. In his old age Tench Francis could still recall with satisfaction the pleasant relations which had always prevailed between the two houses. . . .*[12]

This warm relationship continued until Francis retired in 1768. The Browns, reluctantly one feels sure, had to choose another Philadelphia firm, Clement Biddle and Company, another name that has remained prominent to this day.

These years also saw the introduction of names that would later be important to this chronicle. In 1757 in Philadelphia, Thomas Willing and Robert Morris formed what was probably the most important trading firm in the nation – Willing and Morris. Thomas Willing, uncle of John Francis and Thomas Willing Francis, was one of the preeminent figures in the early financial history of the nation. He was chairman of the Pennsylvania delegation to the Second Continental Congress, he was a leading figure in the establishment of Pennsylvania Bank, which financed the Revolution, along with Robert Morris and Tench Francis. This was succeeded, still during the Revolution, by the Bank of North America, with Willing as president. This bank, on Chestnut Street, was in a building owned by its cashier, Tench Francis. After the Revolution, Willing became president of the first Bank of the United States. He was, in short, one of the most distinguished men of the revolutionary and post-revolutionary period.[13]

Robert Morris, of course, is an even more familiar figure in American history as financier of the Revolution. The unequalled reputation Morris established during the Revolution certainly was responsible for the trust placed in him later when his wild speculation in "wild lands" caused not only his own ruin, but that of many prominent men. This had a significant influence on our story.

It is necessary to dwell briefly on these personal relationships, for during the revolutionary era and for some decades later, the United States was a very small nation in terms of population and its political and financial business was carried on in a personal way by the leading citizens of a few important cities, most of whom were related by blood, marriage, or business and financial ties. The links between Philadelphia and Providence were, as we have seen, particularly close because of the business and personal relationship of the Brown brothers and Tench Francis. Although Philadelphia was the most important city of the time, Providence was rapidly growing in importance as a commercial, shipping and, later, manufacturing center. Yet, despite its growing importance, Providence had a population at the time of the Revolution of only a little more than 4,000 and by 1800 it had grown to only 7,600. Nonetheless (and in this the mercantile, shipping and manufacturing efforts of the Browns had a major significance), Providence became a city of the second rank behind only Philadelphia, New York and Boston, whose populations at the time of the Revolution were only *28,000*, *33,000*, and *18,000*, respectively. This illustrates the fact that the United States at the time of our story was a far different place from the country we now know. It was still a pioneer land with the frontiers close at hand.

The same year that saw the establishment of the great mercantile house of Willing & Morris, 1757, also saw an early evidence of the precocity of John Brown. Although only twenty years old, he was appointed sales agent for the ship *Desire,* the first prize taken by the privateer *Providence.* Within four years John Brown was a leading figure in efforts by candle manufacturers to form a trust to keep down the price of essential materials purchased from the whalers of Nantucket. The Browns, like other businessmen for generations thereafter, established trusts and monopolies whenever they could.

The year 1763 saw, by coincidence, the birth of both John Francis, who would establish the Brown family's first claim on what became the John Brown's Tract, and Carl Friederich Herrschhoff, the Prussian aristocrat whose name was later anglicized to Charles Frederick Herreshoff, and whose tragic life was played out in the solitude of the Tract.

In 1765 the Browns went into the iron business, manufacturing pig iron at their Hope Furnace. This was made into nails and sold in Britain to finance their purchases there. Thus the family began to develop generations of experience that would inform their judgment of the visionary scheme presented them decades later by Herreshoff. An interesting sidelight is that it is fairly certain that the wrought iron fence around the historic Bowling Green in downtown Manhattan was made of iron from the Hope Furnace.[14]

The year 1767 saw Tench Francis on the verge of financial ruin. He invested most of his money in a commercial project with a Godhard Hayne, reputedly a merchant of "great wealth and undoubted integrity." but Hayne reportedly turned out to be a scoundrel and it appeared that the wealth Francis had amassed over the decades would be wiped out at a single blow. It was weeks before he was able to find a ship to take him to London to insitute court action to try to recover his investment. He finally reached England in June of 1767. Although he obtained the finest legal representation, the case dragged on and it appeared in July 1768 that there would be no decision until after the Chancery Court reconvened in November. The situation was saved, according to family chronicles, by Tench Francis' recipe for turtle soup:

> . . . *When the repeated postponements of the hearing had brought my Grandfather to the verge of despair, a lady, intimate with him, feeling the greatest interest in his cause, undertook to bring it to the favorable attention of the Lord*

Chancellor. Knowing him to be a 'bon vivant' she said to Mr. Francis: "If you can procure through some of your West India friends a fine turtle, & direct my cook how to address it in the most approved style, I will ask his Lordship to dinner, & when he is at the height of his enjoyment, introduce you as the purveyor of this luxury!" This could easily be accomplished, as my Grandfather's experiences at the 'Fish Club', and his domestic hospitalities had accomplished him in the culinary arts.

And when Lord Camden was expressing his delight & asking all about the turtle, his hostess took occasion to present her friend, & state his heart-sickness from deferred hopes, & the vexatious impediments of the Court. On which his Lordship promised that the case should be called up at the next session, at which he gave the expected decision against the assignees of Hayne, in favor of my Grandfather.[15]

Whether or not that account of the impartial course of British justice is correct, the essential fact is that Tench Francis' fortune was largely restored, enabling him to retire later that year at the young age of thirty-eight, thus ending the financial, although not the personal, connection with the Brown family of Providence.

The first great land speculation in what became the Adirondacks took place in 1771 when two little-known Manhattan shipwrights petitioned for the right to buy a huge triangle of land not far from what became the Brown's Tract. Joseph Totten and Stephen Crossfield thought they were buying 800,000 acres but it turned out to be 1,115,000 acres. Setting a pattern that was often followed in the wild speculation that followed the Revolution, Totten and Crossfield had never seen the land and knew nothing about it. Presumably they were acting as front men for a group of prominent New Yorkers, including Alexander Macomb, who apparently wanted to keep their interest secret so political enemies would not try to block the deal.

The deal is illustrative of so many between Indians and the white man. The Mohawks agreed to sell the land for £1,135, a travesty since they were getting only a penny for every four acres. The British Crown, which interposed itself in the deal, demanded £40,000 to act as middle man, eight times what the Indians asked and nearly forty times what they got. The new owners, planning to divide the land into fifty townships that would sell, they hoped, at a handsome profit, ordered the region's first survey by an Archibald Campbell, one that was notably vague given the discrepancy between 800,000 and 1,115,000 acres. The vagueness may be accounted for by one of Campbell's entries: ". . . the rum gave out."

The Revolution intervened and the land reverted to the State of New

York but the names Totten and Crossfield have remained in the history of the Adirondacks.[16]

In the last year before the Revolution broke out in earnest, 1775, John Brown was named treasurer of Rhode Island College (named Brown University after the family in 1804), a position he held for twenty-one years. That year also saw the completion from the plans of his brother Joseph of the splendid First Baptist Church of America, of which John was a major supporter.

John Brown was an active supporter of the Revolution, hardly a surprise given his participation in the burning of the *Gaspee.* And the land that was to become his two decades later was the scene of Indian battles for an important route by canoe and foot ran along what became the Fulton Chain of lakes and thus through the site of Old Forge, now the most important settlement on the Brown's Tract.

In 1779 the New York State legislature mandated that the lands belonging to the Crown were "forever after to be vested in the people of this state."[17] This ideal, however, was not to be achieved for nearly a century, for almost as soon as the Revolution ended, the state began selling the land, making possible the great land speculations that led to the John Brown's Tract.

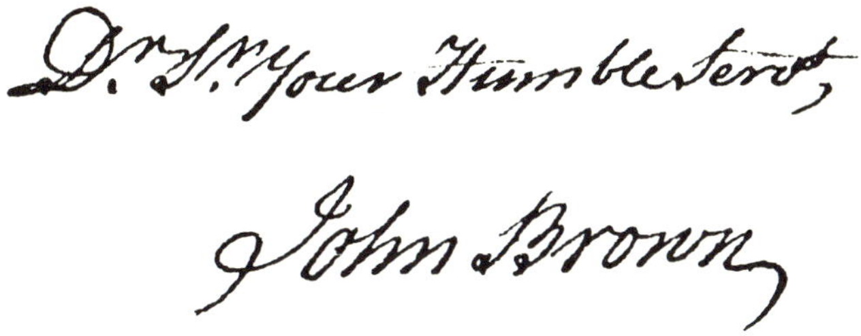

2

Introducing John Francis

... if Mr. Francis comes this way, he shall receive every favorable notice from me, if I can judge from his Parents and Connections he must be a Deserving Young Gentleman.[1]

WHEN THE American Revolution finally dragged to an end with the surrender of Cornwallis at Yorktown on October 18, 1781, John Brown, like American businessmen everywhere in the new nation, began to repair his fortunes. Impulsive and energetic as ever (he was still only forty-five years of age), he struck out in all directions, for in those early years after the war he owed "an Enormous Sum of Money in Europe."[2] He engaged in the slave trade, to the anguish of his abolitionist brother Moses, arguing that it could not be immoral since it had been allowed by the "Supreme Govenour of all things for time Immemoriel." John Brown's spelling, as we shall see time and again, is wondrously atrocious although, since it is plainly phonetic, it gives an indication of how the language was spoken then.

John Brown also ventured into the cod fishing business, something that had long been left to Massachusetts. But most important, Brown began the extensive shipping operations that were not possible during the Revolution when the British Navy controlled the seas. Within a few years he became one of the most venturesome shipowners in the new nation, sending ships from India Point, within view of the magnificent mansion he later built, to India and China as well as continuing trade along the Atlantic Coast, to the West Indies and to Europe. And in the third year after war's end he bought the farm, Spring Green, where this book was written.

Although John Brown justifiably had the reputation of an avid seeker of profit, he was also a most devoted father who must have known great

The main house at Spring Green, circa 1899.

disappointment. Not only did his three daughters have the ill-fated marriages that figure largely in our story, but his son James showed no interest in the family business. Worse he never married to perpetuate the name of his branch of the Brown family. Brown, however, never ceased to try to improve his only son. A year after the Revolution, he sent him to Philadelphia, then the national capital, presumably so he could meet some of the nation's leaders and mingle in society.

Brown wrote to his son frequently and his letters are interesting. It must be remembered that although the Revolution was over in 1782, a peace treaty had not yet been signed, so the United States and its French allies did not feel able to demobilize. He wrote to 21-year-old James in November:

> . . . *our House, wharf, stable and Lott is Jock full of French men, Horses, Waggins, etc., etc. Every Gentleman in town takes the same officers as they did on their March westward last summer. They first told us it would be only 3 or 4 days but the lutenant of the army has been at our house already 6 or 7 days and I see no signe of his Departure, Gen. Rochambeau at Gov. Bowens came the Day before yesterday* . . . .

Then the elder Brown turns to his son's future. After saying that "it will be much more agreeable to Your Parents & Sisters that you come home before winter setts in," he writes:

For my own part I wish you to do that which will be most for your Good and Acquaintance with mankind & with more parts of the World than One is necessary to inable a man to Cut a Figuer in Life, and every man is born for some purpose or other I have an anxious Desire that you should be a usefull member of Society in some sphere or other, as you do not incline to that of a Merchant so much as to spend your time in that Branch, the Law nor Phisich Does not Ingroose your attention, The Statesman therefore is what I wish you to be and the sooner you begin your attention to it the better you'l please me and all your relations.

Then the father ends the body of his letter with a passage that, save for its spelling and grammar, is classic New England:

You have an Education and may probably have a considerable Fortune if Heaven dooth not lift her Rod against us, why should you not give a part of your time to the Publick its a Duty the man of wealth and abilitys owes his Fellow men, I wish you to take a seat in our Genl. Assembly in my Place Next Spring. . . . You must not suffer yourself to be Horty [Author's Note: New Englanders still put their "r's" in curious places.], *high minded nor so proud as to look Down on those of a Smaller kind of Mortalls but to learn so much of the Coutyer as to Please the poore as well as the Rich. . . . Dont Mistake me I dont mean by this that an Acquaintance with Men of a Different Dress & address is unnecessary no Far from it I wish you to be Acquainted with Every kind of Vertuous men, as well the men of fashion as the man of figueres or of Business, both Publick & Privit and that you abstain from the bad habits and Customes & Cleave to that which appears to you, after gaining more experience, to be the most Benefical to your Friends & the Community at large.*

But if John Brown were indeed public minded, he was also a practical businessman and he ended the letter with this postscript:

I have not time to Read what I have wrote, your Descriptions are pleasing Continue them, Even more Lengthy, if convenient, what number of Houses & Soules is the present Estimate of Philade, how many Vessils are build there how large what price per ton Does a Good Ship Cost. I mean the Hulls including Iron work or not but exclusive [words illegible] *& sails.*[3]

An indication of how intimate life was, even in the most important cities, is the way this letter was addressed, simply: Mr. James Brown/Now In/Philadelphia.

Despite his father's earnest exhortation, there is little evidence he was anything but a gentleman of leisure — and a much-loved uncle. The following month, on Christmas Eve, father wrote to son the letter saying that if John Francis "comes this way, he shall receive every favorable notice from me." James Brown and his future brother-in-law, then only nineteen, met in Philadelphia that year. And it is then that we first begin our personal encounters with John Francis.

Two rather humorous letters from a friend, Charles A. Stewart, are plainly meant to cheer up John Francis, who had written that he wished it would please his Maker to call him hence. This was the first of many references to Francis' ill health but never is the malady, which was frequently disabling, specified.[4] That it caused terrible stomach or abdominal pain we know but little else. Quite possibly, he and his family were not sure what the problem was either for medicine two centuries ago was not very advanced. That it was the cause of his frequent distress and depression we can only assume. But a fuller discussion of his health—or lack of it—must await a more appropriate moment.

By 1783, land fever was beginning to mount all over the nation, not least in northern New York, which had the advantage of being close to a major commercial center, Albany, and to water transportation on the Great Lakes or the Hudson River. Washington himself journeyed to western New York and saw the possibilities of "vast inland navigation" that, it was thought, would insure that region's prosperity. For some reason people, especially New Englanders, wanted to buy land in the Adirondacks even though it was known that more fertile land was available not far to the west.[5]

That year also sees the appearance of the first in a long series of affectionate and concerned letters to and about John Francis written by his mother Anne, sister of the financier Thomas Willing. Many of the letters contain references to his fragile health. These first are to him on a trip through Maryland and Virginia beginning in March. Although he was but twenty years old, he was already working for a Philadelphia mercantile house, but it is not certain whether this was a business or pleasure trip, or was, most likely, for his health. He was accompanied by his friend Charles Stewart and there is a reference to visiting relatives. Among them was his aunt, Mary Willing Byrd of the still-famous Byrd estate, Westover, on the James River.

In one April letter to his mother, he wrote of his "continual and excessive pain" that makes his "miserable life not worth enjoying." To his father two days later he wrote that a plaster applied to his side by his Aunt Mary and "three doses a day of some innocent but effectual medicine" made him feel better.

"Perhaps the force of Immagination is the cause but I really feel better than ever," he declared.

And on April 30 from Williamsburg he wrote his father: "Tired to death with a disease become insufferable from its violence and long continuance, I determined to apply to a young and able Physician lately from Europe for relief. . . on discovering my disorder, gave me every reason to hope a speedy relief.

"Three nights and four days I have not felt the least Symptom of a return & such an interruption I have never enjoyed since January. God send it may be an effectual relief."

Again, no specifics as to the diagnosis or the medicine prescribed and again the hope that finally a cure had been found. This characterized the rest of John Francis' sadly short life: hope alternating with a return of the terrible pain.

As always, his mother was concerned about his health:

> *. . . I find by your own account you have trespassed the line marked out by the Doctor for your Stages which was not to exceed 20 or at most 25 miles a day he says, he directed you to take those Pills only when you had too broad a habit of body, (care) to his directions which I put in your pocketbook.*[6]

It is hard to say what "too broad a habit" means. Indeed, in all the written references to John Francis' bad health, there is the assumption that the recipient knows all about it.

It is possible, of course, that the ailment was never properly diagnosed; certainly there was never any long-lasting relief from that "continual and excessive pain." Although a diagnosis nearly two centuries later must necessarily be speculative, there was a good deal of information in all those letters. Thus, Doctor Charles B. Round of Warwick, Rhode Island, came to this conclusion: "From the available historical evidence it seems probable that John Francis had severe peptic ulcer disease which was recurrent over many years. Exacerbations would occur especially at times of stress. The episodes of inflammation followed by healing and the resulting scarring caused obstruction at the outflow of the stomach which in turn produced the pain and vomiting."

In that letter John's mother also reports: "I have received two visits from Mr. (James) Brown who laments exceedingly his having missed you. He would have gone with you had he met you but tis now too late he expects to return home." This indicates what appears to have been characteristic of John Brown's son throughout his life: frequent travel, apparently more often for pleasure than for business.

John Brown's elegant chariot, made in Philadelphia in 1782, is reported to be the oldest American-made vehicle in existence.

Evidently, James was in no hurry to return to Providence, for an entire month later Anne Willing Francis writes to her son that "Brown sets off tomorrow I took an airing with him yesterday and in his new chariot which is most Ellegant."[7] Here she is clearly referring to the famous "chariot" which John Brown had specially constructed for himself in Philadelphia in 1782. It was handsome and exceedingly sturdy since John Brown was a huge man weighing, according to some contemporary accounts, close to 300 pounds. Perhaps because of its solid construction it survived a century and a half of storage on the farm at Spring Green until it was donated to the Rhode Island Historical Society by Frank Hail Brown, Francis H. Brown, and John Francis Brown in memory of Alice Francis Brown. It is now a popular attraction at the society's John Brown House in Providence, called by John Quincy Adams, later president, "the most magnificent and elegant private mansion that I have ever seen on this continent."

Introducing John Francis

Anne Willing Francis often demonstrates in her letters a close attention to the events of the day. Her observations provide a human dimension usually lacking in historical accounts. On April 7 she writes: "Hourly we expect a confirmation officially of Peace. That it has not yet arrived is a matter of amazement to all."

Mrs. Francis and all America still had some waiting to do. Although land combat had ended a year and a half before, a final peace treaty was not signed until September 3, 1783. In the meantime, the British Navy continued to harass American shipping. Mrs. Francis refers to this, writing: "I hope by this time Hostilities will cease on our Coast, their coursers are not yet called in so that our trade suffers as usual." And she also refers to the continued occupation of New York by the British, who did not evacuate the city until November 25. As usual, however, her main concern was her son's health:

. . . I received yours addressed to your dear Father . . . and as you may imagine was distressed to find that your Pain continued however I flattered myself that yesterdays Post would bring me the agreeable news that you were better — but alas how cruelly was I disppointed to find you still obliged to spend your nights over the fire instead of being in a comfortable Bed taken that refreshing Balm *sleep, which is so necessary to our existence. My spirits forsook me on the Idea of your sufferings. I find they are more insupportable to me in your Absence than ever, and I long for your return with more ardour. The company of your friend Stewart with the change of Air I must still hope will revive and restore you for my sake, for your own, do my dear child be carefull of yourself. . . . I have no cause to complain of your neglect in Writing but dont omit any opportunity of informing us of the state of Health you are in. Depend on it my happiness is most materially concern in your Wellfare. I dont wish you to spend your time in fatiguing yourself in Writing long letters, a few lines is sufficient. When you return I shall with pleasure attend to your remarks, particularly if the grand object is Acquired.*[9]

One must assume that the "grand object" is the restoration of his health and also that the trip did not have any lasting beneficial effects, since one gets the picture of poor John shivering with chills by the fire.

Sometime after he returned from his southern journey, young John Francis travelled up to Providence to visit his new friend James Brown. Evidently he did "receive every favorable notice" from John Brown, the man who within five years would be his father-in-law. For in September 1783, while John Francis was at sea, his mother wrote to James:

. . . The kind attention shown to my Dear Son by all your amiable Family, was most gratefully recieved, and will ever be remembered by us . . . . Your Friend lamented much the necessity he found himself under of leaving you so soon, but

his long absence from Mr. Whiteside as well as his longing desire to see his family made him anxious to return. I wish him to make a much longer stay at Providence as I was firmly of opinion that Climate would have proved Salutary to him – a few days after his return his old complaint returned and the Extreme that, with too close an application to Business in his tender state, increased his disorder, which alarmed him, and us, so much that we thought it Absolutely necessary for him to try a serious Voyage, an opportunity offered for Lisbon to the very favorable Circumstance, the Season of the Year & the Climate of that Country, esteemed Moderate & Health. He immediately determined & in a few Hours after Sailed on ye 19th of August went out of the Capes. . . . [10]

John Francis' health problems must have been sporadic, for by August he was able to journey to Lisbon, his first foreign trip, for the commercial house of Peter Whiteside. That he made his first foreign business trip under the best possible auspices is evident from a letter to a Lisbon merchant from Robert Morris, who, just after the Revolution, stood in public esteem only below George Washington. After discussing some business details, Morris writes that "I have advised them (the Whiteside firm, a participant in the deal) to send Mr. John Francis Passenger in the Ship with Mr. Little (nephew of the Lisbon merchant), in order that he may assist in sorting and chosing the Goods."

This young Gentleman is the Son of my particular Friend, and is descended from the first Families of this Place. He is at the moment in the course of his clerkship in the House of Messrs. Whiteside & Co. – An Ill State of Health is the principal reason for sparing him to go on this Business. He has not had experience sufficient to rest the execution of the order to his judgement, we only mean that you should consult him in the choice of the Goods – he knows Bohea & Hyson Teas very well, and altho he has not had an opportunity of being conversant in India Goods yet his general Ideas will enable him to reject Articles that are not suited to the Taste of this Country.

You will find him very deserving of your esteem and I shall thank you for such attention as you will please to show him. [11]

Accompanying the Morris letter was one from Peter Whiteside:

Mr. John Francis will present you this, he is a Young Gentleman of this Place, who has been brought up with us, and has still some part of his time to serve – He takes this Trip, as well for the sake of establishing his Health as to be of some use in executing the Plan – He has been a good deal conversant in Goods suitable to this Country, but is not so perfect as to rest the execution solely on him . . .

Enclosed with this note was a Bill of Exchange for £100,000, a fortune in those days. Then Whiteside added this postscript:

Mr. Francis will be supplied by his Father with about £500 for his own Private Adventure and if you please to furnish him an equal amount in goods should he request it, we will engage to see you paid equable to the Term fixed.[12]

The following day Morris wrote another note to Lisbon:

My regard for Mr. John Francis and his Family induces a wish that he might make some advantage for himself out of the present voyage and therefore I propose that you supply him with such articles as he may choose to the amount of One Thousand Pounds Sterling, and take his draft on himself or his Father, here payable at such Term as you and he may agree in making Insurance to cover the value and I pledge myself that the same shall be punctually paid.[13]

Francis did not reach Lisbon until September 27 and, as reported in a very long letter to Whiteside, conditions were not as Robert Morris had anticipated. The Lisbon firm did not want to participate in the deal, would not extend the necessary credit and, in any case, the goods from India were in short supply and of inferior quality.[14] He wrote a much shorter letter to his father explaining the problem:

I will now quit writing on a Subject truly mortifying to me from many causes. On my return I will fully inform you. At present I am studying the Portuguese Language with as much attention as the State of my Health will permit, but indeed my dear Father it is still very low. By the Advise of the doctor here I attended the Caldas or Warm Baths for the purpose of drinking the water and Bathing. What effect they will have god only knows, it is certain they daily perform amazing cures. In case they dont Answer the Physicians intend applying a plaster of Cartharidis.[15]

Although his correspondence makes it plain that John Francis devoted a great deal of time to business in Portugal, he was always interested in everything around him. Indeed, what young man (remember, he was only 20) would not be eager to see the famous fandango dancers. He did see them and evidently did not like what he saw. There is some reason to believe him, for he was writing in his diary, not to his mother. He wrote that "the different postures in which the [dancers] place themselves would occasion the most obscene Ideas in the most Virtuous of Minds." And he confided to his diary that he preferred American girls: the Portuguese women were "all duggs and Buttocks."[16]

Even before John Francis' ship reached Portugal, his mother began a series of letters. Speaking of his shipboard accommodations, she writes:

. . . I can't help fearing that you may want some Necessaries, many conveniences, and allmost all the Luxurys you have been accustomed to, but I endeavor to console myslef with the pleasing Idea that you have in Exchange fine Health, which will give a relish to very humble fare, particularly after so long and tedious a complaint as has tormented you. I need not my dear Child exhort you to take care of yourself. The pains you have suffered will make you cautious, you'll naturally think, but Experience has evinced the Contrary in older persons than you, therefore I must remind you that relapses is Dangerous, and that much less may renew your Complaint than you can conceive of. . .

But while his mother's first concern was for his health, she was also concerned about his career, in which the voyage to Lisbon was a major step:

. . . I have a presentiment that all will be right, no doubt of your persevering in the line prescribed, Sensible as you must be, that to deviate from your orders or directions, would blast every future Prospect and that as you now Act will your Character be fixed—tis of the Utmost importance that our first appearance on the Stage should be well received, unfavorable impressions are hard to be wiped of, and there are enough to watch the Wrong slip or Ungraceful attitude of a Young performer. . . . be diffident of your own judgement, and seek for knowledge of People of riper years & who are esteemed Wise Virtuous Men. You are now I hope fairly entered on the Commercial Field. View well your ground for be assured there are hidden Snakes, Vipers of many kinds, that will sting if you Approach their meandering to the fair Honest character is above their touch. Day light supports the Actions of the Prudent Cautious Men, their Conduct will bear Strictest scrutiny. Your extreem youth will make you a proper Subject for the Artfull & Designing, their snares may be set to advantage if ever you are off your guard, look well Around before you venture to Advance, remember too that the people you are among are suspicious & resentfull and in general illiterate and of course illiteral, be particularly cautious how you sport a sentiment that dont meet with their taste. Politicks & Religion never on any Account speak on whither in publick or even in the most private party, for you may be overheard & the Penalty would then be severe—pay all outward Attentions that their Customs & Ceremonies call for, with a good grace tis a mark of extreme folly to oppose the fixed established Regulations of any Country where you are only a passenger.[17]

It is difficult nearly two centuries later to know whether John Francis' first foreign business trip was eventually a success or whether it fell considerably short of the expectations of Robert Morris and Peter Whiteside and, if that were so, whether it was because of business conditions in Lisbon at that time or because, as his mother warned him, "Artfull & Designing" men took advantage of his youthful lack of experience. We do know, however, that his career seemed not to suffer by this first venture abroad and that others, extremely interesting to read about so many years later, were to follow. We also learn the melancholy news that the ministrations of his Aunt Mary, the young Williamsburg physician, and the doctors of Portugal were successful only temporarily, for he wrote in his diary of October 3 of the return of "constant and severe pain."[18]

The following year, 1784, saw the dawning of a commercial era that would have profound influence on our story. Robert Morris, ever the financial adventurer, sent the first American vessel on the long and uncertain trip to China. Before long, John Brown would do the same. But times were difficult everywhere in the new nation in that first full post-war year, and especially in Rhode Island, which had so few resources other than its industrious people. John Brown and others wanted to start a bank in Providence. The Bank of North America had been founded in Philadelphia in 1781, even before the Revolution was over, and banks were chartered in Boston and New York in 1784, but in Providence the men of means were not convinced that the time had come for a bank in Rhode Island.

Family letters continued to refer to young Francis' poor health. One, from his cousin Evelyn Byrd (it was her mother who had applied the plaster that seemed to give temporary relief) was addressed: "Mr. John Francis, Merchant to be left at Tench Francis esquires next door to the Bank of North America." When we think of the great men then congregating in Philadelphia – Washington, Jefferson, Franklin, Adams, Madison, etc. – it is difficult to conceive that Philadelphia was just a small town, considerably fewer than 30,000 persons, where men of such distinction often lived in boarding houses and were commonly seen walking along the streets. Contrast that with the rather more opulent lives of present-day politicians of perhaps less distinction.

Letters preserved by the Francis family for decades, hundreds of historically invaluable letters, as well as journals, diaries, etc., languished forgotten in Spring Green and placed in safekeeping by one of the authors, they demonstrated that John Francis was held in affection and high esteem.[19] This would seem an unremarkable assertion were it not for the fact that, as we shall see, he was often disparaged by scholars who did not have access to this recently rediscovered material.

Among the letters of 1785 begin to appear love letters from John Francis to Abby, the eldest of John Brown's three daughters. It is not known how frequently John Francis pursued his beloved Julia, a pet name he often used, in person but it is plain that he courted her frequently and fervently by mail. These letters demonstrate all the passion and fearful uncertainty that his love might be unrequited that have beset young lovers for centuries. In this first letter, he is so distraught that he plunges directly into his reproof without salutation:

Little did I think on this Day last month when I bid adieu to Julia, that I know should have occasion to upbraid her with Neglect, how often did she promise by every sacred tie to let no one opportunity escape without writing me. These were Her last words "dont my dear Frederick [her pet name for him] forget your Julia," if writing will remind you of me I will always write — Shakespeare says, at Lovers perjuries Love laughs, doubtless he does at yours, and does he not pity me? Deluded as I have been — In fact there can be not justification for your Silence. Only reflect on the contents of your last letter, of your severe Indisposition at Spring Green, and then to let a Fortnight elapse without a line — Do you mean to make trial of my Constancy? If so, your Wrong, and as I have told you before it is dangerous to play with Edged Tools, you may wound yourself. . . I will never write to you again except in Answer. I made this promise before our Separation, and will hereafter observe it inviolably — I know well from what little Insight I have had into the Ways of Mankind, that if we do not assume our own consequence We shall assuredly be neglected, therefor if my letters trivial as they are, are to be obtained for nothing, in a short time with you *they will really be Worth Nothing — If you wish me to write long letters set me the example of short ones, only curtail your own, and if none at all never write to me, and depend on it I shall be scrupulously punctual — You see I use no ceremony. I blame or Commend your Conduct as it deserves, if I am wrong convince me — The Tuesday's post will bring your Pappa's answer, to say I am totally resigned to whatever may be his determination would be false, but to assure you that I shall be resolute and not trifle with our Happiness is most true —*[20]

It is easy to smile at such anguish but to smile is to smile at ourselves, for what were we like at the age of twenty-two?

We have no record of what news Tuesday's post brought from Abby's Papa but it could not have been entirely discouraging, for three months later on February 1, 1786, John Brown announced that he was forming a partnership with John Francis.

That more than a business partnership was involved is evident from a letter written to Abby a few months later by John Francis' brother Thomas Willing Francis.

"The Better Day the better Deed" is a saying most people are acquainted with — it just popt into my Head as I was entering my Chamber to dress. I was not long determining what Employment would be most agreeable immediately I took up my pen to write something I know not what, to my dearly beloved Abby.

I had the pleasure of acknowleding the Receipt of your Favor of the 4th Ult. in a postscript to Brother's Letter since which I am not favor'd with a Line from under your hand. Our last letter from Providence is dated the 22 Ult. — Brother,

I find, has suffered a Return after being relieved from that cruel pain near a Fortnight. You can't imagine what real Happiness I felt on first opening his Letter when I read he had recovered much, but on casting my eyes still further down the page in pursuit of a Confirmation of this agreeable paragraph, when unfortunately I met with the Word, Relapse, — *Alas then, all that Satisfaction I was experiencing vanished in a Moment and I was thrown back in the same gloomy Disposition, the thoughts of my Brother's situation has ever occasioned. Four long years has he been tormented with this diabolical pain. I wish to God he could be relieved, sure I am of the continuous long in this Situation it will be the Means of curtailing the Life of the best of parents, our dear Mother. Her mind is constantly agitated and to a person of her kind Sensibility a few Years of Distress must entirely destroy. Be a friend Abby your Affectionate Attentions to him has rendered you more dear to us all than words can express. I always loved you but now feel that Affection more sensibly than ever* —[21]

The year 1787 saw the Iroquois begin the process — completed in 1795 — of ceding all the vast lands of northern New York to the state: for a total of $1,600, lands on which speculators would win, and lose, millions of dollars.[22] And a bill was introduced in the New York State legislature to improve navigation on the Mohawk River, which was eventually to be a major link in the state's great canal system. In Rhode Island, later that year, John Brown's great mansion was nearly completed and he sent his first vessel, the *General Washington,* initiating the China trade from docks at the foot of the hill on which his house has stood for two centuries.

Early in 1787 Anne Willing Francis wrote to Abby that "our dear Johnnys health tis Certainly better" and that although he thought a trip to England and France would very much benefit the firm, "he says positively he won't go unless you approve." She also wrote warmly of Abby's brother James who was on what apparently was a protracted stay in Philadelphia.

. . . . *He is now become Absolutely necessary here having My Sons all from me, he has assumed their rank and fills his Station with great Address. We shall lament his absence more than ever his Affectionate Conduct has secured him the interest of all the Family. In short he is entirely treated in that familiar style that my dear Boys are accustomed to here. And I assure you he has entered with Sport into all the Amusements of the City Gallants, the Ladies and Accompanies Sophia [her daughter] as her Guard & protection whereever she goes.*[23]

James Brown's great gift was not the statesmanship to which his father aspired for him but that of being welcome wherever he went. As far as can be determined, the development of that gift was largely his life's work.

John Brown's "most magnificent" mansion as depicted in a watercolor by Richard Grosvenor, descendant of Alice Brown Mason.

Also, early in the year, John Francis demonstrated in a wild rush of words that he was still achingly vulnerable to Abby's silence whenever he was away from her side. He wrote from Virginia, where he was on a business trip.

I am out of patience with my dear Julia's Unaccountable Silence from when does it proceed? From what suspicion of untowards Events came I thus cruelly be deprived of the only comfort of my present Solitary Life. Dear and best of Girls that loving thee so void of Self Interest as I do, should be productive of such Unhappiness. I lead the most miserable of lives! thy dear Fond Image is ever in my sight but without my reach. Thy Breath so often assured on my lips thy Eyes dear reflections of my Own. Thou dear Arms Around my Neck, and they best of Hearts beating and Throbbing against mine, are all pleasing and Innocent remembrances which distract. Those Hours, Minutes, Moments were the only in my Life in which I have enjoyed pure unalloyed Rapture & those now serve to increase my Sufferings.

The poor lad then declares that "Words are not at my command," so he quotes at some length from memory some lines from Alexander Pope's "Abelard and Eloisa." Then he declares that he would gladly suffer "Danger and Difficulties" for Abby's sake.

. . . All these would I freely suffer, all these have I suffer'd and can I in the End be blessed in peace with my unexampled Julia, the Trumpet of Fame may blow her Fulsome Blasts for those that Covet. Not obscurity but Domestic Retirment with my Adorable partner, not Riches but a Sufficiency, Not Independency farther than being a Service to any Friends for mutual good office. Give Julia & myself Health, the rest will follow. But why this Rhapsody of Language void of sentiment you'll say, I'll tell you my dear, its from a disordered Head & Heart, a Mind Full of Uncertainty—it's—I'll say no more, think for me since you will not deign to write.

Then the young man rushes to an even wilder finish:

. . . Does the Language Displease You? Quit reading it—Does the Subject offend? Have Mercy on the Offender and Consider this as it really will be the last you will receive from me. I have not so small an opinion of my own Consequence as to pass such is uninvited Neglect as you have shown me unresented. If my Silence is any Mortification as the Grave will I be—If My Absence causes any uneasiness why should I not prolong it? Have I received such favors on your side as require a return on mine? You have willfully omitted writing, I will resolutely play the same Game—Adieu therefore—Wise and in future know what I have often hinted that Edged Tools are Dangerous playthings—With all this I will abuse—I am not hardened as to give you uneasiness by informing you when I shall be in Providence. Think no farther of me from this time till you see me in your Best parlour. Say the Month April, May or June. I then may make my appearance, so alter'd you will scarcely recognize me—Worn down with Anxiety, Fatigue and this Attendance to Wealth—Callous to every sentiment of Joy or Sorrow, my Eloisa stern and fixed as Marble Varies but a little. I never never again shall be the Frederick you once loved when I read the pleasing anecdotes of my Youth, my then Gaity of disposition. When I review the Happy Hours we have spent in Social Harmony tho' Attacked with this Complaint my Spirit, kept pace with my Strength when I compare all these past enjoyments with my present mode of Life, I swear if one Leap could place me in Eternity and my Ungrateful Julia Happy I'd take it.

Then poor John Francis ends with an even more melodramatic flourish:

Adieu perhaps forever.[24]

His separation from Abby, her not writing him frequently, the melancholy quite naturally caused by his pain, combined with the vulnerability of youth, almost overcame him. Plainly, he could not bear the separation, for within a couple of weeks he left Virginia, lingered for an impatient week with his family in Philadelphia and then hurried north to Abby's side. We learn this in a letter from his mother to Abby.

. . . Your Friend was deeply wounded at not hearing from you for such a length of time, and from his feelings he was ready to condemn. Reason & Reflection were banished or he wouldn't for a moment censure you. However it was only a Sudden and very short lived Anger if Anger it could be called, for believe me my dear he can't be angry with you for two Minutes. Was I desposed to jealousy I should have felt it at the very time you thought he was displeased with you, all the Arguments his Father, Sister, Friends with mine united couldn't prevail with him to stay a few days longer. Tire & fatigued beyond description with travelling bad Roads, he wouldn't wait for better even under our Roof. Strange Reverse, What won't Love Accomplish. Father, Mother, tenderest Friends all nothing in the scales where love is opposed. This my dear Girl will Compensate for those Unfavorable Ideas that Agitate Your tender Heart, You find the long loved Idea of Visiting Europe no sooner became serious then banished, and Why, because his dear Abby couldn't be with him. Many, Many times, the short Week he was with us he would Exclaim, "Oh my dear Ma, if my Abby was here how happy should I be." Wanting you he couldn't have any real Enjoyment. I hope when he returns you'll Accompany him. You both will be happier when once united, however I shall not say any more on that subject.[25]

Unhappily, we do not have Abby's responses to John's fevered letters. Plainly, however, from what his mother writes, she was unsettled by them. And why not; she was, after all, even younger than John—barely 20.

By mid-1786, the ever-hopeful John Francis was trying a new remedy for his complaint—tar water. As was often the case, it was his mother who tracked down yet another treatment:

. . . . since my last I have consulted Uncle Doctoring Billy on your drinking Tar Water. They both advise Your trying it. I sent you a receipt, the Norway Tar is reckoned the best, but you may get some as Clear of the burnt taste of Carolina or Barbadoes Tar. You must drink it weak at first and if you find it heals you leave it off. Drink at first only one Tumbler a day and as you like it/for you may in time prefer it to most drinkgs/take 2,3, or 4 in a day. Small draughts, but take notice how it affects you. It generally keeps the body Cool, Creasing the appetite and helps digestion . . . . [26]

Although young Francis was often distraught by the unsmooth course of his love, this condition did not extend to his business life. He was always a very keen observer. Toward the end of 1787, John Brown decided to send the first Rhode Island ship to China, so John Francis again journeyed south to assemble a cargo. It was a difficult assignment, for money was scarce with Brown & Francis, as it was with most merchants in those Spartan post-Revolutionary years, especially in poor Rhode Island. On his trip to Philadelphia and Virginia, he kept very detailed ledgers and notes which, discovered among the family papers, constitute an invaluable source of information on the business conditions and practices of the day.[27]

During his trip south he frequently wrote to Abby, his mother, and his senior partner John Brown. Evidently, John Brown wanted his young partner to go to the East Indies, for Francis wrote in October: "You have . . . learnt by my letter the unwillingness of my Parents and their reasons why Voyage to the Indies would be destructive to both A and myself. And I flatter myself you will coincide with us and believe it for the best that I should remain in Providence."[28]

Young John Francis simply did not want to be separated from his Abby any longer than necessary. And a trip to the Orient would, at the least, take months and probably well more than a year. Abby and John had plans that would hardly accommodate his taking a long trip to the Orient.

John Brown was a formidable man, but John Francis was not afraid to stand up to him, as this letter demonstrates:

> *. . . I would not have given the meanest Slave in Existence half the uneasiness your letter of the 18th Instant which I have received yesterday occasioned me, But silence were I to contest the matter it would both create further difficulties and perhaps in some future period render in a disservice. It is sufficient for me to know that I never solicited the Consignment of the Washington that from the first to the last I ever object to it, and that the desire alone of pleasing and rendering one acceptable Service to you made one accede to what from my Soul I ever dispproved and your candid acquiesience must be the case on mature deliberation. Two voyages have thus been relinquished. The next one the consent of my Parents you will first* obtain. *I am sorry their parental anxiety for Abby & myself should argue against them, I am no child and tho dependant on them for advice, yet no dictatorial Command did I ever receive. No my dear Mr. B. never any Man whose government I have been under complain as you have done. The Business I have so often transmited both at home and abroad never yet subject me to the smallest reproof, on the contrary the fullest approbation and am I now to suffer in my Mercantile Character because I omitted giving you advice Current, when in the same Letter I informed you that Nothing would sell but Ginseng, I did not keep a Copy but sure I am that the Construction to be put, was that neither Rum or Molasses wd answer and if my memory does not fail me either the day before or the same Day I actually gave you the Prices—. Have mercy on me I entreat you I never pawn'd myself on you for more than I proved to be and considering the near affinity between us be generous and look to the bright side of my character for satisfaction. I am sensible that I like others have my Foibles,*

Nay I may have a Super abundance of them, yet this you may be content of, they will [never] subject your Family to disgrace, or your Daughter to beggary — . The Origin of your discontent I fear is that abject Situation in Life will not be mended by a Connection, this Truth depend on, she never can be more unhappy than her present unsettled State causes her, and long since would I gladly have removed the Evil, & satisfied the world as to my Intentions, had not that the uncertainties of the times rendered my gain as a Merchant too precarious to trust to — But let me again remind you that I never held up the Idea of Property, nay I painted my situation more dismal than they were — Yet my good Sir parental Estate will be as much as I have the Vanity to wish for, and tho' not at my command yet it so situated that A [Abby] and myself can never want, My Father pointed out a Line that I could well support myself in a moderate Frugal manner till times alter'd for the better in case you should wish a separation — *But as I was bred a Merchant and have borne all the Slavery of one, I refuse acceptance knowing that poorer I could not be and a chance was that I should be wealther. And once out of the Merchantile line it might be difficult to returne to it — . You have construed my offer of going if you requested into an Insult, and* ORDER *me (almost on my Peril) never to mention it again. I will not — here to my sorrow the best Intentions are miscontrued — Oh my dear Mr. B consider my Feelings and let your Native Compassion plead my innocence — Reflect on my Situation dependant on you though* not *for my* Support, *yet what is of more consequence than either the happiness of your amiable Daughter who never was culpable except in loving one, who unfortunately does not possess your Esteem as he once did. — So linked are we together the same pain that pierces my Bosum — Stabs her to the Soul! delicate creature little is she able to bear those severe trials, which in no one view can be productive of good — The subject is distressing to me and tiresome to you, but conscious Rectitude of Heart assure me of self applause, if not of self content. I will bid you good night and consider my future Movements till morning and then inform you. Never never may you or yours feel as I have done is the earnest Prayer of your real disinterested Friend*

JF[29]

The plans, of course, were marriage and exactly when they were made final — for the wedding took place on New Year's Day 1788 — is not clear, for as late as November 13, just six or seven weeks before the event, John wrote to Abby: ". . . my Heart boild on the Rec. of your cruel letter. I will not hurt your Feelings, but never did any Culprit suffer more for Villany than poor Fred for loving his dear Julia." But John does not seem too overwrought for he quickly goes on to say that he is sending gifts of ginger and "Pumgranate" to her and her mother.[30]

By year's end Brown & Francis had succeeded in assembling a cargo, stretching their credit to the limit and, as it later turned out, beyond the

Silhouettes of John Francis (1736-1796) and Abigail Brown Francis (1761-1821) made in London by Miers.

limit. On December 27, 1787, Captain Jonathan Donnison in command, the *General Washington* weighed anchor for Canton, not to return for more than 18 months.[31]

One can only assume that Abby and John were both glad that he was not aboard. On board, however, as supercargo, was Samuel Ward, who later figures briefly but importantly in the story of the John Brown's Tract.

Also by year's end, John Francis received a letter from Rhode Island College thanking him for the donation of a valuable collection of books, and the magnificent John Brown mansion was sufficiently completed that it could be the scene of what must have been one of the most gala events in the century-and-a-half history of this still-small City of Providence.

Although Abby's marriage was cruelly short and often marked with unhappiness (as were the marriages of her two younger sisters), we know the wedding itself was an occasion of "great splendor".[32] Happily details of that auspicious day have been preserved in two letters that confirm what one would expect: that John Brown was not one to do things by halves.

A few days after the wedding, one of the bridesmaids, Elisa Bowen, described it for her friend Mrs. Abigail Goddard. Elisa informed her friend, whom she called "Rosella," that:

Last Tuesday evening witnessed the union of my two friends, Francis and Abbey; I was present and officiated as bridesmaid in unison with Miss Francis and Stillman.

The bride was dressed in an elegant white satin, a very handsome hat, and suite of the most elegant Brussels, I ever beheld. A white ribbon was clasped around her neck with a pearl star, her shoulder was ornamented with the same, to-gether with her hat. Bracelets set in pearl, with fine strings of the same to bind then on her arm, a handome watch ornamented with a new chain, finished her dress, to which a graceful bouquet of white flowers must be added.

She was quite charming, and the most interesting object you can have an idea of. The Bridesmaids, I would inform you, made no despicable appearance, all three of us in white, in pure white, our hats white cane, the crown highly elevated with wire and flowing gauze, finished by a quantity of large white plumes.

Young Miss Bowen then lamented that there were no eligible young bachelors "to exhibit ourselves to, that we should even care a pin whether we looked 'well or ill. . .' "

Well I think I have married the couple, but I was so enchanted with the bridesmaids I had quite forgotten the bride. About nine we had supper, tho' for so large a company the tables were spread with every delicacy, before and after which we had an infinite deal of vocal and instrumental music, sometimes combined sometimes separate. On the whole we had a most charming wedding. On Friday Mr. Brown gave a smart ball at his house on the hill. Indeed it will be a most elegant place, we had four rooms lighted up on the second floor, one for a supper, another for cards and two for dancing. We danced in the large chamber of the hall, and continued it through the door into the next room, which made the whole length of the house. The rooms are already genteel, but will be elegant when finished and furnished. Two of the largest and most elegant mirrors, I ever saw ornamented the rooms. Standing in the door which is in the middle of the partition, you are just on a line with them, so that at the head of the dance you can look down through a crowd of sprightly dancers, and if you are a little elevated above the common race of mortals or chance to be made so by high heels, or long feathers, you can then have the pleasure of contemplating your image and seeing it repeated fifty two feet, so at the foot of the dance, you may see the same, the effect was charming to look on, and such a moving multitude.

Elisa continued her account, which would have done credit to a society reporter, with a plaint common until more recent times:

. . . Well, this is the second time I have been a bridesmaid. I think it is or ought to be my turn next to be a Bride, every dog has his day as the saying is, if so, mine is to come, but if marriage is to make the day I fear it will be without the groom, as there is scarcely such an animal as a man in the Town.[33]

Introducing John Francis

Abigail Goddard, again addressed as "Rosella," also received an account of the ball from Anna Bowen, perhaps Elisa's sister. Her lively account ends with an utterly conventional remark about fortune that, unhappily, was to come true.

The Ball was given at the new house which is almost finished, as yet, they had not any furniture in it, they only sent a dozen or two of the chairs, and for the rest we had long benchs covered with green cloth which looked extremely well. You know the East end of the house is divided into unequal rooms, as those below are unfinished, we danced above in both rooms, and a merrier crew, I never laughed with. We behaved decorum until about eleven and then we set down to a good substantial supper of meats and chocolate. After which somebody proposed an entout Jigg. I forgot who began it, but a ring was instantly formed around the actors and every creature that never cut a caper before now tried the suppleness of their feet. Mr. John Brown, brother Jabez [Bowen], *Col.* [Daniel] *Tillinghast, Mr.* [George Benson] *and in short everybody cut out somebody, never were such shouts, such bursts, such exclamations as when the older gentlemen or the novices stepped in, they were in a moment surrounded by girls who was struggling to dance nearest to them as true a husking frolic as ever you saw. When the novelty of Jiggs were over, we played Blind Man's Buff, and Col.* [Joseph] *Nightingale made a great deal of fun by throwing himself in the way of the Blind man who happened to be Mr. Brown, in the drollest mixture of male and female dress. One of the ladies who had been caught, refused to be blinded, and so we returned to Country Dances again. I should have told you perhaps that the Bridegroom opened the Ball in a Minuet with Mrs. Peck who was succeeded by the Bride and young* [John] *Nightingale, and Mr.* [Thomas] *Halsey flourished away with the lovely Miss* [Sophia] *Francis, he danced a hornpipe too. I know not when I have seen more glee than almost every face wore on this occasion.*

James Brown presumably did the honors of the house with the most perfect propriety, plenty led him to her fountains, and bid him diffuse her nectar with unsparing hand, and decency and bland politeness sat smiling on his face and guided all his motions, I assure you I was half in love with him. The Bride looked the very goddess of tranquil and complete felicity, a sweet and gentle smile enlivened her countenance, and modest tenderness glowed on her cheeck when she turned her eyes on her beloved friend. The poor fellow is far from well, and as well as she, looks miserably, but I have hopes that now all doubts and suspenses are at an end, they will both enjoy returning health among their accumulating blessings.

Then Anna ends her account with this gloomy thought:

To one mortal is given to possess untainted felicity. Where heaven distinguishes anyone by peculiar advantages, does it not also give the Angel of affliction change to shade their sunshine by oft repeated sorrow. Who then sould dare wish for distinguishing marks of fortune.[34]

Affliction John Francis already had and much more was yet to come, but from the depth of feeling that we have already seen in his letters, can we doubt that these were very happy days indeed? These joyous days were also a prerequisite for the John Brown's Tract, for if it were not for the business, and then marriage, union between the Brown and the Francis families, there would have been no John Brown's Tract.

James Brown, who at the wedding again demonstrated his capacity for inspiring affection, treated the wedding briefly in his diary, reporting that for the wedding itself only ten persons outside the family were invited. "Forty-four supped in two rooms at the Wedding which was more agreeable The company all being very sociable. Everyone had retired by one o'clk." And of the reception on January 4, James wrote: "J.B. gave a dance at the new house on the hill upwards of one hundred invitations were given. The four rooms in 2nd story were all open'd and well filled. The Company is remarkable good Sports and supp'd at 11 Oclk, broke up about 3 Oclk in the morn."

The festivities continued for several days. The family dined here at Spring Green on the 6th and on the 15th, the newlyweds, joined by Sarah and James Brown and some friends "Set out for Boston" and at the end of February, sixty people were invited to and thirty-four attended a dance at Spring Green.[35]

The same year that the Brown and Francis families were joined, an adopted son of Rhode Islander, Elkanah Watson, who was to become perhaps the nation's foremost expert on and advocate of a canal system, travelled along the Mohawk River to the region around Fort Schuyler which later became Utica. In this then-remote area he hiked alone, often without food, the territory "alive with savages." This area, less than fifty miles south and west of what was to become the Brown's Tract, was beginning to be developed.

> *. . . . Settlers are continually pouring in from the Connecticut hive, which throws off its annual swarms of intelligent, industrious, and enterprising settlers, the best qualified of any men in the world, to subdue, and civilize the wilderness.*

Watson reported that land along the Mohawk was rising rapidly in value:

> *. . . . A few years past, these lands might have been bought for a trifle; at present, the lands bordering the river, have risen to* three dollars *an acre, and a few miles back, to* one dollar.[36]

Watson was an early advocate, perhaps the most influential one, of connecting the Hudson, by a link of canals, rivers and lakes, and the Great

Lakes, thus diverting what he foresaw as the rich trade of the area to Albany and New York City rather than through British-owned Canada. This, remember, was just five years after the Treaty of Paris and all Americans were still apprehensive, and justifiably so, about the British forces in Canada. Foresighted Americans saw the need to develop economic as well as political independence from Britain, which was then the great economic force in the world as well as the most powerful nation militarily.

Thus, it is easy to see how, to men of enterprise like John Brown, that vast area of northern New York seemed like one great economic opportunity where success was predestined. Before long, entrepreneurs, longer on daring than prudence, would be grabbing this land, the most famous parcel of which is known to this day as the John Brown's Tract.

While great economic forces were beginning to have their effect on the great northern wilderness, John Francis and his new wife Abby were beginning a married life that often saw John away on business for the firm of Brown & Francis. These, of course, were not the days of jet flights and train or automobile trips. Journeys were long, tedious, and uncomfortable by horseback or stagecoach over rough and sometimes dangerous roads. What we can do in a few hours then took days and, especially in the winter, was difficult. Of such a journey Anne Willing Francis wrote to Abby in February 1788:

My dear Son returned from Virginia the extreme fatigue consequent to so tedious and disagreeable journey You may naturally suppose affected his Health and could I detain him only ten or twelve Days I think he would be so well recovered that his journey to Providence would not be Difficult. I fear it will not be in our power to detain him longer than Thursday, his great Anxiety to see you occupys his whole Heart and as much as he loves us, yet tis you Alone that he sighs after, was you here I believe he would enjoy our Society with the highest pleasure imaginable, this long absence has convinced him that a voyage to Europe is no ways necessary for his happiness, he has not the smallest inclination to go, blest with your Society and a tolerable Share of Health, he would Sacrifice every Enjoyment that Europe could give him. Yet such is the Affection and respect he feels for his revered Friend Your dear and Worth Father, that if he insists on his going, he will—but here my Dear you can interfere and I am sure from the tender conduct your Dear Parent has ever preserved towards you & my Dear Son, I can't but suppose your Arguments will have their proper Weight. The delicate situation of his Health is of itself a powerful reason against his encountering the Difficulties of such a Voyage, the next is, that he is highly improbable that the Advantages Accruing from his Voyage should in any degree Compensate for the Expense, you will know his Finances, that he is in no ways entitled from his present Situation to travel.[37]

As far as we know, John Francis, for whatever reason, did not again journey to Europe until 1792, when he made extremely interesting voyages to Britain and France in the early days of the bloody Revolution.

On August 16, 1788, Francis received a letter from Charles Wilson Peale asking instruction for the completion of a three-quarter length portrait of his mother Anne Willing Francis.

By the following year John Brown's commercial dream of establishing a bank in Providence began to move toward realization. Although he properly was given primary credit, it is now evident from family papers that his junior partner, John Francis, also played a significant role. In his journal for Sunday, January 19, he wrote: "Proposed with M(r.) Welcome Arnold to establish a Bank in this Town and concluded the Following Gentlemen w(oul)d join as Stock Holders." And he named a number of the leading businessmen of Providence, among them names still familiar in the city if only as the names of streets: several Browns (of course), Arnold, Power, Bowen, Thurber, Olney and Dexter. The following day he made this entry: "I wrote last evening to my Father and my Uncle Thomas Willing requesting their advice and assistance relative to the establishment of a Bank in this Town."[38] His father, as noted earlier, was cashier of the nation's first bank, and his uncle was president.

The frequent and affectionate correspondence between Anne Willing Francis and her daughter-in-law Abby continued in their homely but irresistible fashion. In one, Mrs. Francis discusses a favorite dish of her son:

> *. . . The Season is over for dressing Rabbits or I should say after they are Skinned Washed & dressed they should be well flour'd & dressed up in a Cloth to boil in Milk & Water till they are tender then have some white onions well boiled in Milk Cream, then put the onions over the Rabbit and pour melted Butter over them. This is the way Johnny has been used to eat them.*

And she cautions Abby not to have children too quickly:

> *. . . Your Pa appeared so anxious that I was induced to mention it to you. I beg you are both young enough to fill your House if you don't begin for several years, and I think tis best to get settled and in a prosperous way first. Do my dear girl make yourself easy & take care of your health. Anxiety will destroy all hopes on it. All's for the best.*[39]

Mrs. Abigail Adams, wife of Vice President John Adams, visited Providence en route to New York, the seat of the government. She wrote:

> *. . . Mr. Brown sent his carriage & son James to conduct me to his House which is one of the grandest I have seen in this Country. Every thing in and about it, wore the marks of magnificence & taste. Mrs. Brown met me at the door & with*

Charles Wilson Peale's Portrait of Ann Willing Francis (1733-1812).

the most obliging Smile accosted me with "Friend I am glad to see thee here." The simplicity of her manners & dress with openess of her countenance & the friendliness of her behaviour charmed me beyond all the studied politeness of European manners. They had collected between 22 persons to dine with me though the notice was so short, & gave an elegant entertainment upon a service of plate. Towards *evening I made a Tour around the Town & drank Tea & spent the evening with Mr. & Mrs. Francis whom I mentioned to you before.*[40]

A letter from John's sister Sophia Francis to Abby's sister Sarah gives an idea how the mail operated in the United States two centuries ago. She writes that when no one they know is bound for Providence, "we send down to the wharf to know wether any vessel is bound to Boston, Newport, or Providence and without ceremony write."[41]

In December 1789, the *General Washington* left Newport on its second voyage to the Orient, preceded by, three weeks earlier, the Brown & Francis brigantine *Providence*. The firm was plunging boldly, the way John Brown did everything, into the risky Far East trade.[42]

The record is sketchy for the year 1790, but it was not without interest for the Brown and Francis families. In February Anne Willing Francis wrote in surprise to Abby: "I had not the smallest Idea you was so near Confinement, as I had never heard you was in that way untill a few days before your Papa was down here." That John's mother was delighted could hardly surprise anyone: "It will give me additional pleasure to have so interesting an object added to our Circle and the Expected Stranger, as *he or she* cannot fail to partake in the Love I most sincerely bear its Parents."[43]

The Expected Stranger arrived on February 24 and, unsurprisingly, was named after her paternal grandmother, Anne Willing Francis. She was to live only eight years.

Anne Willing Francis did not hear of the birth of her namesake for some weeks after the happy event. She promptly responded, on April 4:

> *. . . I am very Anxious to hear of my dear little Granddaughter. I hope Your Mother agrees with me in the propriety of your having an excellent good nurse to suckle it. Depend on it, you have not strength of Constitution for the business—next letter I hope will clear up my Doubts on this very important point, neither my Son, or you, have given the most Distant Hint who Nurses it—and tis of the greatest import to her that her Nourishment should be derived from a very Robust young Person.*[44]

That August, President Washington made the final of his four trips to Rhode Island. That completed his tour of the original United States. He had begun such a tour in New England the previous autumn but avoided Rhode Island because it had not yet ratified the Constitution. That little

Sara Smith Brown (1738-1825). Portrait by Francis Alexander.

state was the first to declare its independence from the Crown and the last to join the Union. Rhode Island joined the other original states in May and in August, as soon as Congress adjourned, Washington sailed from New York to Newport, only his second sea voyage, the first nearly forty years before when he accompanied his ill brother Lawrence to the Barbados in 1751. After a day and a night in Newport, he journeyed up Narragansett Bay to another tumultuous welcome in Providence. We can safely assume that he met John and Abby Francis for he stopped for refreshment at John Brown's, then one of the grandest mansions in the new nation, and he knew well the Francis family from his long stays in Philadelphia, for John's father, Tench Francis, and his uncle, Thomas Willing, were prominent Philadephians.

Introducing John Francis

3

John Francis Abroad

. . . . "Liberty has many enticing blessings". . . .

John Francis July 20, 1792[1]

THE YEAR 1791 must have seemed to John Brown, John Francis and their families an ordinary sort of year in most respects, made special by the death on May 29 at the age of sixty-two of Nicholas Brown, the eldest of the famous four Brown brothers, and the birth two days later of John Brown Francis who, for three decades or more, was to play a leading role in the story of the Brown's Tract.[2]

John Francis, still only twenty-eight, was named a trustee of Rhode Island College, later Brown University. John Brown, with the price of rum high, decided to open a gin distillery and Brown & Francis advertised in the *Providence Gazette* for the necessary grain. And, finally, John Brown was to have his bank. After some advice from John Francis's father Tench who on the 22nd of May writes:

. . . What shall I say to you about Banks and Banking, it seems you want and are determined to have one. You may begin and lay the Foundation, but unless you have a sum in deposits sufficient to pay the Expences of the Establishment it cannot be carried on to yield the Stockholders a reasonable proffit. . . . Every depositor on the average will have in a book about 500 drs two thirds of which may be safely let out on interest, & from this fund Alone you are to look for the Expences of the Institution. You may prove this assertion right or wrong very readily in this mode. Go to every man in your Town who Will make use of your Bank, put down the sum that each had in Hand in Specie, then divide the sum Total by the number of depositors. What ever answer that gives you may depend upon its being always the same under every circumstance. With us ever since the first operations of the Bank of North America in all Seasons of the year the deposits have been the same, that is 500 drs for each customer, the reason is plain, in general

people keep no more money by them than what may possibly be wanting for unforeseen calls. . . . Upon the whole if you are determined to establish a small Bank in your Town, make the experiment with a small Capital say Twenty or Thirty thousand dollars, and you'll soon find wether the Business is worth carrying on or not. Any information that you can want in regard to the mode of keeping your accounts and every precaution necessary to guard against Fraud without as well as within Doors will most chearfully be communicated to any intelligent person you may think proper to send here for that purpose. . . .[3]

In June Brown & Francis invited the leading businessmen of Providence to a meeting. Then throughout the summer and early fall, John Brown consummated plans for the institution, corresponding with his brother Moses, and John Francis with Samuel Ward, merchant of New York. The bank was established on October 3 with John Brown elected president.

Thus, Providence became the fifth city in the still young nation to have a bank, following Philadelphia, New York, Boston and Baltimore. James Brown recorded in his diary that the Brown family had 240 out of the 1,329 shares, which, at $400 a share, came to $96,000, a substantial fortune in those distant days. John Brown himself had 100 shares, Brown & Francis 60, James Brown 40, and Sarah and Alice Brown 40.

In January of that year, John Francis received a very warm letter from Theodore Foster, one of Rhode Island's first two senators, for his letters introducing him to prominent Philadelphians, among them Robert Morris: "And I have a thousand Times thought of acknowledging my grateful Sensation to you which I have felt the more forcibly because the Letters were offered Me without my having solicited them. – The Civilities I have received also from your worthy Father and his Family since my Arrival in this City demand my warmest Acknowledgment. – I dined at his House on the 18th of the month the Day after I arrived in this City when he gave me a general Invitation to call on him at all Times when convenient with a Promise of Introduction to the Family Acquaintances. . . ." Which is to say the leading families of Philadelphia, the most important city in the young nation, as well as prominent men from other states with whom Tench Francis had business, social or family ties. The pertinence of this will become evident later.

Also of interest in Senator Foster's letter is his account of seeking a place to stay. He finally settles on boarding with the family of Samuel Bayard who "has reputable Connexions and Genteel Acquaintance. . . ." The cost? Six dollars a week. How different from life in the national capital now.[4]

That same month, January, the *Providence Gazette* gushed over the latest ship built by John Brown: "To be launched, a most elegant coppered

Thomas Willing Francis (1767-1815). Portrait by Charles Wilson Peale.

ship called the *President Washington* belonging to Messrs. Brown and Francis, launched at the shipyard near Fox Point. She is intended for the India Trade, is 950 tons burthen and allowed to be the best ship ever built in New England." This, one of three ships John Brown named after the first president, was a sore point with him for the rest of his life. Thomas Willing Francis, John's brother, who travelled as supercargo to India, sold it there, exercising his best judgment, with which John Brown, when he learned of the sale, differed bitterly. Years after this, Henry Smith, the clerk who handed to John Brown the letter informing him of the sale, reported: "Mr. Brown read the letter and sat for some time with the tears streaming down his cheeks."[5] This for some time colored the relations between Brown and his son-in-law's brother, although later, in the financial tangle through which Brown bulled his way to obtain title to the John Brown's Tract, he came to rely completely on Thomas Willing Francis.

While John Brown and John Francis were engaged in Rhode Island with their many commercial enterprises, great land purchases that would affect the fortunes of Brown & Francis were taking place in the northern wilderness of New York. This constituted a financial and political maze which in all likelihood will never be entirely sorted out. Probably the best account we will ever have is that of Franklin B. Hough. Hough was not only a medical doctor and a "fondly remembered. . . dean of the history of northern New York" but an authority on constitutional law and a pioneer in the then-young field of forestry. When Congress established the Forestry Service in 1876, President Grant named Dr. Hough as its first head.[6] All subsequent accounts of the astonishing land deals in Northern New York have necessarily relied on Dr. Hough's.

These deals took place in an atmosphere marked by cries of corruption by the legislature and the governor, DeWitt Clinton—accusations that behind the deals were British loyalists who wanted to purchase the land so it could be annexed to Canada, charges that Aaron Burr was involved in shady maneuvering. All of these charges were eventually dismissed but that is not necessarily proof that they were entirely false, for the clearing was done by men, some of whom stood to gain handsomely by the deals.

Whatever the truth or falsity of the various and conflicting charges, it is obvious that enormous profiteering (or the possibility of it, for many of the schemes failed because they were so patently absurd) was made possible by administrative and legislative action in Albany. In any case, Alexander Macomb on June 22, 1791, applied to purchase an enormous tract that turned out to be (to the extent anyone really knew in those days of rather vague surveying practices) 3,816,960 acres, an area larger than several states and nearly five times the area of John Brown's Rhode Island. For this he was to pay the merely nominal price of eight cents an acre. No wonder that Macomb, who had been a member of the New York Assembly shortly before he engineered the idea, expected to make huge profits.

But as is so often the case in this narrative, expectation was one thing and realization quite another. Macomb was involved in other land speculations, things went wrong and he, like others we will encounter, ended up in debtor's prison, perhaps happily, for, according to Hough, men who felt cheated by him threatened his life.

While all this land speculation was taking place, the New York legislature passed its first Canal Law authorizing exploration, survey, and estimates for possible canals along the Mohawk-Oswego route. It is interesting that Elkanah Watson in his journal reports that British troops were still at Fort Oswego in direct contravention of the peace treaty eight years before. This sort of behavior by the British explains American nervousness in the regions bordering Canada and why the New York State government was eager to have the land settled by Americans.

Watson also reported that the area around present-day Utica and Rome was attracting settlers, this less than fifty miles from what would become the Brown's Tract. "Emigrants are swarming into these fertile regions in shoals, like the ancient Isrealites seeking the land of promise."

Then Watson makes an observation that marks him truly a son of Rhode Island, birthplace of American democracy. Speaking of an Onondage Indian chief, he writes:

> *. . . I can safely say, I felt more respect and veneration, for old Kiadote, in the stern of his canoe, than I ever did for the mighty monarchs of Europe; several of whom I have beheld with eyes of contempt—and for this plain reason, that Kiadote is, probably, a blessing to his nation, whereas civilized kings, as they are called, are,* for the most part, *a scourge to the human race, and a curse to mankind.*[7]

Meanwhile, on May 31, 1791, was born the child who was to have the longest and most significant relationship with the John Brown's Tract of any member of the family. John Brown Francis was born in Philadelphia at the home of his grandparents, Tench and Anne Willing Francis. Then, as Francis wrote to his daughter, Anne Francis Woods, some seventy-two years later, "When six weeks old JBF left Phila for Providence where he was Received on the wharf & taken into the arms of his Grandfather Brown who from that moment to the hour of his death in Sept 1803 thirteen years uniformly & unceasingly regarded him with the tenderest care & solicitude."[8]

In Rhode Island there could have been only a dim awareness of what was happening in northern New York as our principals went about their lives. Towards year's end, John Francis was preparing for his long-deferred trip to Europe. In a letter of introduction to a London merchant, he is identified not only as being "of one of the best families in Philadelphia" but "in principle against the African trade."[9] This, of course, opposes him to the views of his father-in-law and business partner, for John Brown defended the slave trade well after New England opinion had turned sharply against it.

John Francis arrived in England on January 25, 1792, where he demonstrated in diaries kept for the English and French segments of his trip, that he had a keen observer's eye, not merely on mercantile matters but as to mechanical devices and social customs.

His intense curiosity about everything around him is reflected in his journal. He, like most travelers from the small cities of the United States, was astonished by London. "And is it possible that a Diameter of 10 miles from the spot I now write in would encircle a Million of my Fellow Creatures, and among that Multitude not one who cares a Button for me. My head turns around I know not how to act, where to go—"

But he was little impressed by the House of Lords where, "by Stealth & Bribe," he went to hear King George III address both Houses. "My expectation was not answerd the room was small, hung with old Tapestry. The Throne but measly decorated. On the one side sat the Prince of Wales on the other and left the Dukes of York & Clarence . . . ."

One evening he lectured a streetwalker:

> *. . . Returning from the Theatre I was accosted by a pretty young girl, 'pray give me a few pence'—'Will you go with me Sir'—I turn'd & accompanied her in the next House when there I reason'd with her on the propriety of her Conduct. On the Misery of her future Life on the Baseness of her Occupation. All was useless, she said she was too poor. Well then work—No, she did not know how—She was too weak—At length she roused into a passion and bid me leave of talking on the Subject, she was poor, but happy, and Sorrow wod come without looking. Having present a few shillings I quit her to reflect on my advice. She was but 20 years. Had a Lively Eye, a fair skin, a very expressive Face, adorned with a fine Person. Seduced at 15, by a Nobleman she is now reduced to the lowest Ebb of Life that of Street walking. How much happier was my Situation on an Easy pillar, thinking of my Abby & my dear Honest born Children.*

He writes about a funeral procession. "two Mourning carriages filled with Mourners not Relatives, Not Friends but hired Mimicks of Real Woe." About the amazing sums of money at the Stock Exchange. About the king: "a large fat man of ruddy complexion & of a tollerable disposition, in common conversation he talks rapidly, but on this occasion he delivered his speech with clearness and precision. Elegance was out of the question."

About the vitality of the London Street life . . . and again about prostitutes: "Once I determin'd to hear again their plaintive Tale but the Image of my dearly beloved Wife – Bid me beware Temptation. For my sweet Angel I will neither Sin or Break your Commandment. I am so much your property here as Transatlantic. Your beloved Idea always hangs present to my view and warns me of Evil."

He writes about the shops, about the process for making lead shot, about the caricatures that are sold everywhere. "Scandal & scandalous sarcasms on all the well born are the subject of all. The King, the Queen, the royal family & his ministers are the main targets they aim at, some hit, a great many widely miss, and a few must wound and cut deeply . . . . In all there prints a strong resemblance is always retained of the characters. The profligacy of all the Princes. The parsimony of the Queen & King. The debauchery of all at court certainly admits of just censure . . . ."

Francis also has a wry sense of humor, as he demonstrates in writing about the ubiquitous English turnip.

> *. . . First Turnips are raised & Sheep Eat these tops changing [their pasture] from Square to Square as the Owner wishes by fencing in with Poles that move at pleasure – Thus Mutton is made of Turnips – The Roots are part boiled as Sauce – Cows are fed only part & you have Turnip Butter – part are ground & (made) into Cyder to drink with your Mutton and part into Port or Madeira Wine to drink After – Fashionable Folks go farther who dine at 5 & 6 oclock by Turnip Tallow Candles and the King himself wears Turnip Woolen Coats – Ergo Turnip here is Every Thing & Ergo pays Taxes for every thing pays Taxes –*

Although everything in the journal is interesting, giving a vivid picture of teeming London, perhaps most important is his visit to Thomas Paine who, it is safe to assume, was an old family friend from Philadelphia. Francis was with his old employer and friend, Peter Whiteside.

> *. . . We thence went in Search of Mr Paine who we found in an obscure Garret dressing himself and preparing to pay me a visit. He had changed from one bad Lodging to another that he might work at ease and without danger of interruption on his new piece called "The Second part of the Rights of Man containing Principle and Practice." This Philippic against the English, their government in my opinion amounts to absolute Libel. Yet they dare not take hold of him.*

A few days later Paine returned the call.

. . . At 9 oClock T. Paine came in and soon entered into conversation about his Second part of the Rights of Man. No reason can convince him of any existing dangers or of the Impropriety of entering any Country he is not a Subject to with an intention to subvert a Government which the Subjects are contented with. A perfect Madman in Principle and conduct. There is no (evil treatment) however Cruel that he would not cheerfully suffer to promote the Sentiment he pretends to inculcate. . . . did they dare to touch him millions that are silent would rise to espouse his Cause.

John Francis' journals are not only interesting to read but contain a number of fine pen-and-ink drawings of various mechanical devices.

A few months later, just before he entered revolutionary France, John Francis wrote to Abby on the seventh anniversary of their marriage. Love letters are seldom exercises in understatement and this, even for one given to some fairly lively love letters, is anything but that. This one sentence will give you some idea of the whole: "Remembrance in all its pleasing forms steals on my Fancy and with cunning address bids Tears Hypocrite, my Heart my Soul my all is THINE."[10]

When John Francis went to France in July of 1792, he knew, of course, that France was in the midst of its Revolution, but he had no way of knowing that he was stepping into some of the most ghastly days of the Terror. His diary, often shudderingly graphic, makes compelling reading and adds a personal dimension to an upheaval that has had such a profound effect on modern history. That he was already well aware of the excesses of the Revolution is apparent by an entry made on his second day in France, July 20: "Liberty has many enticing blessings, and ought to be cultivated in all countries, but here, unfortunately, every effort to regain that precious blessing has been marked with crimes that debase the human race, with conduct that ridicules our reason. . . ."[11]

The entry for the next day is characteristic of his journal. He writes alternately of the beauty of the landscape and the horrors of the Revolution. "The land in general is sandy but productive. This year so great a harvest was never known; wheat, rye, barley, buckwheat, flax and indeed every grain seems to be in full and quantity. Happy France."

But his view of France quickly changes. After describing a quick tour of Lille, he writes:

From there we went to view the spot where the horrid massacre of poor General Dillon was perpetrated, an action too meanly base and cruel to admit of any excuse, a barbarity which will ever stamp on the citizens of Lille a mark of dishonor which a multitude of conspicuous brave actions will never exterminate.

I saw with horror, the spot those savages plunged their bayonets into that brave, noble officer. I saw the lantern where they hung him when dead, and like cannibals cut off his limbs, roasted his body and in beastly revenge gnawed his lifeless trunk. Vengeance was called for by the National Assembly, and inquirey was ordered and the names of the brave Dillons are to be appeased by the death of one poor tailor who was proved to be an accomplice. A woman, it is said will suffer. She, with the usual patriotic rage that fires every man dressed her delicate form in an Huzzars regimentals with the express purpose of embruing her hands in the innocent blood of a noble officer. Such an instance of fore-premeditated cruelty would almost stagger the belief and destroy all that amiable affection we ought ever to feel for the female sex. For me it is enough that I thoroughly know the transcendent virtues of my Abby, and that I believe her merits will extenuate the faults of thousands of her species."

Francis notes that the war—the powerful kingdoms of Europe had arrayed themselves against the republican government of France—"has almost put a period to every honest exertion" and he notes that the big textile factories of Lille are almost at a standstill.

". . . At all events the present division must give the enemies of the new Constitution a great advantage, if not a decided superiority, when they are sufficiently collective to attack France from their encampment at Coblentz. Suspicion operates on the minds of everyone almost one brother suspects his father, and his father his brother. One day brings in an account of the denunciation against the Mayor of Paris, who has been imprisoned; the next paper informs his restoration to office, and the charge against the Marquis DeLafayette. I love France, I admire her people, and as I sincerely wish them well, I cannot but now feel and lament for their present unhappy situation. The cause of mankind is involved in their success, and the fall of liberty throughout Europe with their fall."

The young Francis then notes that on the morrow he heads first for the encampment of the French army under Lafayette and only then on to Paris: "My curiousity and judgment does not in this instance go hand in hand, but the satisfaction of having seen the Marquis and so many champions of liberty in one grand camp, exceeds my desire to be in Paris."

Yet, all he saw and felt could not preempt his thoughts of Abby.

. . . I must now bid good night to my loved Julia, as it is now Saturday and the particular day on which I always toast wives and sweethearts. Indeed, every day and every leisure hour is dedicated to that home I long to see and which I promise never to leave again. The man calls me to the hot baths, and I must off."[12]

Although Lafayette might well have welcomed a visit from the son of a friend of George Washington, Francis was not permitted to approach within two miles of the encampment. Nonetheless, he was able to make a judgment about the Marquis' army.

. . . We had, however, the pleasure of seeing a great number of their troops straggling about the country without any restrictions, poorly dressed, and if I might be deemed a sufficient judge, the most miserable looking men for soldiers I ever saw. If their camp does not boast a better set, I am fearful, for the cause of liberty will be but a flimsy assistance and shield against the Austrian and Prussian bayonet when pushed by old hardened veterans, and conducted by brave, accomplished leaders in the art of war. Besides this inferiority, they have many other disadvantages to encounter. A general distrust of their commanders, which is the cause of daily resignations; a discontent of the conduct of the assembly; and what weighs heavier than any, is the party spirit which exists throughout France and divides the people into every possible faction. For my part, attached as I am to the French people, I cannot view their situation without feeling a degree of pity mixed with horror for their present forlorn and almost lost state. Opposed by two powerful open enemies and secretly opposed by every European power, distracted in their councils and their very inferior country, beset with aristocrats, colored as the strongest democrats, all these backed by the bigotry of the old people under the influence of the non-adjuring clergy, most apparently destroys their present system of government. What will be substituted in its place the Lord only knows.[13]

These observations are plainly the product of a mature and perceptive judgment and of a graceful pen. John Francis was still only twenty-nine, but it must be remembered that he was raised in Philadelphia in the company of the great men of the American Revolution (he was thirteen at the time of the Declaration of Independence) during that extraordinary period as they spoke and wrote their imperishable words about liberty. What an education he had received, living in that unique circle at that unique moment, a moment in American history that has never been equalled.

His French journal is filled with observations acute and perceptive and, when they deal with the people and their trials, sympathetic. In Cambray he describes how coins are struck in the mint, how cambric cloth is spun and woven by country girls and the absurd costumes of the coachmen. He discusses the sale of churches as decreed by the National Assembly:

. . . If the land of the clergy had been disposed of to raise money for the use of the government, the country would have been greatly injured. The cultivation would have been the same, the beauty preserved, but to dispose of those superb buildings, which decorate the country at large, and bespeak almost Roman magnificence, show more than Gothic rage and ignorance. Out of seventeen churches in the town of Cambray alone, fourteen have been sold and pulled to

ruins . . . This public authorization of sacrilege among a people if not bigoted yet religiously inclined, must have an influence that will, I fear, eventually strengthen the advocates for absolute monarchial government. The very children are taught to despise the new form Priests and rather to suffer divine displeasure than make their supposed due confession to those who now perform the public services.

If, then, the present age are taught to despise the only religion they believe because unworthy hands perform the holy office, I fear that even should the Democrats succeed at present, a future Civil War more hideous than the present, will devour the poor remains of the once grand and envied kingdom of France.[14]

Young Francis writes of Picardy as "a glorious country groaning under a delicious burden of almost every blessing any soil can produce" yet, by the mean appearance of the dwellings, poverty-stricken. "One reason, it seems, given for the apparent poverty of the people, is the mean appearance of their clayed hovels, that being liable to cruel extortion from the Revenue Officers, they are obliged to feign poverty in order to prevent its reality."

He writes of a bridge "the most beautiful . . . I ever saw" at Ponte Sainte Maxenne, of the extortionate meal at Sentis and of his visit, shortly after arriving in Paris, to "the Palais Royal where all the world assembles and walks to show their wares or purchase of other." If it should be compared to any bazaar in London, "it would surely be highly to the disadvantage of the latter, where neither taste nor variety could claim scarcely an humble competition in women, in dress or in numbers . . . it is now divided into many habitations and a multitude of shops, richly furnished with every article of convenience or luxury the habitable world wants or ever produced."

And he writes of hiring a carriage to visit "my friend Mr. Go[u]ve[r]neur Morris," the American ambassador:

. . . The streets of Paris are so very narrow, dirty and crowded that no gentleman, much more a stranger, can with safety walk, and as necessity does but seldom sanction custom, where she goes we ought out of complaisance to obey. Here we were, therefore, having agreed for thirteen livres per day in paper, say 6 shillings sixpence sterling for a hansom chariot, and good horses to say naught of the guide who may be a captain of a troop of National Horse, and that no degradation if all men sont Egaux. This vehicle conducted me to our Embassador's who received me kindly, and as kindly gave me every information required.

Everyone agreed that Francis needed new clothes, so he quickly sent for the king's tailor and hoped that by Friday, only two days away, he would be "a la mode Paris," He was already French inside, "up to my shoulders" he told his journal, because of the food he had eaten since

Dunkerque, but he was not so sure about his head, even though "My tongue it is true wags French."[15] Young Francis had an ironic sense of humor and nowhere would that be more suitable than France, where luxury and merriment often prevailed in the midst of the bloodshed and disintegration of the Revolution.

Although Francis was unquestionably a republican, he wrote that his "blood boiled" when a bill, which he thought "merited death" was proposed in the National Assembly, that all the statues of royalty be melted into cannons. He thought the new government should pay "a due regard for the religious and moral customs of the people. Cultivate the arts and sciences and avoid destroying churches, that societies are attached to, fabrics that ornament and give distinguished preference to France. Avoid also demolishing the statues of men who having their foibles, yet had merit in raising France to the great pinnacle of respectability she was placed on when they died; statues which now ought and will hereafter stamp a fame on the age when they were made, a credit on the artist and an emulation in our successors to imitate."[16]

Almost every entry demonstrates Francis' concern over the bloody disintegration of France:

> . . . *In vain thy patriotic efforts poor France, thy liberty like the dew of the morn is vanished, and thy inhabitants like the herbage under the torrid sun will be left parched under the rays of despotism.*
>
> *Thy former situation deserves an alteration. Never had any people so favorable an opportunity of quietly making such amendments as are requisite, nay, further never had any nation so fair an opening to establish that very constitution which your representatives formed, and which is daily destroyed by the frenzy and madness of a portion of monsters who call themselves Jacobins or Enragee. It is not for me to say whether profit or ignorance is the cause, but the world can testify that disorder, anarchy and ruin is the effect.*

And Francis reported that a mob of 4,000 "drunken" Bretons tried to force their way into the King's palace but were held back by the guards.

> . . . *Hand bills are now at this late hour, at midnight, crying about the street acusing the King of treason, the Queen of perfidy and treasonable designs, and LaFayette of every crime that any of the accused parties so prone as they are to evil, could cunningly commit. This moment a mob opposite our house almost at the Palais Royal, have nobly scarrified one man into pieces, dissected anothers arm and occulate (if I may use the word) a bystanders eye, so fares the cause of the supporters of freedom.*

Yet even while the horrors of the French Revolution were unfolding around him, Francis finds beauty. He describes the gate of St. Dennis and St. Martins:

. . . Every beauty that a gate or arch of stone can admit is here expressed. For me all the labor appears lost, when expended on the same species of stone which in England they call Portland, soft in the quarry and easy to cut, the sculptor is tempted to hasten his time and taste on what is not durable. Twenty years wears the angles off, and one, almost the striking beauty. But when you add fifty years, the face of the whole vanishes and your eye is fed by your senses, you are induced to believe that the crowd of figures assembled together on so large an edifice must once have been great, and therefore now continue so, especially as men of taste from whom we dare not differ daily declare that those gates are great.

And Francis found amusement in the theater which he regarded as superior to that in London.[17] He describes, too, the opulent beauty of the palaces at Versailles and Trianon but, as always, returns to the deteriorating political situation. This he wrote after a visit to the National Assembly:

. . . If France ever required men of ability at the helm of affairs, she does now. If ever private and party resentment ought to give way to amity and concord, it is now, and if ever an industrious exertion and attention to the immediate wants of the Kingdom were requisite, this is the moment, or all that had been done will be idly lost and this devoted kingdom again the shuttle cock of Courts and their parasites. . . . For, believe me, I do not exaggerate; no town meeting, no mob, however obstreporous in America and I hope in no other country, ever made more noise, reasoned so little, or seemed to have less reverence for their President, or regard for their own character.[18]

On Sunday, August 5, 1792, John Francis saw the king, Louis XVI, in his chapel at the Tuilleries, accompanied by the queen, the Dauphin and Princess Maria Theresa Charlotte.

. . . The King, a gentlemanly fine looking fellow, blessed with a cheerful happy countenance, and I believe an honest heart exceeded my expectation. He looked firm yet pleasant, and endeavored to throw a gleam of joy where anxious sorrow only dwelt. . . . The Queen resembled no one that I recollect at present more than Mrs. Bennell of Boston, being a little pocked and a little red with painting, but a better person and a finer face. She entered the galley of the chapel with a superior magnanimity and with a view of contemptuous scorn viewed the reptiles beneath her and refused to smile as the good king wished. He poor man had not been one moment in bed during the night. An insurrection among the Marsellors or Marseilles soldiers or irregulars threatened his life, therefore everyone kept awake; fortunately

the Queen was ignorant and slept the night in quiet. . . . Not a face among the crowd except those faces that never had anything but villainy or vacancy in their appearances, but looked sad and melancholy. Distrustful of the future, chagrined at the past, all seemed to be satisfied that more certain dangers threatened the persons of the Royal Family than even I could believe was possible.[19]

For a while he turned from the horrors of the Revolution to inspect the famous Paris Plate Glass Manufactory where he took detailed notes on how the quicksilver and lead are applied to the backs of mirrors.

. . . The wages of the workmen is determined by their knowledge, and as I before have often declared, the danger they encounter. The effect of this metal causes a swelling in the lips and nose, a sore where only a scratch was before, a shortness of breath, a total inability. Wisely and politically only one out of five is worked by those who lay the lead or quicksilver rather; one week's work requires four weeks' delay. . . .[20]

By August 9 Francis was eager to leave for home, but he had not yet heard whether a vessel was available in Bordeaux, where he hoped to embark directly for the United States.

. . . I am distressed, my dearest Julia, and custom hitherto has taught me to fly to you for relief, but alas, only aggravated distress ensues. Yes, my sweetest girl, your Francis has been most cruelly disappointed, and though tomorrow is the day he promised to quit Europe forever, yes tomorrow, and he only quits Paris.

Pleased as I ought to be with the city you almost ordered me to adore, yet my anxiety becomes daily so extreme that unless I have a short passage, to America, all the health my voyage has afforded will be mainly stolen by silent chagrin and morose. . . .

So he did what any anxious husband would do: he went out and bought gifts for his wife and her sisters. And anxious to hear news from Bordeaux, he wrote: "The post boy careless of the tidings he bears, whistles as he trots and boldly delivers letters which convey what causes many a heart-ache, many a tear, and the news of destruction of fathers, children, Kings and kingdoms." His final entry that day records the unhappy news that "The police of the city relative to strangers and emigrants, have refused to grant passports to quit the city."

The horror that young John Francis saw in Paris in previous days paled before what he saw on August 10. A few days later, he dined with Ambassador Gouverneur Morris who made this entry in his diary:

. . . Mr. Francis gives a dreadful account of what he saw on the tenth and says that he shall not dare to tell it in America.[21]

The attack on the Palais Royal, August 11, 1792.

It is impossible, of course, to know how much John Francis told of that ghastly day when he returned home, but so uncommon are firsthand accounts by an American that his journal merits quotation at length:

. . . At eight o'clock my servant with a trembling voice called me to learn that Paris was all in alarm. That the tocksin bell was sounding, the drums beating the alarm. That 20 or more chevaliers of the Order of St. Louis have been massacred by the mob for daring to appear last evening before the Tuilleries.

Instantly rose and had not clothed myself when the captain Ingraham, Mr. Price and Mr. Jarvis of Boston entered. They had been spectators of the brutal destruction of many of those poor victims who lay groaning on the ground in the Square de Vendom, lacerated by a thousand wounds and when dying by inches, their enraged assassins like butchers with common knives cut their heads off and stuck them on poles.

We had but breakfasted and those gentlemen quit our rooms about ten minutes, when out of breath they entered to inform us that the Swiss Regiment were attacked in the Thuilleries by the populace and that a general massacre was expected. 10 o'clock. The streets are now filled with men of every description and armed with every popular weapon fancy could invent to torture and destroy. Regiments seemed now marching to the attack, and a company of half women with pikes and swords seem furiously determined to destroy all they meet. This instance a servant whom

The massacre of the Swiss Guards on August 10, 1792.

we sent for news says the Royal Family are saved and now are in the National Assembly, but that the Chateau is forced and taken.

The young American's account grows steadily more horrifying even though, perhaps because, his language is as restrained as he can manage.

. . . We are now convinced that the Swiss are destroyed. Shoals of men and women are returning crowned with what they deem the triumphal march of conquest.

Their spears, swords and sticks with nails in them have remnants of the regimentals of the slaughtered guards attached to them. Scarce a man but has some mark of blood, gained not from their own wounds, but the dead bodies of their enemies.

The ground almost appears covered with the dead trunks of devoted people, their heads are thrown with less concern than we should stones, and nothing stops the accused cruelty of these cannibals. Not a decent character have I seen among them, all appear the mere scum of the earth. What a stab is such conduct against these supporters of virtuous freedom. And what severe and strong arguments have the advocates for a severe monarchy when they can revert to the unheard of cruelties daily committed by a people who now boast of philanthropic minds, and a universal goodwill towards all mankind, when their individual conduct testifies so strong to the contrary.

A noise in the street called me to view the head of a poor Swiss soldier, only 22 years old, a species of drunken beast somewhat like a man only in shape was bearing it coolly telling the crowd as he passed along to whom the trophy belonged. Behind him came boys, women and men huddled together some with fingers, etc., etc. of the deceased. My God, canst Thou pardon crimes like this?

Francis reports that at three he and his friends sat down to dinner "but who could eat when their eyes have been glutted by the half roasted limbs of their fellow creatures carried in horrid manner on the ends of dung forks?" At five they had finished eating what little they could and "altogether sallied out to see what had been done."

. . . But aghast and trembling my senses could not avoid accusing my eyes. A head grey, nay, white with age, lay carelessly in the first gutter. The body, alas, was perhaps under the feet of a base ignominious crowd, a mob.

The Palais Royal covered with blood offered many lifeless trunks, among the number was that of the virtuous Defender of Liberty and LaFayette, Mons. Duomlard, who but yesterday asserted the rights of man, the virtues of individuals and deprecated those who basely wronged his country.

He lay on the common stones stabbed, cut and bayonetted in a hundred places. His head and his hands off, and his feet hanging but by the tendons that were used to cover them.

The Thuilleries are yet on fire; not the Palace itself, but the row of buildings or barracks in which the Swiss Guards used to live. Here death in every horrid shape rode triumphant over the poor massacred Swiss. Here fell revenge and abominable unparalleled cruelty, too full declared that unlicensed men were worse than furious tigers.

Not a soul have I seen out of perhaps 200 that had not received from 8 to 10 thrusts of the bayonet and all, aye, I say again, everyone cut in three or four places across the throat and their eyes and brains beat out.

Women in decent dresses sat hideously on their bodies, as they naked as when born and with ferocious damnable revenge took sticks and rammed straw and rags into their mouths, or with sticks and knives lacerated the lifeless corps.

Nay, that very altar at which I saw the King, Queen and his Royal Family on the last Sunday returning thanks to God, that very altar was defiled by the innocent blood of the poor sacrificed Swiss. They lay on the steps, monuments of the barbarity of those devils they have hitherto served to protect.[22]

There is more, but what we have quoted is enough, perhaps too much. One can hardly be surprised that he then left Paris as quickly as he could. His last entry is dated August 12, 1792, Saturday:

. . . The defaits of this day required a better pen than I have to demonstrate, a better Republican than I am to exculpate the asserters of liberty. Cruelty and rapine are flimsy advocates in any cause. Cowardice and baseness but savage

excuses for the excess of rage. . . . I must from my bosom declare that what I have seen in France has been the conduct of the most barbarous of the world.

The young man "almost ordered . . . to adore" Paris concluded his remarkable journal with this passage:

But I should be very unjust and unwise were I now to attest in this last of my Journal otherways than I believe.

First: That the French are generally too savage to be free.

Second: That they are too ignorant to choose their own governors.

And lastly: That a punch bowl is better fitted for a saddle than Frenchmen for a Republic.

So honestly believes, J. F.[23]

While John Francis was in Europe, there were important developments at home in Providence and Philadelphia and, although no one in the Brown or Francis families was probably aware of them, up in the wilderness where within a few years the John Brown's Tract would be carved out. The bank that John Brown started with John Francis' assistance was prospering, paying 8 percent interest, a substantial rate in those days.[24] Also, the Brown & Francis ship *Hope* called at Sydney, the second American ship by only a few days to reach Australia.[25] And Anne Willing Francis, ever the faithful correspondent, wrote to Abby commenting on British conquests in India:

". . . a more unjust War can't be conceived. Yet as our dear Tom [John's brother] is in that Country, and has so much of your Fathers property there, I must be better satisfied with the Success of the British Arms as the Advantage is ever on the victors side."[26]

About the same time a letter addressed to Tom Francis in India was written by his older cousin, Thomas Mayne Willing, who was handling his affairs in Philadelphia. Although John's brother had considerable debts, they would, according to his cousin, be easily met if those, including Brown & Francis, would pay what was owed him.

. . . All that can be added on this Subject is that if your Friends in Rhode Island were to give the aid they ought in this business and support your Credit, these affairs would be easily closed; instead of which my repeated solicitations have been neglected by Mr. B (your Brother now being in Europe) who actually has declined entering into any investigation of your accounts, which have repeatedly been furnished by me on your behalf and payments demanded in the warmest manner. The large Balance due you he appears to Doubt and Refers me for a settlement to your Brother on his return to America, which will not take place probably these twelve months, which must procrastinate this business very much

to your Prejudice; leaving your Credit to Suffer and perhaps such (for want of a proper feeling towards you), with the Gentlemen in India who have so Confidentially and Generously served you.

You are a Young Man just entering into the Commercial World, to support your punctuality is essential to establish Confidence towards you—and Mr. B's necessities ought not to Injure your prospects. . . .

John Brown apparently was habitually skeptical of bills tendered to him and this skepticism might well have been augmented by his distress at young Tom's (he was only twenty-five) selling of his favorite ship, the *President Washington*.

Whatever the case, Thomas Mayne Willing cautions his young cousin to keep his business "distinct" from that of Brown & Francis.

. . . Improve this hint Mr. B will always hang on you a heavy load if you are willing to submit and I am of opinion that his speculations are hazardous and imprudent and must occasion his pressing hard on his Connections for support in them, they must prove unprofitable not being founded on Cash or Capital—and this termination may distress you. I do not mean to Doubt the solidity of Mr. B situation by these observations on the Contrary. I think him a man of valuable Candid estate, but at this time charged with some Considerable Demands which may Require time to Discharge.[27]

There is no doubt that John Brown was a daring merchant and that sometimes his actions were "hazardous and imprudent," but it is also true that Rhode Island merchants, because of the state's lack of natural resources, were forced to take more risks than merchants elsewhere. And it is true that, although John Brown often suffered considerable losses, his gambles often paid off. Nonetheless, his impulsiveness apparently often distressed his more prudent brother Nicholas and must have seemed wild indeed to Thomas Mayne Willing, son of the very prudent financier Thomas Willing.

Meanwhile, up in the great northern wilderness of New York, there was speculation of another kind. As we saw earlier, Alexander Macomb had purchased a vast tract from the state. Having made his first payment on January 10, 1792, Macomb received a patent for some 1,920,000 acres of his original purchase of 3,816,960 acres. This still-vast tract included the land in Lewis, Herkimer, and Hamilton Counties in the southeast corner of the Macomb Purchase, that later comprised the John Brown's Tract. Later that year, on June 6, perhaps because of the financial embarrassment that caused him to be lodged in debtor's prison, Macomb sold his entire parcel to William Constable of New City for £50,000, £22,000 less than he had paid for it just a few months before. Thus began a whole series of financial disasters involving the Macomb Purchase. The only one who escaped was William Constable, who soon doubled his money by selling, on December 17-18, 1,281,880 acres to Col. Samuel Ward for £100,000. Not only did Constable double his money, but he kept 640,000 acres for himself. Some of this he sold and some he lived on. Indeed, his home, Constable Hall, is still standing in Lewis County, and his family continued to live on it until recently.[28] Constable, however, lived on good, arable land just west of the barren Adirondacks land where the future John Brown's Tract would be situated.

The sale of the land, including the future Brown's Tract, to Col. Ward illustrates the way that in colonial and post-revolutionary times the lives of eminent men criss-crossed. The nation was still small in popualtion—not much more than 4,000,000 in 1792—and prominent business men in the major cities were often known to one another through the financial, family and social ties to which we referred earlier. Although Professor Hedges in his study of the Brown family does not make the connection, this Samuel Ward was apparently the same one who had sailed five years before as supercargo on the *General Washington*'s first voyage to the Orient and who, in 1806, would represent Brown & Ives in Bermuda when their ship the *John Jay* was seized by the British.[29] When John Brown, a few years later, became intensely interested in a portion of the land previously owned by his old family friend, it is not known whether he consulted Ward as to its value. Nor, for that matter, is it possible to know whether Ward had any significant information about the land. In those days, great speculations were often based more on expectations than on knowledge.

This is illustrated dramatically in one of the great failed schemes in the northern wilderness. William Constable journeyed to Paris which, as we saw from John Francis' journal, was in the bloody turmoil of the Terror. He sold land to a French company that hoped to make huge profits by selling land to aristocrats and other well-to-do Frenchmen wanting to escape the Revolution. The settlement, called Castorland after the Latin name for the beaver, attracted a few Frenchmen, most of whom were ill-suited for carving farms out of the wilderness. Eventually, and inevitably, it failed.

Another great speculation in the northern wilderness involved Robert Morris, the financier of the American Revolution and benefactor of John Francis. He sold 2.5 million acres of land in northern New York to the Holland Land Company, formed by four Amsterdam business houses and

James Greenleaf (1765-1843). Portrait by Gilbert Stuart.

John Brown's Tract

two Amsterdam banks. This brings into our narrative James Greenleaf, who is to become the villain of the piece. As a young man, this Boston native had been appointed United States Consul in Amsterdam where, according to the family genealogy, "he amassed a great fortune."[30] His business activities in Holland must have brought him to the attention of Robert Morris, for when Greenleaf, only thirty-years-old, returned to the United States, he joined Morris in a number of ventures, among them the most grandiose and perhaps most disastrous land speculation in American history – the North American Land Company. His function was to recruit purchasers in Holland.

Although the Greenleaf genealogy says that James Greenleaf returned from Holland in 1795, a respected historian, William Graham Sumner of Yale, wrote that he was engaged with Morris and his partner John Nicholson as early as 1793 in land speculation in the Federal City, as Washington, D.C., was first known. As in the nation at large, there was more land than there were people to purchase it and the speculations soon began to collapse. The land dealings became so complex that even Morris could not follow them. As he wrote in 1800, "It is not possible for me to delineate all the embarrassments that hang over this property, because there are several of which the particulars are not known to me."[31]

In any case, Morris, Nicholson, and Greenleaf passed deeds back and forth and pyramided loans, mortgages, and trusts, and, of course, the personal notes that were the primary means of exchange in those days of almost primitive banking. Their speculations in the Federal City and in the even more disastrous North American Land Company over-reached even their huge fortunes and by the time, in 1795, that Greenleaf became involved in business dealings with Brown & Francis, he was already severely embarrassed, although, as we shall see, John Brown had faith in both Greenleaf's integrity and his ability to meet his obligations.

That year, 1793, saw several other developments important to our story. The *President Washington,* now known as *L'Etrusco,* was captured by the British off Ostend, Holland, charged with violating the Neutrality Act, for Britain, as usual, was at war with several continental powers. This embroiled the Brown family in Admiralty Court for decades and for a time tainted the relationship between John Brown and Thomas Willing Francis, who, as we saw, sold the *President Washington* in Calcutta.

Also, Thomas continued to receive letters from his cousin Thomas Mayne Willing. They continued to shed light not only on family financial matters, but on wider concerns demonstrating anew their value to historians, especially business historians of the era.

John Francis Abroad

. . . Everywhere your conduct has ensured you Friends which is the best test of its prosperity whilst absence has Cost you none on this side, but from the accounts given of your transactions in India every person Desirous of doing Justice applaud your Judgement and exertions. You cannot be uninformed of Mr. B's dissatisfaction at your Sale of his Ship. . . . I wish he had exerted himself equally for the support of your Credit and prevented your being injured by the Non Payment of the Respondenties to Mr. Fairlie but not withstanding his promises to you and myself, and my numerous applications for payments on this acct The small portion of £4000 is all that has been paid and at this Moment Messrs Brown and Francis are your Debtors for at best stg £6000 — a sum sufficient to extinguish the Claims of the London Gent. on you for the Consigned Goods. . .[32]

John Francis, of course, had been back from Europe for several months but it is not known what, if anything, he did to settle the differences between his father-in-law and his brother. It is known, however that John was again being plagued by bad health; this might have reduced his business activities.

A few weeks later the elder Tom writes to the younger that Brown & Francis "is indebted to you at least £10,000" and he cautions him: "in future keep your funds unembarrassed by their operations. . . .[33]

A letter written by the elder Tom on March 4, 1793, illustrates how differently business was conducted in those days, nearly two centuries ago. He refers to Thomas Willing Francis' most recent letter, that "of the 27th of May last." Imagine doing business today based on information more than eight months old and with settlement of bills taking that long and longer.

On May 4 the elder wrote the younger that "America being almost the sole Commercial Nation now neutral, her Flag will be immensely Valuable and under the prudent administration of our affairs Wealth must Roll to us from all the World, our progression in Population and Improvement exceeds the most Sanguine expectation of any American. . . ." He argues that Britain will respect the American flag because the former colonies are her best customers and that the European powers will also because they need trade with America.

Then, Thomas Mayne Willing discusses land speculation. This cautious businessman, who called John Brown's speculations "hazardous and imprudent," writes glowingly of land "investments" made by him, his family and other prominent Philadelphians. While it is true that much of this land was of known, and good, quality unlike much in the great northern wilderness, Willing does say of Robert Morris that "the Prodigious sale of his Lands will clear him of everything and have him a very great estate."

Such was the reputation of Robert Morris that even so well informed a businessman as Willing simply could not conceive of Morris' failing.

Willing again refers to his cousin's dealings which so dissatisfied John Brown. ". . . Messrs B & F will I am satisfied see that thro your means they have made the best Voyage ever made by any American house to India.[34]

Nonetheless, he suggests to his cousin that Francis is not entirely blameless in the tension that has arisen: "As some Jealousy has taken place between your Rhode Island Friends and you it would have been but for you to have advised them oftener Direct, every thing you have communicated to me respecting their business they have been informed of — any under all circumstances it may appear as tho you have not given them as full information as you ought of their Concerns . . ."

Although Thomas Mayne Willing's letters to his young cousin were mainly concerned with business — and as such they in their great detail give a rare insight into American foreign trade of the day — they also deal with important personal matters. It emerges from reading a series of these interesting letters that young Tom was engaged to the elder Tom's sister, Dorothy Willing.

One of the authors, who was not raised with these family names, has sympathy with the reader who must sort out such a genealogical maze, for ere long, Dorothy Willing will marry her first cousin Thomas Willing Francis. We have already introduced Thomas Willing and Thomas Mayne Willing, not to mention Anne Willing Francis. Then, when the Willing and Francis families inter-marry with the Browns, we have John Brown and John Francis, and before long, John Brown Francis. And one of the authors, although named Brown, is in no way related to the original Browns of this narrative, but to the Francis family. It gets even more complex, for later James Greenleaf who, as we said earlier, becomes the villain of the piece, marries into the Francis family, but we'll save that complication for the appropriate moment.

In any case, it often seems that most of the prominent families of that era were cousins, but again, it must be remembered how small in population the United States was. In 1790, the combined population of Providence and the three cities with which it had the most active business ties — Boston, New York and Philadelphia — was substantially less than 100,000.

Thomas Mayne Willing strongly urged young Tom not to follow his inclination to return to India from Europe but to return to Philadelphia, go into partnership with him (noting that as the successor firm to Willing & Morris, it would have enormous capital and reputation) and marry his sister Dolly: "Her affection is Unattenable, her Conduct since your Departure has been marked with the highest propriety and her personal appearance, animation, and good Sense are highly appreciated by the World—in short she will be a prize and make you happy, you will now easily infer what is expected by the Family—from you nothing but your immediately Complying with your engagement will satisfy them or me—"[35]

Before long, young Tom would return to Philadelphia and marry Dolly. Thus, both Francis boys, John and Thomas Willing, would end up in business partnerships with their fathers-in-law.

On September 5 Willing's letter to Francis again asserted his belief that land was the avenue to great profits. "I would have interested you in some lands, but they are all sold by the Government, indeed there is now no lands for sale by any publick Body in the United States. Individuals are possessed of them and must Reap great advantage by their Resale.[36]

Even businessmen as well informed and astute as Thomas Mayne Willing and Morris—and John Brown—were taken with that peculiarly American virus that has affected this nation from its earliest days until now: optimism. America was growing and, caught up in this spirit, men of enterprise simply never thought that failure could happen to them. And land, why land was the best investment of all. One can understand how they could be seduced by the almost negligible cost of wild lands. Sure, the land was cheap, terribly cheap. True, it had—at least the good land did—inherent value. But land, no matter how intrinsically valuable has no monetary value until someone wants to buy it, and in the early days of this nation, farm land was almost limitless. There was far more land than the population could develop for decades to come.

Some land, of good quality and in the path of natural population growth, would return a good, even remarkable, profit in a short time. But most of the speculators, even many who were shrewd and experienced, sank their money, frequently fortunes vast by the standards of the day, often without real knowledge of land quality, into enormous tracts for which there were simply no buyers, except other speculators. And the later you joined this chain of speculation, the more likely were you to suffer substantial, even crippling, losses.

John Brown got in at the end. His land, like that of even greater purchasers, would one day have been worth a great fortune, but American businessmen of that era, like those of every era since, wanted their profits in a hurry. They simply did not want to wait and those who, like Robert Morris, had invested just about all their capital in speculative lands, could not afford to wait. They had nothing left to sustain them and there were taxes to be paid. Even if these were almost negligible, as was usually the case, on hundreds of thousands, even millions of acres, they mounted up. So land investment the way it was carried on in the years soon after the Revolution, was not investment at all. It could scarcely even be called speculation, but rather wild, impulsive gambling. Whatever it was based on, it certainly was not cool, businesslike analysis.

A couple of weeks later Willing wrote Francis that "business is at a stand here owing to a contagious fever [yellow fever] which has carried off many hundreds and banish many thousands from Town. . . ."[37] A more detailed account of the epidemic was given to John Francis by his sister Sophia who, with her husband and parents, had fled to a house outside Philadelphia.

Sophia wrote that none of John's friends or relatives were sick except their uncle [Samuel] Powel, speaker of the Pennsylvania senate, who refused to quit the city because his grapes and peaches nearing harvest were too valuable. But he became alarmed when his servant Philip was taken ill and soon died. Powel "flew" to his farm on the Schuylkill River but became sick and, as was noted on the outside of the envelope, died the day after the letter was written. And she reported that all the doctors who knew anything about yellow fever were themselves dead or ill.

. . . Yesterday & today the weather is favorable, very cool, but still no rain. Sunday, Monday & Tuesday last the destruction was greater than has been at all in the Potters Field alone *— fifty of a day were buried. Poor Mr. Lea that married Sally Shippen fell a Victim on Tuesday. Among Merchants that remained in town the havoc has been dreadful. Uncle Willing has lost two men & one Maid servant, he with the only three children he has with him flew into Mr. Bingham's house, between his house & Walnut Street fifteen died in a few days. We saw a Quaker who has been in town yesterday, he says he walked down Second Street, then Vine to Chestnut Street he saw* not one *house that had a door or even a Window open. This will give you some Idea of our deserted City. Hundreds fly it every day & God knows were it will end. Be not my dear Brother uneasy about us — we are safe at least as much so as we can be so near the City. I often wish myself with my parents under your roof. I think I should have gone to you could I have forseen the present. I know you & my dear Abby would have given us a heardy welcome. I always view your roof as my own, this you have taught me. I know not what to think of returning to town. To judge from present appearances we shall not see it for months. The Merchantile people of Philadelphia will feel particularly hard. For myself I must be happy if it pleases the Almighty to spare all those I love. As yet they are well but if this Fever once gets into the Country I know not what to think. We are most anxious to hear from you, pray write*

us and constantly. We shall receive your letters, for our Servant who is a Black Man, constantly comes to the gate with letters, which are put into a cloth wet with Vinigar. It is extraordinary that no Negros has yet taken this disorder. They are the only people that bury the dead or Nurse the Sick and are most kind and valuable.[38]

Health of a more individual nature was also of concern in the year 1793. John Francis was still frequently ill and, as usual, we learn of it from his mother's letters. She wrote to Abby in January, three or four months after John's return from England and France:

. . . My dear Abbys letter of ye 18th I received yesterday and joy it created was soon Abated as I red the account of my dear Sons Illness my Heart beat in the Flatts all day, poor dear Creature. I vainly flattered myself that the Change of Climate and of living would have perfectly worked a recovery but I fear the dear Fellow has been negligent and perhaps applied with too great assiduety to business since his return. Great care is necessary I am convinced to keep him well and also some attention to his Food & Liquor. I have been always obliged to guard against many things my taste approved knowing that it would not suite my stomach, tis the same with him.[39]

Four months later, on May 31, John Francis wrote to his brother-in-law James, then in Boston, a most melancholy letter. Plainly, he was deeply troubled by his health:

. . . This day your nephew [John Brown Francis] hails second of his birth. God send when he arrives at your age [31] he may with variety claim those virtues your brother knows you to possess. Like you he has not been born to a plentiful estate, and therefore must step forward into this world of intricacies in search of what temptation Heaven ordains that none may ever offer strong enough to allure him from that kind of rectitude you will ever teach him when I poor invalid are buried in the dust.

I may well be jeer'd at for writing you with an intention of enlivening your spirits and at the same time introducing so melancholy a subject. But the day—the Thought—The circumstance—the father—All conjointly bid me sollicit the patronage of a child I may not live to protect.[40]

Melancholy indeed, perhaps even maudlin, but a foreboding that would before long become true.

While we briefly anticipate the mournful end of John Francis, we must also note that the year 1793 saw the entrance into our narrative of its most tragic figure, Charles Frederick Herreshoff. There are parallels between the two lives: both were born in the same year, 1763; both came to Providence to woo and win a daughter of John Brown; both died untimely deaths, leaving their still-young wives long lives of widowhood. Yet, each would leave posterity who would make a lasting mark on the history of

Charles Frederick Herreshoff (1763-1819) and Sarah Brown Herreshoff (1773-1846) when they were forty-seven and thirty-seven respectively, from miniatures painted by Edward Greene Malborne.

his adopted state.

What little is known about Herreshoff's early life will be told later. He was born Carl Friederich Herreschhoff on December 27, 1763, in the town of Minden, Prussia. After a good education (as we shall see, he was an uncommonly cultivated man), he immigrated to the United States in 1787, and became a merchant in New York City.[41] His business took him to Providence in 1793, where he met John Brown and his family, including his twenty-year-old daughter Sarah. He evidently fell quickly in love and began a courtship, over John Brown's objections, that did not succeed in winning Sarah until she was twenty-eight, an advanced age for marriage in those days. Much of the courtship was conducted by mail, but that perhaps, in a letter-writing age, was not a handicap, for Herreshoff wrote English with a grace and elegance that would have been rare even in a man born to the language. We shall read some of his letters, often of beauty and a deep melancholy, written from the oppressive solitude of John Brown's Tract, to his wife and children. Only the stony-hearted will not be moved by his accounts, alternately buoyant and depressed, of his heroic but futile efforts to make of the Adirondacks what nature had predestined they would not be. This episode of a man defeated by natural forces beyond his strength and determination, is the tragic heart of this narrative.

John Francis Abroad

GAUDEO

II

John Brown's Grant

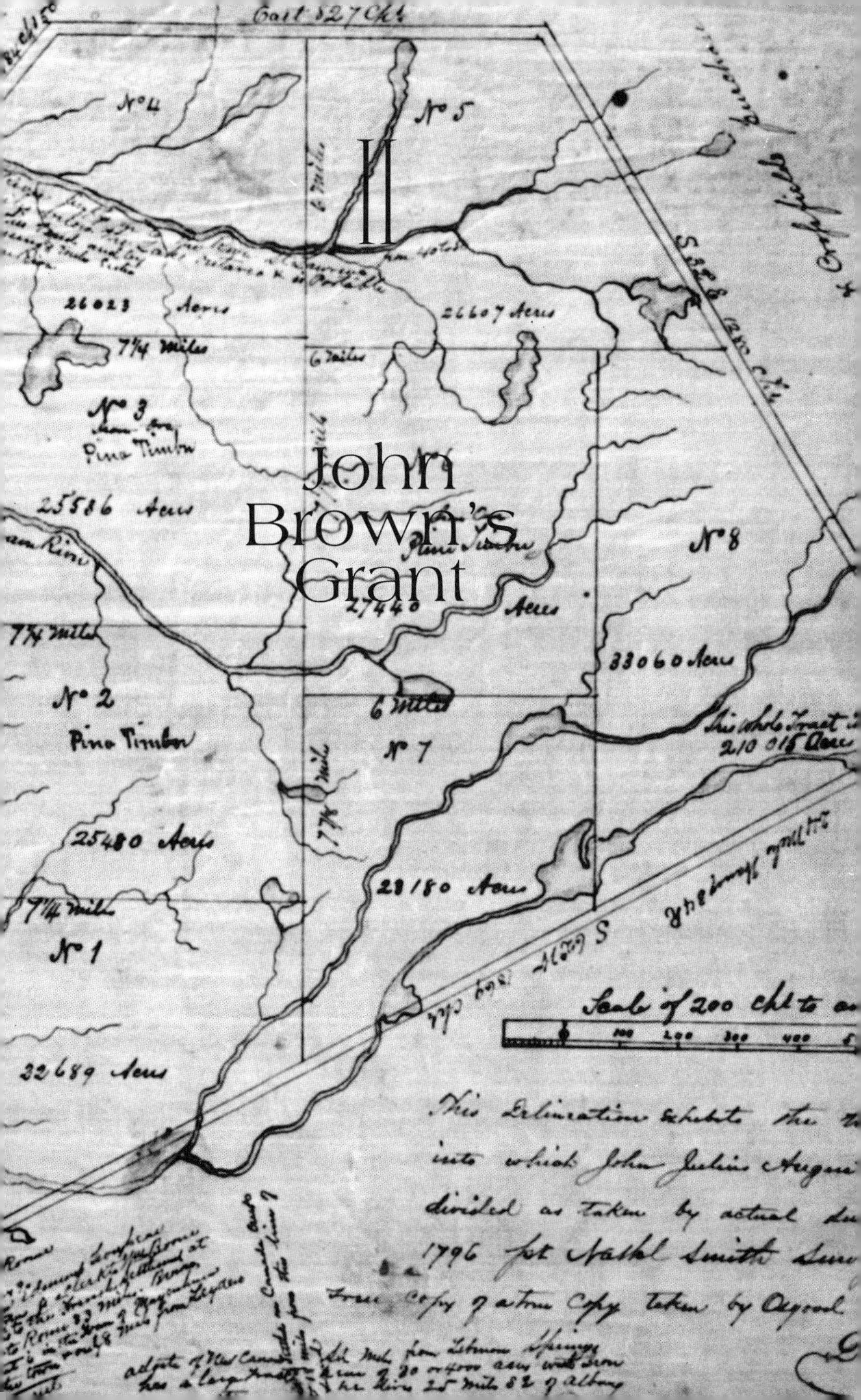

4

That Cargo of Tea

The exact details of how John Brown became the owner of the Tract can never be resurrected for all records concerning it have vanished. John Brown's papers were destroyed by fire soon after his death, and the early records in the county clerk's office of Herkimer have met the same fate. No book, moreover, contains the missing facts and figures. Early writers . . . dipped but superficially into the history of the Tract and allowed it to be shrouded in almost impenetrable mystery.

Alfred L. Donaldson, 1921

IN OUR first three chapters we've seen the threads of our story begin to gather: the history of the land that was to become the John Brown's Tract; the land speculation, including that of Alexander Macomb, without which the Tract would never have come into being; the establishment of the Brown and Francis families and their coming together in both family and business relationships; John Francis' continuing illness; the beginning of the courtship of Sarah Brown and Charles Frederick Herreshoff; the birth of John Brown Francis; all in the context of a setting so greatly different from our own. Now, in this chapter, these threads will be woven together into the single story that for more than another half century will preoccupy the family of John Brown and its Francis and Herreshoff branches, and have a lasting influence on the history of the Adirondacks. It is also in this chapter that we begin to take serious issue with two justly-celebrated scholars: Alfred L. Donaldson, the pre-eminent authority on the history of the Adirondacks, and James Hedges, the pre-eminent authority on the four Brown brothers.

The year 1794 saw the beginning of the almost incredible disgrace of Robert Morris. The financial empire of the Financier of the Revolution, the most powerful and influential businessman of the era, collapsed around him with such stunning suddenness that even his credit, his imagination, and his energy could not save it. He ended up in debtor's prison where he entertained — frugally, of course — such notables as George Washington himself. Before long, he was joined by his partner and friend John Nicholson, and by James Greenleaf, who was by then neither friend nor partner.

That year Brown and Francis sent their ship, another named after John Brown's great hero, the *George Washington*, on its first voyage to the Orient.[1] It was this ship that three years later would have a profound influence on our story. The *George Washington*, like other American ships, was standing out to perilous seas, for now the United States was engaged in an undeclared naval war with its one-time ally France, now in the paroxysms of Revolution. The need for cannon gave to the Brown Brothers' Hope Furnace one last burst of prosperity.

The Browns, as usual, together and separately, were engaged in multiple activities, adding to their pursuits the building of toll turnpikes (experience upon which John Brown could draw when he journeyed up to the Tract in his first attempt to develop it). That same year Brown, who was instrumental in the establishment of the Providence Bank, began to take an interest in establishing an insurance company, a project that required another five years. It was nonetheless one of the nation's early insurance firms, following the lead of Thomas Willing of Philadelphia who founded the nation's second insurance company.

Family matters were an important concern, especially John Francis' health. His sister Sophia wrote to Abby obliquely complaining about not hearing from the Providence Francises: ". . . as to my dear Brother sickness & business take up all the 24 hours with him — tho my friend [her future husband George Harrison] does complain of his inattention to his letters on business — he wrote him repeatedly but has not a line in return."

Sophia also informed Abby that Dolly Willing, Thomas Willing Francis' cousin and future wife, "has rapidly increased in coldness, & now never goes to ask my Mother how she is even & when they do meet — common civility alone is observed. The cause of this change we are all as ignorant of as the child unborn — with all my heart — if she is to be nearly connected with us — I hope it may be explained to the satisfaction of all parties — but Brother is tenderly dear to us."[2]

As to John's health, the implication is that it continued to reduce his attention to business, which may also explain why his brother Tom also complained that he got no response when he wrote to Brown & Francis.

Yet John did have good periods. One was evidently in May when his mother wrote to Abby. She attributed his good health and spirits to some good business news: a ship feared lost and with no insurance turned up safely in Newport. Nonetheless, she cautions Abby to press upon her husband Anne Willing Francis' latest nostrum:

> *. . . Pray my dear Abby press his constant use of Chomomile Tea let no other drink be prepared for his bedside & between Meals. While he accept strictly to it, the change was most wonderful, he was most sensible of the benefit, yet in a few weeks he dropd it, nearly, and resumed his old pernicious drink, for God sake prepare the Chomomile at all events, and never let any cause prevent your having it always ready and he will I am sure take it.*[3]

Family correspondence also indicates a rift between Tom and his brother's firm. Indeed, it appears from this correspondence — which was not available to Professor Hedges — that Brown & Francis was in financial trouble. Thomas Mayne Willing wrote that:

> *. . . it will be impossible to get any reimbursement of the $3425 their strength has been exhausted by means of their wild speculations — in short you will find it a matter of great Difficulty to close your accounts finally with them.*[4]

Tom wrote a few months later that "I have not heard a Syllable from B & F they will not correspondent with me or Messr. Willing. I have written them & brother frequently, but no answer. . . . "[5]

On October 25, Tom wrote that he had not heard from Brown & Francis for nearly two months, even though there were matters on which he needed their response. And on November 2 he wrote to Captain James Worseley of Boston, who was in command of the *President Washington*, regretting that after nearly three years he still has not received payment for his services from Brown & Francis. He says, however, that since "my Influence with the Gents in Providence is not sufficiently great, to induce them to correspond with me — I think it therefore unnecessary to trouble them on your subject." Nonetheless, he expressed confidence that Brown & Francis would treat the captain justly.[6] And in a letter to a Boston merchant that same day he writes: "to this letter we can get no answer and thus they treat all my correspondence.

That Cargo of Tea

A few days later Tom wrote a pained letter directly to his brother:

. . . It may appear strange to find me assert a Doubt wither I received more pleasure than pain from this last token of your friendship — but here it is this point remains undecided in my mind I was, and on reperusal of your letter am pleased with the Idea of still possessing your regards but does not your accusation of my having alienated my affections savor strong at ingratitude — nay does it not amount to an Indictment for ingratitude towards one I have loved from my Infancy . . . [7]

Having only one side of the correspondence, it is hard to know what to make of this situation. It seems clear that Brown & Francis indeed was not answering Tom's letters. One can assume that since John Brown was the senior partner, it was his decision, perhaps because the firm was in difficulties or because Brown still held the sale of the *President Washington* against Tom. And one can only speculate what this did to the relationship between Brown and his son-in-law and between the two brothers.

Nonetheless, despite his disappointment with Brown & Francis, Tom risked his own credit to try to spare his brother's firm discredit. He wrote to the great London firm of Baring & Company to back a bill that would fall due in a few weeks and which Brown & Francis could not cover.

. . . this bill falls due some time in Janr next and without your assistance must inevitable Return to America to the disgrace of my Rhode Island friends & my great mortification. — For your security in the advance . . . I hold myself responsible for the amount you may pay Messrs David Scott & Co on this amount and pledge my Credit for an immediate reimbursement the moment I am advised of the probability of your not recovering the Bond. [8]

Not only did Tom pledge £2500 to Baring & Co., but that same day he pledged another £2400 to David Scott & Co. He wrote: "Induced Solely by motives of Friendship I venture once more to trespass on your generosity and to request your assistance in Saving my friends from disgrace & Loss."[9] This pledge of £4900 (about $23,000) was a substantial sum for the time, many times what it would be today.

The following day he wrote to Brown & Francis explaining that he had pledged his credit to protect theirs. ". . . a wish to save You from Loss & mortification has induced me to stake my credit on your punctuality and honor." But then he went on to express his dismay at having heard from a Boston correspondent of Brown & Francis, Samuel Blagge, that:

. . . you have forbidden his making further remittance on account of the Bill . . . at which I am much surprised and I have written Mr. Blagge to this effect, and must beseech you will remove every Impediment to his effecting what your honor as well as his is deeply interested in. I crave your immediate attention to

the contents of the Letter assuring you that in the event of my not hearing from you Satisfactorily in due Season by mail that I will embrace the earliest opportunity of retracting the request I have made of my friends in London on your behalf . . . [10]

He then wrote to Blagge, who evidently had some responsibility in the matter, asking for "the full and immediate payment of which you are in honor bound to effect immediately. . . . " He also asked Blagge to forward the letter to Brown & Francis to John Brown and "insure . . . that my brother may be acquainted with the contents."[11]

While Thomas Willing Francis was quite cross with his brother's firm, he was at the same time soliciting the business of another Brown firm, Brown, Benson & Ives, a company headed by young Nicholas Brown, son of Nicholas, one of the four original brothers. This firm later, as Brown & Ives, provided funds, often most reluctantly, for Charles Frederick Herreshoff's enterprise in the lonely forests of the John Brown's Tract. After answering some B. B. & I. questions about trade with China and India, Thomas Willing Francis promoted his firm.

. . . Since my return from Europe, I have taken an active part in the mercantile line with my friends & relatives Messrs Willings Wishing to Cultivate an Acquaintance & intercourse with your house we have taken the liberty of sending you a Circular of our Establishment. With a capital equal to any in the U. States and a very extensive credit and connection we flatter ourselves with giving general satisfaction to our employers—Industry and attention to our Constituants will not be wanting to insure success if therefore as a partner of the house I can be of service to you or your friends, I beg you would fuly command me.[12]

While Tom was even younger than his brother John Francis, he represented one of the most powerful mercantile houses in the United States, one certainly at least the equal of Brown & Francis and plainly, at this time anyway, not in B. & F.'s financial difficulty.

Tom again heard from Captain Worseley, who again asked his assistance in obtaining what he believed was his just due from Brown & Francis. He told the seaman that he had done everything he could but nonetheless would again write to his brother. He enclosed the letter to his brother and asked Worseley to "seal and deliver" it.

. . . I can't for a moment suppose you will be longer deprived of what you are in justice entitled to—but you will not consider yourself singularly ill fated when you are told that it has required four years to bring my concerns in the President Washington to a close.[13]

Tom's memory had slipped a little. It had been three years since he sold the *President Washington* in India.

By mid-December Tom had evidently not heard from Brown & Francis, despite his urgent letter of a month earlier, for on December 16 he wrote similar letters to David Scott & Co. and Messrs. John and Francis Barring & Co. in London withdrawing his pledge of credit.

. . . On the supposition that this letter will reach you, before you are led into an actual advance in Consequence of my promise of reimbursement—I beg leave to advise that Mr. Brown's late Conduct towards me, has been such as to induce me to retract every friendly step I have taken to support the Credit of this Establishment I therefore request that you will not consider me responsible for any engagement you may enter into for that account after the receipt of this Letter—In this Determination I only follow the friendly advice you have so frequently given me and which I am at last in opposition to my wishes to serve B & F. under the necessity of availing myself of—If however you have gone actually into advance or prevented the Bill for £6500 from coming back protested you may depend on my Complying with my promise of reimbursement.[14]

He wrote in similar vein to Baring & Co.

Because most of John Brown's business records were later destroyed and because these family letters were not then available, Professor Hedges was perhaps not fully aware of the serious financial difficulties then facing the most adventurous of the four Brown brothers.

The breach between Thomas Willing Francis and John Brown seemed very deep indeed yet, within a couple of years, Brown would become almost totally reliant on Tom Francis in his efforts to obtain payment from James Greenleaf and to obtain the land in the Adirondacks upon which John Francis accepted a second mortgage.

That year, 1794, also saw the land that was to become the Brown's Tract move one crucial step closer to John Brown. His old friend and employee, Samuel Ward, and his wife Phebe, sold the 210,000 acres to James Greenleaf for £24,000. He quickly mortgaged it for $38,050 to the famous New York merchant Philip Livingston.[15] Whether Greenleaf took cash or it was to meet a financial obligation is not known. Remember that at this time Greenleaf was engaged, along with Morris and Nicholson, in multiple land speculations that were rapidly proving disastrous.

The year 1795 was fateful for it was then that John Francis obtained the mortgage on what became the John Brown's Tract. Much of what has been written about that crucial transaction, although accepted as the truth and repeated in account after account, is simply wrong, Much unjustly defames John Francis, as documentary evidence not available to earlier writers will amply demonstrate. We will compare in detail the earlier assertions and the recently discovered evidence, a comparison that will, we have no doubt, forever transform the record of the genesis of the John Brown's Tract.

But this examination will have to await a discussion of developments earlier that year.

The wrangle between Tom Francis and Brown & Francis continued with little improvement and John Francis continued in poor health. In January Tom wrote to Blagge, Brown & Francis' correspondent in Boston, that "neither from you or Messrs B & F have received a line on the subject."

> . . . *I am pained that my correspondence should be loaded with any thing so evidently disagreeable and I hope you will prevent my introducing the Subject in future by candidly telling me what you have done, and what tis your Determination to do in the business of the Bill for which you are responsible.*

And he says he will "employ the whole of my time in stating finally my a/ct with Messrs B & F" and that he believes his "Presence in Providence will place me on the footing I formerly felt myself. . . . "[16]

It is clear from Thomas Willing Francis' correspondence that his credit was "extremely Injured" in London but at this remove in time, nearly two centuries, it is impossible to determine precisely who is responsible.[17] While it is plain that Brown & Francis was not paying to Tom Willing what he believed they owed him, it is also plain that John Brown questioned Willing's statement of what was owed him for his trip to India, including the sale of the *President Washington*. Why this matter dragged on for more than three years, however, and why Brown & Francis so often simply did not reply to Tom's letters, is not so plain. A possible explanation is John's health. Tom evidently did visit Providence in March 1795. That is the inference from a letter to him from John Brown:

> . . . *I wish your Brother would Make it Agreeable to him to go through the Acct with you as Stated & make Such Minnits* [minutes] *or Observations to you their on as he may think proper, and if Agreeable to you & him to Close & Finish the Acct without my going into the Minutia of them, I shall be perfectly satisfied with what you may Mutually Accomplish, but if his State of health will not admit of that Attention and Dispatch your wish in the Business, I will if you wish it give up Two or Three hours Every Morning from all other Ingagements to Attend You with the Accts. I mention Every morng as Your Brothers Ill State of Health has unhappily caused the Habbit of his Laying a Bed Very Late in the Morng, Even when he is in his best State of Health, & which I am happy to obsearve that he Appears to possess a better State sence your Arrival than he has for Maney*

Months past. You will please to Confer with him on the Mode of Prossicuting the Business & being with him.

He will I hope Forward the Settlement as much as may be at his House or I will Attend you at the Store in Such parts of the Day as you may wish & my Other Ingagement will Possibly Admit. I am as Much as You probably Can be Most Hartaly [heartily] *Desire us of the Most Friendly and Amicable Settlemt of All Our Concerns.*[18]

That certainly was a most cordial letter from which one would expect a prompt settlemnt of this long-deferred accounting. But then, a couple of weeks later, after Tom had returned to Providence from Boston, John Brown wrote that "Your Brother has to me Declind saying or Acting Aney thing in the Settlement of Yours accts & My Multiplycity of Ingagements (as you see) has prevented My doing Aney thing in the Business of Your Accts. . . . " He then wrote: "I Begg you to put together on Paper every Charge of Commition You have Made in the Whole Business and I will be with You at 12 oclk at the Stores being Now bound to the Bank. . . . "[19]

In those days, long before the telephone, notes were exchanged the same day, presumably by messenger. Indeed, often a series of notes went back and forth. Thus, that same day, April 11, John Brown disputed some of Tom Willing's charges. He was also still distressed at the sale of the *President Washington*. ". . . JB had no more Expectations at that time of the Ships being sold then he now has of selling his Famely. . . . " And he added in a postscript that he would be "Willing to Submit the above to Tench Francis Esq."[20]

And again that same day another letter from John Brown in which the cordiality of a couple of weeks before had completely evaporated. Brown asserted that "I think it Very Rong in You to Accuse me of Not being Willing to Allow You Aney thing for what Business you did for us in Europe. . . . " Plainly, there was a serious misunderstanding as to the terms under which Tom Willing represented Brown & Francis. Suffice it to say that John Brown's third letter of the day ended rather crossly: ". . . and You May Rely upon it that Nothing but the Connection in the Famely Induces me to make such a Sacrifise of property as I think I do in the offer gave you. . . "[21]

Although it is impossible to know why John Francis apparently was unwilling to work out a settlement, one can speculate that it may have been less his poor health than his reluctance to get caught in the middle between his brother and his father-in-law/partner.

Clearly, Tom Francis' trip to Providence did not accomplish what he hoped, for the following month he wrote to a firm in Calcutta that he had still not received a settlement from Brown & Francis and that his credit in Europe and India had been severely harmed. He hoped to be able to meet all his obligations quickly. ". . . I cannot avoid flattering myself that my London Correspondents will reinstate me in their good opinion & allow me to share a portion of that Confidence they were wont to show me." Yet, although he was confident that his fortune was again on the rise, he still had a jaundiced view of Brown & Francis. "When this affair is settled and I get the amount of the balance due me say £10,000 Ten Thousand pounds, Sterling I am determined never to have a Transaction with the people in Rhode Island."[22] Fortunately for John Brown, Thomas Willing Francis did not stick to that resolve.

By mid-year, about the time that John Francis was in New York on the trip that was responsible for the family's Adirondack adventure, Tom Francis still had "not succeeded in getting a Settlement or recovering a farthing from B & F. . . ."[23]

That year, 1795, also saw the peak, or maybe one should say the nadir, of land speculation. Robert Morris had formed the North American Land Company with more than six-million acres, probably the most grandiose land speculation project in American history. His partners were John Nicholson, former controller of the State of Pennsylvania, and James Greenleaf, whose contribution was supposed to be selling large tracts of lands to Dutch investors he knew from his service as U. S. Consul in Amsterdam. That he failed in this was hardly his lack of skill as a salesman – for he must have been quite a persuasive talker to have piled up such staggering debts – but more likely because of the chaotic situation in Europe. Not only was France in the turmoil of its long and bloody Revolution but it was engaged in war with a number of continental powers. It was not a propitious time to be selling land in America.

The business affairs of Morris, Nicholson and Greenleaf were so complex – and evidently so desperate – that they could not be sorted out by them then. Obviously, it is beyond our capacity to do so now. But it seems fairly clear that by 1795, shortly after the North American Land Company was formed, that a split had developed between Morris and Nicholson on one side and Greenleaf on the other. "Morris always claimed that Greenleaf was dishonorable or dishonest, and chiefly to blame for Morris's calamities."[24] That was an opinion John Brown would most enthusiastically second. Yet, there must have been something in Greenleaf's favor, for within a few years he was to marry into one of the foremost families of Pennsylvania and become related by marriage to the Francis family.[25]

In any case, Robert Morris was in no position to point a finger at anyone. For all his indispensable service to the American Revolution, Morris' postwar financial practices were dubious indeed. His wild speculation led not only to his financial collapse but that of many honorable men who trusted him. And he and John Nicholson resorted to a very questionable practice. They paid many of their debts with drafts on each other, relying on their reputations to cause these bills to be accepted, but they knew (unless they had come to live entirely in a fantasy world) that they were so irretrievably in debt that they could not possibly make good on their notes. Maybe, however, to give them the benefit of any doubt, they really thought they could recover. In any case, they bought Greenleaf out of the Federal City project mentioned earlier, each paying him with notes supposedly worth $124,514.[26]

It was during this time that Greenleaf gave a first mortgage on what became the John Brown's Tract. On July 29, 1795, he mortgaged the land to the prominent New York merchant Philip Livingston for $38,050.[27]

At just about that same time John Francis went down (although he may have said "up," just as Rhode Islanders to this day talk about going "up" to New York and "down" to Maine, a locution surviving from the days of sail) to New York to sell the tea. On that there is agreement, but on many other points—often important points of fact and interpretation—we must take direct issue with what heretofore has been regarded as the classic account of the John Brown's Tract, that appearing in the magisterial two-volume *History of the Adirondacks,* published by Alfred L. Donaldson in 1921.

Because this is, and deserves to be, the standard work on the Adirondacks, Donaldson's account has been repeated time and again in subsequent works by the most reputable writers, including Professor James Hedges of Brown University, whose splendid two-volume economic history of the Brown family is of equivalent stature. Other reputable authors rehashing Donaldson's accounts were William Chapman White and Joseph E. Grady. Such was Donaldson's authority, however, that subsequent writers did not repeat the qualifications to the story that Donaldson included, although it is plain that he believed the story, based on family tradition, was "authoritative." This implies no criticism of Donaldson because there was very little documentary evidence, so he necessarily relied on the only source available.

Donaldson wrote that, "The exact details of how 'John Brown became the owner of the tract' can never be resurrected, for all records concerning it have vanished. John Brown's papers were destroyed by fire soon after his death, and the early records in the county clerk's office of Herkimer have met the same fate. No book, moreover, contains the missing facts and figures. Early writers... dipped but superficially into the history of the tract, and avowed it to be shrouded in almost impenetrable mystery."[28]

However, in recent decades one of the authors has unearthed family papers that throw entirely new light on the history of the John Brown's Tract. This, we have no doubt, will dispel that "almost impenetrable mystery."

But to do this we must address what was written by Donaldson. Referring to the known fact that John Brown's son James had no interest in business, Donaldson writes:

> *... The son-in-law proved to have no more liking or capacity for business than the son. He was a young man of pleasing manners and good education. He had a taste for art and literature and the pursuits of leisure. The social side of life appealed to him strongly, and to share high living with the highest livers was his undermining ambition.*[29]

About John Francis' liking or capacity for business there is limited evidence. It is known that his health often confined him to bed, but in all the voluminous correspondence after his death between John Brown and Thomas Willing Francis, there is no word of complaint about John's work, and Brown was not a man to mince words. What we do know from John's diaries and letters is that he was a most observant and serious young man and, apparently, quite conscientious. As to his "undermining ambition" to "share high living with the highest livers," we have found no documentary evidence one way or the other. That may have been true, but evidence demonstrating it is lacking.

Donaldson then goes on to say that "For a while the firm of Brown & Francis prospered amazingly—just as it would have done probably without a junior partner." That seems a rather gratuitous remark. In any case, the Thomas Willing Francis and Thomas Mayne Willing letters quoted earlier cast considerable doubt on the view, apparently held by Professor Hedges as well, that John Brown's firm was doing "amazingly" well. Plainly, Brown & Francis had a serious cash flow problem largely because of John Brown's (daring or reckless; take your choice) business practices.

That Cargo of Tea

In any case, John Francis did leave for New York to sell the shipment of tea. "The interim," according to Donaldson, "was spent in the social climbing which was his particular weakness." That seems a curious statement. John Francis was related to and on a friendly basis with many of the most important families of the day. And he had been presented at the Court of St. James by Sir Richard Penn, grandson of William Penn.[30] There was little need for him to climb socially (remember, too, that Senator Foster thanked John Francis for giving him entrée to the notable families of Philadelphia).

Donaldson also writes that John's "conviviality brought him in contact with James Greenleaf, Philip Livingston, Aaron Burr, and one of the Morrises — all men, as we have seen, interested in Adirondack land." Since these were all influential men in business and/or politics, they would seem to be the most suitable companions for a young businessman. That they were interested in land, whether it be in the Adirondacks or elsewhere, was commonplace. Almost all men of means were interested in land. John Brown and his brothers certainly were. They had invested, or would invest, in lands in Maine, Ohio, and elsewhere. Yet, what Donaldson wrote about John Francis has the tone of an indictment when he was conducting himself in perfectly normal fashion.

Then, Donaldson goes on to describe the transaction by which John Francis, and thus John Brown, obtained the mortgage on the Tract:

> *The details of just what happened after this are lost forever, probably, but the main facts are reasonably certain. Francis received the price of the ship's cargo, but he took no penny of it back to Providence. Instead, he bought an imperfect claim of some kind to 210,000 acres of land in the New York wilderness.*

Fortunately, for John Francis' posthumous reputation and for those interested in the John Brown's Tract, many of the details, although lost for a century and a half, have come to light. A contract found in the Historical Society of Pennsylvania dated July 30, 1795, signed by Francis and Greenleaf and witnessed by Francis' kinsman, William Tilghman, shows that Greenleaf purchased "one thousand and fifty whole chests of Merchantable Bohea Tea" with an estimated weight of 420,000 pounds. At the stipulated "rate of three shillings (37.5 cents) New York currency per pound," that comes to $157,500, a princely sum in those days. Greenleaf contracted to pay one third in six months, the second third in nine months, and the final third in a year. He agreed to give notes "payable at the Bank of New York" and to secure the notes with "one or more mortgages."

Two weeks later, on August 14, Francis sent a note to Greenleaf saying he would call on him at 5:00 P.M. to obtain "some additional security to the amount now offer'd." He continued: "Indeed, I cannot answer my conduct to Mr. Brown unless you offer it." He said he was sure Greenleaf would "attribute the cause of it not to my distrust . . . but the wish to obtain the entire approbation of my partner who has no knowledge of you." One must assume that the senior partner told the junior to get more security and that that security was the mortgage on the Adirondacks land. In any case, at this time the tea was still in the Brown & Francis warehouse in Providence from which it is hardly likely that Brown would release it until he was satisfied with Greenleaf's compliance with the original contract.

Evidence of unmet notes totalling $40,000 for each of the first two installments has emerged and we calculated from various documents that notes for the third installment totalled $52,500, exactly a third of the purchase price of $157,500. Since the original contract stipulated that Brown & Francis could have the notes divided "as will best suit the convenience" of the sellers, it is reasonable to surmise that Greenleaf made good on $12,500 for each of the first two installments.[31]

Accepting notes in cash-poor America was the normal business practice of the day. Notes for the first two installments were deposited in the Bank of New York, thus a debit on Greenleaf's credit and a credit to Brown & Francis. These were, then, perfectly ordinary commercial instruments accepted from a man whose credit standing was high, for the dimensions of his folly—shared by Morris and Nicholson—were not yet generally known.

Francis was not the least naive in accepting a second mortgage on Greenleaf's property in the Adirondacks, for by the testimony of a subsequent letter from John Brown to Thomas Willing Francis, John Francis had the land appraised by the best available authority, who put a valuation on it that would not only cover the Livingston first mortgage but the third installment to Brown & Francis with tens of thousands to spare.[32] Francis acted responsibly and, we repeat, in all the many letters between John Brown and Tom Francis, there is not a word of criticism of John's deal. Instead, as we shall see, John Brown was eager, almost desperate, to obtain the land and the serious financial problems that developed with Greenleaf were magnified by John Brown's imprudent actions after John Francis' death. This is beyond doubt, for the evidence is plain on the main lines of the transaction, although there is some uncertainty as to some of the details. John Brown and Tom Francis knew what they were writing about, so they did not always give complete details. What John Francis did was with businesslike prudence. What John Brown did later with regard to James Greenleaf was, as he admitted several times in writing, foolish.[33]

A rather different picture, one that has blemished the reputation of John Francis ever since, was drawn by Donaldson:

. . . When Brown was informed of the utterly foolish and incomprehensible thing his trusted son-in-law had done — presumably under the influence of wine — it is reported by an eye-witness to the scene that he dropped his head into his hands and wepted bitter tears of mortification and disappointment.

That the authors have discovered no confirmation of this (we did see that he wept at the sale of the *President Washington*) is, of course, not proof that it never happened. But Donaldson does not document his account and it is admittedly based on hearsay more than a century after the event. What is more to the point is the fact, amply documented, that this does not accord with John Brown's subsequent behavior, his eager, even avid, efforts to obtain the land despite the repeated cautions of Thomas Willing Francis and even his own earlier negative appraisal. A historian would later call John Brown obsessed.[34] If an overstatement, it was not much of a one. When John Brown decided on a course of action, he pursued it regardless of the cost. That was his genius as a businessman — and his failing. Indeed, until the very end of his business career, it was not at all certain whether or not he would retire a rich man. His was, unlike his brother Nicholas's, not the steady accumulation of a fortune but the wild, up-and-down roller coaster of the speculator. Fortunately for John Brown and his family, he also had a number of sound business ventures to sustain him while his more daring adventures worked themselves out.

Thus, according to all the evidence, evidence not available to Donaldson, John Francis conducted a perfectly normal business transaction, one that presumably was profitable. It was not until it became apparent that James Greenleaf could (or would) not pay the notes that the controversy developed. Francis had little or nothing to do with that, for most of it occurred after his death. John Francis, from the time of Alfred Donaldson's account until now (an account that has been repeated in book after book), was assigned the rather gaudy role of the reckless son-in-law whose drinking and careless business habits caused a financial catastrophe that would bedevil the family for three generations. The ne'er-do-well has appeared in literature from the earliest days, but it simply was not the role of John Francis.

While it is true that his acceptance of the second mortgage eventually triggered the events that constitute the heart of this narrative, that simply was not evident at the time. No, John Francis' was a different role, that of a young man with everything to live for who was troubled by ill health, not mentioned by Donaldson, beset by personal tragedy and destined for an untimely death.

The personal tragedy was not slow in coming. On his way back from New York, bearing the good news of his apparently successful sale of the tea, John Francis was met a few miles south of Providence, in the village of Pawtuxet, by a group of friends. They had come to meet him with the dreadful news of the death on August 7 of his daughter Sally, not yet two years old. This sad story is told in a letter to his brother Tom from his devoted brother-in-law James Brown:

My dear Friend—

I have long time wished to address you on a subject which has caused me much affliction but I feared that no communications I could make to you respecting our Brother John, would prove agreeable to you and I utterly despair that any thing you can do or say will change his conduct. However on the whole I think 'tis best you should be made acquainted with it. Since his return to this Place from N. York—On his arrival at a Tavern in the vicinity of the Town he was met by a number of Gentlemen who acquainted him with the death of his Infant, and that his Family were in Providence. Instead of coming here in the stage he engages a carriage to carry him to Spring Green where he passed the night, early the following morn'g my Father went there to meet him having been very anxious for a number of days to see him on the subject of the Sale of the Teas and other Business. He found him in a situation I shall not attempt to describe—Laudanum or Liquors or both had rendered him almost insensible and 'twas in this situation I met him on the Road to Town the Family with me. Poor Abby. I know your heart bleeds for her—Since that Time, Very few days have passed when he has been himself. My Father has written him in very serious terms but he takes no notice whatever of his letters. He also has written to your Father—

James Brown then told Tom Francis that his brother had gone to the house of a man he had often befriended and "insulted him & much terrified his wife."

. . . Such mortification are we obliged to submit to. In short so little attention does he pay to decency that the Coffee house at night has several times been the scene of his intoxication. Three weeks he has been at house-keeping, twice *only during that period have I seen him in his own house, when he is not in Bed (which Indeed is the case most of the time) we know not where he is. But perhaps I ought not to particularise on so disagreeable a subject. Can anything be done to reclaim this Unfortunate Victim? How my sister supports herself in so distressing a situa-*

tion is to me wonderful. I feel that her resolution will not hold out much longer. I have never given advice to anyone unasked, were he my own Brother perhaps I might speak to him but as yet from anything I have said to him he cannot have any suspicion that I know anything of this fatal attachment.[35]

We have seen from John Francis' own writings that he was a sensitive man and frequently subject to melancholy because of his ill health. Thus, it is hardly surprising that the poor man fell apart. But for his wife Abby, it was worse. She lost her baby daughter; her husband fell to pieces and would die the next year,leaving her a widowhood of twenty-five years; and less than two years after her husband's death, her eldest child Anne would die at the age of eight. Her sisters, Sarah and Alice, would also know a full measure of grief. John Brown's daughters, seemingly so wellborn, were not overburdened with happiness.

Although there were periods for which we have many letters of Anne Willing Francis to or about her son John, for the year 1796, the last of his life, there is only one and only a few other passing references to his health. On My 30 she wrote:

. . . a day that must ever be memorable to you and me, 33 years this day was I made a joyful mother, heaven then gave me one of the best sons, and this day 5 years, you were bless'd with a lovely boy, heaven grant he may be a comfort and joy to his dear worthy parents. . . .

The elder Mrs. Francis then launched into a sermon on how little John Brown Francis should be raised. She, incidentally, used poetic license in saying that he was born on the same date as his father; it was actually a day later. Then she reported that John Brown, obviously there on business, "has been with us this day 4 weeks and his whole deportment has been such as to induce from each of our family a veneration and high respect, we have been very highly gratified by this accidental visit and when he departs we shall feel a sensible regret."

Mrs. Francis then expressed the wish that John Brown "had brought my dear grand-son as it would have been highly pleasing to us and most assuredly a very great comfort to him, he is certainly prodigiously attached to that child."

Evidently, however, John Brown had brought along his six-year-old grand-daughter, perhaps because she was named Anne Willing Francis after her Philadelphia grandmother. "I hope my darling will find the way to his heart, she appears all sweetness and every trait of amiability is strongly mark'd in her countenance."[36]

Uncharacteristically, she did not mention her son's health other than to toast it on his birthday. This could cause one to infer that he was enjoying a spell of good health. But such a happy inference was quickly dismissed by a note from John Brown to Tom Francis only three days later:

> *. . . O my Dear Sir that you may see your brother John as he once was and restored to health, he is yet your brother, my partner son-in-law God Bless him and his Dear Family, my Tears are trickling down my cheekes and will say no more only that I am your Friend & that if anything disagreeable has happened ever, between us, I hope it never will again.*[37]

John Brown added a postscript to this alarming note, referring to Greenleaf's last payment, implying that he had already made some payments. But the note does make it plain that John Brown wanted to banish once and for all whatever animosity there was between him and Tom Francis. Perhaps they had finally straightened out their accounts or perhaps Brown's strong family feeling was the cause. Perhaps both.

Meanwhile, life went on. John Brown was not one to be paralyzed by misfortune, even in his own family. Brown & Francis advertised for 1500 cords of wood, a huge supply, for the distillery. Brown was also trying to establish a canal from Worcester to Providence, but it was blocked by Boston interests. They feared quite correctly that Brown and colleagues were trying to divert trade from Boston to Providence.

Up in the northern wilderness a Nathaniel Smith surveyed the Greenleaf tract, dividing it into eight towns, and a Cliff French surveyed Township No. 2, carving it into lots.[38] Greenleaf's finances were growing ever more complex. His erstwhile partners, Morris and Nicholson, bought out his interest in the North American Land Company for $1,150,000. This would seem to have ended his problems, but the payment was half in Morris' notes drawn on Nicholson and half in Nicholson's notes drawn on Morris, a rather dubious payment since each was irretrievably in debt. Once the dimensions of their catastrophe became known, their notes were selling for a penny or two on the dollar and it doubtful they were worth even that.

Then, on November 4 at the age of 33, John Francis died. He was born into one of the first families of Pennsylvania and married into one of the first families of Rhode Island. He had a good and curious mind and a graceful pen. He was one of those to whom happiness and prosperity seemed assured. Instead, he suffered pain for years, his beloved daughter died before she was two, and he himself died young. The cause of death, if known then, has eluded research. One speculation has been a ruptured appendix.[39] But at least, to recall the concern he expressed on his trip to England, he was not without mourners. The funeral took place the next

Brown University from the southwest from an engraving by S. Hill circa 1800.

day and was attended by "the Students of Rhode-Island College, now Brown University, of the Corporation of which he was a Fellow – by the Fraternity of Free-masons, of which he was a Member – and by a large Number of mourning Relatives and Friends."[40]

There are, sadly, no contemporary assessments of this young man and even the voluminous collection of family letters has not produced anything of note that attempts to sum up this short life. We could do worse, however, than quote the assessment of a present-day scholar, one of the very few who has taken an interest in the life of John Francis – Glenn B. Skillin:

> *John Francis was not marked for fame. His view of life in his time, his acute descriptions of those whom he met, his keen ear for what his contemporaries had to say and the way in which they said it, all make him of considerable interest to us as an articulate recorder of the eighteenth-century events in which he participated. His frankness is a refreshing reminder of that earthy quality which was characteristic of his time and which was to fall from favor in the following century.*[41]

5

John Brown's Obsession

. . . a monomania like that of John Brown . . .

George A. Hardin, 1893[1]

ALTHOUGH it was the acceptance of the Greenleaf mortgage by John Francis that was the genesis of the John Brown's Tract, neither he, in the painful months that remained to him, nor his family recognized the significance of the transaction. If business conditions had not been so bad—the United States was on the threshhold of the Panic of 1796-97—if the nation's most astute businessmen had not been so infected by speculative fever, if James Greenleaf in particular had not been the victim, along with many others, of his own greed, the transaction would have, at most, merited a passing mention in the accounts of the many-faceted business activities of John Brown.

Thus, although John Francis indeed set our narrative in motion, he subsequently played virtually no role. The leading player, to no one's surprise, is the enterprising and indefatigable John Brown himself. The famous tract bears not only his name but his stamp. He wanted that tract and he went to considerable trouble (but to less expense than has previously been reported) to get it.

A letter from John Brown to Tom Francis less than a month after his brother's death demonstrates beyond question that the charges that John Francis was guilty of "heedless extravagance"[2] were completely unfounded. Indeed, it would seem closer to the truth that it was Brown who was guilty of heedless extravagance, that the entire enterprise that burdened the family for three generations could fairly be termed his obsession, that rather than try to "salvage something from a misadventure not of his making," as Professor Hedges wrote, it was almost entirely of his making.

On December 3, John Brown wrote to Tom Francis that "I have just

Rec'd a letter from Mr. Greenleaf at Boston date Nov. 30, 1796 in which he says 'I shall leave this in a few days and return back to Phila'd and shall go prepared to submit to Every Sacrifice there that may give me the power to render justice to you and particularly as to the Indorsements given by you in May last for my benefit.' "[3]

This is the earliest reference we have encountered to a supremely foolish business act by John Brown, one for which he subsequently criticized himself. We mentioned earlier that James Greenleaf was to pay for the tea in three installments of $52,500 each secured by the second mortgage on the land, with a first mortgage held by Philip Livingston. The notes for the remaining $80,000 and the $52,500 were held by a bank, a debit on Greenleaf and a credit for Brown & Francis. In May 1796, as the time approached when Greenleaf was contracted to start paying off the notes, he somehow persuaded John Brown to endorse them so the bank would remove the $80,000 charge on Greenleaf's credit . . . "to Give him Cr(edit) to Git the Goods to Raise the money for me to the Amount of 36000 Dolls. & Thoms. Wg. Francis for the same sum."[4]

As reconstructed from a whole series of letters between Brown and Tom Francis, who now was very high in Brown's estimation, Greenleaf convinced Brown that he could not obtain on credit the goods he needed to sell to meet his debts to Brown & Francis unless Brown removed the impediment to his credit by endorsing the notes. Brown agreed, and for $8,000 of the notes accepted a personal note from Greenleaf supposedly backed by a mortgage on an estate in Philadelphia. Brown then persuaded Thomas Willing Francis to endorse $36,000 of the notes in exchange for personal notes secured by Morris & Nicholson notes, with Brown promising to repay Tom if Greenleaf should fail to repay Francis.[5] Brown also endorsed $36,000 in notes without security, solely on his faith in Greenleaf, although there is some evidence that indicates Brown believed he had a mortgage on estates in Pennsylvania that secured Greenleaf's personal notes. Again, despite his unhappy experieces earlier and his resolve to have nothing to do financially with Brown & Francis, Tom Francis was risking his own resources to help Brown & Francis, possibly out of regard for his brother who was, in May, still alive.

Eventually, to anticipate our story, when Greenleaf failed to pay, Tom Francis sold the security for $26,000, leaving $10,000 owed him by John Brown. Brown himself, as will be detailed later, was less lucky. He got virtually nothing from Greenleaf and this, it must be remembered, was because of his business decision, not that of his ailing junior partner.

But in the weeks immediately following John Francis' death, John Brown was still optimistic about Greenleaf:

. . . From these professions I can hardly doubt of your being paid by Mr. Greenleaf very soon. I do believe he possesses the distinct Honour of a gent'm and that his disappointment from others has been the sole cause of his disappointing you and me. I can only add that you shall have my most ardent Prayers for the Immediate payment of the notes & that I will not ask him for a shilling 'till you are first satisfied, pray give him all the indulgence in your power.

A few days later Brown again wrote to Francis enclosing a number of papers that Abby had found amongst her husband's belongings. They involved a number of matters unrelated to Greenleaf, including some that needed attention. "Your brothers state of health no doubt prevented his attention to these two pieces of Business, . . ." A postscript added: "Mr James Greenleaf passed on to your city this Day. I hope he will be able very soone to satisfy you and all the notes you & I indorsed."[6]

Although Brown professed to have confidence in Greenleaf's honor, he was nonetheless concerned about the matter, for a few days later he again wrote to Tom Francis:

I do most sincerely hope that Mr. Greenleaf will have found means before this reaches you to have paid off all his notes indorsed by you and me, in May last, but learnt this may not be the case I have desired the Barer Asher Robbins to call on a gentleman at New York to get the best information he can respecting the mortgage of 210,000 acres of land in the County of Herkimer in the State of New York, which had a mortgage on it previous to ours, & Mr. Greenleaf I am told has since sold it under the imbarresment it lay, if Mr. Robbins finds on inquiry that this mortgage, which I show him is sufficient for $52,500 dollars, I shall have no objection to Mr. Greenleaf selling the Landsdown Estate & House in Town & Lott opposite your brother Harrisons toward discharging the note indorsed by you & me for him in May last, the mortgage deed of both these Estates is at your cousin Tilmons [William Tilghman] *or at the office of Record.*[7]

This indicates that Brown believed the personal notes he accepted for endorsing the notes held by the bank were backed by the property in Pennsylvania, an optimistic assumption since he himself stated "I took no security but Mr. G's note to discharge the sd. Notes or Save me harmless."[8] In any case, by the tone of the letter, Brown is not yet alarmed. However, an explicit expression of alarm appears in a letter dated December 22, 1796.

. . . Yours of the 13th just is before me, by which I hope you'll be able to get clear of Mr. Greenleaf without loss, you may be right in your judgement of him, but I shall hope that I am not deceived in his situation, I am much alarmed at

that part of your letter that says Lansdown is advertised for sale by John Nicholson [Greenleaf's partner or past partner], *how can it be when Mr. Geo. Harrison* [brother-in-law of John and Thomas Willing Francis] *went to the office to examine if there was any mortgage prior to the one to Brown and Francis, and afterwards told me all was well. Pray Sir be so obliging as to speak to Mr. Harrison on the subject and see the deed to Brown and Francis which must be yet in the office, I suppose it taken as security for the tea and in case the Note was not paid, that Brown & Francis had a right to sell the Estate, pray Sir examine the deed and advise me what I have a right to do from the tenner* [tenor] *therefore all the Notes for the third payment of the tea say 52,500 Dollars lays yet against Greenleaf tho have rec'd some part of their amount but not much more than the Note I have agaisnt him for part of the 2nd installment and the interest he agree to allow for his nonpayment to Mr. Robbins well know how the New York mortgage stands, I wish him to see the mortgage of the house and lot in the city and of Lansdown, that he may inform you weither they are simular to the deeds of the lands in the state of New York if they are such or we can sell the two Estates with you and Mr. Robbins, I think from his inquiry in New York that mortgage on deed is sufficient for about $48,000 dollars.*[9]

Although this, like most of John Brown's letters, is not a model of clarity, some things can be inferred: One, that Tom Francis had earlier expressed some doubt about Brown's high estimation of Greenleaf. Two, that John Francis had required not only a mortgage to back the third installment due on the tea but had received what he believed to be a valid mortgage on valuable property in Pennsylvania to back the notes for the first two installments. This is difficult to reconcile with the account of Alfred Donaldson that Francis had done an "utterly foolish and incomprehensible thing."

Although the year 1797 saw John Brown increasingly preoccupied with the Greenleaf matter, he, of course, continued his many other activities, including one last fling at the slave trade, a venture that not only anguished his brother Moses, but got him before a federal court in Newport. Although his ship was condemned, he himself was somehow acquitted, to both the dismay and relief of his Abolitionist brother. But the experience did not much chasten this supreme individualist, for when he was elected to Congress a couple of years later, he was one of only five to vote against a bill strengthening the anti-slave trade laws.[10]

The new year was only eleven days old when John Brown again wrote to Tom Francis, saying that Greenleaf had asked him to discharge the mortgage on the Lansdown estate for a "payment of about 4000 dollars. . . ." Brown said the mortgage was given as security for three notes of "say 8016-⅔ dollars each which was given by Mr. Greenleaf for the Tea payable in 6, 9 and 12 months, the first two notes being given up to him in consequence of the money kept me at Philadelphia in May last, ...[11] He then asked for the advice of the young Francis and his father Tench, saying he would do whatever they recommended. One gathers, however, that Brown had received some $16,000 earlier.

A few days later Brown wrote again, saying that he would leave "my matter with Mr. Greenleaf with you as I think you know the man and can do better with him than . . . I can." And he added a postscript: "Weighing all circumstances togeather, I am fully convienced that your judgement of Mr. G. was much better than mine and I very much fear that this conviction to me is realized to late, but I am happy in the belief that you will do everything in your power to cover Brown and Francis in their indorsement for Mr. Greenleaf as far as you can with due propriety."[12]

By April, Greenleaf had gone down along with his erstwhile partner Robert Morris. He was in debt $1.8 million, a rather impressive sum even today. Then, it was a figure almost beyond comprehension.[13] Plainly, Mr. Greenleaf was a man of some imagination and daring, for to be *that* much in debt was, in a perverse way, quite an achievement. It's doubtful, however, that John Brown was foremost among his admirers, especially when Greenleaf sold Lansdown, which Brown was counting on as security, to the great Philadelphia merchant William Bingham.

Brown learned some of this distressing news in a letter from his young confidant Tom Francis:

> . . . *Greenleafs affairs look more gloomy daily the further we examine the more intricate we find this Transactions — I fear there is too much reason to believe him a bad citizen — Independent of the General tenor of his conduct, we have discovered many instances of his having negotiated obligations of Morris & N. which were previously cancelled and he had promised to deliver up. I mention these circumstances to show the propriety of your taking every step for your security.*
>
> *Lansdown will be sold next week by the sheriff and except so far as the Note for $8000 goes, your claim* [it is thought] *will fall thro. Pray had you not better send me on the note and let me try what can be done. If you approve of this step, I would recommend you forwarding the note immediately by post. The note alluded to is one of the original* [those obtained by John Francis] *secured by the mortgage.*[14]

Later that month, April 1797, John Brown wrote a long letter to Tom Francis which sheds more light on the complicated matter and also, for the first time, expressed an interest in taking possession of the 210,000 acres. Now, Brown is openly distrustful of Greenleaf, writing of his "insufficiency and perhaps I may add his want of honesty." He reported that Greenleaf had told him that "there was not only no probability but no possibility" of bills for £1,800 being returned unpaid. Thus, he sold the bills to a Boston firm, only to be notified that they were indeed returned unpaid.

Brown reported too that the Greenleaf notes for the third installment of the tea, totaling $52,000 (sometimes he adds the $500, other times he does not), were still in the New York bank. He asked Francis to notify businessmen "who hold the notes endorsed by B & F in May last for Greenleaf's benefit and assure them in my behalf that I will pay the notes as soon as I can after the arrival of the Ship *George Washington* from Canton and I expect her in June but should any of those notes be put in suit against me, I shall of course think myself at liberty to extend the payments to the extent of the law and I am told by our laws I cannot be obliged to pay till the holder of the notes first prosecutes Greenleaf and is found insufficient or that he has no property."

Brown argued, vainly as it turned out, that Greenleaf's Pennsylvania property should stand as security for the entire $36,000 in notes he endorsed "considering the pledge in said mortgages to be binding on him till the whole was paid, I did not ask him for any further security for my endorsements for his benefit . . . only his personal promise as above now enclosed you." Later, however, it was determined that the property stood behind only the $24,000 for which it was specifically pledged, two-thirds of which he had apparently already been paid by Greenleaf.

What is perplexing to researchers two centuries later, and may well have been perplexing to young Tom Francis then, is that John Brown wrote one thing in one letter and then something rather different in another. Indeed, he sometimes contradicted himself in the same letter. In this one, for instance, he referred, as he had many times, to the third installment for the tea as $52,000 (actually it was $52,500), with Greenleaf's notes to that amount still being held in the Bank of New York. He had several times referred to that portion of the tea money as backed by the mortgage on the wild lands in New York. But later on in this same letter, he says that the mortgage was to back notes for all the installments. In any case, John Brown, quite humanly, reinterprets his financial arrangements in the light that would most benefit him in any given circumstances.

What is more important in this letter, however, than Brown's shifting interpretations of his deals with Greenleaf is his clear expression of interest in obtaining the New York lands.

. . . Your Brother knew it was mortgaged before to Mr. Phil Livingston, for about 25,000 dollars, which, I wish you could find means to pay off and take the mortgage. If you can, I will redeem it by a consignment out of the ship as soon as she arrives. Mr. Greenleaf has since sold the whole tract in Boston subject to Mr. Livingstons and B & F's mortgages. I know of no other method to receive myself but to purchase the whole tract of 210,000 acres which I have thought of doing if it can be had as its value and the ship arrives safe. I will be exceeding cleaver to leave 50,000 acres of this land to John Brown Francis which to do would make the purchase as some supposed, the 1st mortgage if purchased by those who has bo't it since B & F. Mortgage will shut ours out. I shall be exceeding happy if you or any of your friends could purchase the first mortgage and I am told that Mr. Livingston is about foreclosing ours as soon as the law will admit him so to do which I understand will be some months.[15]

There are not words of a man stuck with property he did not want and reluctantly making the best of a bad bargain. John Brown, contrary to what has been written by Donaldson and Hedges and others, wanted the land and, as subsequent evidence will amply demonstrate, this was anything but a passing fancy.

That letter crossed one in the mail from Tom Francis, in which he reported that he had bought Lansdown from the sheriff for William Bingham for "31,050 Drs subject to your claim" of $8,000.

. . . With respect to Mr. Greenleaf's affairs I see nothing to brighten the prospect. The Trustees are laboring hard to save the creditors they represent—nothing will be forthcoming from the Estate very shortly—What time will effect, God only knows. We are desirous of getting possession of his books to ascertain the real situation of his affairs. To this he refuses unless we become his security in every action and allow him 1000 *Drs* monthly *for his support!!!! This favors much of his having large Property conceal'd or withheld from his Creditors.*

As to the notes I endorsed for your acct, say $36,000 I am still a large sum in arrears. All the security I held I have sold and rec'd therefrom about 26,000$ so that there is a deficiency of about 10,000 for which I have sued Greenleaf and shall obtain judgement in the September Term.[16]

Another letter from John Brown crossed in the mail. ". . . I feel very anxious to save as much as possible of the debt due from Greenleaf, the giving him my order for the notes of the two first installments before I knew how the mortgages run was very unfortunate to me. . . ." And again he pressed Francis to obtain the first mortgage on the New York lands . . . ". . . if you can by any means raise the money for Mr. Livingston, the mortgage can be made over to you till the money shall be repaid you with interest."[17]

On April 26, 1797, Thomas Willing Francis wrote to the great New York financier Robert Lenox, enclosing an order from John Brown that the notes still at the Bank of New York be forwarded to Francis. There were nine notes totalling $52,500 "lodged for Collection by my late partner John Francis." They were dated August 18, 1795, and payable August 2, 1796.[18]

A few days later, on April 30, John Brown sent to Francis the happy news that his ship had come in. "I have now the pleasure of advising you that our ship *George Washington* Capt. Donnison has this day arrived from Batavia with a full load of coffee, sugar, pepper, and some nutmegs, cloves, mace and cinnamon."[19] Although we do not know exactly what John Brown netted from this his last venture to the Orient (James Brown in his diary on May 7, 1797, said the cargo was worth $300,000, a fortune in those days), it was enough for him to pay off his debts and retire, giving him the money and the time to plunge into his next great adventure, the John Brown's Tract.

Brown then proceeded to sell the ship to the federal government for $40,000, exacting a penalty of $400 because the government was tardy. The Secretary of the Navy wrote that it was not "worth disputing about Trifels, and if you insist on it, I must add the 400 Dollars for the expense since you offer; tho' I really think you ought not to ask it." The Secretary then made available $2,500 to fit the *George Washington* out as a man of war, since the U. S. and France were then involved in undeclared naval warfare. He warned Navy Captain Silas Talbot that John Brown was "a complete Master of the Art of bargain making" and urged him to do his best to "let the public be Screwed as little as possible."[20] Although John Brown sold the vessel to the government for $40,000, he earlier wrote Thomas Willing Francis that he was willing to sell it for $36,000.

Things never change, for then, as now, men who regard themselves as patriots sell military goods to the government for more than they could get anywhere else.[21] And in another parallel to the present, the *George Washington* proved to be not only over-priced, but slow and poorly built.

While most of the correspondence between Providence and Philadelphia concerned the Greenleaf matter, one letter from Abby Francis to her brother-in-law Tom demonstrates the affection between them:

. . . *You have generously come forward & beg'd my acceptance of an annual support. This I can not receive from you my excellent friend for various reasons, some of which you certainly cannot be ignorant of. . . . My Fathers ever affectionate attendance to my happiness leaves no* Reasonable *wish of mine ungratified but still as the desire of feeling a little less dependent some time Crosses my mind. I am encouraged by your affectionate zeal in my service & that of my dear* Children *to say that I can receive it only in one way. And that is to call on you now & then for such* small *sum as I* may *want in the belief you'll be willing to grant it by way of loan, to be repaid at some future period. On this principal* alone *I can derive a benefit from your intention of rendering me a service in the pecuniary line . . . the liberty I take in proposing this kind of security to you will not I hope wound the delicacy of your feelings in the smallest degree.*

Then Abby turns to a painful subject:

I recollect to have heard you mention an intention of getting a Tomb Stone cut in Phila for the Grave of my beloved husband. I thought it might not be improper to remind you that opportunities are scarce in the Winter & indeed that Season would not answer for this last & melancholy office, but in this I would wish you to be govern'd by your own personal feelings.[22]

Even as John Brown was trying to obtain the New York land, he received a letter from a New York man, Brockholst Levingston, who asked if he wanted to sell his mortgage. He also notified Brown that Philip Livingston had filed a bill in the Court of Chancery to foreclose his mortgage against Greenleaf.[23]

Again John Brown writes of the tract:

. . . Since I wrote you of my wish to get Mr. Livingston's mortgage . . . I have been fully assured that their is no necessity to do it as my security on the same lands can not be injured by the possessor of the first mortgage, but I should suppose it may be necessary when any part of the tract is sold to discharge Livingson's mortgage, it will be best for me to employ some proper person to be present to sue, that no sacrifice shall be made. I have advise of the land being so poor that shall not think of buying it.[24]

This is the first evidence we have encountered of Brown's being advised not to buy the land. It is not the last.

Then Brown added the alarming postscript:

. . . I have this moment received information that the land mortgaged to me in the State of New York has been owned since the revolution by an inhabitant of Great Britain which it is said will vacate Greenleaf's title and the lands become forfit to the State, . . .

One can only speculate what Brown heard. Since he was in touch with Aaron Burr for his legal advice about the tract, he may have heard from Burr about the brief involvement of John Julius Angerstein, a wealthy London merchant. Burr evidently had contracted to buy the land but somehow, shadily it is reported, wriggled out of the deal. And Angerstein evidently for a time held title to the land as security.[25] Whatever he heard, Brown eventually learned that Greenleaf's title was good. What remained was finding the best way for Brown to obtain title.

As to how much John Brown lost on the deal, it is not possible to say exactly. But from the evidence of these letters, often a bit contradictory, it is possible to make a fairly accurate estimate. Brown plainly lost $36,000 of the $80,000 remaining in notes for the first two installments, Greenleaf apparently having paid an additional $8,000. And he lost the entire final installment of $52,500 for a total of $88,500. Also he might have been responsible for the $10,000 that Thomas Willing Francis did not recover from the $36,000 in notes he endorsed. That could come to $98,500 plus legal costs. Too, there were other Greenleaf notes he had, in effect, co-signed but we do not know if any of Greenleaf's other creditors tried to recover from Brown. This, of course, does not include the fearful aggravation. No wonder that Brown so often ruefully referred to his actions (not John Francis') as "imprudent" and "unfortunate."

The Greenleaf affair dragged on for some months, complicated by the fact that yellow fever again plagued Philadelphia in the late summer of 1797. It hung on for weeks and on September 26, Tom Francis wrote to John Brown of the "deranged State of our mercantile Affairs," reporting that "The fever is increasing, 33 died the 24 hours ending Yesterday Noon."[26]

Time after time in his correspondence with Tom Francis, Brown ruefully admits that he is to blame for much of the problem with Greenleaf. He refers to the notes "which I was so unfortunately gave up by me," the "Notes which I was so imprudent to endorse" and Francis writes of the "notes you unfortunately cancelled."[27] Now it is hardly likely that Greenleaf would have paid, or would have been able to pay, all the notes for the first two installments on the tea even if Brown had not endorsed them, but it was imprudent of Brown to have allowed them to be replaced by personal notes which had a lower payment priority and exposed him as, in effect, co-signer of Greenleaf notes. In any case, this worsened situation was John Brown's doing, not John Francis'.

In October Brown wrote that yellow fever had visited Providence but that the city had been clear "for this past week." He also wrote that month that Greenleaf had applied to the Judges of the Court of Common Plea for the benefit of the Insolvency Act and he asked Francis to represent him at court on November 20. He wrote also of the land in New York, saying "I have lucky information of the badness of the land it being the most rocky and barren of any part of the whole State, there is now a matter of doubt with me weither it will sell for much more if any than the previous mortgage to Mr. Livingston."[28] Again, we have evidence that Brown knew the land was poor.

By the end of the year we learn from son James Brown's diary that his father was advertising to sell "all his navigations and distillery."[29] And that month, December, Brown learned that Greenleaf had been in debtor's prison since the 20th of November. "Mr. G. is consequently still in prison and will not be released till his conduct has been scrutinized into." And Tom Francis reports that a lawyer has been to visit Greenleaf "frequently to obtain evidence from Mr. Greenleaf that you have not recd a bona fide consideration for the notes you have surrendered now in Mr. G's possession. Mr. Thomas has not been successful nor can I flatter you that he will be so."[30]

Tom Francis also reported that land values were collapsing. The speculative bubble had burst. John Brown, as usual, had his own opinion for the collapse of land values:

> *. . . The great fall of real estate with you doeth not in my opinion proceed only from the decline of the rage for speculation, but in fact this rage as well as the fall of property is owing to the great losses and deprivations made on our commerce. If the citizens of those states were now in possession of the great property that we have deprived of by the several belligerent powers with what they yet possess I do not suppose that there would have been any great fall in price of lands in your City but should our nation continue sending their ships unarmed and unprotected till they are all taken or till there is no property left to buy houses or lots left, what will they then fetch when no person has money or other property to purchase.*[31]

Brown was referring to the undeclared naval warfare, especially with France, that took a steady and costly toll of American shipping.

The year 1798 saw John Brown obtain title to what henceforth would be known as the John Brown's Tract. We have already seen that Brown himself at least twice reported that the land was poor and that the wild lands could hardly be termed promising. In considering this evidence the reader should remember what until now has been the conventional wisdom as established by Alfred Donaldson that "the investment was neither of his choosing nor to his liking and was forced upon him by peculiar circumstances."[32]

As the new year began, James Greenleaf was in debtor's prison, soon to be joined by his erstwhile partner Robert Morris, who remained there in frugal comfort for three years, six months, and ten days, entertaining the leading men of the time, among them his Revolutionary comrade George Washington. One wonders if the fortunes of the men Morris had led into ruin might not have been better served if Morris had been out of jail trying to repair the damage he had caused.

Brown hired Aaron Burr, who would soon be vice president, for legal advice in the Greenleaf affair and on February 22, Tom Francis instructed the Philadelphia attorney Joseph Thomas to institute suit on behalf of Brown in Federal Court for unpaid notes totalling $74,316.67.[33]

In March we have one of the earliest surviving letters from Charles Frederick Herreshoff to John Brown's daughter Sarah. Herreshoff, the most tragic figure in our story, demonstrates a graceful pen all the more notable since German, not English, was his mother tongue. This was five years after he met Sarah on his first trip to Providence. The tone of the letter is discreet, as if he fears ardor might alarm her, yet clearly that of a suitor:

> *You would certainly not think it intruding, says our friend* [Thomas L.] *Halsey, whom I consulted on this subject, if in the place of the two drooping myrtle trees, I took the liberty to send you another pair. Confident of his authenticity, and still more of your goodness, I saw no reason to deprive myself of this pleasure. I also suggested that a few dedicatory lines were rather requisite for a dedication, and nothing more, than what every dedicator was entitled to. Therefore, like a respectfull author, I ask leave to lay these little trees at your feet, where they will be envied by him that sends them.*
>
> *Always reflecting with delight on the time I spent in Providence last year, I now feel doubly happy in anticipating the pleasure of another visit, this spring or summer. Till this day I never gave my promise to Halsey's kind invitations; but when he told me that you joined him in his wishes, how could I hesitate: Tis true I should perhaps suspect this to be a contrivance of his, to make me surrender at once, but I will suppress such suspicions until my presence, when, should I find him guilty of treason I shall bring a charge against him, before a Tribunal, whose justice in this, and candour in another cause, I may have to implore.*[34]

That same month Tom Francis wrote to John Brown that Greenleaf's efforts to get out of prison failed, pending a hearing on April 5. In the interim his creditors were "to have free access to his Books—in order to a full Investigation of Villainous Transaction. . . . I shall be glad you would write me on the subject and enclose a letter to Mr. Thomas with Directions to make every opposition to Greenleaf's release unless you obtain Security.

"I am convinced from the slight view I have had of Mr. Greenleaf's books that he is the greatest rogue in Existence—his *Liberality or Prodigality* is astonishing!!"[35]

And Francis reports the capture by the French of a New Jersey ship bound for home from China. "She was out 95 days from Canton with a Cargo worth 400,000 Dollars when those *free Booters* carried her to Porto Rico. Her value will ensure her condemnation.

"The late European Intelligence has created great Alarm – and enhanced the premiums to French Ports in the West Indies & Europe. Pray what will become of us."

The John Brown of 1798 was little changed from the youthful John Brown of the burning of the *Gaspee* twenty-six years earlier. He knew what the answer was.

". . . we shall be much better off if Congress would grant letters of reprisal against France, Spain and Holland."

His blunt opinion was that if the nation was ready to take on Great Britain when the colonies were much less equipped to wage war, the United States shouldn't hesitate to take on France and its allies, especially since the U. S. would have the assistance of the powerful British fleet. ". . . we have nothing to fear from their navies compared with what we had in our infancy to contend with in our Revolution from England." And he added: "I am ashamed of the government of our nation."[36] Clearly Brown had little patience with the attempts of President John Adams to keep the young nation from being crushed between the sides in the great European power struggles.

On May 20 misfortune again visited the family to which it was no stranger. Eight-year-old Anne Willing Francis died. Abby Francis had already lost her daughter Sally and her husband and now her eldest child. An obviously affected James Brown wrote this in his almanac on a blank page opposite the data for May:

. . . At one Oclk at night after Sunday the 20th of May 1798 My beloved Niece Anne Willing Francis expires. She had been ill a forthnight. She lived eight years & three months in this painful World.

Her loss leads me to wish I had less feeling on this painful occasion. If there is a heaven and happiness hereafter, my darling must be among the blessed.

The lovely angel sleeps in peace. Storms and tempests can't o'ertake thee more.[37]

Early the next month John Brown pursued his interest in the New York lands with this letter to John Hammond, a surveyor of Schuyler, New York:

. . . I observe by yours of the 2d of April 1797 that you have discovered Iron Oar & copper on the Tract of land I have mortgaged of say, eight Townships in all – 210000 Acres and that you wish to do any surveying I may have to do,

pray what season will be the best to survey it and what will be the Expense to survey the whole lay it out in quarter mile squares describe the Rivers and kind of Land or waters in every Division with what kind of wood and whether much wood or less and mention the Iron Oar, Lime Rock Salt springs the kinds of timber & on every piece or No. how did the coper oar turn out that you sent to New York for trial what quantity of copper does ther appear to be and what extent of Iron Oar and what kind, whether Bogg Oar rock oar or Mountain Oar or whether it is on dry level ground or in swamps or mountains and what appearance—how far distant on the Moose River did you discover a plenty of Iron Oar; If the mill seats are good and the Iron Oar is good it appears to me the Land must be valuable the soil may not be rich and proper for raising Wheat, but is the whole 210000 Acres so generally bad as not to afford any good wheat or Corn farms; as yourself & Three of your Family are surveyors I suppose you will undertake to survey it with accuracy for a Reasonable Sum as you may do it at leisure and miss no other employment please to mention the lowest price you'll do it for to give me a particular description of every quarter mile square affixed to its No. say from N. 1 to 1200 or 1300 which will comprehend the whole tract.[38]

That same day, June 2, John Brown also wrote to Tom Francis, saying "I have had two pressing letters from Greenleaf to be released from prison. Will you desire your friend Thomas to answer my letter to him on the subject *and you or he advise me on what part of my Demand against him is secured*, as I am left entirely in the dark, know not how to act."

Brown also wrote rather defensively of his continuing interest in the New York lands:

. . . I cannot remember to have ever signified to you that the 210,000 acres of land in Hercermar County was worth nothing and the Land may be bad in genneral, out of such a large tract it will be strange indeed if there is not some good. At ⅓ of a Doll per Acre for the whole will amount to Livingstons mortgage. The notes remaining of our mortgage say about 70,000 Doll. and I am told there is plenty of Iron Oar upon it. . . .

Yet, while Brown is obviously concerned with the Greenleaf matter, his concern as a family man is paramount, for his letter begins with a reference to his daughter who had lost her daughter less than two weeks before: ". . . our Dr. Abbey appears to enjoy no society. She keeps her chamber and looks like a poor Disconsolate goast."[39]

At just about that same time Thomas Cooper, Master in Chancery for the State of New York, who had been appointed by the Court of Chancery [a court of equity] to investigate the matter, reported that James Greenleaf still owed $27,070.27 on two promissory notes originally totalling $38,050. With interest, Cooper set the amount owed Philip Livingston and his wife

Cornelia at $29,550.93. Cooper decreed that if the payments were not made within six months, the property could be sold and gave John Brown, holder of the second mortgage, preference.[40]

Thus, John Brown had some time before he had to decide whether to obtain the land or not. By now he had rather a more optimistic value of the tract than he had earlier. He wrote to Tom Francis:

. . . I cannot conceive how you could have understood me or others that 210,000 Acres of Land within 100 miles of Albany is worth nothing, although it might not sell for much in cash over & above Mr. Phillip Livingston's mortgage, say 29,150 dol Now if exposed for sale together and no one appears for our mortgage, yes I can have no doubt that from the rappid settlement of that country if must soone be worth as much or more than Livingstons & our mortgage together, as it is settled on several sides of it within 7 or 8 miles of the Tract and has many good mills and plenty of iron oar upon it as I am well informed. I therefore do think it would be unpardonable in me to suffer the loss of that mortgage for the want of the above sum to advance and pay off Mr. Livingston or to make the purchase at vandue which will be the 7th of Novem next if the mortgage is not purchased before.

This surely is not the reluctant man making the best of a bad bargain that earlier writers have portrayed.

Brown added a postscript the next day: "I am sorry to advise that the most of my Family with myself have been much unwell ever since the loss of our Dear Little Ann, for the first time since Mrs. Francis has this fine deliteful day taken an airing in the carriage with her married sister."[41]

This final reference is puzzling, since neither Sarah nor Alice was yet married. He may have been referring to Abby's sister-in-law and dear friend Sophia Francis Harrison.

Tom Francis quickly replied and explained why he understood Brown to have a low estimate of the land by quoting from Brown's letter to him of October 27, in which Brown termed the land "the most Barren & Rocky of any part of the whole State." Francis then tactfully added that "I hope the Ideas you then entertained will prove erroneous, but I think I would be well ascertained of the Value of the Lands before you involve more property in them." Plainly, the young businessman was more prudent than the much older one, demonstrating once again that experience is not always the best teacher.

Francis then discusses in most unhappy terms his dealings with Greenleaf, who has accused him of being "Greenleaf's persecutor. His impertenance is only equalled by his villainy toward me. He has defrauded me of thousands and pays the debt by illiberal & false accusations." Francis then describes the situation of the various suits against Greenleaf. "Thus the suits against Greenleaf stand and you can best judge what you ought to do with him. I do not know that detention of his person will produce any good, whatever you determine please communicate to Mr. Thomas as Mr. Greenleaf's behavior towards me does not admit of any intercourse with him. Your letter should be sent to him in jail."[42]

Within a few days Francis decided that circumstances did admit of one final intercourse with Greenleaf. He wrote to Greenleaf saying he had a letter for Greenleaf from Brown and that Brown had also sent a letter to him from Greenleaf in which the following paragraph appeared:

> *. . . The object of the present letter is not Sir to operate on your feelings by a detailed exclosure of the extreeme hardships, not to say cruelty of my case, but is simply to disclose to you that Mr. Francis is altogether an improper agent to act in this business as his own* personal Interest *(not yours) prompted him to opposition on my subject therefore can the exercise of Impartiality, of humanity and of Justice.*

Francis' response is stern indeed:

> *. . . I shall not trouble you with any observations on the false, unfounded Insinuations you have taken the liberty of making against my character — or to remind you of the Immense picuniary Injury you have occasioned to me & to my connections — nor will I take a retrospect of the mildness of my treatment of you in every Instance when I had sure Int. but shall confine myself to the duty I owe to my character, in declaring that Mr. Brown ordered the suits against you in the manner they were instituted, for the declared and express purpose of preventing your release from prison under the Insolvency Act of this State, untill he was satisfied that you had fairly and honestly given up all your property and fully secured the debt to Brown & Francis . . . . . It is true Mr. Brown had frequently written me & referred the matter to my* Decision, *but I never have acted since Feby, nor is it my intention to meddle where no good can arise to my friend & possibly nay most probably more injury to myself. Mr. Brown is sufficiently capable of Judging what is more for his Int. Presuming you are unable to rectify the Injury you have caused I must request you will do justice to the Character of,*
>
> *Yours,*
> *Thomas Willing Francis*[43]

By the end of June, John Brown was wondering whether there was any point in keeping Greenleaf in jail and he suggested to Tom Francis that it might be better to allow Greenleaf's release if he paid all costs including Brown's lawyer's fees. He suggested that the suits be withdrawn and the notes preserved "till some better prospects of getting something from him . . ."

John Brown then returned to his now constant preoccupation, the wild lands:

> *... Thought it may be a doubt weither the 210,000 acres of land in Herkimer County State of New York would sell at veandue or otherwise together for much more money that Mr. Livingstons mortgage, I never had it in view to relinquish our claim profided I could* [be] *assured that the title would be good which Wm. Bogert and others assures me is the case. At only a quarter of a dollar per acre, it amounts to 52,500 dollars which is certainly a very low estimate for land within 100 miles of Albany, tho much of the land may be very bad. If one quarter of it is good it must together be worth this price. When your brother took the mortgage* he had it valued by the best judges he could get [author's emphasis] *and they then supposed it worth in cash 120,000 over and above Livingston's mortgage which with the interest and charges will not excede 30,000 dollars on the 7th of November next when it is to be sold by the judgement of court to pay Mr. Livingstons mortgage.*

Brown referred in a postscript to his earlier letter in which he said Abby had finally gone out to take the air.

> *... I was mistaken. She did not go nor has she ever been out of the house since the loss of her dear Ann, only once with her sister she went to weep over the grave. All the persuation of her parents and friends has not yet prevailed on her to see company or go out. If it is in your power or that of your family to prevail on her to shake off the fatal catastrophy, infinitesimal service will thereby be done her.*[44]

Plainly, John Brown meant infinite, not infinitesimal, but he had a wondrously random way with language.

In July, Tom Francis reported to John Brown that Greenleaf had been released from prison under the terms of a Congressional bankruptcy act. "... his person of course is liberated as far as regards the suit you commenced against him – but his property if he has any or should ever acquire any, remains liable."[45]

Not much was ever recovered from Greenleaf but it must be remembered that we have seen his business dealings from only one side, that of those who suffered. They, quite humanly, regarded him as villainous but those were difficult financial times and it may be that he was honest but imprudent. After all, a great many men, among them the formidable Robert Morris, fell victim to the times – and their own eagerness for fortune.

Although John Brown plainly had his mind made up to obtain the tract, he did send his son James up to the area in August. According to notes he scribbled in his almanac, James visited Utica and Rome, the two largest settlements in the area, and also Boon's, now Boonville, a small settlement about a dozen miles southwest of the southwestern corner of the tract. He noted that "These regions altho settled only about 10 or 12 years are thickly inhabited and many of the inhabitants are again emigrating." And James reported that "land not cultivated sell for about Six Dolls. Per Acre." The next day he traveled the twelve miles to Boon's. ". . . the vilest roads."[46]

Even while James was up in northern New York to take a look at the situation, his father urged Tom Francis to provide, on credit, the money necessary to obtain the land. He assured Francis that he would pledge the "land or any other part of my Estate" for the money and that there would be no risk since he would soon have available three or four times the amount needed.

> *. . . pray remember that my securing the 210,00 Acres Land will be fixing a certain and hansome fortune to your dear nephew John B. Francis who is a fine fellar and now well with his dear maw at Point Pleasant* [John Brown's farm in Bristol, R. I.]. *I think it is not unlikely but that land will be worth 400,000 Dolles if not half a million by the time my Grandson is of age.*[47]

We cannot know if John Brown Francis ever saw this letter, but if he had during those years when his most fervent wish was to unload the Tract at almost any price, he must have winced.

While John Brown was moving closer to obtaining the Tract, Charles Frederick Herreshoff intensified the courtship of Sarah Brown that would eventually culminate on a bleak December day nearly twenty years later in the tragedy of the John Brown's Tract. Plainly, the relationship between Charles and Sarah had developed during the six months since the last letter we quoted. It is fair to assume that the then projected visit did indeed take place and that, despite the disapproval of John Brown – he clearly thought no one was good enough for his daughters – a romance was blossoming, albeit one that would take three years to result in marriage. The formidable John Brown's disapproval was not easily swept aside.

As to what it was based on, we can only conjecture. Herreshoff's foreign birth may have been a factor, although in those early days of the Republic there was a close kinship between America and Europe; nationalism had had little time to develop. More likely it was Herreshoff's spotty record as a businessman. He seemed much more the polished gentleman than the ambitious merchant. But, of course, it may have been some personal quality or the chemistry between two very dissimilar men, although, as we shall tragically see, Herreshoff too was capable of obsession.

Of biographical facts about Charles Frederick Herreshoff, especially of his early life, there are relatively few. There are two major sources, "The Chad Browne Memorial," a genealogy of the Brown family, published in 1888, and the account of his grandson, Lewis B. Herreshoff, who must have been in his early seventies when he spoke to Alfred Donaldson. Although Lewis was born twenty-five years after his grandfather's death and was only two-and-a-half years old when Sarah Herreshoff died, he plainly must have heard a great deal about his grandfather from his father, also named Charles Frederick Herreshoff, his uncle, John Brown Herreshoff, and his maiden aunts, Anna Francis and Sarah Herreshoff, all of whom lived in Bristol.

The Chad Browne account, which was contributed by the family nearly a century ago, is short enough to quote at length:

Carl Friederich Herrschhoff (original spelling), b. Dec. 27, 1763, was the only child of Carl Freiderich and Agness (Müller) Herrschhoff. His mother dying when he was but three years of age, his father entrusted him to the care of a friend living near Berlin, and went to Italy, where he soon after died. The son continued during his youth with his father's friend, an author and professor. In 1779, April 1, he entered the Philanthropin, *an educational institution, then recently founded at Dessau. Here he remained eight years until 1787, when he emigrated to America, and settling in New York, became associated in business with a Mr. Goch. The affairs of the firm led him about 1792 to Rhode Island on a visit to John Brown, the merchant, who introduced him to his family. . . He was a man of polished address, highly educated, an accomplished linguist in seven languages, and a good musician. His educations and tastes were illy adapted to frontier life, and were not conducive to success in the pursuits in which he was engaged.*[48]

Although it is anticipating our story a bit, it is fair to record that, although Charles Frederick Herreshoff may have been "illy adapted to frontier life," he nonetheless demonstrated perseverence and inventiveness in his attempt to make a success of the John Brown's Tract. It was not any lack on Herreshoff's part; the tract was then, as it remains today, wholly unsuitable for agricultural, mining, or any other commercial exploitation save timber or recreation, for neither of which was there a demand in those early days. Herreshoff, like John Brown, was a stubborn man, but he paid an infinitely greater price for his stubbornness.

The Donaldson-Lewis Herreshoff account somewhat fleshes out what appeared in the Brown family genealogy. It tells us that the founder of the famous American sailboat building family was named after his father, "an officer in the famous Potsdam Giant Guard established by Frederick William I, and later abolished by his son Frederick the Great." His mother was Agnes Mühler (notice the slight difference in the spelling of her maiden name) Herreshoff, of good family, and herself both beautiful and accomplished. The son inherited the dominant traits of both his parents. His fine physique and towering height – nearly six-foot-four – came from his father; his grace of carriage, charm of manner, and marked artistic inclinations from his mother.[49]

According to the family account, when Charles was only three or four his mother was injured in a carriage accident and died shortly thereafter. His father consequently suffered from melancholy, left for a journey to Italy and disappeared for good, leaving little Charles in the care of a dear friend. "This friend was a professor, a man of marked culture and learning, who lived a short distance from Berlin. He was, moreover, like many intellectuals of the time, on a certain footing of intimacy with the ruling monarch, Frederick the Great. It thus came about that the king saw the professor's youthful ward and took a strong fancy to the boy. The story runs that the king used to take the little fellow on his knee, and delight in the keen, quick answers he would make to the royal interrogatories."

Young Herreshoff was fortunate enough to be entered into a school at Dessau known as Philanthropin, "the most famous and exclusive school of his day." Under royal patronage, Johann Bernhard Basedow carried out his theory which was to teach, under one system, boys from childhood to manhood. Since the school was for the nobility, it is assumed that Herreshoff had some influential patronage, perhaps even the emperor's, to be admitted.

Herreshoff left school at about the age of twenty. "There is no doubt that he left [the school] in possession of an excellent liberal education and fully equipped with the accomplishments of a cultured gentleman. Among these were a well-trained voice and the ability to play the flute with taste and skill. This latter accomplishment was undoubtedly traceable to his royal patron, for Frederick the Great was an ardent and excellent flute player, and encouraged the gift of music wherever he found the germ."

The young man traveled widely across Europe for several years and then, about 1787, he found his way to New York, where he entered the import trade with two countrymen named Goch and Emptke. This trade took him to Providence in 1793, where John Brown introduced him, then thirty, the same age as John Francis, to his second daughter, Sarah, then twenty.

No doubt his interest in music helped establish a bond with Sarah who was "especially proficient in music and education, deriving consolation from and giving pleasure to others by her skill on the piano, which she played in a remarkably correct and brilliant manner."[50] One can easily imagine piano and flute duets in the music room of John Brown's splendid mansion. And since Charles was a product of a rigorous German education, he might well have shared Sarah's interest in astronomy and mathematics. But maybe this is over-rationalizing. Maybe they just fell in love. However it happened, by late summer of 1798, Charles Frederick Herreshoff was writing unabashed love letters, his language as graceful as his hand. This was written in Boston and then, a couple of days later, in Salem:

. . . You must not expect a very interesting journal, my dear Sally, from a man who did not set out to see and to observe, but who thinks himself exiled from your company, and wishes only for the end of his journey. Besides this, the incidents of such a little tour, are commonly so trifling as to afford little pleasure when related, not that I should not be pleased with a Point Pleasant journal from my dear little Sally, should it contain nothing more remarkable than a walk to the western shore or a ride to Mount Hope, but you know I am a foolish creature, that thinks every thing highly interesting that comes from little Sally, even her faults should he ever discover any, would, I am afraid, appear amiable to him. —

He wrote then of the "melancholy sight" Boston offered because so many shops were closed due to a fever. And he wrote of visiting a woman friend of Sarah, or Sally, as he usually calls her:

. . . I have been three times to see her; I am happy where I can speak of you, and where I find somebody that is worthy to praise you. I know every thing she can tell me of that angel, and nevertheless I always listen to it with pleasure.

Then he mentioned a lovely pond about five miles outside of Boston that "with a little assistance of art, could be made a paradise of, worthy to be the habitation of two happy faithful lovers, like little S. and her friend. I always pity the poor taste of those rich people, that place pompous buildings as near as possible to the public road, exposed to the admiration and the dust of every one, in preference to a beautiful solitary spot."

He ended with:

. . . What fine weather we have, I wish my dear Sally may enjoy it and take better care of her health than she did when that foolish boy walked with her so late in the evening. Adieu you charming excellent girl. Yours in all eternity.

And he signed it simply, "Herreshoff."[51]

John Brown's Obsession

A few days later he wrote to Sarah from Portland: "Since I wrote to you from Salem this is the first moment I am alone, how else could I employ it otherwise than to write to my dear Sally, whose image is my constant companion. Every fine prospect creates the wish that you might be present, and every rock that offers a pleasant seat brings the recollection of some happy moments to my mind." And he described his thoughts on September 5, Sally's 25th birthday. "I sent that day a thousand thanks to heaven for the birth of the dearest little child that ever was born and a thousand times I wished to be with you at Point Pleasant retired and happy." How differently his life would end. "I thought then my absence a real penitence; I hope I shall soon be rewarded for it by many a delicious moment." And toward the close Charles Frederick Herreshoff penned these elegant lines in saying that he hopes to receive a letter from her in Boston: ". . . and if I find none, I shall frown, not at you but at the goddess of indolence whom alone I shall accuse for the loss of that pleasure."

John Brown was a formidable man indeed but what daughter's father had a chance in the face of so ardent, and so eloquent, a suitor.

Meanwhile, John Brown was continuing in his single-minded pursuit of the wild lands. But his letter of September 7 to Tom Francis in Philadelphia also concerned an expected order of "Pigg iron" so the Brown brothers could manufacture cannon at their Hope Furnace for use in the undeclared naval warfare against France and its allies. He supposed that the lack of communication from Philadelphia was caused by "the unhappy state of your city occasioned by the Fever . . ." presumably the same fever that Herreshoff reported in Boston.

Then Brown turned to the subject that so preoccupied him:

> . . . *My son James has been to Herkimer County in the State of New York to investigate the real quality and value of the 210 Thousand acres of land mortgaged to Brown and Francis by James Greenleaf. And has returned fully convinced of the importance of our getting the fee of said land at all events, as he verely believes the land to be worth as many dollars as there is acres say 210,000 dollars and in a few years with a few settlements may be worth double the money as the settlement of that county is rapid beyond description, as the time now draws near when the money must be paid or the opportunity lost forever.*[52]

This is the first time we have encountered a documented reference to the land being worth $210,000. It is not inconceivable that this is the source for that oft-cited figure, although that figure has been misconstrued as what John Francis should have brought home for that sale of tea.

Although James Brown's journey to the region was a laudable and serious attempt to learn about the Tract, it must be remembered how extremely difficult travel to the area was in those days. The unhappy fact is that James, and thus his father, thought he knew more about the Tract than in fact he did. Although he came within a few miles of the property, there is no indication that he actually set foot upon it. Yet, in that region a few miles makes a vast difference. To the immediate west and south of the Tract, the areas James visited, the land is fertile and productive. Travel, however, just a few miles east and north and the character of the soil changes drastically—for the worse. For now you are in the Adirondacks and even though the elevation rises gradually, the soil is that of the uplands, stony and barren, inhospitable to the farmer. Beautiful land, but barren. The earlier reports "of the badness of the land it being the most rocky and barren of any part of the while State" were indeed accurate but, as the old saying has it," There are none so blind as those who will not see." John Brown wanted that land and disregarded any information to the contrary. And his son James' trip played into Brown's prejudice; he assumed that the land on the Tract was much the same as the fertile lands nearby, a natural enough assumption were it not for those negative reports.

Although it is outside the scope of this book, we should note that John Brown, besides his efforts to obtain the wild lands and liquidate his business before retiring, was also running for Congress, to which he was elected in August as a Federalist candidate. He served only one term. When he sought reelection two years later, he received only 138 votes, compared to the 2,680 he had received in 1798, running third among the three unsuccessful Federalist candidates. That year, the year Thomas Jefferson was elected President as a Republican (what the present Democratic party was then called), Republican Congressional candidates led the field.[53]

It was nearly a month until Tom Francis replied to John Brown, who had been right that fever had crippled Philadelphia. Writing from outside the city, Francis reported that "Shortly after my last letter to you on the Subject of the Pig Iron, the fever commenced, which now desolates our City & put every mercantile management at a Stand—thus circumstanced it has been impossible to attend to your Commands, wither in Phila or even at NYork from whence our friends have been driven by a similar calamity. The number of deaths are daily very considerable, and altho the *new cases* reported are diminished. I do not believe we shall be able to return to Phila until next month."

Then he turned to what interests John Brown most: "I observe by your letter of the 7 Sept. that Jimmy has returned from a Visit to the Lands in New York & sincerely rejoiced I feel to learn they are likely to secure the payment of your demand on Greenleaf."[54]

The mail service was astonishingly good, for John Brown replied to Tom Francis' letter of October 3 only four days later and wrote that "I am really concerned for your Fathers Family and am surprised at their remaining in the city. . . ." He reiterates his concern in a postscript: ". . . am exceeding fearfull that your Father will meet the Fate of Capt. Anthony, beg him in my name to quit the city, a short time will bring a Frost to restore the health of the city—"[55]

He writes also of the health of his daughter Abby: ". . . my Family are well Mrs. Francis with her dear Boy & her sisters quited their summer residence at Point Pleasant and return to me on the Hill a week past."

But the bulk of the letter is concerned with the wild lands.

. . . Alexander Hamilton Esq. whome Messr Loomis & Tillinghast employed for me to investigate the business of the present State of the Mortgage of the 210,000 Acres land in Herkimer County advises that the sale will commence early in November and that by all means I must provide myself with the money say 30,000 dollars or more and be on the spot myself or send the money by an agent to make the purchase at vendue and thereby get the Fee of the land which he prefers to the paying of Mr. Livingstons mortgage to him as in this case the persons to whom the land was sold after our mortgages will come forward to redeem and thereby prevent any improvement. I must therefore request you to have the money ready for the bills in New York by the 6th of November as I shall take care to have the residence their in person or by some able hand to accomplish the Business by the 7th of November. . .

A couple of weeks later John Brown sent an urgent letter to Tom Francis saying that he was so concerned about getting the money on time that he was sending son James down to Philadelphia to get it and the Greenleaf notes, totaling just under $40,000. And he said that he himself planned to be in New York by the 4th of November. He feared "the mortification of loosing the whole, which I hope you will prevent, by a punctual complyance with the above. . .[56] Then there is a notation dated November 1 and signed by James Brown—who stayed with Thomas Willing Francis outside Philadelphia because of the fever—that notes totaling $39,816 67/100 had been received from Thomas W. Francis. It is not quite clear why John Brown wanted those particular notes, since the notes for $52,500 were presumably still on deposit in the Bank of New York. Perhaps John Brown merely wanted to have in his possession at the sale anything that might buttress his claim to the land.

While John Brown was moving closer to obtaining the land that had become so dear to him, and which was to become so dear to him and his heirs in another sense. Charles Frederick Herreshoff was pursuing his courtship by correspondence. He wrote that a letter would be handed Sally by a colleague going to Providence on business. "He will tell you that I arrived here safe on Saturday last, could he but tell you how much I love you, how constantly I have thought of you during our journey, he would be received with a smile of that tender faithful angel. But he is happy enough in seeing you, spare then those smiles for your loving little boy till he comes to tell you, that he will not leave you again, that he will never never love but you."[57] How ironic those words must have seemed some years later when Herreshoff, obsessed by his determination to make a success of the John Brown's Tract, spent long, lonely months on the land, separated from the woman he romantically declared he would never leave again.

James met his father on November 4 just north of New York City at Rye, where he presumably turned over the Greenleaf notes. John Brown was accompanied by his grandson, John Brown Francis, and by two daughters, the boy's mother Abby, and Alice. They all then proceeded to New York, possibly so John Brown could attend the sale of the land. The next day, James continued home to Providence while the rest of the family journeyed on to Philadelphia. John Brown and daughter Alice visited for a couple of weeks – plainly, the fever had finally left the city – while Abby and John Brown Francis spent the winter, presumably with his Francis grandparents.[58]

There is some uncertainty as to the exact date that John Brown obtained title to the land. The date he kept speaking of in advance was November 7, and his visit to New York on November 4 and 5 would seem to suggest that perhaps the transaction did take place then. But Donaldson, a most meticulous scholar, states flatly that it was December 5, although he offers no documentary evidence to support his assertion. However, there is support in the report of Thomas Cooper, the Master in Chancery, who was assigned to make a report on Greenleaf's mortgages to Livingston and Brown:

> . . . *And whereas the said Thomas Cooper, one of the Masters of the said Court, did on the fourth day of June in the year of our Lord, one thousand seven hundred and ninety eight, . . . report to the said Court, that there was due from the said James Greenleaf to the said Philip Livingston on the said Mortgage on the day of the date of the said report, the sum of Twenty nine Thousand five hundred and fifty dollars and ninety three cents. And whereas the said defendants, . . . did*

not within six months after the confirmation of the said report, or at any time since pay to the said Philip Livingston the said sum of money . . . due to him on the said Mortgage . . . And whereas the said Thomas Cooper, . . . did cause the said Mortgaged premises above described, to be set up at public auction for sale, at the Tontine Coffee House in the City of New York in the State of New York aforesaid on the day of the date of these presents, . . . And whereas the said Mortgaged premises . . . were struck off to the above named John Brown, party of the Third part to these presents, for the sum of Thirty three thousand dollars money of the United States, being the highest price bidden for the same, and he the said John Brown being the bidder.[59]

That may be enough of that charming, archaic language, but while it established that John Brown finally achieved his fervent wish, it does not specify the date. However, allowing the passage of six months from June 4, we come to December 4 with the first day after that period, of course, December 5. Whatever the date, the indenture quoted above was dated December 29, 1798, and recorded on February 22, 1804. We should perhaps add that John Brown had to pay an additional one dollar to Philip and Cornelia to complete the transaction.

We can now speak of the land, without qualification, as the John Brown's Tract. And we can finally attempt to answer the question: How much did it cost? Donaldson writes, as he never would have had he the documents that have finally emerged from long-lost family papers, that "it had cost him over $250,000. The later expenditures on the tract, it will now be seen, were not the mere speculations of a visionary (which, of course, is precisely what they were), but futile efforts to retrieve another's mistake."[60]

Donaldson obviously got the figure of $250,000 by adding to the $210,000 that John Francis purportedly should have received for the sale of the tea, the $33,000 John Brown paid to get title to the land, plus, presumably, legal and other expenses. Well, a quarter of a million dollars certainly makes a nice round figure, but a more accurate figure would be about $131,500: $36,000 left in notes for the first two installments, $52,500 for the third installment, plus $33,000 he paid to obtain the deed. Perhaps we should add to that the $10,000 he paid to Thomas Willing Francis for the sum Francis did not recover on the notes. All this totals $131,500; plus whatever he spent on legal costs.

But there's another way to look at it: the $36,000, the $52,500 and the $10,000 were lost in any case because of Greenleaf's inability, or failure, to meet the contract and because Brown so imprudently (his word) signed, and convinced his son-in-law's brother to sign the $36,000 in notes.

Thus, it could be argued that the land cost solely the $33,000 Brown paid for it. What cannot be argued is that Brown took the land reluctantly. As we have seen, he sought it avidly. John Francis, already dead, cannot be blamed for that.

One can however, certainly argue that John Brown was throwing good money after bad. The speculative bubble had burst and land that in 1795 seemed like more than adequate security for the purchase was scarcely enough to pay off Philip Livingston's first mortgage, and then only because John Brown wanted the property.

If Brown had not bid on it, the land's selling price, if anybody wanted to buy it, would have been much lower, not even enough to cover the Livingston mortgage, Plainly, there was nothing left for Brown & Francis. That money was gone, through no fault of either John Francis or John Brown.

While it can be argued that John Francis should have held out for cash, one must remember that those were difficult times, cash was very scarce indeed, and promissory notes were the customary way to do business. Greenleaf was believed to be a reputable businessman with great resources, so one can assume that John Francis felt quite comfortable in selling the tea to Greenleaf, especially when the notes were secured by a mortgage on lands assessed by experts as having ample value. After all, John Brown, a much more experienced businessman, continued to have faith in Greenleaf even after Thomas Willing Francis cautioned him.

One could indeed argue that the land cost only $33,000, for the security was no longer worth anything, that John Brown being amply, and frequently, warned about the poor quality of the land should have swallowed his loss and retired, content with the fortune provided him by the final voyage of the *George Washington*, augmented by his handsome sale of the ship to the Navy. Surely, two generations of his descendants must have wished he never bought the land. But he wanted it and what John Brown wanted, he always did his damnedest to get. If he hadn't, there would have been no John Brown's Tract, no financial embarrassment of three generations of the Brown family, no Charles Frederick Herreshoff tragedy and – no book.

John Brown did get the land and, as we shall see in the next chapter, plunged into it with his customary gusto.

6

John Brown Goes North

It has been said that all these social virtues are needed for the settlement of this region.[1]

John Homer French, 1860

THE JOHN BROWN'S TRACT it now was in fact, and so in legend it has remained for more than a century and a quarter after a greatly-relieved family finally rid itself of a vision turned nightmare. Well might the name persist for the inimitable John Brown would soon place his lasting stamp upon it. Two decades later, his son-in-law Charles Frederick Herreshoff, in one moment of despair, climaxed years of soul-destroying frustration with a desperate act that would forever lay upon the Tract a melancholy but undeniably romantic legacy, for happiness can seldom compete with tragedy as the stuff of romance.

But Charles Frederick Herreshoff would have dismissed with a laugh, or perhaps a frown, such a prediction, for at about the time that John Brown was finally gaining what he fervently sought, Herreshoff was deep in the throes of love and swore, indeed believed with all his heart, that he would forever cling to the side of his beloved Sally.

We know what he professed to John Brown's daughter, for his family preserved his letters and they are now safe in the archives of the Rhode Island Historical Society. He wrote to Sally from Charlestown on November 27, 1798, after a stormy passage by sea.

> *. . . Those four days I think were the most miserable I ever passed in my life, but how little would I have felt of all the inconvenience I suffered, if instead of being driven from you dear Sally, I had been on the way to see you. This I hope will soon be the case, and if you promise to write very often to your little boy, he promises to go back by land, perhaps as soon as the month of February or March.*[2]

A few days later he wrote again:

. . . o how happy would we be if we were together. But more than a thousand miles distant from her, whose happyness is dearer to me than my own, nature in her mildest form, smiles in vain on me; she cannot make me forget you, she only reminds me of your absence, and that without you, there is no happyness for me in this world. Your picture lays open before me, you seem to look with tenderness on me, but I do not discover that smile, which I sometimes see in it, and it puts me in mind of a passage of a letter you wrote me once from Point pleasant to Bristol, where you say, that while you were pleased to see how well I loved you, you felt for the weakness of my heart. Dear girl, I should not make you more melancholy in reading my letters, than you may be already in those solitary hours of reflection; I should only speak of our hopes, of our future happyness, but I am not master of that heart which is really weak when I think of you; . . .[3]

On the first day of the New Year, 1799, Herreshoff wrote:

. . . I know your heart is mine, no fear of losing it shall ever give me a moments uneasiness; for my greatest aim shall be, so long as I live, to be worthy of you, and to love you, dear angel, with all the power of my soul . . . Consider, that as cruel as our present separation is, we have reason to hope that it will be the last.[4]

Herreshoff mentioned in another letter that he heard from "Sister A.," presumably Abby, that "little John had the small pox favorably," a rather unusual way of saying he had recovered from an inoculation while visiting his Francis grandparents in Philadelphia. John Brown Francis would later be a collaborator with Herreshoff in attempting to develop the Tract, and, after Herreshoff's death, was for years the member of the family most involved with it.

It was not until mid-April that Herreshoff's business permitted him to leave Charleston and, in his final letter from there, there is a note of doubt about Sally's love for him. Evidently hoping to hear from her enroute, he writes ". . . and in the meantime learn if she wants to see me at all." But of his feelings for her, there is absolutely no doubt: "I shall not tell you anything now, except that I love you as much as I ever did, and that my heart can never change, you shall soon see dear girl, that I am as foolish a boy as ever you saw."[5]

While the romance between Charles and Sally was taking the slow course necessitated by his long absences on business, and by John Brown's opposition, Brown himself was pushing ahead on his last great project. Impatiently, we can be sure, he had to wait for winter to relent before he could begin working to develop his new northern empire. John Brown

Moose River and forest outside of Boonville.

did not have to wait to start organizing his project.

While it has long been known that John Brown spent several weeks on the Tract in the late spring of 1799, we have discovered that he made *two* trips to the area. Characteristically, John Brown wasted no time; he journeyed to the area in the middle of winter. Bitter cold though it must have been, the travel perhaps was a little easier, for the rutted, bumpy roads were snow covered, permitting, if the snows were not too deep, travel by sleigh. Since we have few details of the trip, we must assume that he traveled somehow to Albany and then by road to Utica, and then to Boon's settlement, now Boonville, a dozen or so miles southwest of the Tract. The inference from the scanty evidence is that he did not venture onto the Tract itself, but at the edge of it made plans for the spring with local surveyors, builders, and so forth.

We don't know how he got to Albany. In a milder season he almost certainly would have sailed up the Hudson from New York City, but usually in the winter the river was closed by ice. An overland trip would have been arduous indeed unless the frozen Hudson was used as a superhighway for horse-drawn sleighs. However he did it, the determined John Brown indeed did it.

How do we know? Well, in family papers there is a letter dated February 27 from James Brown to Tom Francis in Philadelphia. The letter, which otherwise has nothing to do with the Tract, begins this way: "In the absence of my father who is gone to see and to settle a part of those lands in the State of N.Y. on which he had Greenleaf mortgage. . . ." However unlikely it would be for John Brown to journey to northern New York in the winter, that brief reference caused us to re-examine our documents.

A letter to the surveyor, Elder Hammon, which we quote below, says as quoted in Grady's popular *The Adirondacks*, ". . . I told your son at East Brayton that I would give you the same as I gave them (other local surveyors)." That passage had not clicked earlier, but curiosity caused us to go back to a photocopy of the original handwritten letter. The letter, and it is easy to do so in the scrawl of a faded letter nearly two centuries old, had been slightly mis-transcribed. It was "Esq. Braytons" not "East Brayton" and since a Brayton is mentioned in the John Brown letters to James Sheldon from which we will quote, that suggests that Brown was in the area. Finally, in a letter to his son James dated December 23, John Brown discusses the expenses for the Tract "in going up twice."[6] The clue was present in evidence long available but not likely to be detected until made plain by evidence more recently uncovered.

In the meantime, on March 31, he wrote to the surveyor, Elder John Hammon Sr.:

> *. . . If you have Concluded to Survay on the Same Terms as Mr. Arnold Smith and Mr. John Allin has, I Desire You'l begin the Business Immediately, Indeed I hope You'l be at work on the Ground before this reaches you—as I wrote Mr. Bellews Some time past, that I told your Son at Esqr. Braytons that I would Give You the same as I Gave them. You'l be very particular in Your Field Book & Note Every thing of Importance, so as to Give Me the Value of Every Town as near as posable by its Number, You'l be Sure to Note Every Mill place, Every Good place for a Compact Town, the ore, the Salt Springs if Aney, the kind of Timber, the Lay of the Ground Weither Good or bad or Indifferent, Weither Broken, or Even or Weither Large or Small Hills and Every other Observation You think worthey of My Knowing, I Shall be on the Ground in all April & if You & I both like I may Continue You at the Survaying till the Whole Tract is Layd out into Four Rod Rhodes Within one Mile of Each in Every Town & the Rhodes at right Angles within Two Miles and Every Farm to be Laid half Mile Squair & Fronting one of Said Rhodes and of course one half the Farms will Lay on Two Rhodes.*

John Brown ended his letter with a characteristically blunt postscript:

. . . If it is Not Convenient for You to begin Immediately I Shall not want you at all —[7]

John Brown did not think small. He was proposing to lay out about 500 miles of roads before he even set foot in an area that he knew was rocky and covered with forests at a time when it would have to be accomplished with hand tools and animal power. Glance now, nearly 200 years later, at a road map of the area. There is scarcely a road to be seen. Despite the availability of power equipment that can do in an hour what it then took days to do, there is little reason for roads, for John Brown's Tract today is what nature intended it to be, a wilderness, populated year round by only a few of those hardy souls who serve those nature-starved vacationers who come to enjoy the wilderness.

John Brown, however, did not see it that way, not before he got there and not even when he saw with his own eyes the difficulties. He was a formidable man, which is no doubt why Tom Francis in a letter to his brother Charles referred to him as "old *Thunder*."[8] You can judge for yourself by the tone of his many letters to James Sheldon, from which we will soon quote handsomely, how well the name is deserved.

Before we join the aging John Brown on his rather daring plunge into the north woods, we must briefly rejoin Charles Frederick Herreshoff who on May 3, when Brown was enroute to his lands, wrote to his Sally from Baltimore:

. . . I feel as if a great burthen has been taken from my heart, that I am so much nearer to you again, and that I may now hope the moment is near when I shall hold you in my arms. . . . I am more than ever convinced that my heart did not betray me, it cannot love but you, and nothing in the world will ever be able to lessen my affection; I did not want this trial to convince me of it, but I feel happyer after it, and seem to feel more confident that I can never forget your worth, never become unworthy of the best noblest saint.[9]

A month later from New York, Herreshoff wrote that he hopes Sally has taken residence at Point Pleasant for the summer. He asks if she has found "That cherry tree again under which you promised me your heart, tell me a great deal of your favorite place, which of course is mine too, ..."[10]

John Brown was pursuing his own romantic vision: carving out of the Adirondack wilderness a flourishing farming community or, rather, a series of such. He gave names to the eight townships into which the Tract had been divided: 1) Industry; 2) Enterprise; 3) Perseverence; 4) Unanimity; 5) Frugality; 6) Sobriety; 7) Economy; and 8) Regularity. J. H. French, the New York State historian, wrote dryly in his 1860 Gazeteer: "It has been said that all these social virtues are needed for the settlement of this region."[11]

Brown certainly possessed most of these virtues in abundance and, as we shall quickly see, and if he himself did not possess frugality and economy, tried to enforce them on those in his employ. We learn from the diary of his son James, who a little later journeyed up to join him, that John Brown was on the Tract beginning on May 5.[12] It must have

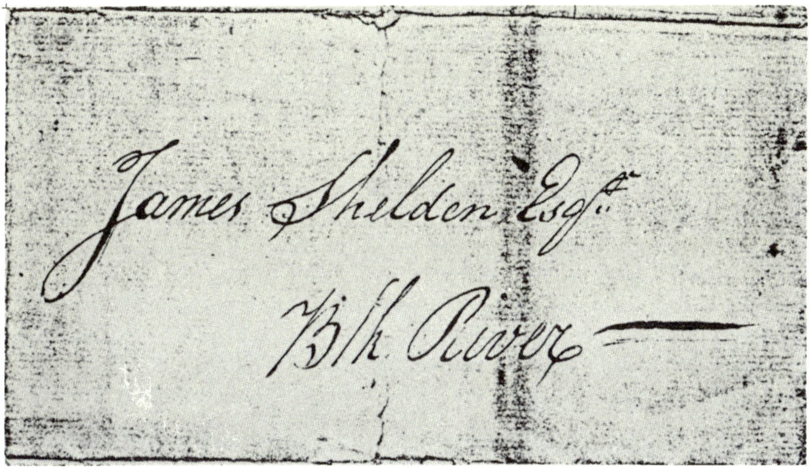

been a terrible trip for the elder Brown, even though he was traveling in his specially-built chariot, the elegant carriage that can now be seen at the John Brown house in Providence. He was, remember, 63 and reportedly weighed about 300 pounds. Roads to the Tract were few and those almost impassable. He must have slept and eaten under the most primitive conditions, for there were no other. Yet, there is not a word of complaint in his many letters which, happily, found their way to the fine Oneida Historical Society in Utica. They are classic John Brown, an often amusing amalgam of impulsiveness and frugality. His vigor is manifest in every sentence and the possibility of failure simply never occurs to him. Grammarians will wince, but those who believe a person's writings should reflect his personality will rejoice. The letters are all addressed to James Sheldon,

Brown's agent. The first is from "Township No. 1 near the north East Corner," which would put it about five miles west of the present town of Old Forge. And it is dated "Fryday May 24th 1799." Since it is the first of the series, it is worth quoting in full so the reader can capture the unique flavor of the man. If the spelling perplexes you, just sound it out. Brown believed in phonetic spelling.

. . . Sr we have beene on hard Timberd Land for a mile & half back how Far Forward it will Continue I cant Determine. I suppose we are about 6 Miles from your Settlement on a Strate Line & about 8 Miles as the Rhode Is Cut [from Sheldon's place at the small Moose River settlement just west of the southwest corner of the Tract]. *The Land has not beene too Stonney since we turned of from Mr. Goulds Rhode Yesterday morning which is now about 4 miles if the Land continues as good as it is now & has beene for a mile back. I shall make a stand and build a House. I have more men then works to advantage—their is about 4 axes more wanted. If aney of the survayers come in from No. 2, 3 or 7 you'll please to desire them to call on me as they come out. The Bread Baked at Lydon I think is too Slack baked & the people complain of its being Sower. I wish you to have all the Bread baked in our own oven & and that it be made as good as possible & baked sufficiently to keep Sweet & Good at least a week. I think you gave an Extravigent price for clearing & believe their never was so high a price given before for clearing Land so lightly Timbered. 14 Dollars Per acre would have been fully adequate & found themselves victuals & drink. Mr. Angell has agreed to work for 12 Dolls per acre. I desire you'll not agree to give 14 Dolls for aney more unless they will find their own Boding* [Boarding?] *& liquer also clear it all off & desire it in a Workmen like manner. I have not seen Major Pease since I came from you, if he chuses to give up his contract I shall be quite willing to Requit him as I have no doubt of the land which he will Chuse being Richly worth double the money—is to give me for it. As soon as Mr. Gould returns you will desire him to come on as soone as possible as his men will not do more than half the work in his absence that they will in his preasance. I hope you'll have 2 acres of wheat at least in the ground by tomorrow nite as Mr. Baker, who I am sorry is Lame will accommodate you with his oxen. As soone as you have got in the wheat, corn etc in the land cleared, with you & your Lame group will admit you'll come out & see us.*

I shall send our Team in tomorrow to go to Leydon for a load of flour meal & potatotes. In the mean time you'll be contriving all possible means to bring on these and other articles you want from Leydon. When your son comes on if you Don't come out please to send him out with the cow & some meal so that I may have some Hasterpudding [Hasty pudding, remember the Rhode Island practice of sticking an "r" in odd places] *and milk. I think I shall stay all next week & shall be glad that Mr Baker & his son may come on as Soone as may be, as I don't expect they will suit you tho. Major Pease may.*

John Brown was a big believer in postscripts and often added one, sometimes two, as here:

> . . . *4 men came out to day, I don't want them and shall send them back. I never heard of more than 15 Dolls per acre being given for Clearing the Largest & heaviest land & they who cleared it find themselves* [provide their own food] *Fence it, and Sr. that was when wheat & other things would fetch 1/3 more money then it will now. Money is very scarce and hard to git. Land has fell in price why then should I raise the price of Clearing. The very men that you'll Employed certainly ment to work for the Value According to the Timber & I had agreed to Leave it to Mr. Edmunds or you but I certainly had reason to Expect you would consult me before you gave 14 Dolls & find & their Victils & Drink. Pray Sr. Send for the Beens that was Left on the Rhode, it is said their is now about half a bbl* [barrel] *Full, & are about four miles this side of the Black River.*

Then Brown added still another postscript:

> . . . *they may be Brot. in by Men on Foot.*[13]

Since John Brown did not say exactly where he was, one cannot be certain where he was at work. But from bits and pieces of evidence, it is probably safe to deduce that he was at or near what later was called Middle Settlement, a short-lived settlement that appears on early maps and is marked by a good-sized body of water known as Middle Settlement Pond. What little is known about it we owe to a late 19th century lawyer in the Town of Herkimer who was also a careful local historian, Charles E. Snyder. He delivered a solid paper on John Brown's Tract, to which later historians will always be indebted. On December 8, 1896, Snyder told members of the Herkimer County Historical Society—which is still active and was most helpful with research for this book—that:

> . . . *The Middle settlement is now a mere tradition among a few old people. The remains of three houses are said to be still discernible in the woods, about six miles west of the Fulton chain along the old Remsen Road. This is all there is left of the Middle settlement. What was once a clearing has lapsed into a forest with only a few traces that it was ever the abode of man. The only mention made in the records relative to this settlement that I have found is in the will of John Brown wherein he states that upon Township 1, "There are two log houses, a good barn and a considerable improvements of cleared land."*

In one of the conveyances from Brown's grandchildren of Township 1, three lots were excepted "at or near the Middle settlement, sold or contracted to be sold to one Wilcox," presumably one of the settlers.

Two days after his first note to Sheldon, John Brown received two in return. He said, "Your Remarks on the Importance of Giting Some Land cleared & Sowd or Planted Immediately is very just" and he urged Sheldon to "Sow & Plant the Ground Immediately." He referred also to "4 men from Situate and Cranston," indicating that for some reason he wanted some Rhode Islanders working on the project. He said too that he wanted the ox team "by this Day a week at the furthest I wish to go out & be on my Return by this way of Balltown Springs and I do not know of aney way I can git out but with the waggin." He further instructed Sheldon to

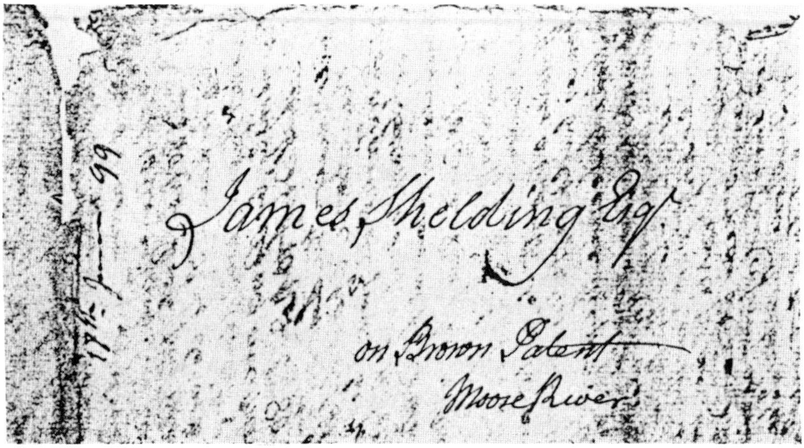

make "cosways" [causeways] on the "bad Swampy Places between you & the Black River." He said that Gould, another of his road builders, was going to construct causeways on another road "at a Dollar Pr rod the poles to be 14 feet long. He finds him Self & men with every thing" and he refers to that Mr. "Brayton" we mentioned above.

Throughout the correspondence with Sheldon, he keeps giving his agent little pep talks to encourage him to move onto the Tract with his family, for he knew that nothing sells land like the sight of someone prospering on it.

> *. . . I have no Doubt in my mind but before the Year comes Round You will find 500 Acres of Land on the Tract that is really worth double the Money. I agreed you should have it for I wish you to bring your Famely here as soon as you can with convience. I should have been happy if it could have Beene while I am here that I could have had the satisfaction of Drinking some of Mrs. Sheldons small Beer but this I despair of. . . ."*

Then Brown explained why he thought the first mill should be built in the township where the flourishing resort town of Old Forge now stands:

. . . I rather think it will be best to build the First Mill on the North Western Branch of the Moose River in Town No. 7 now surveying by Elder Hammond. I think should the Land be Favorable it will be Good Policy to Have a Mill & Settlements on or Near the Direct Route from the Middle of the North East Side of the Tract to Johnstown or as Near the Middle of said Line of my Lands as may be all other advantages Considdered.

Actually, John Brown built not on "the North Western Branch" (now called the North Branch) but a mile or so east of the confluence of the North and Middle Branches of the Moose River, perhaps because that provided a better mill site or because Brown saw that the situation at the head of what became known as the Fulton Chain of lakes put it right on a natural route of water transportation.

Brown also reported to Sheldon that he found "it Very Slow Giting Flour having no wood that will split – are obliged to hew all & to go to a Great Distance to get Spruce of which there is but Little in this Vicinity." Nonetheless, "Tho very little Flour laid – in but one Tire [tier] of Bark on the Roof, the Rafters & Ridge Poles are all on & it will be a Good Rommely (roomy) House with a Chamber over the Whole." And John Brown, as in so many of his letters to Sheldon, cautioned him to "make the most prudent use" of money he sent him for "paying Such Contracts which Require Immediate payment."

Brown enlisted the support of one of the men working with him, a Mr. Angell, in his continuing campaign to convince Sheldon to move on to the Tract. In a postscript to Brown's letter, Angell wrote: "After my respects to your honor I would inform you that Esq Brown has made a stand on the most beautiful place I ever saw in the country and it is my ardent desire that you will be on this delightsome spot with your Honored family as soon as possible."[14]

That John Brown suffered setbacks should be no surprise in surroundings so difficult. On "Tuesday Morning 7 oClk May 28, 1799" he wrote to Sheldon of his dismay at hearing that the scow used to ferry provisions across a river, presumably the Moose, had, in some manner, been lost.

. . . Sr I have Rec'd no Letter from you since my Two Last. I suppose the Reason is that you had Nothing Pleasing to Communicate. The Careless and Shameful neglect of the Security of the Schow is very mortifying to me, of Mr. Brayton

Lives their as Ferryman as I expected he did & he alone ought to have the Sole charge of the Schow & never Suffer her to go a Crost or to be Loose only when he is in her, which is the Case of all Ferry & indeed in all Business some one should have the charge of Every Department, and if I agree with Mr. Brayton at all it was for the sake of haveing him Stiddyley [steadily] *their as a ferry man & to have the care of the Land Improved near the House, which Must be the Case in Futer or the Schow will not be preserved. She is Lost now.*

But Brown was not one to linger over misfortune, but plunged ahead to repair the damage.

. . . You must Immediate set 3 or 4 Smart ax Men to Hollowing out 3 of the Largest Trees that grows by the River & Lay them all Side by side . . . & Lay Acrost them Poles of Hemlock or Spruce 4 or 5 inches over of sufficient Length for the Wagen to Stand upon to pass over & that one Yoke of oxen at a time may be tacon aCrost with Saftey, if you think 3 Canues [canoes] *besides the old ones is not sufficient have 4 Dug out they may be all Made in one Day, but I hope You'l have got the Schow to her place before you Receive this. I send the Spade & one Hoe to have the Landing on this Side, the Ferry dug away and made better to Git the Waggin up the Bank, I shall Depend on Your Sendg* [sending] *My Waggin with a Full Load of Bread, meal, Grind Stone &&& by Thursday.*

Then, in a postscript, John Brown changes his mind:

. . . if you go up the Falls above the House near ware the Schow was built, perhaps you may find that Temperrley [temporary] *Bridge maybe be built in Two Days to Last all Summer if so & the Schow is Lost I should prefer this plan & that you Imploy Every ax man about you to Affect this in Lue of building Canues and Laying on Poles as Mentioned within, . . .*

Brown then notified Sheldon that he had sent a surveyor and several men "to Explore both branches of Moose River & find the Most Elligable place for a Mill to be built as soone as possible I want the Waggon to Cary me to the place they pitch upon." Brown did not fancy heaving his huge bulk through the woods the few miles to the mill site so he ordered the wagon which, incidentally, the inventive correspondent misspelled three different ways.

Then he added a P.S. to his P.S., "I am Sorry to hear your Flour is all Baked up we shall be out of Bread by nite."[15] One assumes from reports of John Brown's ample girth that he loved his victuals, yet here he was almost out of bread and it's worth mentioning only in a postscript. Plainly, when he was seized by an enthusiasm, nothing else mattered.

On the 30th on the farm site at the Middle Settlement, he was firing off another letter that is combination instruction and pep talk.

. . . *I have this moment Rec'd Yours of this Date &* with pleasure *observe you have got the Schow to her Moreings, I have one Request to make to you which Beg Your Attention too,* Without Delay *that is that you Weight out accurately as much Flour as Mrs. Brayton can bake at one Batch and have it all Mixed & all Baked Well and then Cooled in a Dry place and Weighed with the Same Exactness as You Weight the Flour, when this is Done I shall know how to Contract for the Baking, I pray You to have the Experiment make tomorrow without fail. And that Kingsley be Constantly Imployed in bringing out Flour, Meals, Potatoes & Beenes as fust as possible with the white Horse as I may want the Waggin hear some Days. If you can bring out all the Jobbers* [workers hired for small jobs or chance work] *you have I think You may yet Git in Ten Acres of Corn & potatoes hear and a fue Acres of Otes in allso. I wish You to Make Every Exursion* [exertion] *to git Every Hill of Corn in the ground that probably Can be Done by the 15th of June at this Place* . . .

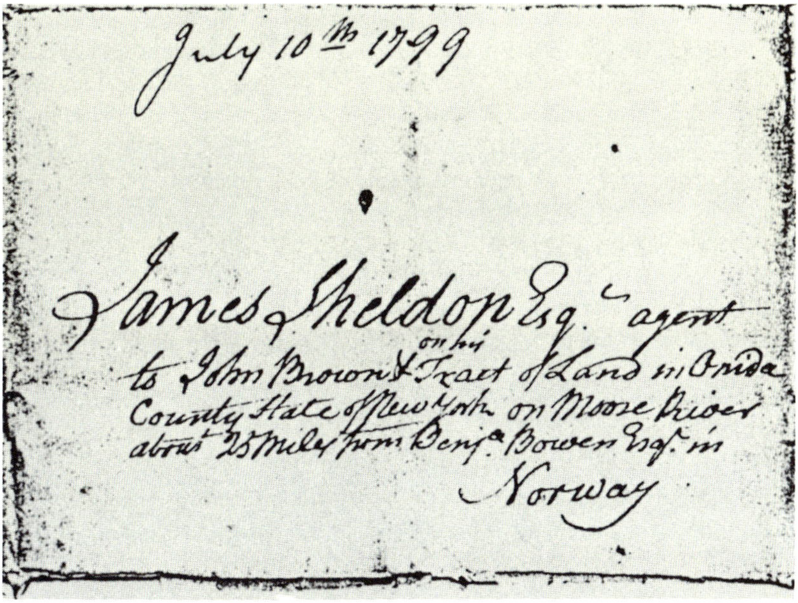
July 10th 1799

James Sheldon Esq.r agent on his
to John Brown's Tract of Land in Oneida
County State of New York on Moose River
about 25 Miles from Benj.a Bowen Esq.r in
Norway

John Brown then explained that by his calculation it would be cheaper to raise cereals on the Tract than to buy them elsewhere and haul them in. There would be another important benefit:

. . . *In this Case we have the Land Cleared an other Year all Reddy for Improvement & the Expense of Clearing Reimbursed by the Produce. I Begg you to Finish there at Moose River as soone as possible by havg* [having] *all the Ground*

Planted that is Cleared & bring every ax man you can bear by the Day after tomorrow if possible, Leaving only Brayton & his wife to Bake and Tend the Ferry.

The pep talk comes in one of Brown's customary postscripts:

. . . I wish I Could see Mrs. Sheldon & Your Famely all Well arrived at this Farm which I Think well Worth Improving but when the Mill place is fixed upon you can then Remove to that if the Business of the Settlement Requires it, I think Mr. Smith has found a Good Bed of Iron ore within three Miles of this House & Near a Good Mill place and I Flatter My Self of haveing a Forge & a Furnace on the Settlement the next Summer if you Don't git Discouraged but Act the Man of Business.

Brown went on to list the advantages Sheldon would discover before he had lived on the Tract two years: good water, stones (Lord knows there were plenty of them, as in much of New England, the most bountiful crop), iron and salt. Brown ended by saying, "I shall kill the ox this afternoone & Let him hang all Nite to Coole & have it Cut up and Salted in Morng Researving a Good Rosting Peace for You to purtake of the next Day when you will beg hope able to Leave the Stand you are now at & Join me."[16]

That same day Brown again wrote to Sheldon saying that he is "Sencible that the want of oxen & the loss of the Schow has prevented your Giting the Ground Planted. . . ." Yet, he urged Sheldon to get it started "as Soone as possible so as to Leave the Compleation to Mr. Brayton and you come on hear Leaving Such Direction with Brayton to presearve the Schow as you think may prevent a Simmuler Misfortune to the former, and as soone as the Rhode is coswayd which I suppose will be to Day or tomorrow I hope they will come on with you & clear out what you can clear for Corn, Potatoes & Otes which may take a Month or near it." And Brown made a cryptic reference to an untoward incident of some kind. "Mr. Baker can Inform you of Mr. Ross's wild Conduct."[17]

The following day, Brown sent a letter to Sheldon, carried by a Mr. Hall, who "offers to Come on as a Black Smith & find his own Costs from Rome, I suppose a Smith Will be wanted when the Mill is Built, but he is a Stranger to me & I can not Determine on hiring him till I see you & the place for a Mill is Fixed, . . ." He said that Hall "asks 15 Dolls Per mo." but Brown told him "we May by & by want a Smith when my Iron Steel Etc is got here from Fourt Scyler (Fort Schuyler, the earlier name of Utica) and if he will work for Twelve Dolls he shall have the prefference if you think his General Charector as a Workman & a Sober man will answer."[18]

For nine days we have nothing from John Brown. The likelihood is not that he fell uncharacteristically silent, but that Sheldon had joined him, making notes unnecessary. Now, however, we have a new source of information. John Brown's son James had journeyed north to join his father and they met on June 10 a few miles east of the present Boonville, where James had spent the night at a place owned by a Mr. Edmunds, "have Trout for Supper—a good accommodation."

On June 11, James recorded that he slept on the floor, "a cold night," whereas "Sheldon now is in a Snug hut."[19] That afternoon the Browns and their party began the trek out of the Tract. Although some early writers spoke vaguely of John Brown making subsequent trips to the Tract, there is no supporting evidence and it is unlikely in the extreme that John Brown ever again set foot on the land that for nearly two centuries has borne his name.

James recorded that land just outside the Tract, near what is now Port Leydon, was selling for "8 Dolls." That must have encouraged the Browns for they did not yet recognize—John Brown probably never did—that in that region, even a few miles made a vast difference. In the Black River Valley, the farmland was fertile; a few miles to the east where the Adirondacks began, and where the John Brown's Tract was situated, the soil was sparse and stony. Those few miles made the critical difference between a fabulous investment and a disastrous speculation.

As soon as John Brown left James Sheldon, the stream of letters resumed and continued, although with diminishing frequency, for months to come. Brown did his best to communicate his fervor through the mails. Even as he was leaving the Tract, Brown on June 10 notified Sheldon that he had hired "Mr Soram the Barer who Informs he Sarved 7 years Apprentiship to the Carpenters Business, to work all the Season with his Tooles with Mr. Kindal at the Mill at Fifteen Dollers per mo & you'l employ him Accord(in)g after planting all You possably Can this Week with corn at Seat No. 2," presumably the Middle Settlement.[20]

Writing from Utica on June 14, Brown told Sheldon of the various provisions he has purchased and enclosed $600 in bills and $100 in cash which "will I hope carry you through the Summer but Shoud You find it Nesessary to Imploy So Maney Men or to Require More Provisions then all their is procured by Messrs Belew, MySelf & Your Self You Must in this Case purchase it on the best terms you can, advising me in due time." He signed his letter thus, "My Money is all Gone & am Your Obt. Servt."

As usual, there was a postscript: "When Mr. Kinsley and Mr Burr is their I hope you will Imploy them in Clearing some good Meadow So as to Git a Plenty of Hay this Year for the Oxen & Horses through the winter & the Cows. Your Son has just returned, I am Exceeding Sorry he Did not cary the 20 Bushels of Otes to You but Boys will be boys, weither you will git them from Stormer Ware he Left them or Not I cant say I have Repremanded him for Not going to You as I know [you] want the Otes & to See him"[21]

The following day Brown informed Sheldon that he had hired a Mr. Brewer for "Ten Dollars per month for the Season from the time he begins to work in the Seat till he Quits it & the Mony to be then paid him Say about 4 or 5 months work." Brown also reported that he had "bot. half Ton of Flour hear which with the Ton at Boones Settlent & the 47 Bushels of Wheat at Laydon will I hope Supply you till Fall."[22]

A couple of days later Brown wrote from Johnstown, his optimism still at flood stage. ". . . the Two Branches of the Moose River will give a good chance for the settlers to transport their boards & timber Etc etc by water and if the land Suteable [illegible] may be a thick Settled place from the Mill seat at No. 1 to the Mill seat or Bridge at No. 3 which I suppose must be a Distance of about Ten miles. You'l imploy Mr. Gould to make such other one rod Rhode all to be cust Clost and well cleared out for ten Dollers per mile as you think best for my interests. . ."[23]

As usual, John Brown had no doubts. The Tract was going to be "a thick Settled place" and that was that.

A couple of days later he wrote to Sheldon from "Baul Town Springs" (Ballston Spa). Again, he cautioned his agent to watch the money:

. . . You must be cautious not pay Mr. Goald (Gould) too Fast when he has got his pay he may not be so carefull to Cut the Stumps Clost. I wrote you by him what I had pd him which is three times as much & perhaps ten times as much as his Two Rod Rhode yet amounts too & he ought not to ask for aney more till the whole 30 Miles of Good Two Rod Rhode is Cut According to Contract. . . .

With his customary optimism, Brown wrote:

. . . The more I think of it the more I am Convienced of the Importance of the 300 Ten Acre Lotts to be Laid out as nearly on a Square Adjoining three Street to be Laid Parrell with Each other and three Streets at Right Angles so as to Comprehend 300 Ten Acre Lotts as near the Mill as the Situation of the Ground will admit or if the ground suits better pray have only Two Streets parrelel and of cource Longer as I propose to Build a City at the Place or between the two Branches of Moose River in Such place as you & Mr Arnold Smith with such others of the Survayers as you chuse to, may find to Imbrace the Most Advantages.

He continued that "I therefore Contemplate the Receiving Many Thousands Bushels of Wheat at Albaney from my 210,000 Acres of Land in a fue years. . ."

He claimed "I have seen many people of this State who wish to go on the 210,000 Acres on Lease haveing a fue years before anye Rent is payable." Brown said he would offer the land at three dollars an acre with no interest for two years. Or the land could be paid for in crops, "in Good Corn at half Dollar, good Rye at 2/3 of a Doller, good wheat at a Doller to be dd. [delivered] yearly at my Store to be built in the City above contemplated as fast as they can Raise it to Spair they allowing Interest after two Years till paid."

Not only was John Brown confident of settling the land, but he told Sheldon that he expected to "See Maney of the Proprietors of the Land their on Each Side of that Town between Johnstown & my Tract in Albaney & Schenectide, I shall without Doubt git such encoragement or assistence as will Induce me to Cut the Rhode to Johnstown or north of it. You'll therefore desire Mr Goald (Gould) to Discharge no good men but to hold him self in Reddiness to come out to the west Canneda (Canada) Creek with the Two Rod Rhode after you can find the best possible Route to the place for the Bridge. . . ." And he instructed Sheldon "to set Mr. Goald to cuting the Rhode Two Rods wide Clost to the Ground and make the Bridge or Bridges without waiting my Further orders." Such a road, he said, "will Save us 50 miles at Least in going from Albaney. . ." Cutting a road 40 miles through virgin, largely unexplored forest seemed not to faze John Brown a whit.

Brown then went on to instruct Sheldon and, through him, Gould, on how the roads should be cleared, using adzes instead of axes. "I know a man will trim off the Stumps close to the Ground Espically Round the out Side of the Stump that can hardley be cut clost with an axe Evin with much time be cut with a good Adz with Ease & convience as the man using the Adz may Stand nearly upright ware as with an axe he must Bend to the Ground & perhaps not affect the object at Least."

Then, in one of his postscripts, Brown tells Sheldon to plant potatoes "in the Rhodes" and casually remarks "if you can find good clay you must have 20 thousand or 30 Thousand Brick made this summer."[24] One cannot know if the bricks were ever made, but it is safe to assume that the Johnstown road was never constructed, for surely there would have been some record of it, as there were, however sketchy, of the three roads that were believed to have been cut.

John Brown must have found the spa at Ballston agreeable, for he was still there six days later when he again addressed Sheldon. Apparently, Sheldon took one of Brown's letters as criticism and responded accordingly, for Brown replied:

. . . I fully agree with you that without confidence no Sattisfaction can Subsist between the Imployer & his agent & I do believe that fue men is Less apt to Shift or find fault with his Tenants or Agents then my Self & hope I shall never have aney cause to complain of your Contract.

Brown then lamented that some seed proved to be bad and expressed his regret that Sheldon's son had left some oats at Leyden instead of carrying them on to his father on the Tract.

. . . The very next Day I saw him Returnd to Utica & when he told me he had left oates at Laydon & no one to carry them to you. You may Judge how I felt. I hope a bad beginning will make a good Ending and that buy the buy things will go on like Clock work as you mention it would have Done had you have begun the Business, You have Reason to Suppose I was not fully Satisfied with those on whome I rely to procure the Supply before I contracted with you; but Every Little Man *is not made to conduct Large Business but Sr Let us look Forward & do the best in our Power according to our abilitys.*

That last constitutes classic John Brown.

As always, the owner encourages the agent.

. . . I have not the Least Dought but that Your Five Hundred Acres would Sell for Ten Dollers Per Acre if you chose it In Ten Years but before that time I hope you will make a Handsum fortin by the Distelling Business.

John Brown added that "As I think the waters of the Spring hear helped my Reumattick I may possibly come up again towards Fall Say in September . . ." There is little likelihood that he did again journey to the Tract, but plainly he did feel he was profiting from the spa at Ballston for he remained at least another couple of days, more than a week in all.

In Albany he added to the letter that "I have seen the Gove(ernor John Jay) & Surveyor General on the Important of the Rhode to the River St. Lawrence through Johnstown and my Tract. They both are pleased with idea and will promote it as also the Geneleman in Sannactida (Schenectady) who owns land in the Jersey Fields & allso those of this town."[25]

His next letter burst with optimism:

. . . I would not sell an Acre of my Land to be picked under Ten Dollars was it not to promote the Settlement of the Country and theirby make the other Lands the more Valuable and affect the Completion of the Mail State Rhode through that Route Sooner much Sooner Evin You *have an Idea.*[26]

That letter was written at five o'clock in the morning. Only four hours later he wrote another long one, perhaps even more optimistic:

. . . when I hear the people on this Rhode mention the short time to me it was allmost unpassable and the country all New and when I compair the Soyle to that of my Tract and the Size of the Timber & Hills, I am allmost Shure that in a fue years the Land of my Tract must bare a higher price than the Lands in General of this Country which are now generly from Ten to Twenty Dollers per Acre, tho it is True that there is an amazing Large Country of Unimproved Lands in the Western & North Western part of our Nation to Fill up Yet it is as True that the Sett[l]*ed part of our Nation is allso Extenccive & from Every part of it the people are Immigrating to the Westward. Their is nothing in My Mind that can Impeade the Rappid Settlement of my Lands unless their is too Maney Stones which from the Account of those who had Reconorterd* [reconnoitered] *to Westward I confess give accts of more stones that I wish to have had, tho a large proportion of Stones Would in time be an Advantage Rather than Disadvantage to the Land, as no Fence in the World is Equilly Valuable to a Good Stone wall, and tho you now have a super abundance of Wood & Timbrr Yet time will come when Every Tree will be of Grait Value & that time can not be farr Distant when we consider that this Country in Which I now Write but a few years ago was Full of Timber and but Very thinley Inhabbeted. Yet nearer the Less Mountainous as it is the people found the way in & have Distroyed the Timber So that Wood Land is Scare & Dear from 10 to 20 Dols per acre and the Country Generly So Crouded with Inhabitants. . . .*

Even in his optimism, John Brown could not help noting the factors that would prove fatal to his vision: there was plenty of land, better and cheaper, farther west and his Tract's soil was richer in stones than nutrients. While it is certainly true that few things are lovelier than a New England stone wall, and few things more durable, it is also true that many a curse must have been muttered as those hardy Yankees dug out the stones and carted them to where they still stand. A virtue of necessity, to be sure, but there can be few New England farmers who would not rather have skipped the whole thing. Rocks and farmers have been antagonists since time immemorial. And while timber would indeed one day be valuable, demand for it was still decades off, longer than John Brown's descendants were willing to wait.

John Brown Goes North

Evidently, even his agent James Sheldon was expressing doubts, for John Brown wrote in this letter:

> *. . . I hope you will be Firm in Your Mind & no Longer Wavour in Your Mind of uncertainty Weither to Fix for Life on my Said Tract, but that you will be Fixed and Determined on Remaining for Life and Setting all Your Famely on that Central Tract of 210,000 Acres as I am Determiend Ever to Reach My Famely.*

He ended by instructing Sheldon "please to Enguage 200 Good Apple Trees of a Good Size. Set out this Fall or in the Spring without Fail. . . ." And his final words had the customary Brown optimism. ". . . Giving Two Years Cr. (credit) without Interest, You may Git as Maney Real Settlers Next Year as Can be accomodated Say 100 Fammelys. . . ."[27]

On July 10, 1799, John Brown reported to his agent that he had arrived safely home on the 1st and lamented, "I have not heard a Word from You Sence I left You, only the first Letter which You wrote before I had got out to Layden what makes me the More Anaxtious (anxious) that you should have a Good Rhode to & from My Land through the Grants and if practicable Direct to Johnstown at Least one Rod Wide this Summer. . . ."

And he said that some of the landowners in the area were more "Inclined to Discorage that Incourage My Settlement" by asking too much for wheat, flour and other supplies. If Sheldon built the road, it would "Give You a Larger Field for Supply of Every kind, and for Settlers in particular. . . ."

Brown estimated that the road from what is now the Old Forge area to Johnstown should not cost more than $3,000, including bridge and causeways. If landowners along the route would not subscribe money, Brown authorized Sheldon to take land at $2.50 an acre. He said he would advance the money for the road and pay one-third himself.

Brown also notified his agent that he was sending eighty large potash "kittles" from his foundry at Taunton, Massachusetts, to Albany, and that he could have as many of them as he thought he could sell."[28]

In his next letter to Sheldon, John Brown was cross indeed. Evidently, Sheldon had paid Gould before he finished a road construction job.

> *. . . pray Sr. keep the Sterl*[ing] *in Your hands or let Me keep it in Mine, and not put it again in to Mr. Goald hands Nor No one Else—I thought You had Sufficient Experience in Business to have Seen at once that the Bill was Drawn in Your Name. To prevent his haveing aney part of it till he had earnt it by Fullfilling his Contract. He must pay the part he Borrwd of me or it must be chd* [charged] *to his acct as well as Every other Advance.*
>
> *I Begg Sr you'l pay No Man aney more money on my acct till he has Earnt*

it besides what had been advanced previous to it — I find money is Exceeding Scarce and Very hard to git, I therefore must Insist that you Considder it so in every part of my Business and that you Git Labour and Every thing Else, that you do git on My Acct Very Cheep, or I wish you Not to git it at all.

Again, he urged Sheldon to build the road between the mill seat and Johnstown and instructed him to build it one rod rather than two rods wide if he cannot get enough subscribers to pay for a two-rod road. And he suggested that Sheldon sell two hogsheads of sugar provided by Brown, save what was needed on the Tract.

. . . This Two hhds of Suger will I hope with what Bills I sent you pay all or Nearley all the Money You'l have Ocation for on My Acct till Spring. I Join you that Some Course Goods would be Useful to pay Wagers [that New England "r" again] *etc, etc. & as Soone as You Git a Good Store built I Shall take Care to have them procured. Please to Furnish Me with an Inv°* [inventory] *or memorandum of the Most Nessary Articles & the wts* [weights] *of Each to be sent by me to Albany to be Reddy. Their to go on by Slaying to the New Store You Will have built this Fall or Early in Winter to be Ready to Receive the Goods. Perhaps you May barter the Suger for Labour or Some Articals You have bot or May Want for the Use of the Settlement.*

John Brown also had to deal at great distance with some difficulties between Sheldon and men with whom he did business. At issue in one dispute was some pork and cider that had spoiled. "I hope No Difference of Annemossity between You and O. Ballew Will Cause My Interest to Suffer . . . Pray Ask him about it & Not Suffer Aney Bickerings between You & the Famely to Injure Me or my Interest."

Another incident concerned a workman named Burr:

. . . I am supprised at Burrs turning out as you Represented, Expetially as Mr. Baker thought him a None Such, but I confess I considered him as a prittey Smart Boy. If he stole Gin, if he Imbezzled property or if he Disguised him Self Frequently with Liquor You Certainly Did Right to Dismiss him. The Fact is that he was too much prejudicied Against you I hope that Was Not Your Case Against him.[29]

Several weeks passed and then John Brown wrote to Sheldon with bad news. His correspondence merchants in New York, Loomis & Tillinghast, were, because of business misfortunes, no longer paying bills he had drawn on them. Because he had not received a specific accounting from the failed firm, Brown did not know yet how many of the bills he had given to Sheldon would be returned unpaid, ". . . this failure is unfortunate for me, as they have Sold about Four Thousand Dollars worth of my Gin & have not paid me more than One Thousand Dollars towards it . . ."

John Brown Goes North

I will endeavour to place Funds in New York to pay the Bills which are not paid by Loomis & Tillinghast as soon as I know what Bills are remaining not paid. I have received none of yours since the 3rd ult. I hope you'l be able to raise Money frm the Pot Ash Kittles, Sugar & Gin [he had sent at least 120 gallons from Providence] *so as to have no call on me this Fall only to pay the above mention'd Bills which has not been paid by L. & T.*

The letter also refers to more trouble between Sheldon and people in the area.

. . . I had thoughts of sending or ordering 12 of them [potash kettles] *to be delivered to the Ballous, but since your Letter advising of the* Low & infamous Conduct *of O. Ballou, I have alter'd my mind and concluded not to deliver Messrs Ballou any more Property of mine.*[30]

Lacking further information, it is not possible to know whether Sheldon was simply having bad luck in his relationships on and near the Tract or whether he was, in whatever degree, responsible for the problems.

The next letter we have was sent in September or October of 1799. We don't have the exact date of this long letter because the first four pages are missing. In it, however, there is reference to a letter from Sheldon dated September 4 at Middle Settlement in which he reports having sold some of the potash kettles at $70 a pair, what Brown had instructed him to ask for them. Brown also discusses what he will pay Sheldon for boarding his family on the Tract.

. . . James Sheldon Esq his wife three sones & one daughter making Six in all. The remainder you said should keep at school. I therefore do not expect you will exceed 6 in your family this winter to be boarded by me that will be 1½ dollars pr day for your provisions allowing ¼ dollar pr day to each & a dollar for your wages will make 1½ dollars pr day, but the wages pr Agreement I expect will go towards the 500 acres of land sold you on which I hope You'd raise provisions next season in plenty for sure I am till we begin to raise Corn, rye & wheat on the lands as well as Beef & Pork & all kinds of sauce [culinary roots and vegetables eaten with meat], *the Improvement or Settlement must be made to great disadvantage. I must therefore urge you in the strongest manner to prepare for the raising a large quantity of grain both on your own Lands & mine the next summer as it will be in vain to attempt Iron Works or other manufactorys without Bread & other provisions to feed the people & the moment we succeed in raising a good plenty of provisions there will be no difficulty in getting Settlers to any number, but to get men onto the disadvantage of supplying them as has been this season will never answer for my interest.*

That, of course, was the crux of the situation. Settlers could not be attracted until it was demonstrated that the land could feed them. Despite all John Brown's optimistic talk (and probably conviction) and that of Charles Frederick Herreshoff a generation later, the land simply rejected all attempts to farm or mine it.

In that same letter, John Brown returned, as so often, to his conviction that he was being overcharged. Certain it is that Brown was hawk-eyed when it came to scrutinizing the bills tendered him.

> . . . *Now I wish to know by Mr. Allin how he can charge 510 days for Surveying 22689 Acres when Mr Godfrey has done 25236 Acres in 344 days including every man that worked with him on the business & Godfreys wages by agreement was 9/ L My* [9 shillings legal money] *per day and he find himself whereas Mr. Allen has charged 12/L My pr day. I have not got all the Acc't of Elder Hammond & his men before me but I believe the number of days of him & his sons & all the other men that worked with him will not exceed 344 days the same as Mr. Godfreys & his Town No 7 contains 23180 Acres so that Mr. John Allin must have made a mistake in his charge of 510 days or has been very slack & dillatory. You'l please to read this statement to him & desire him to reduce his a/c to make it as good to me as Mr. Godfreys or Mr. Hammon's.*[31]

That letter also lists some supplies that John Brown had sent to Sheldon, among them bellows leather, a mill saw, a crosscut saw, two grindstones and associated equipment, presumably for the saw mill and grist mill to be built in the area of what is now Old Forge. There was also a large barrel of gin and two hogsheads of sugar, plus five barrels of "Cyder" that Brown wanted Sheldon to sell.

The last Brown-Sheldon letter we have for 1799 is dated October 23 and is a short note in which he says he could "not ascertain the Exact sum due to Mr Smith and the men who Survay'd the Town he undertook to survey but if I had Judge from what Mr Godfrey and Elder Hammons Town cost, the whole survey, it can not exceed 300 Dollers including the provisions found by them. . . ."[32]

There is one final letter surviving from 1799 that deals with John Brown's efforts to develop that grudging land. It is from Philadelphia, where Brown is serving in Congress, to his son James in Providence, dated December 23.

> . . . *I have had Mr. Gould the man who cut the Rhodes and made 7 bridges to & on our Lands with me this Several Days at intervals he ses pot ashes is now at 200 Dolls per ton at New York & that 10 Acres of Land will make Ashes Sufficient to make a Ton of Potash if the wood is of sutable quality & the Ashes well Saved, at this Rate the Land suteably wooded for a Farm of 160 Acres, And as to Iron works their is no Dought of their advantages when we find a good & sufficient Bed of ore, but this has not yet been found tho I think we shall find it in the Course of a year or Two, that the Land will by & by become Valuable I have not a Dought*

& the Question is how much money we ought to spend or how Fast we ought to press the Settlement, the whole Expense I was at Last Year in going up twice *with the money Expended for wages & provisions & in making Rhodes, Schows, Bridges, Cosways & the Mill will not be less than Eight Thousand Dollars, & Esqr Sheldon is now making the preparations of Provisions for the Next Season & I shall order some Potash Kittles carried to the Mill place. . . . the Fact is that the First Settlers of all new countrys must have good Incoragement, as Mr. Peregrine Foster now writes me from Belpré 12 miles from Marietta that our Township, he calls it, of 18,000 Acres in that country will not Settle without Giveing some Land or Selling it allmost for nothing to the First Settler.*[33]

This last refers to land the Brown family has purchased in Ohio, land squarely in the path of the westward migration rather than unfertile, hilly land easily bypassed. But even there, it was necessary to lure settlers with very cheap land or, at first, by giving it away.

While John Brown was trying to develop the Tract by mail, and, of course, carrying on his multifarious activities, including serving in Congress, there were personal developments in his own house that would affect our story: his daughter Sarah and Charles Frederick Herreshoff were getting impatient, and his youngest daughter Alice was involved with a man in a way that would lead to much unhappiness in the family and cause a scandal that must have been impossible to cover up in so small a town as Providence still was at the turn of the 19th century.

Herreshoff had been courting Sarah for six years and he was tired of waiting. In mid-August he wrote to her from New York expressing concern, as he often did, about her health. She was evidently in Ballston Spa, whose waters, a couple of months earlier, had so benefited her father.

. . . I wish you to consent to your union this fall, and to go with me to London to spend the winter there, and thus I give you my solemn promise to return with you early in the spring and probably I shall then be able to take a fixed residence in this country, for wherever you are I shall be happy, and proud. . . [if] *I be doomed to be separated from you, I wish only for the grave. You will tell me if I shall ask the consent of your good father and in what manner?*[34]

Although he would found a family that would be, and still is, famous, Charles Frederick Herreshoff was one of those people who seem perpetually bedeviled by ill fortune. Whether it was the bad business conditions in Europe or the imprudence of his partner, or his own faulty business judgment, toward the end of 1799 his partnership suffered great losses. The evidence now available is not detailed enough, so we cannot say whether Herreshoff was entirely wiped out, but it is obvious the losses were very serious indeed. The bad news got to Herreshoff's beloved Sally and, we can infer from what he wrote, also insinuations that his partner had been guilty of some malfeasance. On October 30 Charles Frederick replied to Sally:

. . . How thankful I am for your two letters, and what a salutary effect they have had upon my mind, is more than I can express my dear friend. I was not under any apprehension that misfortune could make an alteration in your sentiments and yet to receive such an undoubted proof of it, has made a deeper impression upon me than any other event could have done. To possess what a world could not purchase from me, will be a support for which I am thankful to heaven and to you, I hope it shall in a great deal reconcile me to my fate, let it be ever so miserable in other respects. To hear that you have entirely recovered your health and your spirits is another great comfort, could I be a witness to it only for one single hour, what a satisfaction it would give me. But it is impossible and perhaps my dear Sally it may be better for me not to see you in my present condition. To leave N York at this moment could render me blamable in case of some accident and it would perhaps raise suspicion in the mind of some people who are interested in the fate of my bills on Europe.

Then Herreshoff told Sally what had been happening in Hamburg, the European seat of his import-export business:

. . . The late accounts from Hamburg are very melancholy, from the unhappy turn trade has taken there. The embarrassment became more and more general, immense sums of money are lost and a number of the first houses are agitated, several of middling consequence have failed. Unhappily for us we have this year been engaged in larger speculation that almost any of them. By the sudden fall of sugar not less than a half million of our money has been swept away.

He then turns to the unspecified allegations against his partner:

. . . Till this moment I cannot however in justice make any other reproach to my partner, than that he has been too enterprising, which has compelled me also to undertake more than I was inclined to. Though certainly if circumstances had remained the same as they were twelve months ago we might now perhaps be the richest house in Hamburg. I have been in the greatest intimacy with my partner many years before we had an intention of forming a commercial connection. The firmness of his character and his strict principles of honour were the first things which attracted me toward him, in no instance have I seen him yet to deviate from the latter. What you communicate to me is the first charge of the kind that ever came to my ears. Should such a thing be proved to me I would be the first to condemn and despise him but not merely my confidence in his honor but the circumstance took that our books have been laid open before an assembly of respectable men, that under the inspection of three of them, our business is

continued and a delay of payment of 4 months allowed us and that further in the letters from Hamburg written to several people of this place, in speaking of our situation, no such things have yet been mentioned, makes me believe it is to be a piece of malice, or at least a premature judgement of people who have been only half informed on things on which they give their opinion.

With his customary courtesy, Herreshoff asked Sally to tell him where she heard the unspecified allegations about his partner.

. . . How far it is in your power to give me an occasion for procuring either an explanation or a satisfaction concerning this matter and how far you are willing to do it, I must leave to you. You are too just and I hope too partial to a friend to refuse me a favor of that kind without reason. I will give my conjecture respecting the probable origin of that observation, though I am afraid my dwelling longer on the subject must be tedious to you.

After a long and detailed explanation of how his property in the United States had been pledged to back up his drafts, Herreshoff said that he believed it was Thomas Willing Francis who told her father of Herreshoff's financial problems and introduced the allegations against his partner. "I shall not urge you to tell me whether my conjecture is right but I have no reasons to doubt of Mr. F ill will towards me since I charged him so justly with a breach of confidence.[35]

Herreshoff then changed the subject and we get the first intimation of a scandal brewing that involves Sally's young sister Alice, then only twenty-two, and James B. Mason, himself only twenty-four or twenty-five. Since, as we shall soon see, bitter accusations were made against Mason, it seems only fair to point out that he came of a most respectable family and, in his mature years, had a most distinguished career. His branch of the family sprang from Sampson (or Samson) Mason, an officer in Cromwell's army, who came to the Boston area about 1650. A Baptist, like Roger Williams, he later moved from that Puritan area to Rehoboth and then to Swansea, towns near Providence, "for conscience sake."

James Mason's father John was a prominent Providence businessman who, like John Brown, was active in the China trade. He also was a founder of the Washington Insurance Company (which still flourishes), a rival of the Providence Insurance Company of which John Brown was a founder.

James himself was born in 1774 or 1775 just across the Rhode Island border in Connecticut, where his father ran a tannery and later a grocery business that expanded to reach Providence and Boston. James was graduated from Rhode Island College (Brown University) in 1791 and studied medicine and surgery with Dr. Bowen of Providence. After prac-

Alice Brown Mason (1777-1823).

James Brown Mason (1774-1819).

ticing in Rhode Island for a time, Mason went south, reportedly to Virginia or South Carolina. There he married and, upon the death of his first wife, about 1798, returned to Rhode Island, evidently giving up the practice of medicine. On his return, he met, or renewed acquaintance with, Alice Brown, youngest sister of Abby and Sally.

Later, James B. Mason became a prominent businessman, trustee of Brown University, Speaker of the General Assembly, Major General of the Rhode Island Militia, and for two consecutive terms, a member of Congress. In one of the many coincidences that mark our story, he died at an early age in 1819, the same year that Herreshoff met his lonely fate. Two of John Brown's sons-in-law were born the same year and two died the same year. Lacking any witness for the defense, this brief sketch will have to suffice.[36]

Anyway, we again refer to Herreshoff's long response to Sally's two letters. Evidently, she mentions James Mason favorably, to which Herreshoff replied:

> *. . . I am a little surprised to read what you say of M. (Mason) it is singular that our opinion of the character of this man should differ so vastly, as in most instances we judge so much alike. That you should find him an agreeable compan-*

ion is no wonder, but that you should not very soon discover, that the very candor of this intriguing fortune hunter is his greatest piece of art, seems to me impossible from the justness with which you use to penetrate into the character of men. If I had a sister I assure you upon everything that is sacred to me, that I would with pleasure see a dagger plunged into her heart than to see her fall a sacrifice to an artful wretch who would stop at nothing to carry his point and in whose heart corrupted by the deep rooted habit of the loosest dissipation there is not room more for a virtuous attachment. To think that such an excellent girl as A. should be a prey to so much baseness makes me shudder.

One can imagine what Sally thought when she received that letter, but Herreshoff was just getting warmed up. His next letter said:

. . . I received this morning your letter of the 6th inst. I am alarmed my dear friend about the unhappy attachment of our good A. I would write to her but to think that perhaps matters have already become so decided as to be irretrievable deters me from it as in that case I would rather do any thing to make her fate less unhappy. What little I have seen of that mans conduct was enough to make me shun him. . . . But there exists only one opinion of him amongst all his acquaintance I know, and friends. I always concluded that he was one of the most corrupt and deceitful young men I came across south.

Herreshoff then expressed the hope that somehow the family can stall for time, hoping, as they say in the soap operas in such circumstances, that Alice would come to her senses.

. . . Truth will at last conquer, if therefore you can only gain time and if yet possible, prevent A. from taking a precipitate step, it cannot fail but she will soon be undeceived respecting his real character. You say he has for several months past given up the gaming table and declares *he got the better of that propensity. But can anyone believe that an abstinence of a few months from* ones *view is a certain proof of reformation, especially when such a prize is to be gained by a short dissimulation, and gracious heaven, could even a reformed profligate be a desirable object to such an exellent girl? Is it possible that mere negative virtues could suffice her?*

As if his previous remarks were not enough, Herreshoff then wheeled out the big guns:

. . . If he has given up the gaming table there are other propensities, inconsistent with an uninterested virtuous attachment, such as one as alone should entitle a man to A heart which I am sure he has not given up, and without a true and lasting attachment, of which I think him incapable, never will give up. Since I wrote my last letter to you I had a conversation with a man to whom M. views seemed to be no mystery . . . and so far dispelled my apprehensions that I almost repented what I had written, could not refuse myself the satisfaction to learn

wether... he thought his attachment sincere. He then told me that M. had a connection with a woman of dubious character in B. [Boston] *who when she heard of his attentions to A. made her remarks upon it, and he to ease her mind and not to lose the good graces of this favorite, had the baseness to speak in a very slight disrespectful manner of A. of which that woman has since not failed to boast against her acquaintance. This happened very lately. The man who told me has no interest in it except that he professes an esteem for your whole family. Let errors find forgiveness from a loving heart but you judge wether such perfidy ought to be forgiven and wether a man capable of it more likely to add to the happiness of a girl like A. or to destroy it. May she be wise enough not to give an opportunity of doing either. I could now tell you the name of him who told the above to me, I believe it would rather confirm than destroy the authenticity of it in your opinion, but I am not authorized to do it. I shall however try to procure you an opportunity to inquire nearer into this fact, which if proved will be enough to make him* [at this point the letter is torn][37]

Herreshoff was so concerned that he took a drastic step, as he reported in a letter to Sally.

... I was not at home when Mr. Ward [Richard Ward, a merchant in New York, who was married to Elizabeth Brown, daughter of Joseph Brown, John Brown's brother] *brought your letter of the 19th Novr and I was obliged to go out of town on some business that same day, so that I could not visit him but several days after. I have only seen Mrs Ward* [Sally's cousin] *yet, she told me she had been disturbed the night before by a terrible dream, that made her feel quite unhappy because she was afraid it might perhaps soon be realized. It was nothing less than that Alice was engaged to M. She thinks it one of the greatest misfortunes that could happen to your family and says she had never seen anybody yet that did not despise the man in his heart, but she says it is no secret now that A. is attached to him, but that it is generally believed he will succeed in his intrigue. For nobody doubts but what it is a speculation* [fortune hunting]. *I pity our beloved A if passion has made her blind to the views and ungenerous designs of a man whose character is so unlike her own. I have written to her though I am afraid I shall lose her friendship by my letter, which is perhaps not written in a stile which any body else would have chosen in so delicate a subject. But I thought that I just either tell her my real sentiments or not write at all. If she has not shown you my letter it was because I requested her to destroy it after perusal.*[38]

We do not know whether Herreshoff's letter cost him Alice's friendship but we do know that, whatever effect it may have had on that young woman when she read it, it did not change the course of events, for by mid-December it was too late. Nature had taken charge and propriety, not for the first time, had succumbed to what: love or passion? It depends on your point of view.

John Brown Goes North

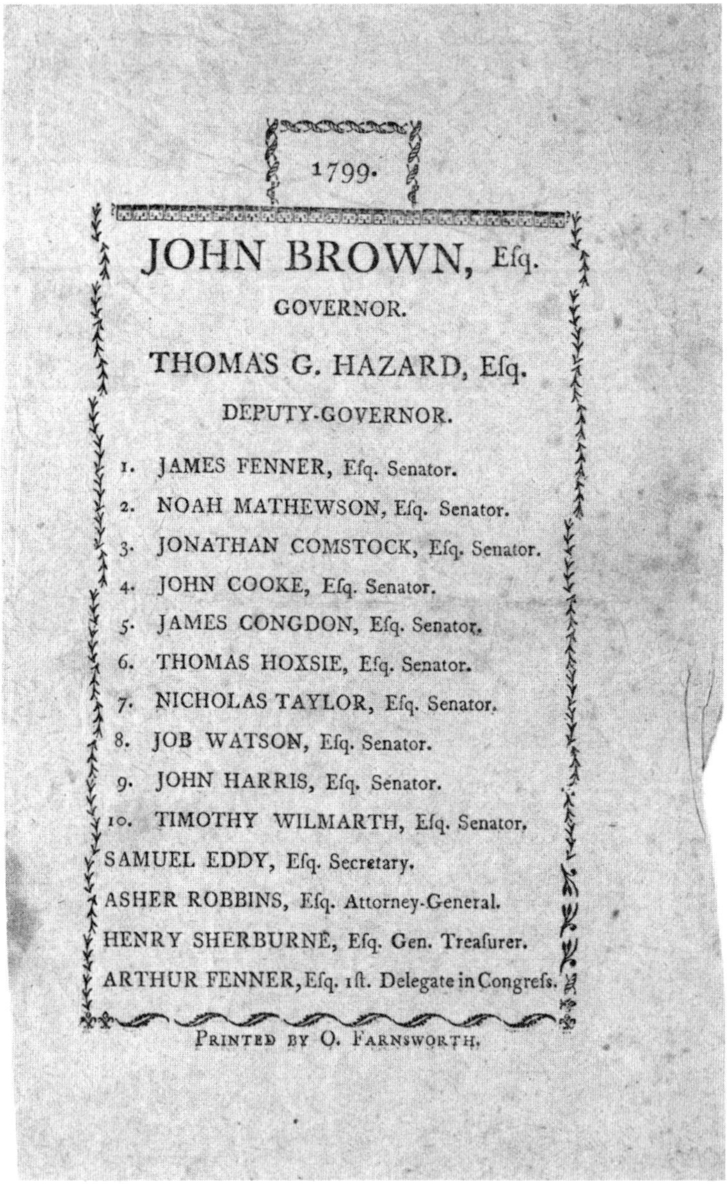

1799.

JOHN BROWN, Eſq.
GOVERNOR.

THOMAS G. HAZARD, Eſq.
DEPUTY-GOVERNOR.

1. JAMES FENNER, Eſq. Senator.
2. NOAH MATHEWSON, Eſq. Senator.
3. JONATHAN COMSTOCK, Eſq. Senator.
4. JOHN COOKE, Eſq. Senator.
5. JAMES CONGDON, Eſq. Senator.
6. THOMAS HOXSIE, Eſq. Senator.
7. NICHOLAS TAYLOR, Eſq. Senator.
8. JOB WATSON, Eſq. Senator.
9. JOHN HARRIS, Eſq. Senator.
10. TIMOTHY WILMARTH, Eſq. Senator.

SAMUEL EDDY, Eſq. Secretary.
ASHER ROBBINS, Eſq. Attorney-General.
HENRY SHERBURNE, Eſq. Gen. Treaſurer.
ARTHUR FENNER, Eſq. 1ſt. Delegate in Congreſs.

PRINTED BY O. FARNSWORTH.

1799 election ballot advocating John Brown for governor.

Herreshoff, incidentally, believed in destroying letters, but happily those who shared these pages with him did not share that view, for if they had, there would have been no book and the John Brown's Tract would forever have been known as the folly of John Francis and not the vision of John Brown.

We do not know what John Brown thought of the courtship of his youngest daughter by that young man reputed to be a rake, but just when the family was most concerned, he had to leave for Philadelphia to attend a session of Congress. Son James, in his diary, records that his father set out on November 23, adding that "he has been before elected but never accepted the appointment."[39] Since there is no record of John Brown's having been elected to Congress in the first five elections after Rhode Island ratified the Constitution, James must have been referring to the Continental Congress, to which his father was elected in 1784 and 1785. He evidently did not attend its sessions for, according to the Rhode Island Manual of 1917, he and several other Rhode Islanders were "Duly elected, but their names are not in the Journals of Congress."[40]

On "Novem 27th, 1799 at ¼ after 9 Oclock on the Morng," John Brown wrote a chatty note to his son recalling that he, daughters Abby and Alice, and grandson John Brown Francis had stopped in Stamford a year before on their way to Philadelphia and "they will allso Remember that we met James the same day in the Rhode 12 miles from hear in New York State. Our Horses Purforms well the coalt doeth much better than I expected he Eates & Drinks his Full allowance and I have no Dought of his purforming the Journey to Philad by Sunday Eveng or Monday morng."[41] That trip the year before is presumably the one on which he obtained title to the John Brown's Tract.

On December 2 John Brown wrote to James that he had arrived safely the previous afternoon and had spent the evening with Tench and Anne Willing Francis, their daughter Sophia and her husband George Harrison. ". . . they are all well, only Mr Francis complains of a coald but is not near so bad as your Marr was when I left you."

Brown then discussed some business and, in the same sentence that he mentions "Spice & Syder" announces, "I am Situated at Mrs Whites in the 8th Street North of Market Street only a fue Dores, to give rest to the Horses I shall attempt to walk to Congress Hall to day." After scribbling, "I am in Haist," he adds one of his postscripts.

. . . PS the Horses purformed better than could be Expected but was som Dull when got hear. I wrode all the way with them, our Carrage wheels Running 6

inches wider than the Stage hear made it go much harder as the wheels Jamed in the Ruts, I shall in due time propose a Genl Law to make all the wheels throughout the Nation Run of one Width.[42]

The full dimension of Herreshoff's financial catastrophe becomes fairly clear in a letter from the Hamburg trustees of his business holdings to the Philadelphia firm of Wachsmuth & Soullier, which was to be their representative in Pennsylvania, John Murray & Son, having that doleful assignment in the other states. The letter confirms Herreshoff's version of his affairs and paints an even bleaker picture.

. . . No doubt you allready know that ye Arrangement of the affairs of Messr Eimbeke & Herreshoff at this place by the horrible Decrease of value of goods and by the untoward behavior of some of their Creditors, hath unfortunately turned to total Ruin.[43]

On the next to last day of the year, James Brown, according to his diary, wrote "to J. B. on the Subject of J. B. M. (James B. Mason)."

Before we take leave of the year, and the century, there are a couple of final interesting notes. One is distinctly a curiosity. Among the Brown family papers was found a political poster dated 1799. On it is a slate of candidates headed by "John Brown, Esq. Governor." At the bottom of the slate, which includes candidates for Deputy-Governor, State Senator, Secretary, Attorney-General, and General Treasurer, is the name of Arthur Fenner, who had been elected Governor annually since 1797 and would be until 1806, as a candidate for "1st. Delegate in Congress," the office John Brown then held. The electoral records for that period are sketchy, so we have not been able to determine whether Brown actually ran for governor hoping the incumbent would be willing to take Brown's seat in Congress, or whether the poster was just a gambit in the kind of maneuvering that has taken place in American politics from the beginning until now.[44]

Since December 1799 saw the death of George Washington, this is an appropriate time to recall the story that Elizabeth Francis, daughter of John Brown Francis, told about her father's playing with Washington's sword when he was visiting the lad's grandfather, Tench Francis. This hardly comports with the well-known picture of Washington as cool and formal, but perhaps with children he unbent a little. No date is given for this charming incident, but since John Brown Francis was born in 1791, it could have been while Washington was president.[45]

7

Romance, Marriage . . . and Death

Mr. Brown died, however, before he realized any of his anticipations, and no doubt a great many more men will die before that wilderness will be seen to blossom as the rose.[1]

Natheniel S. Benton, 1856

The turn of a new century, even more than the advent of a new year, is a time of optimism, not that John Brown's optimism ever needed much encouragment. He expected, as we saw from his letters to James Sheldon, for settlers to turn up in number, plant crops, have good harvests, and attract more settlers by the hundreds. It seemed not an unreasonable expectation, for it was happening just a few miles west in the Black River valley, as reported by a clergyman, the Rev. John Taylor, who found the area already under cultivation when he toured the river valley in 1802.

> *. . . People frequently raise their provisions the summer of their settling; if they go on in season, they chop down the trees, and get them off as soon as possible; and they sow spring wheat and plant corn. The wheat is sown and dragged; and if there is no blast* [a plant disease], *they reap from 25 to 35 bushels the acre. Corn is only planted upon the ground without plowing, and is seldom hoed more than once—and then no more is done than to cut up the fire weed: and corn planted and tended in this manner, I have measured, which was 11½* [feet] *in height.*
>
> *Poor people have, in general, been the first settlers. They have bought farms of about 100 acres—have cleared 10 or 20—built a log house—and then sold to*

Adirondack settlement "Among the Pines" as depicted by Arthur Fitzwilliam Tait, Currier and Ives lithographer.

others, for a sum as much greater then they gave, as to purchase them another 100 acres—and by this means have placed themselves in a short time in a good situation.

It is considered here but a small affair for a man to sell, take his family and some provisions, and go into the woods upon a new farm, erect him a house, and begin anew.[2]

With information of this nature coming from the region, one can understand John Brown's optimism, for despite his weeks on the Tract, he did not discern the fatal difference between his land on the slopes of the Adirondacks and the fertile land just a few miles to the west. Nor did his descendants until they had wasted decades, and a life, on John Brown's dream.

At that time, Lowville, along with Boonville, the only settlement of any size near the tract, had a population of just 300. And a contemporary account from that small trading center reported that the people of the region subsisted on salt pork and corn bread in the winter, with the occasional treat of venison or turkey. Cane sugar was hard to come by, expensive, and bulky to transport, so people often used maple sugar they produced themselves. They drank tea (coffee was almost unknown) and they wore garments of wool which the women spun on wheels in their gloomy log cabins.[3] It was not an easy life.

Providence was growing, but its population was still only 7,614, although it had overtaken Newport with a population of 6,739; and it was small enough so that a letter needed only the recipient's name (no address) for it to be delivered.

The year 1800 also saw a wonderful irony. James Greenleaf, the bane of John Brown and Thomas Willing Francis, that year married Anne Penn Allen, granddaughter of William Allen, Chief Justice of Pennsylvania, who by blood or marriage was related to the foremost families of his state and the mid-Atlantic region, including the family of William Penn. His father-in-law, James Allen, was the brother-in-law of Sarah Coxe Allen, granddaughter of Tench Francis the Elder, founder of the Francis line in America and grandfather of John Francis, whose acceptance of a second mortgage from Greenleaf was the genesis of our story. Thus, James Greenleaf was related by marriage to John Francis' cousin.[4] As we have noted earlier, it sometimes seemed that everyone of prominence in America was related. To finish the story of James Greenleaf, we should report that he lived for another 43 years near Allentown, Pennsylvania, the city named after his wife's family. In those days, if there were any disgrace attached to debtors' prison, where so many famous men resided, it appeared not to be lasting.

A final note about the infamous James Greenleaf before he disappears from our chronicle. An aggregate fund to be financed by the sale of his assets was established, with Thomas Willing Francis as a trustee. But, there is no record of John Brown's family receiving anything from the fund.

Although George Washington had died on December 14, it was not until January 9 that services for him were held in Providence. In those days, of course, when communication was by stage or boat, things took a lot longer to arrange. Some 3,000 people, nearly half the population of the city, attended rites at the Baptist Church, according to James Brown's diary, "to hear the oration by J. Burrill. The Procession of Civil & Military was numerous & respectable – in all the large Towns of America similar processions have taken place to honor the Memory of the deceased – That in N.York far exceeded in brilliancy the one of Philadelphia."[5]

John Brown was in Philadelphia attending the session of Congress which, needless to say, also marked the death of Washington with appropriate ceremony. He wrote about it to son James:

> *... Yours of the 6th Int. with the paper enclosed of the 4th came to hand yesterday by which I obsearve the Inhabbetents of Providence are possessed with the same Condolence for the Grate Good man as seemes to be so universelly felt to much Esteeme Cannot be bestowed on the memory of that Hero Whome you have*

offten heard me Say was the Best Man in the World *I now Enclose You the Oration dd.* [delivered] *by Govr.* [Henry] *Lee by request of Congress in both Branches and beg my Daughter Francis to keep it Safe till her Son my dear Boy Learns it by hart which he will Soon do by Learng, one Paregraft at a time till he gits it Fixed in his Mind, and then take the next and, so on till he Can Repeet the whole I wish him to learn to use his arms Orationly to give Ellegence to the Body with a proper Inlivend motion at the proper periods, I wish my Abby to mention this in due time to his Teachers that is my Desire That he should not only Learn to Speak Distinctly and Properly, but that he should allso be Lernt the proper gestures of his Body and Limbs, . . .*

John Brown went on to say that "tho their may be many more Butifull and brillient orations Given on this Subject," Governor Lee's deserves a special place "being the First, and that by order of Congress. . . . " Another factor, perhaps no less important, was that Lee was "one who in a particular manner has Congrattulated me in the most Complementary tearms on My Sentiments in polliticks Considering so Exactly with his every Instence. . . ."[6]

After a lapse of several months, we again have letters from John Brown to James Sheldon. In the first he refers to having heard from Sheldon in a letter dated January 10. As was often the case with past letters, much of Brown's reply was a discussion of who owed whom what and about purported mistakes in the accounts. Brown reported that the road builder, James Gould, had visited him but there is no information about the roads.

Brown also discussed the production of potash on the Tract.

. . . I remember Very Well that Mr. Angell & All Agreed that the Wood or Timber ware we Cleard at the First & Second Settlement was Not Suteable for Ashes, but I Understood You or Mr Baker that the Timber up the Mill pond or on that Branch of Moose River Sum Distance above the Mill was Elme & other Suteable Timber of Pot ashes, but if You think their is No Timber Suteable to make Pot Ashes from, You certainly will Not Carry Aney Pot ashes Kittles to the Mill as I proposed, but if there is Good Timber Land suteable to make Pot ash I think their ought to be 2 or 3 of Pot Ash Kittles Carried to the Mill Seat by slaying . . .

Brown also mentioned that Sheldon was thinking of "Removing Your Famely," allowing the inference that the Sheldons did spend that one winter on the Tract. And there is reference to a forge, presumably at or near what is now Old Forge.

. . . Observe You have found a Man who Inclines to Erect a Forge at Moose River. I hope he will prove a Good Man . . .

Then John Brown launched into a discussion of liquor on the job.

. . . as to Rum the Less You use the Better. You'l employ No Men but such as will do without Rum, if they Must have Rum Let them find it them Selves. Mr. Goald You know gives his Men No & I do beleave he got more work out of them when with them then was got out of My Men who had Gin Every Day. If you cant do without Spirits Your Self I have no objection to pay for it but you had better first find it Your Self. I do assure You that I have found by Fifty Years Expearence in Buissness that those who Suffer no Rum or Spirits Among their Workmen do Much Better & Git More work Done with Less trouble and Quarrilling then those who use Spirits.

Brown informed Sheldon that Gould would be carrying $800 up to him to use for wheat and corn to make bread. Sheldon was to buy beef with proceeds from the sale of potash kettles. The bread was supposed to

Last till the Next Harvest when I hope you will of Every kind Say wheet, Rye & Corn that the Grist Mill will be Reddy as you mention Early in the Spring till which I suppose you'l prefer Flour, or Git the grain ground before you carry it on the Tract. You'l Remember the Man that Lives clost by the Black River, 2 miles from Layden, I spooke to him for his Grain if he will Supply you as cheep as aney other person it will be as Little Carrage from their as from aney place you can git it.

Then there was this rather plaintive ending:

. . . I must close by beging you to make use of all the Oconnemy in Your power and Reduce the Expenses allready Exceeded my Expectation. More than Double Considering their is no produce Yet Raised & but Little Land prepared.[7]

About ten days later Brown wrote again:

. . . I wrote you Fulley a few Days past & Expected then that Mr. James Goald would have Returned to you before now, but he now promises to go in 3 or 4 days and that he shall not stop on the way more than one Day, the money Say 800 Dallas has beene all counted out and Reddy for some time, and I shall allmost a mind to inclose it by the Mail, but so maney Robbery's of the male has Lately taken place that I am a Frade and therefore shall prefer the Send'g of it by Mr. Goald with his Receipt and List of the Bills, this Sum I hope will give you Full Releaf and as the Spring is now so near advanced that should aney more money be wanted You'll advise me and I can give you orders on Messrs. Bleeckers as by your Letter of the 20th Ult. . . . [8]

The final letter of any substance we have from Brown to Sheldon is dated February 9 and written from Philadelphia, where Brown was attending a session of Congress:

. . . As the Rhode and Bridges are now made & mills done I must Begg and interest you to lay out to raise as large a quantity of wheat and corn next year as you possibly can with a reasonable number of hands, as till we show the people

who wishes to go in to the new country That we raise our Bread kind we can not expect many people will be willing to purchase the Lands, but as soone as a plentiful crops is raised we shall not only be able to Feed those we wish to imploy at building houses & clearing Land etc, etc but we shall have people from all quarters to purchase or lease the Lands and settle thereon. I must therefore begg & intreat you to ingage some of the best and most industerious men you can git to be ready as early in the Spring as the weather will permit to go to Sowing and planting as much ground as you think bids Fair for good crops and as I have expended so much money allreaddy without aney produce from the Lands I do hope that the crops of next Summer will give full encoragement to me to you and every one that Soil is well worth spending money upon.

As usual, there was a postscript in which he reported that he had given Gould a letter to people in the Johnstown area "to try to git them to have the Rhode cut from Johnstown through the Jersey Fields next season."

. . . *Which Mr. Gould thinks may be done for 600 Dolls including Bridges, cosways & every other expense making the Rhode ful one Rod wide. I mean to see you in the Spring but I wish to go through the Royal Grants & over the Bridges made by Mr. Gould from the West Cannide* [Canada] *Crick to the Mill place on my Tract but Mr Gould seems doubtful wither that Rhode will be so good as that by Mr Boones Settlement which you must remember how bad it was when we passed it in May last and in June when I came out it was not much better. I then confess I have little encoragement to go on the Lands again till I can have the Rhode made good through the Jersey Fields or the Royal Grants. Should I go to the Springs perhaps the Rhode may be so well settled and be made good by the time I Leave Baul Town* [Ballston] *Springs that I may go on in a Carriage without diffulty to the Mill seat. You'l give me your advice in this purticular in your next.*[9]

Poor John Brown had been making the same entreaty for months—clear the land and raise crops or no one will want to buy my lands. By March he was beginning to think his entreaties were in vain. As he wrote to James:

. . . *I have thought as Ballew doeth for some time that Sheldon is not the man to git Settlers, but I am sorry to Inform you of Sumthing more Disagreeable that this. Mr Bogert was to have attended the Gen'l assembly at Albany with my Potion* [petition] *to the assembly to establish the Title, as it was once in the name of a Fourener by the name of Angersteene & which I have Ever been told by all that no difficulty would happen in the Business, but Mr Bogert now writes me that his Ill health had been such as that he could not go to Albany & that he had Desired Genl* [Alexander] *Hamelton to attend to it but that the Genl had Returned and said that Col Burr claimed money due from Angersteen & was trying to Injur my title to the land. Indeed to Defeat it if he could and that it was the advise of Genl Hamilton for me to go Immediately to Albaney & that the Genl Assembly would not probelly Set Longer than towards the End of this month. I have wrote to Genl Hambleton very Pressingly to go to Albany and act for me, or if he can not go to write to some able council to act for him, and I have Desired Mr Henry P Franklin to pay Genl Hamelton aney Fee he Demands in Reason, and have mentiond to Genl Hambleton & to Mr Bogert that my being no Lawyer I do* [not] *see aney material advantage my presents could be and that to Impossible that I can now Leave Congress and Suppose to be Col Burrs object to squeese a Sum of Money out of me if he can . . .* [In this single passage, Brown spells the name "Hamilton" three ways.]

If the matter is not settled, Brown supposed, his petition would be continued. ". . . one consequence will natturally Result from a Continuance of the business Viz that I shall not be Fond of Laying out money on the Land as I did Last year."

This might be a good time to point out that James, contrary to what has been written about him as something of a gentleman of leisure, did indeed spend a good deal of time on his father's business. Although he did seem to relish travel for pleasure and seemed to enjoy his role as favorite uncle, the great number of business letters to and from James make it plain that his father often relied on him in important business matters.

In the final paragraph of his letter to James, his father made it evident that he was beginning to think of what he would leave behind when he died.

. . . You see how many ways their is to spend money, it is like to go but hard to come, when I was active & in FULL business I did not mind give money by subscriptions too Publick Buildings and Publick Rhodes & other uses but now I am so much Indebt at Bank & Col Potter that without selling Real Estate and making use of Reasonable Econommey I may be too much Involved when I depart this Earth.[10]

Since this is the last letter from John Brown to his agent James Sheldon,[11] this might be the right time to try to figure out exactly what John Brown had accomplished on the Tract. We can be fairly certain from a variety of sources, not the least his own will, that John Brown or his agent James Sheldon built at least one road there. However, it is impossible to say with certainty exactly where that road was, except that it terminated about where Old Forge now stands, for there is direct evidence that there was a log dam at the site of the present state dam, a saw mill, a grist mill, a store and a number of houses. That is specified in John Brown's will. We know the road crossed the Moose River on or near the Tract, but where it started is uncertain. Charles E. Snyder of the Herkimer County Historical Society, in his well-researched paper of 1896 (when settlements on the Tract were still within living memory or in the memory of those who had heard stories from their parents), says flatly that the road began in Remsen. That is certainly possible, although Remsen is some 25 miles from the Tract.

A more likely possibility is Boonville, for in his letters, Brown made frequent references to Boon's settlement, among them this one:

> *. . . Mr Gould seems doubtful wither that Rhode will be so good as that by Mr Boones Settlement which you must remember how bad it was when we passed it in May Last and in June when I came out it was not much better.*

If Brown entered and left the Tract by Boonville, it suggests that is where his road began, for a man of his bulk would certainly choose the easiest route out.

There are also references in early accounts of a road from High Falls, the present-day Lyons Falls. Although there are a number of references in John Brown's letters to nearby Port Leyden, there is little or nothing directly pointing to High Falls. Almost certainly there was a road from middle Settlement to the Old Forge, and if that had continued west out of the Tract, the logical terminus was Lyons Falls because that was the nearest hamlet.

In any case, there were reports of three roads, but in all his writing about "rhodes" and "cosways" and bridges, John Brown is not specific as to location, except that one terminus was plainly the Old Forge area. There were also reports long after that time of twenty to thirty families living around what came to be known as Mill Pond near the grist and saw mills. That was almost certainly true some time later, but not likely during John Brown's time. His letters suggest that Sheldon, and maybe a very few of his workmen, lived briefly on the Tract, but the tone of his letters almost demands the inference that Sheldon was almost entirely unsuccessful in attracting settlers. However, it does seem likely that some crops were planted, probably wheat, rye, barley, oats, peas and potatoes, but there is no record of any successful crop, as almost certainly there would have been had the planting not been thwarted by the grudging soil and short growing season. In short, for what remained of John Brown's life, he had little factual evidence for whatever optimism persisted. If indeed there were any optimism, it was entirely a function of Brown's unquenchable ebullience.

As to how much John Brown spent in his futile attempt to make of his vision a reality, we have a good source. His grandson, John Brown Francis, wrote to his uncle, Thomas Willing Francis, that Brown had spent

$25,000 in making improvements on the Tract.[12] Now that was a considerable sum in those days, but for a man of John Brown's wealth, it was hardly a reckless expenditure.

For the time being we must turn away from the still "wild lands" to family developments that would have a major impact on the Tract – the difficult, and in one case rancorous, courtships of John Brown's daughters Sally and Alice by Charles Frederick Herreshoff and James B. Mason. Although it is hardly uncommon for fathers to think that no man is good enough for his daughters, here the evidence of that is unmistakable.

Before we turn to that, we must take quick notice of the fact that John Brown was again having what today are termed "cash flow" problems. A number of letters show that he was attempting to sell what was presumably his last ship, the *General Washington,* to a Captain [James D'Wolf] of Bristol, to Brown & Ives (the firm started by Nicholas Brown) or to Thomas Willing Francis.

In a letter to his son James in Providence Brown wrote that he wanted to sell the ship for at least $15,000 to pay part of his debt to the bank and to Colonel [Simeon] Potter. But if he could not sell the vessel quickly at his price, "I shall Rigg her & if no one chuses to purchase her shall send her to Sea this Spring or Fore part of Summer, but if [I] can Sell her my mind had reither do it. Then to Fit her out as I have no one in my Famely who is Anxious to do Business in Navigation, if aney other, and according to the cource of Nature I can not Live Long and have been Declineing in Navigation for three years past and so Inactive that its Imposable I can attend to Shipping as I once could. . . ."[13]

In John Brown's letters there begins to appear frequent references, like that above, to the approach of death. In a letter a week later to James, he mentioned the expected death of a Mrs. Bowen. ". . . be Ye allso Reddy for you know not the Day nor the Hour. . . ."[14] A couple of weeks later he complained mildly that his grandson, "Little John finds time to Write to Jonathon [his young Negro servant] but not to me, I should Suppose that he thought to Find time to Write a Short Letter and nothing will Learn him to write a Letter if or well as to coppy a Short Letter from the hand writing of H [Hezekiah] Sabin [John Brown's clerk and cousin] who writes a good hand & I am shure will, with pleasure make the Copy." In that same letter he again alluded to him and "Marr" getting old "and can not help our Selves as we once could. . . ."[15]

Perhaps his preoccupation with his own mortality was hastened by the condition of his old friend Tench Francis. As Brown wrote to his son,

"Tench Francis dying sent Jona[thon] to enquire 11 oclock Mr T Francis is still alive but Mr Harrison thinks he is struck with Death, and that a Fue Hours must Finish his course, thus from Dust we come & to Dust we Return. Serious as it is that we must all have our turns in this most Sollumn Event, yet it is as Full as it is Serious, ...[16]

Tench Francis, whose friendship with the Brown brothers led to the marriage of his son John to John Brown's daughter Abby, and thus to the James Greenleaf mortgage and the Brown's Tract, did die that day, May 1, 1800. He was seventy years old.

A few days later Abby wrote this in her diary: "Letters from my Dr Father announced the death of Mr Tench Francis which was the 1st of May 1800. This dear Mans amiable Deportment toward me during my Knowledge of him left pleasing impressions on my mind.[17]

John Brown sent a constant stream of letters back to his family in Providence, and one emphasizes how different Congress was in those days:

> . . . *Exceeding Sorry I am to have to advise you & other Friends of my collegues through you of an affair of* Honour as it is caled, *which took place yesterday jest before nite between Mr Champlin* [Christopher Grant Champlin, the other Representative from Rhode Island] *& Mr* [James A.] *Bayard of Willimmington in consequence of their Respective Speeches in the House on the Bill to Raise the Sallerys of some & Lore the Compensation of others etc They with their 2nds say Mr J* [John] *Rutlage to Mr C and Mr* [Lewis R.] *Morris of Vermont Nephew to Governor Morris was 2nd to Mr Bayard they took the ground, in the Jerseys, 12 paces a Sunder & Fired both together as Mr R Informes me & Mr C was shot through the cheek & spilt much Blood, Mr Bayard was shot by the Ball on the side of his Thy & is only a Flesh Wound. The Doctor Proudfoot ses Mr C will be out in a Fue days he is Now Comfortable in his bed. I have jest beene up to See him, I do not Expect he will attend Congress aney more this Session in Deed their is but 4 Days more Including this day, Mr. Rutlage Jest now told me that Mr Bayard will he thinks be able to atend the House this Day, they both behaved well and stood their Ground after both being shot but from the Interfearsome of their Seconds they closed the Business shuk Hands & all Returned back to the city in the one boat. Thus is the Frayelty of men one Hour the best Friends the next Hour Indevering to shoot Each other, then Shake hands & Returns to order. Mr C made his will as he now Informs me & prepared for the worst, and feels very Fue Inches Variation of the Shot which went in through one Side of his Face & Out of the back part of the Neck would have kild him Ded in an Instant.*[18]

Again, beginning in June, we have a series of letters from Charles Frederick Herreshoff to Sally Brown. We infer that for some time Charles has been discouraged, but that something in one of three letters he just received has encouraged him to hope again.

... I am glad to know you at your favourite place [Point Pleasant in Bristol] *and the more so as I am well convinced you will think of your absent friend, on visiting those spots where we have been so happy. That moments like those should ever return, I thought it folly to hope until a few weeks since; a little lonely spot, where I could quietly reflect on what is past and love you with a pious resignation, was all I dared to wish for, but my love is too powerful for my reason; one beam of light was sufficient to give another turn to my imagination, and your last letter has compleated it. I begin already to see a chain of melancholy days in my solitude; I begin to think myself entitled to more happyness, whatever reason may say to the contrary; but taught by sad experience, like you my dear Sally, not to anticipate much happyness, I shall guard my heart from being to sanguine. One happyness I am now determined to enjoy, let the consequences be what they will. I will see you, dear excellent girl, I will hear it confirmed from your lips that your heart is above the caprices of fortune, that it is as constant as my own.*

But he wrote that he could not visit as soon as she would like, that first he had to spend a few days in Philadelphia, but that on his return to New York, "The first packet shall convey me to you." He said that he hoped she would be at Point Pleasant, for "I feel very averse to go to Providence." One assumes that is because he is not eager to see John Brown, who has opposed Charles' courtship.

... From all my mind has suffered these ten months past, since I have entertained the prospect of meeting you again, I feel as if there had been a great change in my fortune.

And, as he did so often in his letters to Sally, he turned to the difficult situation of her sister Alice.

... I lament that our pleasure will be checked by the situation of poor A. Let us be ever so good, we cannot escape our share of misery in this world, every one must have his turn.[19]

Alice was also on the mind of her other sister Abby. This is her diary entry:

... My beloved sister Alice is at this Date June the 23 at Point Pleasant a very Unhappy Woman owing to ill health as Well as that her family disapprove her connection with Mr. Mason to whom she is engaged. I pray to God in case my Sister Marriage to him that all opposition which is made mayn't create a Parting Dissention & that Real Merit may triumph over every report to his disadvantage. But Alas the prospects at present is by no means favorable either as it respects her health or future settlement.[20]

The fact is that less than a month before the marriage of Alice and James Mason, it was still not certain that the marriage would indeed take place.

Romance, Marriage . . . and Death

Whether it was John Brown alone who was the impediment, or his wife Sarah, or general family opposition, we do not know. It is amply clear, however, that there was plenty of opposition. The presumption is that the "ill health" Abby mentions is a euphemism for pregnancy, for according to several sources, Abby Mason was born the day after her parents were married, which, by the mores of that time, was even more troubling than it would be today.

The "private Marriage" was performed by the Reverend Stephen Gano, pastor of the First Baptist Church from 1796 until his death in 1828, on July 16.[21] Little Abby arrived the next day. That is the commonly accepted date, although James Brown wrote in his almanac: "19th July 1800, my sister Mason has a Daughter since named Abby." James, however, usually made his entries well after the fact, so his dates are not always precise.

This, needless to say, occasioned a certain awkwardness and, later, presented genealogists with a problem. Which would they choose: accuracy or propriety? Each of the foremost genealogies of the Brown and the Mason families dealt with it in a different way. The Chad Brown Memorial recorded the birth date but discreetly omitted the marriage date. The Genealogy of the Sampson Mason Family also recorded the birth date but put the marriage a year earlier, on July 16, 1799.

Charles Frederich Herreshoff heard of the marriage on July 21 in a letter from Sally:

> *. . . The one in which you inform me of your sisters fate happened to be the last I perused. Poor Alice! She has not deserved it, Heaven has destined her to be an excellent wife, an affectionate mother, but alas a villain has robbed her of all her happy prospects, there is one place more where she will find peace again; a tear of pity shall follow her, whenever she goes to it. As for the wretch that betrayed her, he has murdered an innocent girl without passion, a premeditated murder is less criminal, with smiling satisfaction could I send him to his grave; a much greater punishment I hope awaits him beyond it. . . . What a world is this, every day I become more disgusted with it, in your arms alone can I forget all its miseries, you are the only hope of my sick heart. . . .* [22]

We should, however, point out that Abby, in her diary four months later, noted that the marriage "appears to render my Sister happy." Surely, that's what mattered.[23]

As genuinely concerned as Herreshoff was about Alice, he and Sally had plenty to be concerned about in their own lives: his grave financial problems and John Brown's continued opposition to their marriage. Poor

Herreshoff was so desperate to see Sally that he was prepared to sail to Newport, and then journey to Bristol just on the *chance* that he might see her before she left on a trip.

. . . I am ready to go in a Newport packet if there is one going next Friday, in hopes to meet you in Point Pleasant before your departure. I cannot bear the idea of staying an hour in case I should not be so happy to see you, and therefore if you have left P. P. for your journey I shall go right home again. At all events I request you to leave a few words for me at the tavern where I used to stop, that I may immediately on my arrival know my good or ill luck . . . . I should be sorry if any one of your family taxed me with indifference for not going to see them, being so near; under other circumstances it would certainly add greatly to my pleasure to see them well, I would be particularly happy to see Mrs. Francis but I am this time unfit to speak to any body unless I meet you, therefore little Sally will oblige me not to tell of my coming if she expects to be gone before I arrive. — A favorable wind will I hope carry me to Newport toward Saturday noon; I shall then be in Bristol in the evening, how will I feel if I see my charming little Sally walking under the cherry trees, it will be one of the happiest moments I ever had. Adieu till Saturday night, but if I should not see you then, at least think of me, think that I am then praying for your happyness, forget not to write me from the springs [presumably Ballston Spa of which her father was so fond]; *I cannot follow you there, nor go with you if even I land in time. For ever yours . . .* [24]

Poor Herreshoff. Thirty-seven and writing with the passion of youth. John Brown's daughters could not complain of a lack of romance, or at least emotional turmoil, in their young lives.

James Brown, in his diary, reported that yellow fever which, as we have seen, often plagued Philadelphia, finally brought widespread suffering to Providence, "50 people die of it."[25]

By mid-September Herreshoff's firm had been declared bankrupt in Hamburg.[26] Although plainly shaken by his financial collapse, Herreshoff was not the least bit less determined to marry Sally, as he made clear in a letter sent from New York on October 1.

. . . It is a week to day since I parted from you my dear little Sally, eight days of a short life, lost for ever, and how many more shall we lose before our fate is to be united; if I reflect how happy how truly happy we feel when we are with each other, alone and without fear of being molested, I look with indignation upon every thing that puts itself in our way. There is no new trial wanted to convince us that our affection is sincere and constant, and that we would live happy without a brilliant situation, in one word, I grow more impatient every day to see this unnatural situation terminated. Whatever may happen I could never be reconciled to lose you, it answers then no purpose to wait much longer, you are deter-

mined to share my destiny and I am no more afraid of the future, I have no doubt that with our moderate wishes we shall not suffer any want, there is but little required to make two people happy, who are so content with each other; you observed but lately that there were certainly but few equally so.

Herreshoff was tired of waiting. It was time for them to take matters into their own hands.

. . . Let us my dear girl be the masters of our own fate, and let us begin by showing our resolution to that effect. I believe this is the only way to put an end to all further opposition, for I perceive that the longer we wait quietly for a change the less hope there is of it. If you think proper to let your father know that our union is unavoidable, and that we are determined not to postpone it longer than three months, it would in my opinion be the best and most proper step at this present moment, for our conduct must have no appearance of mistery; whatever we do we will do it in a free and open manner, we will tell to every body whom it interests what our intentions are and let every body use his persuasion or whatever means he thinks proper to hinder it.

Charles Frederick, like people in love since time immemorial, was confident and bold one moment and uncertain the next.

. . . I wrote the above two days ago; I expected to have a letter from you today, but received none, what can be the reason of it, it is now ten days since I left you, and if you had only written last Tuesday, the letter would be here.

A few days later he expressed the fear that her "tender health" had been affected by the "sudden changes of weather" and told her that the approach of winter "makes me feel gloomy; it would not be so had I the prospect of spending it in your company." He said that "if I receive not a letter by next mail I shall feel very uneasy." But then he added something more cheerful. "Mr Eimbeke formerly my partner writes me that his wife has given him a daughter, and that he named her after you."[27]

Plainly, their wedding plans were advancing, for in less than three weeks Herreshoff wrote Sally a chatty letter saying that he was renting a house, rather than arranging for them to live in a boarding house which he thought she would not find to her taste. There was talk of servants (whether she should bring hers or engage new ones in New York), of bringing the smaller rather than the grand piano, and of his buying furnishings as good "as my little share of taste will afford." And he recommended that she send things soon "before the ice prevents it or makes it too dangerous."

. . . I have not altogether changed my mind respecting the resolution to postpone our marriage till my affairs were wound up, but the news I received since of those two vessels and some other favorable circumstances have in great measure altered

my situation for the better, and what little you understand of what I told you of it, must at least show you that I see my way pretty clear. . . I approve very much of your pride my dear Sally not to ask any thing of your father. I would much rather tell him that we did not expect nor wished to accept any thing of him, let us be content with what we have, and let us not place it in the power of others to disturb the happyness Heaven offers to us. . . . [28]

A couple of days later he wrote that "I walked by a long round about way to our house on the Greenwich road, to rent it for the winter season; and did accordingly. I could not suppress the wish that we were that very moment already settled in it to enjoy a few such mild serene days, before the snow comes on; however I shall be supremely happy under all circumstances, as soon as I see you there, the few days that are yet to separate us will soon fly away. I have besides taken some arrangements for the furniture of the house, and in a short time everything will be ready, and I shall only have to wait for your summons."

Herreshoff also wrote of Sally's "insurmountable partiality" for living in the neighborhood of her "native place, and that you wish that sometime hence we may take our fixed residence there."

. . . It is true that I never promised you yet to return there for such a purpose, nor have you ever asked such a promise of me, but you know very well my dear girl that to promote your happyness is promoting my own, our wishes will always be the same, not only because mine will always be directed by yours, but because I know also by experience how much our feelings and tastes are alike, I am convinced that we are born to make each other happy; therefore do not be uneasy about things which I do not promise. . . . The idea of settling somewhere near Providence is extremely pleasing to me, I do not know this moment a place in the world, where I would rather live with you, if even I felt less attachment for the very persons you love most.

He went on to say that he is "anxious to know the result of your conversation with your uncle," presumably Moses Brown, the only brother of John who was still alive.

. . . If I understand you well, it is not to have his advice, but merely to reconcile him, and if possible through him, your father with our resolution, you will begin by convincing him that it is no more in any body's power to alter it. It is not always good to follow old people's advice in such cases; they forget too often that they once possessed a heart, and that there are other sources of happyness than those derived from riches, especially are those not fit to be our judges, who never look upon marriage but as upon a contract of conveniency. [29]

By November it was evident from a Herreshoff letter that Sally's and Charles' expectations of an early marriage were again frustrated. The inference is obvious that there was still too much opposition for her to leave Providence that winter.

Herreshoff:

. . . But after all I am extremely happy to see that you still entertain a wish that our union might be near, and I have only to complain that you should find it singular that I wished it still more.

Herreshoff wrote that "Any thing I could do with propriety to remove the doubts of those who are still determined to doubt, I would undertake with pleasure, but I must confess my dearest girl, that I dred to make any more fruitless attempts. – I will join you the moment there exists no doubts more on either side."

Perhaps then, he went on, this was the time to carry out a plan he had designed for after their marriage. He said he was about to purchase a 200-acre farm, twelve miles from New York and one mile from the East River, presumably on nearby Long Island, for £4500, about $11,250. It supported the family of ten of a farmer who paid $500 rent a year and saved $250 a year.

. . . The deeds of this farm shall be made out in your name, without any encumbrance; it shall be your own indisputable property . . . How happy would I feel if by that means we could reconcile all those whose consent you think indispensable to your tranquility; and to those only I request you to communicate it, and that even with the desire not to divulge it, for as long as I am engaged in any mercantile business, I would have it believed that your father made the purchase for you.

Two inferences leap to mind here. One, that the objection to Herreshoff was primarily financial because of his ill fortune in business; and, two, that he did not want his creditors to know that he had more than $11,000 to spend on a farm.

. . . I told you before that I intended to do the same thing after our marriage (I do not mean with the same place) it is therefore not so much for your father as for the sake of your friends, that I do it at this period – It is not enough that you are sure in your own mind, that those for whose approbation you wish, have no longer any objection to our union, but whenever you are convinced of it by their own expression, and when you see yourself no obstacles more I shall feel content. I shall then wait only for your consent to fetch you to New York. I do not wish for a precipitate resolution; consider it maturely. It does not follow that through this acquisition we are bound to New York; but it is absolutely necessary for me to make it my chief residence for some time, perhaps – two years – longer.

The intrinsic value of the place [the farm] *is such that I belive it could at all times be sold again without loss. If you should wish me to put the deeds in your fathers hands on his passing through this place, please let me know.*[30]

A couple of weeks later, Herreshoff wrote again. Although the letter is primarily concerned with his financial situation – which he said was not as bad as someone had been telling her father it was, he began by saying "How sincerely do I wish for the moment when we may be sure of our happyness, that of being never separated again in this life, it seems now as if every day produced new obstacles, but at last we will conquer them all, and the calm that is to follow upon all these tempestuous and gloomy days, will be so much sweeter."

He protested that the man who had been her father's informant was wrong.

. . . the truth is that the house of Eimbeke & Herreshoff failed for more than double the sum, your father mentioned, and if I should be answerable for what remains unpaid, I would think myself in a forlorn condition. But the fact is that my responsibility extends no farther than that I am obliged to give an account of all the funds in my hands belonging to the house, and that after the settlement in Hamburg nobody has a right to demand a farthing from me. I am answerable though for the bills I have drawn, if they are not paid by the house, and that is the only debt I have.

Herreshoff then expressed the hope that John Brown, on his way through New York to the session of Congress in Washington, will stop so he can explain his financial situation.

. . . I will try to explain to him every circumstance that respects my situation, though I have very little hope that I can convince him that he is wrong in his opinion, if he has more confidence in what a fellow like Adamson tells him. . . . if therefore he has not confidence enough in me to believe that I tell him the truth, he will never be convinced that my situation is not bad, at least not but by the experience of a number of years. . . . I entertain some hopes that Mrs. Francis may have advised him not to pass through New York without seeing me, we may then know at least whether there is a shadow of a hope for his consent now or hereafter. I repeat it, if your father had the least confidence in me, it would be the easiest thing in the world to convince him that there is not [illegible] *fear respecting my circumstance, if he can persuade himself that with the means which remain me, it is possible for us to live happy . . . .* [31]

Whether as a result of that letter or previous correspondence or her own judgment that it was time to press John Brown for an answer, Sally, on November 29, wrote a very stern note to her father. Presumably she was living in his house but, for whatever reason, she wanted her words on paper, where there would be no mistaking them. We quote the entire letter.

Dear Sir

To judge from your conduct towards me the summer past and the extreme prejudice you have all along entertain'd against Mr. Herreshoff, I have little reason to think you ever mean to give your consent to our marriage, this is different from the idea you expressed in one of your letters to me two years since you then said that if he proved to be the man of honor & integrity he appear'd you should no longer withhold your consent, I dont know that he has in any instance deviated from this Character and I am very certain he has never shown any disposition to deceive either you or me. What induces me to trouble you with this is to request as a particular favor that you will have the goodness to see Mr Herreshoff on you way thro' New York, and hear his account of the situation of his affairs, he lives now near the battery No. 27 white Hall. I do not at present ask your consent to our marriage I wish to wait till the Spring, when if his property is sufficient, as he now thinks it is, to maintain a family, I shall unite my destiny with his, to have the entire approbation & consent of my parents is what I have always wish'd for and if there was a prospect of obtaining it I should feel happier than I do at present, there are however three months between this and the Spring with the hope you will think more favorably on this subject before I subscribe myself your affectionate Daughter

Sally Brown[32]

John Brown, "Old Thunder," as we have seen him described, was a formidable father, but Sally, to use current slang, had had it. On the day he was leaving for the first session of Congress in Washington, she wanted him to understand that she and Herreshoff were tired of being stalled. We infer from subsequent correspondence that Brown did not visit Herreshoff in New York or that, if he did, there was no resolution of the impasse.

We must note in passing that on December 5, 1800, John Nicholson, partner of Robert Morris and James Greenleaf, died in debtors' prison.

By December 13, John Brown wrote to son James about the political maneuvering between the supporters of Thomas Jefferson and Aaron Burr for the presidency.

. . . I board at Mr Stills with 15 or 16 Federal Members. I have to walk 600 of my steps to Congress Hall, the Horses Mr Still has being miserable and I know not ware I could hire a Desent Horse & Carriage if I was so minded, Hay 25 Doles per ton, not a drink of Syder to be had for Love nor money, so that you may Judge weither I had Reither be at my own Table or here.

I hope however to Rub through the Winter & bid aDue to this city for Ever, no Inducement would prevail on me to come to this country again. The Town of Baltimore Excepted their is less Houses on the Rhode from this 80 or 90 miles towards Philada then their is from Coopers Town to our new Lands being about the Same Distance and yet this is the main Stage Rhode from the Northern to the Southern States, from aney thing that yet appears the Government will be carried on much as it has beene tho a Change of men no material change of measure is Expected will take place, the collectores it is hoped will be continued Loan officers etc, etc but of this we shall no more by & by

I am called to Dinner kiss Little John for me[33]

It is perhaps worth noting that, although John Brown said that "no Inducement" would ever cause him to go to Washington again — the city in those days was new and raw — he had run for Congress again in August and been badly defeated, the Republicans [now Democrats] defeating the Federalist candidates for Congress handily. Brown finished by far the worst of the Federalists, receiving only 138 of the 3,240 votes cast.[34] However, this election, for the term beginning in 1801, was held before Brown had ever served in Washington. One can only speculate how he might have felt about the new nation's capital if he had been reelected.

A couple of weeks into the new year of 1801, a letter from John Brown to James mentioned that James B. Mason was in Alexandria, Virginia. One gathers that he was in the mercantile business, but not yet employed by his father-in-law.

Again, we see Brown's concern about his mortality, no doubt heightened by his attending the funeral of a House member from "Georgie."

I made my will Last August at Point Pleasant but never Executed it but have Redrafted it here before the Death of Mr [James] *Jones who Lay Ill but 10 or 12 days but have not yet signed it but think it shall not pass over an other Day till Done as we know not the Day nor the moment we may be Rendered Incapable of Such an Act and we are admonished to be Reddy.*

Then he asked James, "What is your opinion of Salley's attachment to Mr H will it ware off or will she have him as the Sayers Ses 'Shirt or no shirt.' " Given the fact of Sally's stern letter of a couple of months before, and the fact that the courtship had been going on for three years, Brown should have been able to answer that question himself.

In February Herreshoff wrote to his Sally a letter that makes everything seem up in the air: ". . . I have less confidence in our meeting next summer . . . I believe my hopes to see you this year, depend chiefly on one circumstance, which is, wether your father will make a journey to his new lands in the course of next summer, which I flatter myself is very probable." Plainly, Herreshoff did not want to encounter John Brown, a feeling that was mutual. ". . . I believe it is in vain with our little foresight, to form plans, and the wisest resolution is to swim along with the current of time, as chance or some superior hand directs us."[35] Poor Charles Frederick sounds like a man resigned to defeat but still playing the game.

There seems little improvement in his spirits in his next letter.

. . . If you have one comfort yet for me in store, one hope, near or distant, I beseech you to point it out to me, at least tell me that you continue to be well, and that you can never doubt my sincere affection for you. . . . Adieu my dear Sally, if I had more hearts than one they would all belong to you, the one I have will be constantly yours as long as you think it worth while possessing, for ever yours"[36]

Maybe it was the approach of spring, or perhaps a letter he received from Sally, but the melancholy tone of resignation was not present in Herreshoff's next letter.

. . . I am very much pleased my dear little Sally to entertain a hope that you will not be visited by your usual indisposition this spring; I believe a great deal depends in that respect on your faith in your own strength, and especially the state of your mind; as you say yourself that nothing seems to affect your health when your mind is not troubled, you must repel then all fictitious and real sorrows till the season returns when you can breathe the soft air of Point Pleasant, in which you always find a relief. Though I shall not think it arises from forgetfulness or from a decrease of your affection when you observe too long a silence, yet I cannot consent to be very long without any news from you; if I knew your health to be as constant as your heart your silence would not make me uneasy. You are right my dear girl that this winter has been a long and tedious one to me, and you are also right to believe that I would have spent a part of it much happier, if I could have known how things would turn out; but I am happy to see the Spring begin, I anticipate some pleasure since you give me some hope to see you at Newport in the month of May. How eagerly will I embrace the first opportunity to see you; this last separation seems to me longer than any before, we shall have a great many things to discuss, a great many important things to communicate to each other.

Charles then explained why he did not send a letter he had begun a week earlier.

. . . my dissipation was the cause that I neglected to send it. I was at a large and very brilliant party that night at the miss Murrays, where I danced without interruption till 2 o'clock in the morning to make it up for my abstenence during the whole winter; there were a great many fine girls present, yet I cannot say that I felt any pleasure, I sighed for the only little girl I love. I think it is a fact greatly

to my honour that whenever I return from such company, I think of you even with more tenderness, and feel always more convinced that there is no little girl like my dear Sally. . . .[37]

About this time, James B. Mason returned to Providence, and his family, after a three months' absence on business in Virginia and thereabouts. A couple of days later, John Brown returned from his final session in Congress and, some time thereafter, Mason accepted Brown's invitation to join the firm, although Brown was more or less semi-retired.[38]

In this month of March, we have the last letter we know of from John Brown to his agent James Sheldon, written to him at Remsen, off the Tract. It is not terribly informative. It indicates that Brown had earlier written from Washington, enclosing some funds in the form of bills of exchange. ". . . I think I mentioned Seeing You on My Return or that perhaps You Might Incline to Come to this State to See Your Remaining Friend here, as I think You have a Brother at Newport, but as I have not Rec'd a Single Line from You Since I am at a Loss to know weither You Mean to Come Down or Not." The rest of the letter concerned, as did so many of the previous ones, a financial wrangle between Sheldon and a local businessman. "I do Really Wish You to Attend to The Business & Get the Accts. Settled by Some Good Disinterested Refferees, if possable, if You Can Not Agree with Mr. Bull Yourself."[39]

Although that is the last letter of which we have knowledge, it is possible that there were more. Perhaps there was a formal ending to the relationship that, as we saw, John Brown thought was unsatisfactory. Or maybe it just petered out. Whichever, one should not be too hard on James Sheldon. Although he was the first agent to fail to develop the Tract, he was hardly the last. It is probably fair to assume that Sheldon did his best but that he, like all the others that followed, including members of the Brown family, was defeated by nature. We can also assume, for surely there would have been some record, that John Brown did not make the trip to the Tract that he contemplated and to which Herreshoff referred in his letter of February 5. It is difficult to conceive that John Brown would ever give up on a project, especially one so dear to him as the Tract, but we simply have no further knowledge of it in his lifetime, although, as we shall see, two more generations would for another half century attempt to settle lands that nature, with greater authority than any legislature, seems to have decreed would be "forever wild."

Romance, Marriage . . . and Death

The situation between Sally and Charles still appeared to be unsettled in early April. In a long letter Herreshoff wrote: "I cannot blame you for disliking upon reflection the idea of meeting me in Newport, it would be better to do it in Providence, but the latter is impossible without an invitation from your father, and little I can expect that you know as well as I do." He suggested, however, that if Sally went to her beloved Point Pleasant, she might spend some time at Mrs. Ives' place just across Narragansett Bay, a short trip by boat (Potowomut in Warwick) ". . . could we not meet there, if only for one or two days." It was necessary to observe the proprieties.

He also mentioned the possibility of buying a farm on Shelter Island, a lovely island in the eastern fork of Long Island. "I must observe here that what I told you respecting the farm ought yet to remain between us, especially as it is intended for a speculation in which I will not appear to be concerned." This, we assume, is to substitute for the farm near the East River he had earlier said he intended to buy.

Herreshoff also discussed the farm he had just rented in West Chester:

You will think the rent of 500$ I pay to Mr. Guerlain rather high when I tell you I have no profit from the farm. I have only some cows and food for them and the horses I wish to keep, and the flower and kitchen garden, which are both in excellent order, but you know that I then expected to live there with you, and it was certainly very convenient and profitable to have a furnished house and everything we wanted to our little household; it was certainly more advantageous than to pay nearly as much for an empty house in town. The house is by no means large nor elegant, but I think pleasant and convenient enough for a country house. . . .

Then Herreshoff discussed the possibility of soon living in Rhode Island:

. . . I find no difficulty my dear girl to persuade my heart that you would share a small fortune with me and be happy; but if even you were determined to surmount all the obstacles to our union, I am afraid that the failure of one attempt would discourage you for ever, and when I think of that I feel discouraged to wish for such an attempt. If my willingness to settle hereafter in R. I. and any assurance that I would prefer it to any other residence, was my circumstances such that I could live without doing business. I say if this was sufficient to make our wishes succeed, I could with sincerity satisfy you; but to promise it without any reserve you know very well I could not, nor would it be of any use, for with the best intentions, circumstances might render the fulfilling of it impossible. . . .

It was beginning to look as if their marriage would never take place. Yet that letter did have some good news.

. . . A proposal of partnership has lately been made to me by a man whom I consider the most able merchant without any exception in this city, whose house is undoubtedly amongst the most solid and has an opportunity of doing very extensive and lucrative business, not only by the means of its funds, but through its great connections in Europe. A circumstance peculiarly acceptable and flattering in this offer, is that it exempts me from giving any funds to the house, but that only the exertion of my little capacities are expected, which at the same time must convince you that the man is my friend, and has some confidence in me. Without saying that I feel inclined to accept this, I think it is worth to reflect upon it before I reject it, and I should like to know what you think of it. I would at all events make in a condition that I would not be so much a slave of my business, as not to enjoy the pleasure of a country seat in summer.[40]

By May, Herreshoff had moved out to his rented house in West Chester and said he would go to New York only when business required. As he wrote to Sally, he intended to:

. . . devote the greatest part of my time here, to gardening, amusing myself and but little to reading and writing; you must therefore not be surprised my dear little Sally if on our meeting I have no more the appearance of a genteel town lad, you must overlook my sun burnt face and course hands, and you must take back what you said about three years ago, when we rode from Point Pleasant to Warren bridge with L. Howard that you would never marry a farmer. I am already half a one, and since according to your own plan we shall probably spend our old days at P. pleasant, it is you own fault if I turn a complete clown. It strikes me very forcibly, the more I reflect upon your plan, that you can live no where happyer than at P. pleasant in the midst of all your relations and dearest friends, who I dare hope will in time also become mine, and I wish that the time was already arrived when we were quietly settled there and employed with nothing but to make a little paradise of our home and to make each other as happy as it is reasonable to expect in this world.

How ironic these words, in view of how Charles and Sally would spend their last years. We must also note that, although the name "Herreshoff of Bristol" is one of the most famous in the annals of American yachting, it was Sally Brown who planted their roots there.

Again, plans for marriage were going ahead.

. . . You cannot doubt that I heartily consent to your project of our uniting this summer at Mount Lebanon, after having previously convinced some of your friends that in the manner we intend to live we may join our fate without imprudence. This satisfaction I certainly owe to you and as I have no less confidence in Mr Ives than you have yourself, I will with pleasure lay as true and as exact

a statement of my affairs before him at our next meeting, as I am able to give, as he is a merchant, your friends will rely more upon his judgment than upon their own.

And he expressed pleasure that he and Sally were of one mind when it came to her father.

. . . I am glad my dear girl that you are inclined to do me justice in respect to my refusing to address your father again. It is true that I wrote him last year that I had not come then to demand his daughter, that I would wait till I had in some measure repaired my losses, of which if I had succeeded I would inform him, but I also told him that I came to hear of him, that a deficiency of fortune was his only objection to our marriage and that as to the rest he did not consider me unworthy to become his son in law. You remember what singular answer he gave me, of which you seemed more offended than myself and that from the tenor of my reply he could not expect that I would ask for his consent again . . . that we were determined to get by our own judgment. You have likewise intimated to him, you told me, that it was our resolution to be married this Spring. No one certainly can charge us to have acted with rashness or inconsistency.[41]

We can safely assume that Charles Frederick did indeed meet his Sally at the Ives' summer place and that his presentation of his finances passed Thomas Poynton Ives' scrutiny, for James Brown's diary for July 2 reads: "my sister Sally is married to C. F.—Herreshoff."[42] That scant reference is all the information we have encountered about the wedding itself, compared to all the almost rapturous detail about the marriage in "great splendour" of Sally's sister Abby to John Francis 13 years before. But given all the obstacles in the way of Sally and Charles Frederick, can we doubt that they were happy—and relieved?

James' diary also indicates in a few words how well James Mason had been accepted into the family, although not necessarily for himself but out of concern for Alice. His entry for June 20 says "Ja^{s} Mason moves into the old house," meaning the house that John Brown "built in the year 1760 & moved into it with my Wife & Family the day after Marriage and remain'd liveing in it till June 1788 when we moved on to the Hill."

And James' diary says: "The married Pair, after dining once at Mr Masons & once at Mr Ives set out 6th for West Chester via P^{t} Pleasant. 7th they imbark in a calm—I return to Providence. very hot*****

By July 15 Charles Frederick Herreshoff wrote to his sister-in-law Abby Francis that he and his bride were settling happily in. They had already been to New York to the theater and a concert, but "this evening our dear little Sally felt very happy to be at home again, and expressed a wish that we might not see town again for a long while, in which I join her most heartily, for we have real pleasure at home, and every hour spent in town is a loss. . . . Sally has enjoyed the most perfect health and excellent spirits since our departure from Rhode Island but if she did not calculate with certainty upon the pleasure of seeing soon some of our friends under our roof she would not be quite so content."[43]

That letter crossed in the mail with a very nice one from Abby to Sally, in which she said how much she missed her sister. Yet "I am consoled when I extend my reflections on your subject — because my heart is fully persuaded of the excellence of that Being who's tender care & Amiable deportment altogether will I hope render you delighted in the performance of All your new Duties. . . . "[44]

Letters passed frequently back and forth, with those from the Herreshoffs always including the warmest invitations to visit them at West Chester or Shelter Island. James, not surprisingly, for he was the family visitor, was the first to come. He arrived on August 8, stayed a couple of days and then returned to Providence, where he soon gathered up sister Abby and nephew John Brown Francis for a visit to the Ives at Potowomut.

By September, it was apparent that John Brown, who was always inclined to make the best of things, was reconciled to Sally's marriage and was writing to his new son-in-law about business and personal matters. Remembering that Brown was supposed to have retired from active business, it interesting, and amusing, to read how he was spending his retirement days.

> *. . . Sr by the time this will reach West Chester I suppose you will have returnd from Shelter Island to which Island I should have Liked to have gone in a Boat to meet you, could I have Left the Various workmen I am Every Day overseeing and directing to the numbers of about 40 men in Various Branches Viz the Distillery, the Repairs of the Ship Hope, the Removeing the Hill at the Point to fill up the Pond Hoole at India Point, paveing up the Hill North East of India Bridge and allso up the Hill in Frunt of my House Ware we Live compleeting the Fence & Paveing in Frunt of the Same West of my Said House all these attentions together with a New Wharf at India Point has kept me in my Sulkey from the Brake of Day till nite Exception only an Hour at Breakfast and an Hour at Dinner for this 2 or 3 mo. I thought Indeed have added the makeing the new Rhode from India Bridge & the cultivation of my meddows & corn Lands, Say about 50 acres which I am Gitin under the Richest Cultivation & to do which, have made more than 1000 Loads of manure at India Point this season.*

Brown also inquired about a shipping venture that Herreshoff expected to be very profitable, and he attempted to attract Herreshoff and Sally back to Rhode Island.

... Is Your Mannufactory of Tobacco proffitable & if so could it be as well caried on here as at New York, if your connection in that & other Business may be agreeable to you and Salley to spend the Summer at Point Pleasant you may Manage that farm the next Year. As I propose to Discontinue my Present Tennent Mr. Chace, or would it be pleaseing to Live in this Town or at India Point or near it, in the Massachusetts State ware I have it in Contemplation of building an Elegant Seat, Should the Ship Genl Washington Return safe.

John Brown then reported that "James B. and Abbey Francis with John B. Francis Setts off by Land the Day after tomorrow to pay you a short Visit."[45]

According to James' diary they arrived at West Chester on October 3, spent twelve days there and then journeyed on to Philadelphia for a few days, leaving Sally's house on the 15th and returning there on the 22nd, staying overnight before beginning the trip home.

John Brown continued his campaign to get Sally back to Rhode Island in a letter to Charles Frederick Herreshoff soon after the three got back home.

... as Salley has mentioned in her Letter to her Sister Alice that their is no place she should like to Live at So well as at Point Pleasant provided the Farm was her own, I have thought proper to make a proposal to you & her on the Subject.

Tho I have Ever concluded it is Impropper for a Man to Give much of his Property to his children till his Debts are First paid, My Point Pleasant Farm & Prudence Lands are under Mortgauge for Twenty Five Thousand Dolls Inclusive, I will however if Its Convenient to you to purchase one half the Farm I will give her the other half, the Lowest price I value the Farm at is Twenty Thousand Dolls without the Stock, if You Chuse to purchase one half at Ten Thousand Dolls. I will Discharge the Mortgauge & Give a Warrentee Deed and give all the Stock on the Farm to Salley besides the one half the Farm.[46]

Although this proposal never came to pass, for the farm was left to Sally in John Brown's will, there must have been some agreement about the Herreshoffs living there, for, about four weeks later, there is a very long and detailed letter from John Brown discussing Herreshoff's prospects if he carried on the tobacco and sugar manufacturing business in Rhode Island, with a suggestion that Brown would be willing to invest in such ventures.

... I am of the opinion that Mannufactory well adopted and Strictly Attended to will produce More Cartin [certain] *a Proffit to Support a Fammely then Other Trade and Navigation, Tho it Offteen happens that Large Estates are made by Successfull Voyages, Yet Unsuccessfull Voyages & the Extrevigent Mode of Life*

Facade of main house at Point Pleasant farm at Bristol, R. I.

too Offten Practiced by Those in Trade, Under too high Expectations of Proffits from this that and Other Voyages, as offten Brake or perhaps More offten than they Succeede and Evin the most Discreete Frugall and Desearving Merchants Sometimes Fail from Unforeseen Accidents and Disappointments, ...

In the middle of an extremely detailed discussion of business, Brown asked, "Shall I look out for a man & womon to live on the point Pleasant Farm next Summer Under You or will You procure them"

He then returns to business:

. . . The Suger Mannufactory Might be caried on at Bristol but I think India Point much prefferable and Evin if You Live Most of the Year at Point Pleasant I should prefer the Manufactory to be at India Point reither than at Bristol.

If you are sufficiently acquainted with Dry Goods and Incline to go into the Importation Business at India Point the Shop Keepers of this Town who now go to New York & Boston would be glad to purchase 8 or 10 Thousand pounds Sterlg Annulle Which I think would give You a Proffit of One Thousand Pounds per Annum at Least Which with the Suger & Snuf Mannufactory would Inable You to Live in as high a state as Aney in this Town.[47]

That month of November also saw reference to a couple of entirely personal matters. Abby wrote to Sally that "Mr Mason is I believe to be *an* Adventurer as well as to own a past, he is *now every* Moment engaged by *her*—scarcely gives himself time to Eat. Alice is if anything a more attentive house wife than formally. She appears not to dream of any pleasure greater than that which her domestic scene affords." And John Brown, in a letter to his old correspondent Thomas Willing Francis, noted the resemblance of his grandson John Brown Francis to the boy's father, Tom's brother.[48]

We have no record of anything important until March 18, 1802, when, as James Brown records in his diary, "my Father was upset & much hurt, does not leave his room during the remainder of the month—and not untill the 2d April when he goes out in the Coachee—" As we learn from other sources, John Brown's sulkey overturned.[49] We do not know the extent of his injuries, but, presumably, no bones were broken, for he was back at work within two weeks.

To the extent that we have knowledge, the next year and a half passed uneventfully, at least as far as the Brown's Tract was concerned. But then, well, the words of his family tell it best. From Abby Francis' diary:

. . . My dear Father expired on the Eveng of the 20th of Sept 1803 just one Month after he attended the Funeral of his much Esteemd sister in law. His malady was first observed by us in the beginning of the preceeding July & it continued most alarmg at night time until at last symtoms of a Dropsy of the Breast, were I believe consider'd by his physician to be the cause of his disorder, altho he had other most distressing complaints Notwithstanding which his Sweetness of temper was such as I never before witnessed in a sick room. Blessed be God without a struggle on Tuesday Even the 20th of Sept 1803 after having past an eveg with us in good harmony of Spirits, without bodily pain.

Sixty years later, when John Brown Francis was 72, he wrote about his beloved grandfather to his daughter Anne Francis Woods:

. . . When six weeks old JBF left Phila for Providence where he was Received on the wharf & taken into the arms of his Grandfather Brown who from that moment to the hour of his death in Sept 1803 thirteen years uniformly & unceasingly regarded him with the tenderest care & solicitude.

This affection evinced itself in a most touching way on the night of my dear Grandfather's B's death—It was customary for me to rub his legs with a Flesh Brush—

As I left his Bedside he bade me "good night my dear Boy Good Night my dear dear dear Boy." These were his last words. Ten minutes afterwards John Brown, my grandfather, had ceased to breathe at the age of 68, having died of dropsy - So I am his Senior in years 4 years & my Grandfather Francis 3 years—

The longest, and most informative, account comes from the diary of his son James:

> . . . *My Father John Brown was born January 27th, 1735/6. He expired September 20th-1803, aged 67 years, 7 months, 13 days.*
>
> *He had been infirm for many years, having a weakness in one of his leggs occasioned by the Rheumatism.*
>
> *He walked out very little after 1795* [remember he twice made the difficult trip to and from and spent five weeks on the Tract in 1799] *but he constantly rode out, generally in a Sulkey—July 2, 1803 he rode to P. Pleasant, soon afterward a difficult of Breathing came on, which his physicians, William & Pardon Bowen declared to be occasioned by a Dropsy; after this, sound Sleep was seldom enjoyed by him, But he retained his Passion for business as formerly—*
>
> *He went out two days before his Death, and on the Afternoon & Eve on which he expired, seemed better than he had been, particularly between 7 & 9 oclock his spirits were higher than I had known them for many months. He laughed and took part with in a long conversation. at 9 oclk we left him for supper, at which time he went into bed, intervals of sleep intervened till half past 10 ocl when my Mother & sister Francis sitting near perceived an alteration in his breathing which did not alarm them thinking it was a sounder sleep. But now a shriek from my Mother, and his last groan, reached our ears. a moment brot my Sister Sally and Brother Herreshoff into his room where we beheld our departed Parent. Doctor William Bowen arrived in a few minutes, but my father's pulse no longer beat—*
>
> *In 1802, my Father had a Fall from his carriage & was much injured a mortification in the leg ensued, and his constitution withstood the shocks of continued pain, but after some weeks extreme suffering his health was again restored—He eat and drank hearty and his spirts were good—In the Autumn of 1802, he began a new road leading from the Bourne Lot to the Boston Road, leading to Newport. This he finished with great Labor of body and of mind—early & late he attended to the Laborers—*
>
> *About the first of September & indeed before that I perceived a depression of Spirits and particularly when Doctor Stilman came to visit him the day after Commencement but I always indulged the hope of his continuance till three days before his exit when it appeared to me thre was no longer any hope—*[50]

Thus died one of the extraordinary men of his time. His dream, however, did not die with him. For two more generations his family would struggle with that intractable tract.

III

End of the Empire

8

James Mason's Turn

You may depend that if God spares my life, the settlement shall flourish — [1]

James B. Mason, 1807

THOSE WERE THE WORDS of James B. Mason, whose entrance into the Brown family was, as we saw, hardly conventional. Nonetheless, it appears from this remove in time that he was quickly accepted by the family, and it was he who was first in the second generation to make efforts to settle those still "wild lands" on the western slopes of the Adirondacks. They, and all future efforts, were John Brown's legacy.

Although he left an estate valued by him at nearly $600,000, an immense sum in that day, what concerns us, of course, is John Brown's disposition of the Tract. That portion of the will that describes the Tract was dated September 13, 1802, little more than a year before the peaceful death of John Brown. It tells us how much (or more accurately, how little) had been accomplished with the expenditure of so much of John Brown's energy and money.

The arbitrary value that John Brown set on the Tract — and it must be emphasized that this is indeed an arbitrary value that existed only in his mind, for in a half century of trying, even with values rising generally throughout the nation, the family received only about $33,303.50 for all the land they sold — was $210,065 which, by coincidence or design, comes to a dollar an acre.

The work listed by Brown is meager indeed. Although all eight townships had been surveyed, only five had been sub-divided into farm lots, merely lines on pieces of paper. Improvements are recorded for only two towns, No. 1 and No. 7. For No. 1, Brown lists "2 Log Houses, a good

Barn & considerable improvements of cleared land." For No. 7, "through which the large & fine River called Moose runs & on which I have made great improvements, of a Grist Mill & Saw Mill, House, Store etc on this Town is the best of Pine Timber which may be floated to the Mill & saw'd in to the best Pine Boards, very cheap." For all John Brown's urging, that was all that James Sheldon was able to accomplish. Sheldon himself had left the Tract and, at most, there were a handful of families clustered in what is now the Old Forge area. If there had been any substantial settlement, Brown would have mentioned it.

Township No. 1, Industry, of 22,689 acres, was left to his wife Sarah and then to his daughter Abby and thus, eventually, to John Brown Francis.

Township No. 2, Enterprise, of 25,486 acres, was left to his wife and then to John Brown Francis.

Township No. 3, Perseverence, of 25,436 acres, was left to his wife and then to Sarah (Sally) Herreshoff.

Township No. 4, Unanimity, 26,023 acres, was left to Abigail (Abby) Francis and thus, eventually, to John Brown Francis.

Township No. 5, Frugality, of 26,667 acres, was left to Sally Herreshoff and eventually to her son, John Brown Herreshoff.

Township No. 6, Sobriety, of 27,440 acres, was left to Alice Mason.

Township No. 7, Economy, of 23,180 acres, was left to John Brown Francis.

Township No. 8, Regularity, of 33,060 acres, was left to James Brown, who eventually left 5/6 of it to his sister Sally and 1/6 to John Brown Francis.

Thus, eventually, 4-1/6 of the Tract's eight townships were eventually controlled by John Brown Francis, and 2-5/6 by John Brown Herreshoff, the third generation family members who made the final efforts to develop the Tract. Yet, the first efforts after John Brown's death were by James B. Mason, husband of Alice, who owned the smallest share.

Before we get to those, however, we must take one final look at the will, for one passage of it has routinely been cited as proof that John Brown was angry with his son-in-law John Francis for getting them involved with the Tract.

In the section leaving No. 7 to his grandson, John Brown made the

express condition that his deceased fathers Relations or Representatives never made any demand on me as the surviving Partner of the late firm of Brown and Francis or on my heirs or Executors in consequence of such Partnership as they can certainly in Justice have no claim for one shilling by reason of said Partnership, as John Francis my late partner and Father of the said John Brown Francis never put any property in the Company stock and from his almost constant sickness and our bad fortune during the Partnership, I do not think my Estate was worth as much including the whole stock at the Expiration of the Partnership as at its commencement, . . .[2]

True, that is not a cordial statement but since we have established that John Brown was avid in his pursuit of the Tract, it seems obvious that these words should be taken to mean exactly what they say, no more, no less. Which is how they should have been taken by Alfred Donaldson and others, for John Brown, although his grammar and spelling may have been wondrously atrocious, never had any difficulty in expressing himself. He said what he meant and he meant what he said.

In any case, such language hardly seemed necessary, since John Francis' only heirs were John Brown's daughter Abby and his beloved grandson John, each of whom received handsome bequests in the will. One infers that Brown, although he seemed genuinely concerned about his son-in-law's persistent ill health also, as healthy people often do, held it against him.

By 1804 the first substantial mining in the Adirondacks region began at Mineville, a few miles west of the lower end of Lake Champlain. It was the only truly successful mining venture in the region, despite the high hopes of more than 200 mines and forges in the Adirondacks.[3]

Also that year, the New York State legislature finally passed the bill that John Brown had tried to hire Alexander Hamilton to lobby for, one confirming his title to the Tract. And that year Rhode Island College changed its name to Brown University in recognition of many years of benefactions from two generations of the family whose name it adopted.

While, as far as we know, John Brown's descendants made little attempt in those first years after his death to develop the Tract, settlers were moving into that general area, and we are fortunate to have a lovely account of life during the first decade of the nineteenth century in Lewis County, where the western portion of the Tract was situated.

It was written in 1884 by Lydia Herrick Pitcher, then ninety-one. When she was fourteen, she lived in Martinsburg. Because her large family had little money from their farm on a hill, she worked outside the house, presumably as a general helper with another family. "I tried it, but soon found it was very different from living with my kind mother. In fact, I was homesick, and said, 'I will not follow this very long; I will get married and have a home of my own the first good chance I have.' "

James Mason's Turn

She soon met Reuben Pitcher, who "had come to this wilderness country from Massachusetts with a numerous family of boys and girls."

. . . Their young folks gave a party to which I was invited, and there for the first time I saw my future husband. It was quite a large party for a community so thinly settled, and everything passed off pleasantly, singing being part of the entertainment. Reuben Pitcher, Jr., sang several songs. The first was "The Exile of Erin," and I thought him a splendid singer.

Somehow or other I got the impression that very night that we should marry and he afterward said it was the same with him. He called on me afterwards, and in ten months we were married. I was 15 years and 15 days old, and my husband was 21. We were married in December in my father's log house on the hill, and had quite a wedding. We did not commence housekeeping until March but lived at home with my parents.

Lydia Pitcher's husband had, before the marriage, bought a piece of land, and his brother Daniel had bought an adjoining parcel. "They were intending to commence plowing their land early in the spring, but where was a housekeeper? After careful and deliberate thought, they came to this agreement: They concluded to cast lots, and the lot fell to my husband. Both were satisfied as Reuben was a year or two older than Daniel."

About a month before they were married, Reuben built the shell of their house, planning to roof it in the spring.

. . . Accordingly, Reuben and Daniel took their axes and went to see what could be done. When to behold, their house was filled with snow! Their house was big enough for those days, large enough for one room, and well it was no bigger. What an everlasting job it was to shovel that snow out, and they saw no other way. They could not wait for it to melt out, so they set about it with a will. In a few days they had the roof all covered with nice bark, a floor made of rough boards, the wall chinked with moss, a cupboard made, an opening in the roof for smoke to pass out, trainel to hang the kettle on, one door and two windows, and all was ready. The fire was built right up beside the logs and the coals were raked out to set a bake-kettle on, in which bread and pies were to be baked. A long-handled frying pan was used to cook the meat. Oh, what a beautiful little palace it was, so snug and nice, all in the thick woods.

My husband had bought a yoke of oxen, a cow, and a barrel of pork, and now all was ready for the woman. He yoked the oxen and put them forward of a sled and started for the hill. He found me with my furniture and things all ready. I had one bed and bed clothes sufficient to keep us warm. Daniel furnished his own bed. I had a table, a low chest, four chairs, a teakettle, a pot, a frypan and bake-kettle, six teacups and saucers, six large plates, six small plates, four iron spoons, six teaspoons, six knives and forks, a milk cup and sugar bowl, a teapot, one tablecloth, two towels, three sheets, two pair of pillow cases—and that completed my outfit.

Young Lydia spun flax into threads enough for twenty yards, and her mother wove it into cloth.

. . . Was anybody so rich? I thought I would whiten ten yards of it for a pair of sheets. They had a little spot cleared off just around the house, and I wet my cloth and spread it out to dry, but while the men came in to eat dinner, the fire from the burning brush was blown by the wind on my cloth, and burned half of it before it was discovered. Oh dear! Here was my first grief and child like and woman like, I cried. Never shall I forget how bad I felt. I needed it so! My husband and his brother were sorry as I. But after awhile I gave up and worked on, and soon found I was as cheerful as ever.

The men planted potatoes and beans and "quite a garden." Our cow furnished us with milk and butter in abundance, though sometimes flavored with leeks a little too much to suit us, but we couldn't help it as she ran in the woods. She wore a bell, and one night when the men were busy I thought I would go after her. It was almost dark and just before we got home a wild animal rushed across my path. It frightened me terribly. I described it to the men and they said it was a deer, but what I dreaded most were the wolves. Almost every night we heard them howl and sometimes they came very near our house, but we never got sight of them. We often saw a great black bear trudge across the paths. I was rather timid about going out alone much, though I ventured sometimes. Our nearest neighbor did not seem near at all.

With their first winter came their first child, Paulina. The mother had just turned 16. But with her mother's help, she got through the winter. The men chopped wood and hunted, and Reuben "had partly learned the making of shoes and boots," so there was plenty to do.

. . . Father Pitcher gave me more flax and I could sit and spin linen with my baby in my arms. Happy golden days! Precious, fleeting hours!

Ours was a home of peace and love. I never saw two brothers agree as Reuben and Daniel did. They lived together three years and then Daniel got married and built himself a log house. They still changed work with each other, and it was so pleasant to have neighbors so near! We built a log barn for our stock. We prospered in our work and we had land cleared so that we set quite a number of apple trees. The second spring I made 30 or 40 yards of cloth. The same mother wove it for me as before. Our neighbors were increasing in numbers.[4]

But the increase was coming on the fertile lands just west of the stony slopes of the Adirondacks. Nonetheless, in April of 1806 we have the first evidence that a family was again attempting to attract settlers to the John Brown's Tract. James B. Mason went to Sturbridge, Massachusetts, where he hired a Joseph Shaw to go to the Tract, repair the roads, bridges and buildings and serve as the family agent to attract settlers to what is now the Old Forge area.

James Mason's Turn

"The Mills, houses & other improvements you will use for the assistance and encouragement of the Settlers now going on with you. . . . Keep your mind steady to work, give them plenty of beef, pork bread & what vegetables you can procure—as little rum or spirits as possible, & no expense in other superfluities." And he instructed Shaw "not to expend more than $1200, including all the expenses of this undertaking."[5]

A separate "Memorandum of agreement" between Mason and Shaw went into more detail. It gave Shaw the use of the buildings at No. 7 "except the house where Solomon Clark now lives the Blacksmith Shop the workshop Near the Mills & the Saw Mill." He also got the use of "one pair of oxen, two cows, one cart & generally all the farming tools on the farm, as also some Articles of Household furniture now in the house an Inventory of all which he has this day given me." This last implies that Shaw had been on the Tract and came to Sturbridge to meet Mason. He was also instructed to visit James Sheldon in Remsen and collect any tools he might have "belonging to the late John Brown Esq."

Shaw is also to have use of the grist mill, keeping it in good order, and "the use of one eighth of the Saw Mill, he taking & always having the Mill keep in good order by himself and the settlers who are to have the use of the other 7/8 parts"

The agreement provided that Shaw would get "five dollars for each settler that may come on & settle permanently this Autumn or next Spring—An addendum says: "If people come on to view the land you must give them all the Assistance you can, in every way—& you may tell them if they like I will move on to my township & perform settlement duties next spring, they shall have fifty acres given them & what more they may want on the most reasonable terms, not to exceed two dollars per acre. The same terms will no doubt be given for all the other towns, except those of J. B. Francis & on his also I have no doubt in asuring the same encouragement."[6] This matter of Mason's visiting the Tract would be a frequent point of a contention between him and the settlers.

That same month there is some evidence that Charles Frederick Herreshoff was in some financial difficulty, for he signed over his "Peck farm" to James B. Mason, who agreed to return the farm once Herreshoff had returned what he owed. No figure is specified, however.[7]

In January of 1807, there is a promissory note from a Jeremiah Crosby to Mason that includes the receipt in Providence of "Twenty dollars . . . in Cash with which I am to move up Asa Leach's family to Browns tract. . . ."[8]

We can assume that, for whatever reason, the relationship between Mason and Shaw did not work out, for in June of 1807 we have a letter from Mason in which he attempts to persuade an Amasa Dow to move onto the Tract and serve as his agent, for which he will receive 120 acres of land. And he says that if the settlers "dont flinch, I will not desert them."

If Dow does move onto the Tract, "I am convinced it will be more to your Interest than any move ever you made – you will find those people who now are so backward will be firm eno. after you have made a beginning – I expect all these unpleasant circumstances, – but I have yet no doubt of the lands settling."[9] Already we are seeing a resemblance between Mason's letters and those written by his father-in-law to James Sheldon.

Dow clearly accepted the offer, for ten days later, Mason wrote, authorizing him to take possession of the house Shaw was living in and to take over operation of all the buildings. And, like John Brown, Mason urged "your exertions to have as much crop in the ground as possible, . . ." But unlike Brown, he offered a bonus: "I hereby Authorise you to Offer a bounty of One dollar & a half for every acre of Wheat & Corn & One dollar for every acre of Rye that shall be reaped by the Owner next Year."

Mason also sent $300 for provision for the settlers, including "Cows for the use of the families on the tract, also some lean Hogs & lean Cattle to turn into the woods to fatten, . . ."[10]

A month or so later, Asa Leach signed an unusual promissory note.

> *. . . Borrowed of Jas B Mason one Cow, brindle 4 years old – which he has loaned to me & which I promise to return to him or his order when called for Aug 31st 1807.*[11]

Toward the end of that year we have the first recorded sale of land on the Tract. Alice and James Mason sold 1,000 acres to Oliver Ingalls of Windham, Connecticut, for $2,000, reserving, however, the iron ore, mill seat and water works.[12] Although the Mason branch of the family was the first, some years later, to lose interest in the Tract, it was the most successful (although the success was certainly limited) in selling parcels to settlers. And at this stage Mason seemed very determined indeed, but that, of course, is the pattern – determination, strenuous efforts, and then, sooner or later, exhaustion and frustration.

His determination is evident in a letter (from which, unhappily, large sections have been torn) in which he instructed Dow to get a plow and a "pair of cattle for the use of Leach, Sizer & yourself together with the pair you now have you will take care that every person shall not want a team to get in all he has cleared, you will also be sure to provide plenty of seed, & in time, of all kinds — You may call on Sheldon for one pair of the cattle & if he will furnish at a fair price, I will discount the same on his note, also call on him for wheat if he will furnish — "[13] Evidently, Sheldon still owed the Brown estate some money.

Mason also spoke of promoting the settlement "by selling 5000 acres to several persons at 7/6 or 9/ (at 8 shillings to the dollar, that meant $1.00 to $1.13 an acre) & give them clear deed take mortgage back & take back all they cant sell at the same price at the end of from 6 to 10 years — " This, of course, made sense, but, to the best of our knowledge, Mason never got any such buyers.

He also wrote Dow that "If Moose river Bridge goes I shall open the road to the high falls (now Lyons Falls) — Clark says he will contract to open it & build the bridges clear thru for $200. I would give this — "

Mason also gave Dow bad news about a load of venison he sent to Providence:

> *I am sorry your venison does not answer better a great deal has been sent down & has been sold very low, a load came in the day before yours & nearly supplied this market . . . I have purchase of your venison 3 saddles 120^{lb} at 8/100 & I took the remainder of the hind parts that he could not sell at 6/100 . . . .*

Imagine nowadays venison at 6 and 8¢ a pound.

He ended his letter with a firm statement of determination, "You may depend that if God spares my life, — the settlement shall flourish — " His life was not spared, for James B. Mason died a mere dozen years later in his forty-fifth year.

In May of 1808 James and Alice Mason sold parcels to three potential settlers, a total of about 940 acres for $1,850, approximately $2.00 an acre.[14] We don't know how many settlers were actually on the Tract then, although there is reference to Asa Dow, Asa Leach, Lemuel Seiger, Henry Daniels and Jeremiah Crosby, in letters and promissory notes.[15]

In October, Benjamin Bowen of the Newport, Rhode Island, family, then living in Newport, New York, about forty miles south of the Tract, received $20 from Mason to purchase wool at Albany and deliver it to the families on the Tract.

Promissory notes toward the end of 1808 give a good idea of what costs were on the Tract. One cow cost $18, and another $17, while a 205-pound hog (whether slaughtered or alive is not clear, probably the latter) cost $10.25. Red flannel, useful indeed in Adirondack winters, was 60¢ a yard, while woolen cloth was about $1.25 yard. And on the last day of 1808, we first encounter a name that would be important on the Tract for some years—that of John Joy, Jr. "Value received Dec. 31 1808 in Cash advanced me for the promotion of my settlement on Brown Tract. I promise to pay to James B. Mason on order One Hundred & Twenty five Dollars on demand with Interest."[16] Joy was to serve as agent; we do not know if he was related to Major Abiathai Joy, who was later a prominent figure on the Tract.

The new year of 1809 had scarcely begun when Charles Frederick Herreshoff, who seemed plagued by bad business luck, had to pay out $5,608.56. It seems he had decided to go into the marine insurance business in Bristol, and one of the first vessels he insured, perhaps the very first, the *Truxton*, was lost.[17]

In February, Mason received one of those optimistic reports that was forever raising the hopes of the family. A man named French, who had received a letter from Joy, said that he "writes very favorably as it respects getting on the first twenty familes & seems to fear nothing but the failure of the road's being cut thro as we talked when I saw you last— . . . matters seem to go on swimmingly except your Mr. John Joy . . . has not yet returned to New York & I fear no good will come out of the thing if he should not return—"

French wrote that the bearer of the letter, Sam Whitney, had moved "into the house by the mills" and "wishes to be secured in his possession by you, & States his intention to remain on the Tract & is in hopes of some encouragement from you, ... this Mr. Whitney is the person that was employed to repair the Mills last fall by Mr. Bowen & from the charac[ter] given him by judge Bowen, I should think him a usefull man on the Tract. . . ."

In a postscript, French asks Mason to provide Whitney with money to purchase nail rods (from which nails are cut) and potash kettles, with Whitney to repay French by working on the road. Mason complied.[18]

The only information about the Tract that we have for the rest of that year is that Mason sent a half bushel of flaxseed each to Asa Leach and Jeremiah Crosby so they could produce flax from which linen and linsey-woolsey could be made.[19]

Almost a year passed before we have any further news. Benjamin Bowen wrote in March 1810 to James Mason:

I am requested by Franklin & Curtis Two of Your settlers under Major Joy that you would inform me weather Joy is to supply them with provisions this Spring to enable them to Get in a crop for themselves or weather they are to be at the call of Mr Joy to pay for provisions as they may want I am of opinion if you intend they ever doe any thing they ought to be at liberty this spring as it will be all important they get in grain for the suport of their families after which they may be able to assist Mr. Joy.[20]

A couple of months later Mason heard from a Thomas M. Palmer, who owned land near the Tract. ". . . I had occasion to pass over much of your tract, and contemplate a Road from Thence to my Land." Having heard that Mason planned to visit in June, Palmer proposed a meeting "when some plan might be arranged which will eventually be of advantage to both parties — Allow me to add that your visit is looked forward to with the greatest anxiety by your settlers —"[21]

This would be a constant theme in the coming months — the settlers felt abandoned by Mason.

The short Adirondack summer was coming to a close when Mason again heard from Palmer, who had taken up residence on the Tract, presumably at the settlement near the present-day Old Forge. His letter demonstrates that situation on the Tract was not very good.

. . . I take the liberty of troubling you with a second letter to request you will inform me if it is your intention to visit your Tract this present season — If not, I wish to propose to you to take the Mill Farm & Mills for three or five years as may be agreed upon — By permission of Major Joye [sic] *I am at present in possession, but as They are very much out of repair, indeed, so much so, as to render them useless for the ensuing season unless the necessary repairs are made, which he does not seem inclined to undertake. And not having the pleasure of your acquaintance I am adverse to doing anything myself without your authority — I shall therefore be obliged to you to signify your wishes upon the subject —*

He said there were other things he wanted to discuss, but that he would wait in the hope that he would be able to discuss them with Mason in person.

. . . On my arrival here I found the Road from Remsen to the Settlement Totally blocked up by fallen Trees — The settlers were unable to clear it, and were suffering very much in consequence — Major Joye [sic] *declined having it done — They applied to me, in consequence I undertook to have it cleared from Remsen to the Beaver Meadow, which has been done for 15 Dollars — Mr. Gould with the people from hence turned out and have cleared from the Beaver Meadow to the settlement so that the Road is now well open, which before was all but impassable. — If you think I have done right you will I have no doubt permit me to look to you for the repayment of the fifteen Dollars.*

I found the Buildings on your Farm in sad order, I have done what the short time I have been here would allow me, to put the Barns etc. in a good shape, but much is still necessary to be done, I hope however in a little time to make it have another appearance.[22]

The very next day, August 14, 1810, John Brown Francis, the third generation to visit the Tract, wrote a business letter from Utica, in which he said, "I shall remain in the Black river country till the latter part of Sept -"[23] He was only 19. John Brown's favorite grandchild would make several visits more to a Tract that would often preoccupy him for another four decades. But what he did on this first visit, we simply don't know. It is safe to assume, however, that he visited Palmer and, during that month or so, familiarized himself with the vast estate that would so trouble him for so many years.

About this time our old friend Thomas Willing Francis, uncle of young John, reappeared briefly. Although he wrote not about the John Brown's Tract but about a piece of land he owned, his observation is one that two succeeding generations of John Brown's descendants must have often wished he had heeded. Himself stuck with an expensive piece of property, Tom Francis wrote, ". . . I perceive tho' rather too late for my interest – that a man should only possess property which lies within the sphere of his own controul. –"[24] But on the John Brown's Tract, while absence insured failure, presence, as we shall sadly see with Charles Frederick Herreshoff, did not insure success.

In November, Palmer wrote two very long, and very candid, letters to Mason. In the first he regretted not having received authorization earlier to repair the mills, for it would have been much easier a month earlier "when the waters were never known to be so low" but now "the heavy rains within this last Week will make it a more difficult undertaking. . . ."

. . . It will I am sure be some satisfaction to you to know the crops here have been generally very good, much better than I had thought possible, and I am sure that industry & prudence combined, would insure to the settlers a good support, but the latter has been much wanting, with some of them, and indeed some deficiency in the former, but altho I say this, I do not attribute so much blame to the parties as I should have done, under other circumstances – They have been full of the expectation of seeing you on the Tract, but that not being the case, and not hearing from you, they suppose themselves forgotten, and grew dispirited. Indeed I was fearful that with the exception of Mr Gould's and Clarke's families, the whole would have abandoned.

James Mason's Turn

Palmer added that "I hope as soon as your health is reestablished you will pay us a visit, upon which be assured the settlement of your land alone depends." One is reminded of the old French proverb: The best fertizilier is the owner's footprints.

Palmer also reported that the people in and near Remsen appeared "particularly hostile to the success of this place" and that only Mason's presence would remove the hostility. He added that Gould's crops "by the industry of himself and Boys" were in good order and that Clarke had also done well with crops, "but his want of health will probably very much impede, if not totally prevent his future progress.'[25]

Just five days later Palmer wrote again, saying he had received a September letter from Mason and would do all he could to repair the property. He said he had been on the Tract since July 7, having taken possession of the farm left by a tenant. With Major Joy's permission, he was to pay the same rent which he did on October 4, paying $25 in produce. By the following summer he expected to have eight or nine acres in grain, plus corn and potatoes and other crops. "And I hope in one Year to have the whole Farm in very different order to what you have ever yet seen it."

Palmer also estimated it would take $200 to repair the mills. He also had plans for a road from No. 6 to his property adjoining it on the northeast that he hoped would join a road from Johnstown to St. Lawrence. This needed discussion, which he hoped would take place on the Tract "or should you wish it or that you continue unwell I will upon your answer make a Journey to Providence—"

He continued with the fullest description we have encountered of the state of the settlement in this early period.

> *. . . When I arrived here, I found six families—their crops generally looking well and the people appeared to be trying to get on—In fact they existed themselves very much in the hope you would see what they had done—After a time however, finding you did not come, and not hearing from you, they grew dispirited and I really feared a general abandonment of the Tract—Two Families have quitted, but I hope the Letter I have received from you will stop the panic—You may be assured I will do all in my power—But indeed Sir, if you are anxious that the settlement should progress, it is absolutely necessary that your sentiments should be known, in order to do away the present prevalent opinion that you are indifferent about it—Establish this and the settlers will not be wanting—*

Palmer then reported on the stock he found at the settlement: "3 yoke of Oxen, three Cows and about 20 Sheep, all in good order, except one Cow which I think will not get thro' the Winter—"

. . . Gould has one Yoke, Clarke another, the Third was in the case of the Families which have gone off – The remaining settlers do not want or rather cannot keep the Oxen, if you choose it, I will buy them at 55 Drs which Gould & Majr Joy think their full value, be good enough to mention this in your next – Clarke has a Cow, a Bull & a good stock of Hogs – Gould also has a Cow and some good Hogs, the others have little to boast of & want help – My opinion of the Land is that it wants nothing but industry to make it produce every necessary, The Crops have all been generally good, some of them abundant for the Quantity sown, particularly, Oats, Pease & Potatoes – Clarke has cleared 13 Acres since you were here – Gould has nearly 20 Acres cleared in all – The Leach Farm is much as when you saw it – On the Crosbie Farm there has been about 4 Acres cleared in addition to what you saw, & about the same quantity on the Gibbs Lot – Some other small choppings have been made but nothing of consequence – There is nothing to prevent the settlement from increasing, and that rapidly, if people knew your sentiments and the Road from Remsen (or the Grant) here was made good, with a House at the Beaver Meadow, another at Moose River, and an active Agent on the spot, ready & desirous of carrying your plans into execution – Upon all this I wish much to see you & shall not hesitate going to Providence if you wish it – From the best information I can collect there has been raised about 70 Bushels of Wheat & about 60 of Rye – the Corn was unfortunately almost totally destroyed by the frost in July which I find to have been general –[26]

Unhappily, the rest of the letter disappeared. Nonetheless, it is invaluable, for it provides more information about the John Brown's Tract, than has heretofore been discovered. Thus, for the first time in a century or more, we know how many families were on the Tract, who they were, what status their farms were in, and what livestock they had. Perhaps even more important, we now know their state of mind. The importance, therefore, of this account cannot be overstated.

We should note that whoever of the Brown family took the initiative at any given time, he concerned himself with the entire Tract and not just the portion under his control. Thus, Mason, who owned No. 6 and sold several parcels there, devoted most of his efforts to the Settlement at No. 7, the Old Forge area, recognizing that, until one settlement on the Tract prospered it would be difficult to sell land elsewhere on it.

A couple of weeks later Palmer indeed set to work repairing the mills, for Bowen advanced him $30 and some materials for the project. Bowen also notified Mason that Palmer would soon leave the Tract "to return to Duchist (Dutchess) County & N York from which if he does not Receive a Line from You – he intends seeing You before he Returns to Your Land in the Spring."[27]

The year 1811 was crucial to the John Brown's Tract in many respects:

the relationship between Palmer and Mason, which now, all these years later seemed so promising, came to an unhappy end; Robert Fulton, made a brief appearance on the Tract, leaving his name on the beautiful chain of lakes that begin at Old Forge; and Charles Frederick Herreshoff, along with his nephew John Brown Francis came to the Tract beginning a tragic episode that still has the power to move readers of his lovely, often melancholy letters.

Early in February, Palmer wrote another of his gracious and informative letters to Mason, in response to one in which Mason plainly said he would visit the Tract in the spring when, presumably, he would have gained his health. He reported that the mills "with much labour & difficulty put in good repair . . ." and that he had to hire workers from other settlements because there were so few men on the Tract.

Palmer also recalled his last letter, in which he had explained "that with the exception of Gould's & Clarke's families, all had quitted the Tract, the latter of these is from his misfortunes prevented doing any thing, therefore all the assistance I could get on the Tract was from Gould which he has readily and industriously contributed – He has hauled all the Logs for the Works, and has been very exact in performing it by the time limited – "

He wrote that he had given up the idea of going to Providence, since Mason said he was coming to the Tract. He also reported that "Some of the old Causeways & Bridges are so much out of repair as to make it dangerous to pass them. These for the present Must be rendered passable to keep up the communication and for the Transport of some families who are now preparing to come in – "

. . . *Have taken care to communicate your message to Gould who appears in consequence to have become another Being – Poor Clarke is in a miserable state, his expenses & his wants are great, if you will authorize me or any other person to contribute a small sum to his relief it never can be better timed, as I am apprehensive there is no cure for his malady.*

Palmer closes by establishing that he is well connected:

. . . *If you should pass through Albany or have occasion to write there before the breakup of the Legislature – Governor Lewis near whom I have lived some time I can venture to refer you to, or his Brother in Law Jno Th. Livingston – I am connected with some of the first families in that County – My Daughter has married Maj^r Prevost of Stratsburg* [N. Y.], *and I trust our future transaction will be mutually beneficial.*[28]

The next day Palmer signed an agreement with two Indians, Hamal Bagoagona and Jacob Miscoabimis, to pay them $50 for showing him a mine "which they firmly believe to abound with lead and a portion of silver, they also solemnly engage not to disclose the matter or enter into any treaty with any other person than the beforementioned Thos. M. Palmer." The agreement provided for an additional 1,000 dollars "only to be paid in case the future profits arising from the works makes the proprietor or/Proprietors such returns as might fully enable them to complete the agreement –" The purported mine was supposedly "situated near a Tract of Land known by the name of Brown's Tract in the Northern part of the State of New York."[29] That anything came of this is doubtful. Nonetheless, Palmer reported the agreement to Mason.

> . . . *Circumstances have . . . occured which lead me positively to think the discovery of a Lead Mine on your Tract will lead to infinite future advantage. The testimony I have received and the exhibition of the Ore which I have sent to Albany to ascertain the proportion of Lead has induced me to enter into an engagement of which I now send you a Copy, and I was the more induced to do so from finding other persons endeavoring to procure the information with certainly no other view than to enable them to make a good bargain with you –* [30]

The following month Palmer again urged work on the roads and wrote that the storekeeper and taverner on the route to the Tract would "contribute toward the Road *in works*, . . ." Plainly, they thought that development on the Tract would improve their businesses. And again, Palmer expressed the hope that Mason's health would permit an early visit.[31]

In May of 1811, Palmer, whose earlier letters have been gracious and cordial, wrote crossly to Mason. The letter speaks for itself.

> . . . *Mr Cunningham has this day informed me of your refusal of my draft for 250 Drs in his favor – In consequence I have made a statement of the account between us which I now inclose, by it you will observe a Balance in my favor of 210 Drs 60 Cents, which has arisen by executing the Directions you have given in your several Letters – From this state of the account, and your desiring me to make occasional advance to Clark I thought myself Justified in drawing upon you for the sum I did.*
>
> *In this account you will also see I have not noticed any of the responsibilities I have entered into for Clarke* [particularly to his Physician] *and respecting which I wrote you in my last – It will I am sure also not escape your notice that I have not made any charge for the time I have been employed in executing your directions, or for the trouble I have had in transporting the several supplies necessary for the Works, and the people who were employed in it –*

From a thorough conviction in my own mind that I have done all in my power to execute the several directions I have received, and not being able to advance the Money, I have again requested Mr Cunningham to forward a second draft for the same amount, which I have no doubt upon the receipt of the present account you will honor immediately—I have Vouchers for every Shilling I have paid which shall be delivered to you upon your arrival here which I am glad to learn will certainly be in the course of next Month—I shall forbear saying any thing further upon this subject, more than to request your immediate reply in order that I might as early as possible be released from the disagreeable, indeed disgraceful situation I am at present placed in—

Since I wrote you last I have been with the Indians to the Mine, which is evidently upon your Land, & I believe on the 8th Township. Samples of the Ore which appears good I have sent to Fairfield Academy to ascertain its properties and I hope by the time you arrive to be in possession of full information respecting it—[32]

The itemized account that Palmer enclosed totalled $246. Since we have only one side of the correspondence, it is difficult a century and three-quarters later to make a confident judgment, but it is difficult not to be persuaded that in Palmer the Brown family had found an exceptional steward, one that, given the circumstances, they could ill afford to lose. But however it ended, end it apparently did in mid-1811, for the last letter we have is dated July 27. It is solemn, even sorrowful in tone.

. . . Upon my arrival . . . today I have been afforded the opportuity of forwarding you a small sample of the Ore found on your Land, and at the same time to acknowledge the receipt of your Letter of the 15th May last—I had long before this expected the pleasure of seeing you here, and to say barely that I have been disappointed would be far short of the truth—For three Months past I have felt myself in consequence of your suspicions in a most unpleasant situation—And conscious of the rectitude of my intentions in every point in which I have been concerned for you I have looked forward most anxiously to the period pointed out for your arrival.—As every thing I hold dear points out to me the necessity of a clear & full explanation of my conduct I request you will inform me as early as possible whether we are able to expect you on the Tract—If not, it is a duty I owe myself that the business should be elucidated without further delay, and I am sure you will be as ready to do me justice as your informants have maliciously endeavored to ruin me in your opinion—I therefore request your early reply . . . .

Palmer added this doleful postscript:

. . . Clarke is alive, and that is all which can be said, he is reduced to a perfect shadow, and his countenance is become ghastly—There never was a greater sufferer and it will be a happiness when he is released—The crops upon the Tract are abundant, as far as our strength could admit of cultivation.[33]

With those words, Palmer largely vanishes from our narrative, another demonstration of the difficulty of attempting to develop a wilderness at long range, with the proprietor forced to make decisions with wholly inadequate information, entirely dependent on the skill and good will of his informants.

Just as Thomas Palmer leaves our narrative, Robert Fulton, known to every school child as the inventor of the steamboat, briefly enters it. In 1811 the New York legislature established a commission to study the possibility of a waterway between the Hudson River and the Great Lakes, a dream long held by visionaries. Fulton was appointed to the commission, and he visited the Old Forge area, where a lovely chain of eight lakes begins, a natural waterway that Indians had used for centuries. Although he saw the difficulties—why build canals through mountainous country when it is possible to by-pass it—he was enthusiastic about the beauty of the lakes and, in due course, they were given his name—The Fulton Chain.[34] They and the other lakes, and the serenity of the scented forests, turned out, in the long run, to be the most valuable resources of the John Brown's Tract, not the soil, not the minerals, not the timber.

It was nature itself, as a refuge from the tensions and ugliness of industrial society, that would one day bring prosperity to the entire Adirondacks, including the Tract. But that never occurred to the next, and the most tragic, major player in our story—Charles Frederick Herreshoff.

9

Tragedy on the Tract

I will settle the tract or settle myself.[1]
Charles Frederick Herreshoff

TO SAILING YACHTSMEN the world over, the name Herreshoff is legendary because, for generation after generation, it has meant excellence in the design, construction, and navigation of sailboats. Yet, of the many for whom the name Herreshoff is part of the basic yachting vocabulary, few indeed know that the man who brought that name to the United States two centuries ago died a lonely death far from the sea in the vast and icy solitude of the John Brown's Tract, about which he uttered the prophetic words with which we introduced this most tragic chapter in our narrative.

Why Herreshoff went to the Tract is not certain. Donaldson wrote, and it has been echoed and re-echoed in book after book, that John Brown's legacy to his wife Sarah was dwindling and that Herreshoff went to try to restore the family fortune. That may be so. We have encountered no evidence that would disprove that, nor any evidence that would prove it, either. Nor have we discovered any evidence – the sale of lands by Sally Brown, for instance – that would indicate the family was in any want. Lacking any specific evidence, we assume that the simplest is the most likely reason: John Brown had faith in the Tract, as did his son-in-law James B. Mason. When the latter, for whatever reason, ceased his active interest in the land, it was natural for others in the family to look into the situation.

That is exactly what Herreshoff did in September of 1811, taking with him his nephew John Brown Francis, an entirely reasonable course since Francis, then 20, was the heir to four of the eight townships.

Herreshoff, of course, wrote to his beloved Sally, reporting that "We passed five whole days on the tract very pleasantly; if it was only peopled it would be one of the finest & healthiest counties in the world, and there is every possible reason to believe that there is nothing but roads wanting, to see it settled very rapidly indeed."

Herreshoff, like John Brown and James Mason before him, was captivated by the Tract. That is easy to understand. It, hardly at all changed from then, is still very beautiful, there is plenty of water and wood (for building and burning) and the air is absolutely wonderful, tonic in its effect. Not yet aware of the grudging soil and the short, sometimes prohibitively short, growing season, Herreshoff and young Francis saw no reason to doubt the Tract's promise.

Although Charles Frederick and Sally had been married ten years, he was as romantic as ever, "I remembered you on the 5th inst. (her birthday): we were then on the tract and went to see a very remarkably fine spring on a large Beaver meadow, from which I drank your health out of my hand; . . ."

Unfortunately, Herreshoff did not say who guided them around the Tract or anything about the state of the settlement. Indeed, much of letter is about young John. "John is growing fat, but ever since his disappointment at Utica he is cross and morose." Evidently, John was used, whenever he was away from home, to be showered with letters from his mother Abby, but there was, for whatever reason, no mail awaiting him at Utica. ". . . a number of his friends had also promised to write him to Utica, which increased his astonishment on finding not one single letter; but it will be a good lesson to him not to depend upon promises; and to teach him that even he may be neglected." One gathers that young John, spoiled by his late grandfather, continued so as the only surviving child of three.

In this first Herreshoff letter about the Tract, there is one final final mention of it. ". . . we have seen many a beautiful village and a great deal of most excellent land, we have however found none so healthy, as by all appearances our tract, and no where had we seen such water, while all those rich tracts through which we passed to the westward were parching, their brooks and springs dried up, our horse even suffered sometimes for want of a mud puddle."[2]

But while Herreshoff said little about the Tract, his 20-year-old nephew reported much of value in a letter to another uncle, Thomas Willing Francis. He passed on the discouraging news that although his grandfather had spent $25,000 in roads and mills and his family "have since added to that" only "one *real* settler is on the tract."

Tragedy on the Tract

This enormous expenditure has had no other effect than to create the false belief in the minds of people that the land is worth our money [but] *has been unthinkingly squandered. A good road must be made, no settlement will succeed, were the land as rich as that of the German flats on the Mohawk even the Genesee without a road, passable at least for waggons. Our land is indeed not so luxurious rich as the Genesee but the fever & ague will never rage there & the inhabitants will always find an abundance of the purest water.*

Without realizing it, young Francis had noted what would one day make the Adirondacks a celebrated resort: its wonderful air and water. He described the land:

We tarried *there one week & explored the country as much as was consistent with our strength. We found it broken & uneven but not mountainous, extremely well watered, the timber prime Beach, maple, & hemlock all exceedingly high and large. We saw no open spots some places rough but none free from trees excepting the meadows which were occasioned by the dams of the Beavers. They exhibit astonishing traces of the talent & industry of these wonderful little animals. They are as level as your Valley Forge & the wild grass grows very high & thick. They are generally near some lake or pond, or a stream runs through them.*

But contrasted with this idyllic description of the great resort area-to-be was Francis' account of the state of John Brown's improvements of twelve years earlier. Writing of the bridge over the Black River "constructed by my grandfather," he said, "it is weak & tottering, too much so for use."

. . . The road from here was also made by him; it was never good & it is inaccessible, large trees have blown over, bushes & branches have grown up, causeways gone to decay & bridges swept off or broken down. The path crooked & the branches of the lofty trees obstruct the rays of the sun. We were often obliged to dismount & lead our horses round the prostrate trees or compel them to jump over. The fatigue was such as cannot be expressed, in fourteen hours we reached the destined goal! Having seen nothing like the abode of civilized man, nothing but one continued forest.[3]

Plainly, despite John Brown Francis' description, Herreshoff was taken by the Tract, for he journeyed there again the following April, quickly followed by a letter from his nephew.

Uncle Mason & myself agreeably surprised to hear of your intended departure altho you have previously declared your intentions . . . I feel very curious to know the history of your adventures? how you found poor Gould & his family together with his coadjutor *Col Palmer & other Expectants. What new lights you have gained of the course of our projected road of the expediency of commencing & If you really concluded to make contracts before returning in June, I hope that you will first secure all necessary intelligence all the experience of the Country & that then no bargin be entered into without an exertion of your wonted sagacity. Repose confidence in none but such as have been tried and found faithful. Believe with the celebrated Parson Whitfield that nearly one half of mankind are fools & the remainder knaves, Let your schemes be founded on the principle & disappointment will not be the result. You will smile at receiving from a youngster like myself such skeptical misanthropical opinions but experience fatal experience will prove their soundness.*

Francis was not yet twenty-one, but his soundness was already apparent. Later in that letter he asked his uncle to send "a detailed account not only of affairs relating to the proprietors in general of the Tract, but concerning the contemplated Sheep Speculation; the scheme which you handed me I shall take with me & investigate in more closely *hereafter at my leisure.*"

He had reason to investigate it more closely because many sheep had died on the Herreshoff (really the Brown) farm at Bristol.

. . . dead Bodies seemed to be strewn in every direction at Poppasquash. The earth was literally shrouded in wool. Is this infection caught from the Merinos? are they generally affected with cutaneous disorders on arrival in this Country, or does it arise from our ignorance of the mode of treatment of large flocks? we had better investigate the secret cause if possible & not plunge heedlessly into the unexplored oceans of experiments.[4]

Although Francis suggested in his letter that his uncle would return in June, only a couple of months away, Herreshoff, in fact, was to remain on the Tract until November when, with the onset of winter, he returned to Bristol. How different his life was becoming from all that he expressed in those moving letters of earlier years in which he said he would never be parted from his beloved Sally. Herreshoff was becoming obsessed, perhaps even possessed, by the John Brown's Tract.

During Herreshoff's final seven years, his correspondence from the Tract was sporadic, but many of the most moving letters were exchanged by him and his eldest child Anna. (Although her name was Anna, she and others often used the name Anne.) The first one we have from her is dated August 25, 1812, when she was but ten. She referred to Aaron (Thresher), plainly a hand on the farm, who was about "ready to take his departure for your part of the world where I hope he will find you in good health."

His daughter wrote that they all wanted him "home on every account but particularly on account of our apples as we have reason to fear we shall not have an apple left to ripen in the Trees,

The Bristol people take the same liberty in the Orchards that they did with the Cherry trees and would you think it, in Cherry time I saw two men with their horses stop and take your hay out of the Barn to feed them whilst they ate Cherries. I know you will wish to hear something of your dear little Frederick he is very good at all other times but when he is at his meals then he wants his dear Papa to Doctor him from your Affectionate little Daughter—

Anne F. Herreshoff [5]

To which her mother added a rather bleak postscript. She reported that the children's penmanship had not improved "since you left us for a very good reason they have not taken a pen in hand but when they have written you." She wrote that "I cannot perceive that they improve in any thing at School" and that actually "John's aversion to his Book appears to increase. . . . As to every thing relative to farming etc you will hear from Aaron your next I hope will inform me when you think of returning. Some times I think of great deal to say to you, but at present I am not in disposition for writing.

It does not appear that the long separation was without effect on the Herreshoff family, children and mother.

Charles Frederick responded on September 27 to the letter given him on the 9th by Thresher, who arrived accompanied by Jarvis Mason, from Cummington Village, Massachusetts, a hired hand.

. . . *This will be handed to you by our Cousin John* [John Brown Francis] who is preparing to leave this in the morning. He has stood it out like a brave fellow, but now I can no longer hold him, I should have wished him to prolong his stay, for I shall feel rather dejected after he is gone; . . . *I have therefore nothing interesting to say but to confirm that I continue in good health and though not sick of the wilderness am very impatient to see home again. . . .*

He expressed concern at his son John's lack of interest in his studies. "I am told that the little boys in the Fairfield Academy study very hard and are very forward in reading & writing. I shall feel mortified to see him so far behind them when I carry him there next Spring; if he does not wish to be laughed at and called the Pappasquash dunce by those little rogues, he must be very diligent & try to make up for lost time. . ."

Although most of the information about the settlement is to be carried by his nephew, the letter does have something of interest:

. . . *How glad I would feel if I could accompany John tomorrow but it is quite impossible; it is only 4 weeks since I have been able to obtain a mill wright and with all our exertions we are now only so far advanced in the repairs of the mills, that everything is put down and every thing to be put up again. The materials however are for the now in readiness and as soon as the dam only is standing again I expect we will make rapid progress. Toward the end of next month I calulate certainly to be at home. Aaron went off this morning on a Sheep cruize* [to purchase sheep] *from which I expect him back the latter end of this week; He will however make one or two more & may not set off for good till about the middle of next month. We had the first frost here on the 20th inst since which the weather has been pleasant but of a different temperature. Jarvis will stay here this winter to draw logs for the Saw Mill & take care of the sheep.*

Herreshoff closed the letter with detailed instructions on how the tulip and hyacinth bulbs should be planted and says "you may safely write one more after you receive this. Your last letter came here in 6 days from Warren."[6]

He did not succeed in leaving the Tract until the middle of November, at which time he wrote to Sally from Utica.

. . . You see my dear Sally that I have at least made my escape from the wilderness though still very far from you. I have already been several days in this muddy village where I intended to stay only 2 or 3 days and expecting Capt Gould from the tract, to carry back a couple of Merinos; not being able to find any body here to trust them with. I could of course not expect to hear from you after telling you that I should be at home the end of last month but I feel not the less anxious and cannot help feeling dejected in spite of reason every night on the arrival of the mail without tidings from my dear wife and children. Everything is attended with so much difficulty in a situation like that of our settlement so far remote and of so tedious an access that it is impossible to make any correct calculation as to time, nor any thing else; it takes a week often what I calculate to achieve in a day and I have especially towards the last had my hands full of trouble. I intend traveling on horseback from here to Albany as I cannot dispose of my horse here without too much loss. Besides the roads are so horrible that people are afraid to trust the stage unless absolutely compelled. I hope I shall get rid of my [horse] *Buciphal at Albany and then take the steamboat.*[7]

Although it is not possible to know exactly what Herreshoff accomplished in his first prolonged stay on the Tract, certain information is available for his accounts which, happily, have been preserved. We know, for instance, approximately how much he spent. For board for himself and workmen, occasionally as many as 13 but usually less, he paid at least $814 to Captain Gould through October 25. Subtracting what he owed for an earlier period, $43.00, that means Herreshoff had 771 man-days during the months of August, September, and October, something like 128 man-weeks of work, a considerable amount. How many men he had working for him in May, June, and July we do not know. Clearly, however, the work force was big enough, even discounting the difficulties of working in the wilderness, to accomplish a good deal.

His other expenses, of course, included wages (say, something on the order of $1,000 at a dollar a day or less) and supplies. We have a record of his having paid $810 to Joseph & Levy Ballou of Utica. And we have records of smaller amounts to other purveyors. So it is safe to assume that Herreshoff spent at least $3,000 for that first summer and fall.[8]

From these old account books, we are able to determine exactly what he paid for some supplies. Whiskey, an important item for men stuck in the deep woods with little to do after hours, then cost 16¢ a quart. More important, potatoes cost 50¢ a bushel, pork 10¢ a pound, and rye bread 3¢ a pound. The diet was terribly monotonous. From one purveyor all that was bought was pork, bread, potatoes and whiskey. From another, coffee and brown sugar was purchased. Presumably, the monotony was slightly broken by milk from the farmer or two still on the Tract, some vegetables and, most likely, venison.

As to other expenses, we see that a scythe cost $1.25, cloth was 35¢ a yard, iron spoons six for 75¢, and a yoke of oxen cost $70, but whether that was to purchase or rent is not specified. Often, all these years after the Revolution, prices were quoted in shillings.

What he did accomplish, we cannot know for sure, but we know from the account books that some of the labor was devoted to road work. Quite possibly—for we do know that the work was accomplished early in his years on the Tract—it was to start building a road from the Old Forge area to the tannery village of Moose River, just outside the Tract, and thence to Boonville. That road, other than the personal legend, was almost certainly Herreshoff's and John Brown Francis' legacy, for it served as the main western gateway to the Adirondacks until 1892, when the railroad came up north from Utica and then cut eastward into the mountains.

Also, within the first few years, Herreshoff built a fine home for himself, a two-story, six-room manse at what is now Thendara, a couple of miles from Old Forge. This handsome dwelling stood for about 80 years, used for a time by the Arnold family as an inn, and eventually abandoned to the elements. He also cleared some land, repaired some of the old structures and built a few new ones, and put in some crops.

Although we don't know the exact date, there is a nice story about Herreshoff. It seems he was at what is now called Fourth Lake, the easternmost lake of the Fulton Chain within the John Brown's Tract. He was there one September with some men to pick some good pine timber. He went ashore on Bear Island and, in lighting his pipe, somehow set the dry brush

The Arnold family at Herreshoff Manor near Old Forge circa 1869.

afire. A stiff breeze fanned the flames and Herreshoff, to escape, climbed out on a branch hanging over the water. As the flames reached out toward him, he threw himself into the icy lake and called for help. "When at last he was rescued by his companions, Herreshoff was half-drowned, half-frozen, and shivered for hours."[9]

The War of 1812 did not affect the John Brown's Tract much, even though there was a constant threat of invasion from Canada, not many miles north. But there was little on the Tract to interest anyone other than the Brown family. Some military roads were constructed north and south, just east of the Tract, and they remained passable for some years, but had virtually no influence on settlement on the Tract.

In 1813 the first gazeteer of New York State was published by Horatio Gates Spafford, who traversed the entire state gathering material. He noted that the mountains now called the Adirondacks were then called the Peruvian and he speaks of the northern part of Herkimer County

with vast forests of evergreens, pine, spruce, hemlock and fir, characterize its mountain temperature, and a cold sterile soil. But, when I penetrated the northern wilds of this country, while collecting the materials for this work, I may have judged too hastily, and perhaps unfavorably, though of the mountain character, and its influence on the climate I cannot be mistaken. In a country wholly wild, however zealously bent on precise examination, the traveler, in time, ceases to examine mole-hills, till he have found a breakfast.[10]

Spafford did not judge too hastily.

Those forests would seem to suggest timbering, and indeed, in 1813 a timbering industry did begin to grow in the Adirondacks until, some years later, it was rapaciously stripping the land.[11] But on the far western side of the Adirondacks, there was an insufficient market for timber and no convenient way to get the wood to more distant markets.

In the spring Herreshoff again journeyed to the Tract. About all we have for that year is a letter from Sally to her nephew John Brown Francis. Prophetically, she writes, ". . . of his success, I have only gloomy presages."[12]

One interesting tidbit survives for that year. James Brown was up on the Tract in September, presumably visiting his brother-in-law. For some reason – maybe it was a commentary on the wildness of the Tract – James was conscious of his mortality and drafted a will.

. . . I James Brown of Providence, State of Rhode Island, being on a Journey and uncertain of the continuance of my existence on this Earth, Do hereby declare that in case of any Accident that may prevent my return to my native Home, that tis my desire that after my Death and all the just Debts due by me shall be Paid, that my Property may be divided in the following manner. In the first place I do hereby give and bequeath to my Nephew John Brown Herreschoff, provided he shall take the name of John Herreschoff Brown, the Mansion House in which my late honored Father expired when he may or shall have arrived at the age of Twenty one years – To each of my other Nephews & Nices, children of my sisters, I do give and bequeath an equal share of my property . . . .[13]

James obviously was conscious of the fact that the Brown name of his branch of the family would expire with him. Even if his suggestion had come to pass, it would have done no good for his nephew also died unmarried. Notice that James spelled Herreshoff in the old style, hardly surprising, since the name was spelled in many ways in letters and documents of the time.

We hear nothing else from the Tract until the following spring, when Herreshoff again returned. In May 1814 he wrote to his most faithful correspondent, his daughter Anne. It was a chatty and informative letter.

. . . I arrived here on the 29th ult. since which we have remarkable fine & some very hot weather some days last week the thermometer was above 80°. Vegetation

is very forward the trees are as green as they were on the 20th May last year if not more so. Our grain sowed last fall looks very fine & promises a great crop. We are now very busy sowing and planting; we shall begin planting corn the day after tomorrow. I found the people on the tract in very good health except Mrs Joy and Mr Slocum. The former has a sore finger which is very painful and makes her unfit for any business. Mr Slocum returned unwell from a journey to Albany beginning of March and has been sick with a swelling in his throat ever since; his friends were afraid it would terminate fatally but he is now nearly recovered and is beginning to work. Owing to his sickness there has not been so much sugar made this Spring as they calculated upon; there has been however one thousand pounds manufactured in all.

Herreshoff then explained to his daughter that traveling to the Tract was now much easier.

. . . We have now two Taverns established on the road between this and Remsen; one 6 miles from here on a very pleasant hill near the Moose River run by a Mr Weeks and his two sons; the other 11 miles this side of Remsen of 19 miles from here kept by a Mr. Hale who has a wife and three children with him. The land lady is an uncommon smart & industrious woman but he is a drinker. These two houses make the journey through the woods a great deal easier though the accomodations are not very elegant. We have had the misfortune of losing one of our bridges in the great freshet which happened this Spring, the one over the Moose River 6 miles from here and the largest of all. We now cross the river in a scow, and I do not contemplate building a new bridge this season.[14]

Nearly a month later he wrote to his daughter Sarah, then eleven, acknowledging the receipt of a number of letters from his wife and daughters.

. . . We are going on pretty smoothly so far with our operations this year, and thus far we have had a fine growing and pleasant season. I do not know that I ever saw a finer month of May and it was such a one as I did not expect in this part of the country; it was a real summer month, and everything is much more forward that it was last year. The grass near Capt. Gould's house is up to my knees; our rye is earing out and looks very promising. We have about five acres of corn which we shall hoe for the first time next week. Twelve of my plum trees which I planted last year bore blossoms; they are too small yet to have fruit but we may have some next year. Capt. Gould has set a little orchard of apple trees, about 70. Next year we shall have a great many to transplant.

Herreshoff then discussed some of the people living on the Tract.

. . . All the people seem happy, we have no malcontents there this season, and they are all well, except Jarvis Mason, who had a jaw bone injury the other day, pulling out a tooth, which gives him some pain, and makes him unfit for work.

Tragedy on the Tract

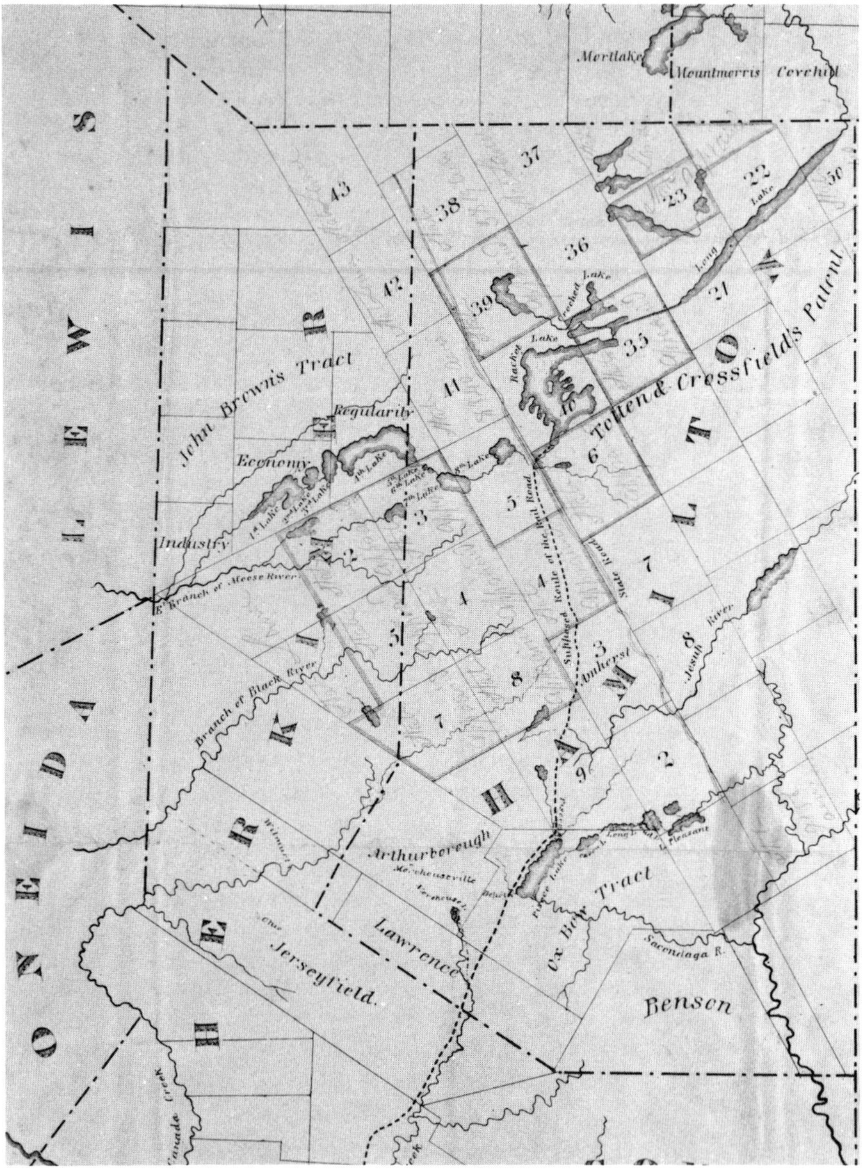

Portion of map of Herkimer and Hamilton Counties published by Miller's Lithography circa 1850 showing John Brown's Tract, with annotations attributed to John Brown Francis.

He is going out tomorrow to recruit; I think he will go home to Cummington and will most likely stay there until Aaron comes this way, for his constitution appears to me rather shattered, and not able to bear much fatigue in hot weather. We have an accession of a very clever family, a Mr Thomas who moved out here with his wife and five children; the oldest a girl about 15, the youngest an infant 6 weeks old. They came on an ox cart without accident or much fatigue, for you know we have two taverns on the road.

Father then reported to daughter the arrival of Casper Meier, who would be his partner in the Brown's Tract venture. He arrived in the company of Mr. Ballou just as the carpenters were finishing "my new room in Capt. Gould's outhouse and were carrying out their tools to let the girls come in with the broom."

. . . *In an hour after two beds were fixed up; the rest of my furniture consisting in a handsome table made of cherry wood, and two small benches. The room is 18 feet square, has three windows and three doors but not yet plastered. On Sunday following we went to the lake not so much for fishing as to see the country, but a dark thunder cloud threatening to overtake us we stopped at the end of the first lake on the island, when presently we saw a fishing party in a skiff coming towards us, they had about 50 lb of excellent trout, the largest weighing 6½ lb, we then clubbed together and had an excellent chowder. After dinner we went as far as the end of the third lake and then returned. Mosquitos and flies are very troublesome this year; those excepted Mr Meier was pleased with the country, and found it very different from the description he had had of it; he was particularly struck with the pleasant and fertile appearance of our sheep farm, which now belongs half to him, and has it yet in contemplation to move his family to Utica. . . .*[15]

That mention of a "fishing party" is the first we have encountered on the Brown's Tract. Although it would have been most unlikely for it to have occurred to Herreshoff, for the crowded industrial cities that made a retreat to nature so important were still some decades ahead, he that day glimpsed what would be the real future of the Adirondacks.

In a letter to his wife, apparently written in June 1814, Herreshoff said that Aaron must come to the Tract because "my bargain with Mr. Meier is such that I am bound to have him (Aaron) come and stay here all winter. It would in every respect be a monstrous disappointment and a total derangement of our plans, if he should fail." Thus, she must find a replacement for Aaron "even at exhorbitant wages. If I should give 20$ a month it would be nothing in comparison to the loss that Aaron's failure would occasion."

We infer that Sally asked him to come home, for he wrote, "It is however impossible to trust my business to any one else, nor could any body else that I know do it with any prospect of success."[16] Plainly, Herreshoff recognized that absentee management was bound to fail.

Another chatty letter was sent to daughter Anne on the first of July.

. . . I have not been from the Tract since my arrival and hardly think I shall till I return to winter quarters; every day brings his care, I am like a shopkeeper behind his counter always expected to be at hand. We continue to have a most unusual season, in a whole month we have had one rain, for a number of days now have hardly seen a cloud and every thing begins to suffer, yet nothing essentially except the grass; we shall have but a small crop of hay. I am afraid it will be the same with you. Our other crops look so far very promising yet, and they say are not surpassed and especially our rye not equalled by any in the neighborhood. We had several large fires lately, they broke out by accident in the choppings which was all burnt, about 70 acres, before they were wanted to, but fortunately exceedingly well; one of these fires came very near consuming Mr Thomas house; every thing was removed and the roof caught several times, but with great exertions we saved it.

Herreshoff then discussed his plantings.

. . . I have sowed between 30 & 40 acres with oats, grass & clover and am now preparing the ground for 10 acres of turnips. Tell Aaron I have it in contemplation to sow between 20 & 30 acres of the side of a hill on the new choppings with turnip in the fall; for pasture only, as soon as it is logged, say to the latter part of August. I have an idea that this will produce a fine early pasture for our sheep next Spring and will give time to the young grass to gain before it is fed down too close. Let me know what Aaron thinks of it. After the Turnips are fed off it is to be sowed with oats. Our rye is now in full blossom from 5 to 7 feet high. Mr. Slocum expects to eat new potatoes from his garden on the 4th of July, but his peas are only just in blossom, so are some of our field peas. Tell brother John his peach stone has come up, he must send some more by Aaron if he can get any. I wish you also to save some seeds from our best gooseberries that have been ripe; the best way is to pull some for the purpose and lay them in a dry place to rot, then wash the seed out and dry it; he may likewise bring a few tulip roots, if he can conveniently; they will be a monstrous show here, and fetch a bushel of potatoes apiece.

Herreshoff then sent instructions for Aaron to start for the Tract by the middle of August, "he will find a very clever couple with only one child to board with, by the name of Vincent. A snug house for his flock, shingled on the roof, 300 feet long by 15 feet deep, and a fine barn 60 feet by 40." The Vincent was presumably Nicholas Vincent, who had married Major Joy's daughter Elizabeth in what was long accepted as the first marriage in the area, and their child the first born. As we shall soon see, however, it was not the first. It was after Aaron became landlord that Nick's Lake was named.

This long letter ended with a sad but amusing story.

. . . I must now relate to you the sorrows of poor Captain Gould; how he has been lately crossed in love and in all his future bright prospects. He was courting a smart widow in Russia, the next town to Remsen, with a property of 1500$. She had accepted of his person and the match was fixed upon provided she should have no particular dislike to Brown Tract. It was agreed upon that Capt Gould would come out this spring and introduce her to her new abode. Accordingly he rode out in stile about a week ago, equipped with a new pair of boots, black velvet pantaloons—and a brand new waistcoat, made out of an old one, which it seemd fate had saved for this solemn occasion from the ravages—of words and time, in a snug chest, these 27 years. Every one felt glad at the prospect of so valuable an acquisition to the family & the whole settlement; we all agreed she would be pleased with the appearance of things and her friendly reception, though we felt a little concerned about the accomodations she was to find. The potatoes were [about gone] *and to tell the truth, our pork was a little rancid. But on the other hand I had hired a cow a few days ago and we had now at least milk in the house. Every body wished to be the first to see them ascend the hill, when one evening, the dog barking, which we saw Capt Gould on his Rosinante* [Don Quixote's horse] *creeping slowly up hill, nobody* [was with] *him nor behind him. This sorrowful countenance told the story; nobody asked any questions. The particulars we learnt a few days after. This sagacious widow heard not long since that the wife of a rich neighbor by the name of Col Wright, was very sick; off she posted to see her, and found her very low, that very night she dreamt she would be the Colonels wife and told her dream in the morning. O why did not the poor Captain also dream; but Mrs Wright died, and yet he dreamt no wrong, but unconscious of his fate went to add to his disappointment the mortification of being rejected. Before that same week was out, his bride was married to the Colonel, just 4 weeks after his last wife's death. This valiant Colonel has buried three wives, and the longest time he ever was a widower was 6 weeks,—twice he married 4 weeks after the funeral. What do you think of such people my dear Anne? A disregard of decency and the opinion of the world they may find pretty convenient at times; but they are planting a thorn in their own breast which soon or late may produce anguish in return. If Mrs Wright should be taken sick, she may enjoy the sweet consolation to think, that her dear husband is already courting her successor for they say that is his way, and celebrate his fifth wedding should she die, before the grass has time to spread on the grave.*[17]

His next letter was brief and not so amusing, but informative. It was to his daughter Sarah.

Tragedy on the Tract

. . . We have had a very severe drought here, by which our hay has suffered much; our grain however is excellent and will be set for reaping in a few days. We have now plenty of new potatoes, turnips & field peas, and a great abundance of rasberries, Mrs Slocum picked a pail full the other day to make wine of, and some of the little boys picked 10 quarts for me in one day, but those and blackberries are about all the fruit we have at present; I believe this to be a fine country for fruit however such as apples, pears, plumbs & cherries, and by the time that you come to live here, we shall have some to console us for the loss of our apples & cherries. I shall prepare the ground for a garden this fall on my sheep farm, where I am going to setup a small house early next spring, on a little elevation in view of the river to the south, and sheltered from the N. W. wind by a high hill, the summit of which is about ½ mile from the house, on a part of its side cleared of for sheep pasture . . . .[18]

For several months we have no further word. We do not know whether Herreshoff fell silent – in later years, he often did when he had no good news to relate – or whether his letters somehow strayed from the family collection. It is not until October 1814 that we have any definite information. That month Major Joy, who apparently served as agent when Herreshoff was not in residence, purchased a section of 160 acres just south of Old Forge for the bargain price of $50, obviously an incentive for settlement. Evidently, Joy spent part of the time on his new farm and part at his place in Remsen. His son-in-law, Nicholas Vincent, lived on the Tract and spent at least part of his time manufacturing nails by hand.[19]

Herreshoff, to the best of our knowledge, did not specify who the settlers were but, other than the families we have already mentioned (The Gould, Clarke, Thomas, Vincent and Slocum families), a handful of others are listed by Joseph Grady in his *The Adirondacks*: the Joslin, Justin, Morgan, Pritchard, Sweet and White families, although a couple of these householders may have been bachelors. He also mentioned an Emmiline Sperry, "a young school teacher" who "when weather permitted, gathered the Brown's Tract children in an untenanted cabin for instruction in the three R's." Although we have no disinclination to believe Grady, his interesting book does not have notes, so we cannot know the source of his information.

The next definite word we have is in December, when Herreshoff wrote to John Brown Francis from New York City that he had left the Tract on November 15. There is also reference to Francis' attending the New York Legislature session in February to pursue a grant for constructing a road. This probably refers to an attempt by Francis and other nearby landowners to have a road built between Boonville and a road proposed

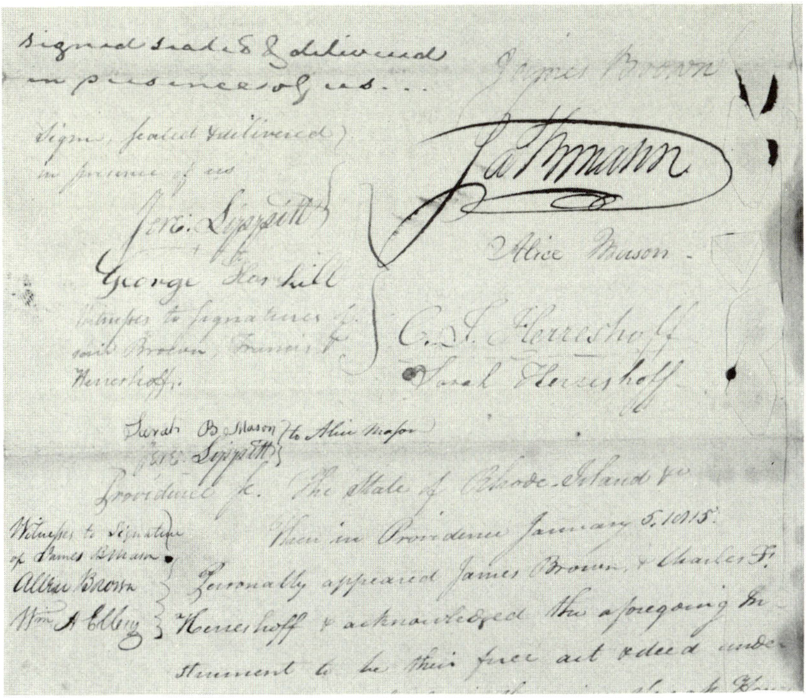
Signed sealed & delivered in presence of us...

James Brown

Alice Mason

C. F. Herreshoff

Sarah Herreshoff

Jere. Lippitt

George

Sarah B. Mason to Alice Mason

Providence Sc. The State of Rhode Island &c

Then in Providence January 5, 1815

Witnesses to Signature of James Brown

Allen Brown

Personally appeared James Brown & Charles F. Herreshoff & acknowledged the aforegoing instrument to be their free act & deed

1815 deed showing family signatures.

between Albany and the St. Lawrence River. A road crossing the Tract roughly from west to east would, of course, have been an incentive to settlers. In 1816 the Legislature, by an Act entitled Chapter 152, did appoint Francis, along with Stephen Smith II and John G. Post, as "commissioners for exploring and marking out a route for a road, from the northerly part of the town of Boonville, to intersect the road leading from the city of Albany to the St. Lawrence, in and near township number forty-one, of Totten and Crossfield's Purchase, in such place as they shall judge to be most eligible and advantageous for a road." There was a great deal of such hopeful legislation passed in that era but, as was usually the case, nothing much came of it.[20]

Of the intervening year, 1815, our knowledge is limited. That was the infamous year of the eruption of the volcano Tambora. The eruption on the island of Sumbawa, in the Indian Ocean, east of Java, was the worst recorded in 10,000 years. The debris it cast upward for thousands of feet slowly drifted around the planet causing in 1816 the "year without summer," lowering by 1° the global temperature. Its effects, which we shall soon note, were serious indeed on the John Brown's Tract, as on all of the northeast, especially the northern portions.[21]

We do know that John Brown Francis sold to his uncle Herreshoff and his partner Casper Meier 5,060 acres in No. 7 for $10,000.[22] We do not count that, however, as money earned by the family, since it was merely transferred from one member to another.

Herreshoff apparently arrived on the Tract in mid-May.[23] He did not, however, write home for a month, and in this letter we see, for the first time from the Tract, the tone of melancholy that would increasingly mark his letters home. The letter was to his daughter Anne.

. . . *Waiting from day to day to have a more convenient opportunity to send and to be in a better mood for writing you a letter, a whole month has this day elapsed, before I have fulfilled this duty towards you. I begin now to feel more settled and you shall not remain so long again without hearing from me. I cannot thank you enough, nor express in words the love I bear for you, my dearest little Ann, for your frequent tokens of remembrance, and I beg you all to continue to write me without long intervals, for I assure you that I enjoy here no pleasure equal to that of opening your letters and finding you are all well.*

Plainly, he was deeply affected by his separation from his family. Yet he was to spend increasingly long periods away, and we will see how his unhappiness grew from year to year.

Writing of his son John, he said, "Tell him that the tulip root he sent me last fall by Aaron has been in full bloom and much admired by the natives. I have also six little peach trees from the stones he sent me."

He then turned to the curious weather that year.

. . . *I find you have not had a very pleasant Spring; here the season has been most extraordinarily cold, wet & backward, we had frost on the 9th & 10th of May in New York, a thing which I never recollect to have heard of before, it snowed & froze in Utica a few days before I left it. Here the tree buds just began to be tinged with green on my arrival. Every thing has however taken a rapid start of late; our rye has eared and our wheat looks promising beyond every body's expectation, and if nothing happens to our crops this first trial of raising that grain will tend to establish the character of the Tract for being a fine wheat country. I found all the inhabitants in good health, our sheep too are in very good order, we lost 5 lambs we have 50 alive, as handsome a little flock as I ever saw, Aaron will keep up his name for being a good shepard, he has besides been very attentive to all my concerns and has done a great deal of work; we have a considerable garden on the new farm but cannot boast yet of much in it, every thing is backwards not even lettuce or radishes fit to eat yet; last year I had new potatoes the 10 of July & ripe raspberries in plenty. We are in other respects rather better off this year; we have 10 excellent cows on the tract which supply the inhabitants with plenty of milk & butter; Mrs Joy is even making cheese. We shore* [sheared] *our sheep on the 5th inst . . .*

He ended by expressing the "hope I shall soon have the pleasure of seeing my solitude interrupted by the arrival of cousin John, yet I feel as if I had some doubts about his coming. I feel most grieved at the great loss he has sustained in the death of his uncle (Thomas Willing Francis). The loss of a friend is worse than death."[24]

Although we don't know exactly when he arrived, John Brown Francis was on the Tract for at least two months that summer. We learn something of what he was doing from the first letter Herreshoff wrote home in almost two months, despite his declaration that he would write frequently.

. . . The letter I promised to write to you has been a long while coming, so long indeed that I begin to think I may as well omit writing at all before my departure from here, if I postpone it much longer. The more you get out of the habit of some things the greater effort; but the chief cause of my procrastination is that I always look for something more interesting to tell you than the old story that I am well, that I constantly think of my dear children and bemoan my hard fate of being so much separated from them. Yet after all my delay I have now hardly any thing more to say. Our summer season here is pretty much over, we are today celebrating the equinox with a chilly comfortless North East storm which has kept us in the house all day. I expect many more such during the remainder of my stay here which of course will make my absence from home doubly illsome.

One does not have to be a psychologist to know that Herreshoff was responding in a not uncommon fashion. He missed his family so much that he could not even bear to write to them. He could, so it seems, deal with his misery only by pushing them from his mind. After writing of his unhappiness, Herreshoff gave some detail of what John Brown Francis had been doing.

. . . Cousin John is very busily employed making arrangements for opening a road next season; he has made one trip with a surveyor and several more to measure the route to the east road, and has just returned from a desired one to the westward to the high falls [now Lyons Falls] *on Black River and Boonesville.*

Herreshoff then wrote about life in the settlement.

. . . Mr. Watson who was taken with so melancholy a disease last fall has returned perfectly recovered from France and is now at his settlement in our neighborhood: (The Watson settlement was to the west of the Brown Tract and the name is preserved in a village on the present road from Lowville to Number Four.) he has written to invitation [sic] *to cous^{in} John who received them however too late. We live very comfortably now since we have a young couple in the house which Capt Gould occupied, it is a young man by the name of Vincent who married a daughter of Maj Joy's. A little before their wedding we had another; a Mr Brown was married to Pheobe Briggs who lives in Mr Slocums family. From the middle of June to the beginning of September we had a most delightful season, a fine crop of hay and as good weather to secure it. Our harvest time has not been so favorable some of our wheat got somewhat damaged and especially the spring wheat, some of which grew standing in the field which spoilt it for bread.*

Then he described, to a limited extent, what came to be known as Herreshoff Manor.

. . . I have built a very snugg fair house, it is not quite finished, the masons are now building the chimney. A gentleman by the name of Wilbur, a brother to the former Lieutenant governor of our state was blowing rocks in our neighborhood about 6 miles from here; just as I was about preparing to send clay from our clay pit to the new house, expecting the mason every moment they brought me some samples of various stones and matters which they had blown out, one of which stones I immediately recognized to be a beautiful white lime stone, in consequence of which I set off immediately to the spot with two men and extricated a pail and in a few days we had some excellent lime instead of clay to build our chimney and plaster the walls. We had long ago given up the idea of finding lime stone in this part of the country not the smallest symptom of any having ever been seen, this was therefor a very unexpected but welcome discovery. The stone is of a solid rock under ground and seems to afford an inexhaustible quantity, it looks like a coarse marble of the purest white, we bring it partly by water to the mills with about 2-½ miles of land carriage.[25]

Nearly a month passed before Herreshoff wrote again, this time to his daughter Anne.

. . . Your cousin Francis will leave me to morrow, you may well judge, to my great regret. After having enjoyed his company for two months, and the season beginning now to frown, I shall pass many gloomy hours in my solitude, independent of other circumstances. We have so far had an uncommon pleasant autumn, not a single flake of snow yet, and have been pretty lucky in securing our late crops. Cousin John has been scouring the woods a great deal of his time to explore the country and find out the best ground for roads, and has been most lucky in finding good land for that purpose as well as for settling along the roads,

than we had any idea. I cannot tell you anything about our situation and way of living, but what he can describe you much better verbally, but yet I know and you tell me so that my letter without any matter of interest, will however give you some satisfaction as a token of life. It is some time since I heard from you, that is, not since your letter, my dear Ann dated [blank]. *But a few days ago we received a bundle of newspapers, as late as the 30th ult which contained the most melancholy tidings I ever received from our quarter when there. You can easily imagine how much our hearts have been filled with sadness since; we can hardly talk or think of anything but that deplorable scene of horror. We know no other particulars but the few which the papers contain;*[26]

Herreshoff might have gone on to explain to which horrors he was referring but the rest of the letter is missing. And perhaps he might later explain why it was necessary for him to remain instead of leaving with his nephew. We can speculate, however, that the papers were referring to the great hurricane of 1815 which took place on September 23. The hurricane wrought terrible damage all along Narragansett Bay, and contemporary accounts tell of enormous destruction in and along Providence Harbor. Since many of the Brown family businesses were conducted along the waterfront, we can assume they suffered substantial losses.

Charles Frederick Herreshoff returned to the Tract in June 1816. His first letter, about six weeks after his arrival, is anything but optimistic. Life was beginning to weigh heavily. This sometimes sombre letter was written to his daughter Anne:

. . . Your letter by Aaron my dear daughter has afforded me a great deal of pleasure. . . . I would have sent you one by Aaron, but in truth I did not think fit to trust him, and after he had set out I was glad of it, for I did not think from his beginning that he would ever reach you. He had travelled about 20 miles when he fell down dead drunk in the woods and lay there bear like all night. He left the Tract to take a trip to the westward, but I find he is still loitering around here. I have been bodily well ever since I left you, but have not had many hours of comfort; I shall not however annoy you with a long list of great and petty troubles. I left the Tract last Monday and shall return to morrow. We have had a most gloomy season till within a few days, nothing but draught and frost, for a month after I arrived on the Tract which was the 10th of June, the grass instead of gaining, lost every day; since the last fruitful showers every thing has taken a rapid start, but it being so late in the season, our crop of hay cannot be but small; with a common season I would have had a large crop, I had upwards of 100 acres to cut. The only thing we have to boast of is our rye, I have seen none equal to it coming here. Aaron gives me a melancholy account of the prospects all through

the country he passed, our farm not excluded; the only thing that makes life supportable is to hear that you are all well and the hope of finding you so on my return. The sickness of our little Agnes, though she has got over it, gives me some concern, from fear of some relapse.

Then Herreshoff discussed something about the trouble his wife "endures from the stone house" which, out of context, has little meaning now. In themselves, he wrote, they "would weigh but little." However, "added to the realities & disasters I have to contend with here, . . . they give me some uneasiness; in fact the only thing hopeful that one can think of in these gloomy times, is the end of all things."

These unhappy words, so prescient of what would happen three years later, could hardly have cheered his family, especially when he continued: "I will make no promise of writing oftener in future; I will leave it to chance, but that ought not to prevent you my dear Anna, as little Pip says, to write to me, you can easily conceive how much more necessary it is that you should inform me frequently of your situation, you may conclude that I am well when you do not hear from me, you know that I am always well. I cannot sleep of late without taking much fatigue, and that always agrees best with me." And he scribbled to the side: "John & Agnes have added a little scrawl to your letter, I have seen nothing from little Queen Sheba's hand yet." This, presumably, was a reference to his 13-year-old daughter Sarah.[27]

On August 12, 1816, as his nephew was nearing the Tract, Charles Frederick Herreshoff was writing a long (17 pages) and urgent, even courteously desperate letter to Brown & Ives in Providence, asking for a loan of $5,000 to establish a nail factory on the Tract. One readily infers from the letter that he already owed a considerable amount to Brown & Ives.

. . . The discharge of my engagement to you, if nothing else, is a necessary step towards the retrievement of my affairs and has of course been one of the first inducements for the toils and privations to which I have subjected myself, perhaps for the remainder of my days.

He expressed confidence in the future of the Tract. "My first impression too of the character of this country and which has acquired strength ever since, was that nature had peculiarly formed it for a place of business, and that with such, together with agricultural pursuits for which there is a sufficient scope, it must eventually flourish."

Herreshoff pointed out two great advantages. Even with the bad weather, such as a big snowstorm on June 8, (he did not suspect, and why should he, no one suspected, that a volcano halfway around the world was causing such detrimental effects on the climate, that more killing frosts were soon to come), "We have suffered no want in this time of distress but have maintained more than our own population with our grain." They would have a surplus, he wrote.

Also, the great road directly from Albany to Ogdensburg, just 16 miles east of the settlement at No. 7 (now Old Forge) was now complete and easily accessible because the chain of lakes went ten miles of the way.

> *. . . One effort only is required to give us a spring and to insure our prospering: the establishment of a safe and regular branch of business that can be constantly pursued to advantage. And there is one to which our particular situation and all other circumstances seem strongly to invite & for which we are fully prepared. It unites the greatest possible safety & simplicity with a prospect of enriching the undertaker and of being of more immediate advantage to this property than any thing else that could be devised under present circumstances. Such is likewise the opinion of several intelligent men in Utica and this neighborhood whom I have consulted on the subject.*

Herreshoff wrote that he had been confident of his ability to raise the money until

> *I learned the failure of Murray & Sons in New York with whom I had come to some terms . . . this unexpected disappointment may frustrate all my hopes in this quarter, and I have none, I conceive, anywhere else; unless enabled by some early assistance, to pursue and accomplish my object. My hope to derive that assistance from you, rests much on my intention not to propose anything, but what to the best of my perception is reasonable and consistent with propriety.*

After this long lead in, he wrote, "the business I have alluded to is a slitting & rolling mill in connection with the manufactory of cut nails." He explained how great the demand was in northern New York. "It is the only article which always commands cash. . . ." And he then went into a minutely-detailed explanation of markets, transportation, and costs. As a particular advantage he mentioned the site at what is now Old Forge.

> *. . . In the first instance our mill seat is not surpassed by any I have seen or heard of. Of the whole body of water in the lake, 10 miles long and in many places about 1 mile wide, the mill stream with a fall of water perhaps 20 feet forms the only outlet; the supply of water is inexhaustable. A dam of about 30 feet secures the whole, unaffected in the smallest degree by freshets, drought nor frost. By means of a wooden trough only, sufficient water may be taken out of one of the flooms to supply any machinery. Our water work therefore is cheap and suffers never any interruption all the year round.*

After presenting his detailed arguments for the project, Herreshoff got down to costs.

. . . The whole work as near as I am now able to calculate may be put in operation with somewhere less but certainly not exceeding 5000 Dr. including a large building for the works, a small dwelling house, the water works & running gears, machinery for rolling and slitting, cutting & heading machines, and all necessary implements & tools, for the working of 100 tons a year and upwards. — That sum I would propose you to advance, offering you as security a deed of the establishment and all belonging to it, and of 5000 acres of land in this same township (all I have to dispose of in my own right) Both which deeds shall remain in your possession until the new as well as the old debt are cancelled with interest. But to the discharge of the new debt of 5000$ & interest, I would further engage to apply 3/4 of the neat [net] *proceeds of the business, and account for them as far as they may arise to any agent you may appoint (J. Francis for inst.) After paying that debt, for which I flatter myself less than two years will be sufficient, making allowances for some difficulties & impediments in the beginning; you may fix on the proportion of the neat [net] proceeds thereafter, for the redemption of the old debt, according to what you think equitable.*

He ended this long letter in moving fashion:

. . . Perhaps one half of what I have said, (and I wish it may be the case) would have been enough to convince you of the greatest merit of the business: its unquestionable safety. Can there be any danger of loss in it, without the utmost want of attention and care: The object of my ambition is of too serious a nature to lose it by such means. Once more I wish to live through one day — not owing onc cent — my wife & children secured from penury, the most grating most unhappy of all feelings, next to a guilty conscience. For the enjoyment of that day I would cheerfully assign the remaining. I will only add that I look for your answer with an anxiety of suspense, I may truly say, never felt before, . . .[28]

One can fully understand such an "anxiety of suspense," for to Charles Frederick Herreshoff his sacred honor was at stake. By his conception, a gentleman did not remain in debt and he did insure that his wife and family would, whatever happened to him, live in comfort. The terrible wound to his self-esteem that his business reverses caused is movingly apparent in this letter, despite (or perhaps because of) the restraint of his language. How different an attitude from that so current today, when the entire economy seems to float on a sea of debt. To us, so far removed in time, his proposition sounds reasonable, but to Brown & Ives, whether rightly or wrongly, it did not. The Brown family, it must be remembered, had decades of experience in the iron business and B & I, like the founder of the firm, Nicholas Brown, was a prudent house not given to speculation. Thus came this cordial but short and direct response three months later:

. . . We duly rec^d the original & duplicate of your favour of the 12 Aug. & the delay in our answering it has arisen from the difficulty we found in complying with your request—as well as from a conviction that the business in which you propose employing a capital in the interior of New York cannot possibly succeed. Nails are made in this vicinity & in various other places by great manufacturing establishments to the extent of two or three tons a day—the facility of a transportation is very easy & the expense quite light.

On your return we hope for a full conversation and on this and other subjects connected with your Black River Establishment—when should there be a reasonable prospect of advancing your interest—it would give us pleasure to contribute toward it.

They attempted to soften what they must have known from the tone of Herreshoff's letter would be a severe blow by signing the letter: "We are with great regard Your assured friends Brown & Ives."[29]

To poor Herreshoff it must often have seemed that he was doomed to live in bad luck, but he was determined to restore his fortune despite that rejection and, as we shall see, neither his determination nor his ingenuity was yet exhausted.

John Brown Francis also returned to the Tract in 1816, just after Herreshoff sent that letter that bore with it so many of his hopes, and spent much of the summer there. From his diary and from the few letters written by Herreshoff, we learn a lot about the Tract. Francis left Providence on horseback on August 6 and his diary is frequently funny. We cannot resist quoting a section from the first day.

. . . Very much diverted in Burrillville with the Taverner. A sing song sort of man at first sight but very cute *withal. He questioned me for the space of 20 minutes in every ingenious way to ascertain my profession etc. etc in which he must have undoubtedly succeeded had I not had one to boast of in spite of myself. He is a man of taste & always takes a* nap *of an afternoon. Wears a whig which does not conceal a very good deal of hair. All the family have a nasal twang.*

Pray sir do you live on the street? No, on the hill? Then likely near Squire Thurbers? No—may be you keep an office near the market: No—you belong to the College, I suppose? No—a pause again. Then as you keep a store you can tell me the price of flour? I do not keep a store, sir. Here the poor man's ingenuity ran out & he determined to let me rest. His name Walden.[30]

The diary is interesting and well written, filled with details about the country through which he passed and the people he met. In Albany his diary discussed "drinking, whoring & gambling." Against all three. Also at Albany, on August 10, John Brown Francis paid the taxes due on the road to be built from the Watson Tract eastward across the Brown Tract to the Totten and Crossfield lands, $636.66 for Francis on No. 4 and $74.67 for Herreshoff for Nos. 3 and 5.

On his way to Little Falls, Francis traveled the last ten miles with a Presbyterian clergyman. "Had a long controversy with him about Popery and Infidels." Not impressed with his powers of reasoning, Francis concluded that "most people take up their opinions on trust & may be said to borrow rather than beget their ideas."[31]

The night of August 15 he spent at Fowler's in Remsen. "Found no letters at the Post Office & feeling like a cut throat to go to bed. The confusion & vulgarity of the bar room enough to sicken one with plebian manners. The next morning this was what he found:

. . . The news of my arrival has given the Bar Keeper more than his usual custom from mere curiosity or the desires of hearing from R. I. A mob had collected. My horse was to be admired, my motions watched & everything attended to with that sort of scrupulosity which people in low life on the confines of a wilderness might be supposed to entertain towards the proprietor of a neighbouring Tract of Land—the only property of which they have any conception. If say one I am well off with a lot of one hundred acres & log hut what may be said to be his situation with one hundred thousand acres.

Francis then demonstrated that he was both philosophic and cynical, not uncommon with educated and intelligent 25-year-olds.

How true the doctrine that every heart knows its own bitterness. These people are disposed to call in question the justice of that disease which makes them hewers of wood and carriers of water & leaves me to consume only but little do they think that the most unfortunate of their clan has fewer moments of care. Less concern about the future than the object of their envy. A being who has discovered at the early age of twenty five that almost everything in this life is flat, stale & unprofitble & that there is scarcely any thing worth living for. . . .

Life did not sound like much fun for young Francis, and, as for his philosophic musings about the carefree life of the poor, there are few poor who would not be willing to make the sacrifice and exchange their lives for those of the rich.

Francis then goes from the general to the particular.

. . . The man who is planted at Beaver Meadow, 12 miles in the woods insisted on accompanying me for he wanted as he said to Talk sentiment to me. *I could not help exclaiming. Even the wilderness then is no defence against these sentimentalists if I escape the verbiage of pious, pedantic, lifeless, sapless declaimers of*

one sex I am to be pursued to the very mouth of my cave by a satellite of the opposite gender.

Good Lord deliver me. I saw the storm gathering however & prepared for it. In other words I guarded myself against a sermon from this long winded wiskey drinking Hall by dosing him with his favorite beverage till his ideas could no longer get utterance & then we rode to his chanty very peaceably not meeting a living thing—man or beast. His wife boiled me eggs as hard as a rock before I thought of giving direction. The poor woman had sent out for materials & actually made pies *for me several times expecting my arrival. She was an inconsolable interesting little woman. This her first child. She described her suffering from a broken breast. Women certainly endure pain better than men.*[32]

If Francis sounds self-centered, it is hardly surprising. With the death of his father and both his sisters, it was natural for Abby Francis to lavish attention on the last remaining member of her family. Nor is it surprising that his bachelor uncle James made a fuss over him. But, as we will see, he does mature with the passage of time.

Across the river, the Black River probably, he, on August 16, 1816, found Herreshoff waiting for him. Thus, it had taken him ten days on horseback from Providence. The next morning he awoke to this:

Fine summer weather, the thermometer at 70 in the morn'g. The last frosts had injured the potatoes, Wheat looking well where it took seed but the greater part poorly seeded or perhaps winter killed. The rye always good here. One field of about 12 acres—surpassing any crop I ever saw. Thirty bushels to the acre undoubtedly. Some of the ears on measurement not less than seven feet from the earth.

Who can talk of the impracticabality of settling a country where the yield is so abundant & the climate so healthy—absurd.

John Brown Francis, like John Brown and Charles Frederick Herreshoff, was not to be discouraged. Three generations refused to be put off by such things as frost-damaged potatoes and winter-killed wheat. Nature would soon make the lesson even plainer.

Francis recorded that "old Hunter White," hearing of his arrival, brought him a mess of trout. White had killed seven beavers within the last week that averaged twelve dollars apiece in value. He reported, too, that an "old hump-backed dwarf is now living on hard rye bread & water" and salmon trout. Francis declined his invitation to stay overnight and determined to press on to the settlement.

. . . The road damnable it made my heart ake to press the poor animal thro' mire & over stump & stones, where her legs were in so much danger of being broken.

Tragedy on the Tract

The road was so bad, the bridges and logways worst of all, that Francis was forced to dismount "& actually stand in front of the poor devil to prevent her from precipitating herself into the gulphs." The bridge was gone at Moose River, so they had to ford, the "water was not above her shoulders."

... *In 6 miles I alighted at Betsy Vincents who came to receive me in the* attitude *of suckling her babe. One she seemed to have chose on the occasion — certainly the most interesting situation for tho' our women would shudder at the idea of exposing a breast but their chastity or delicacy is no greater than Betsy's, a very honest hearted communicative well meaning* [person].[33]

Francis may have been self-centered and cynical but, like his father, he was also observant and open-minded.

The following day Francis again visited Betsy and then her mother "& the old Lady Grandmother Joy 90 years old, a well bred, mild, ancientless." He records that the daughter Susan, about 17, was handsome and Millee, an old maid even though she was only 25, "rated in the old maids row these two years."

... *Cole the man who is clearing fifty acres for Mr H* [Herreshoff] *arrived today with a gang of hands & a woman to* serve, *as Betsy shrewdly suspects, as women serve in camps, the mistress of the company. Well done Betsy — A cow, two horses & one yoke of oxen compose the retinue.*

Francis summoned Major Joy and learned that a barn at the middle settlement had been burned down, "a damage of a cool five hundred to me. Joy the unintentional cause."[34]

As the proprietor (or, more properly, the heir), John Brown Francis seemed to supercede his uncle when he was on the Tract. Thus, the settlers turned to him for decisions, often of a personal nature.

... *Joy kept me in the house all morn'g on a consultation about his whipping Mrs. Clarke. Advised him not to let the affair go to Court. The woman was enceinte* [pregnant] *& a damned bitch undoubtedly but no man is justified in my opinion in striking a woman but in case of defendendo.*

Francis went on to record that "Ice was seen this morn'g about the houses for the first time since the *ninth of July*!! A large fire put out comfort again — This would be a most excellent place for a studious character: a winters residence would convert me." One wonders whether this frost tempered his optimism. These dates, July 9 and August 21st, correspond exactly with those cited in "Volcano Weather," the book about "1816 and froze to death."

In that same letter Francis again emphasizes his reservations about religion, occasioned by a report from a man from Remsen that there was "a great religious stir there which he attributes 'to the cold snap.' "

> . . . *All Methodists they fall by the dozens he says but always on* their bottoms, [rather than on their knees]. *These Methodists have their run at intervals as much in this country as in England. Religion goes by fits and starts, as one sheep leads a whole flock over a wall so one or two conversions sactifies a* leash *of gossips. They are as wild & mobocratic* [Francis did not hesitate to coin his own words] *as in Cromwells time & only want the power to do the same mischief.*
>
> *A plague on this influence of priestcraft – I say.*[35]

On August 27, Francis left Boonville in the company of "Smith the Surveyor" and three pack men "to explore & mark a route for a road to our settlement. We forded the river but the stones being slippery & my shoes off, fell in and bruised my ankle." They struggled for hours over gradually rising land and ridges, but eventually found land "as smooth as a house floor."

> . . . *Then on the same kind of land covered with hard timber a little more than three miles & a half & night coming on obliged to chanty without water – a serious evil – no one can be aware of the disappointment who has not felt as I now feel. We have built an excellent chanty, the spruce peeling easily; the rain pours at this moment but it does not leak. Men employed in cutting wood & breaking hemlock boughs for a bed soaking wet.*
>
> *Nothing but salt pork & poor bread & whiskey – hard fare by the Lord. I write now by the light of a tremendous fire – a flaming Etna. Men weary & faint hearted – feel well myself physically but would rather be at home.*[36]
>
> *Finally it cleared and at one o'clock they saw stars. The men waked me from a profound sleep insisting upon it – it was morn'g. My watch made them quiet again. All hands complain of cold. The frost must have been severe. No complaint from hard fare. Caught no water in our kettle. Moved as soon as we could see & breakfasted on the outside of a dismal swamp. Chocolate & sugar hardly palatable.*[37]

More difficult land was ahead, but eventually they found a better route, ending up on the last day of August with "an excellent route – for miles as level as a house floor. Little is to be said in favor of it however in the vicinity of the Moose river country thereabouts as well as the stream itself from this circumstance is the most interesting stream I ever saw." And he writes of crawling "along the banks & thro' deviltry of every kind. . . ."

Finally Francis "presumptuously ordered the men to lay down their packs & build a chanty tho' the light from the river might have enabled us to see much later than usual, but we were all just dead with fatigue & the night required a roaring fire. Never slept better."

The next day they got lost, "I fearful the whole time too that this wretched country was a part of my inheritance till we were arrested by the roaring of a river which we immediately ran to & found to our astonishment one of which no one had any knowledge." Francis concluded that it was a branch of the Moose and that they were south of the Tract. They changed their course and eventually found Major Joy. "—took some of his boiled pork & beans—a great treat for dinner. . . .

After a few days of this difficult life, he headed for the tavern.

> *. . . Recrossed Black River the water having risen waist high. I had reserved a private flask of brandy to swig after this baptising but lost it all in taking it from my pocket. This one of the miseries of human life unquestionably. The river two miles & upward from the tavern.*

And on September 1, Francis then rode off to Lowville. "The country more settled as you follow the river." His diary is then filled with descriptions of people he encountered in Lowville. As usual, they are sharp in both senses of the word. For instance:

> *. . . Next Bostwick the great land agent naturally eloquent, enthusiastic & fond of company too. The most violent man I ever met—a violent swearer & drinker sometimes according to ill report—but withal a very pleasant companion for it is amusing to meet with this sort of irrationality if it is only in a transient acquaintanceship.*[38]

After a few days in Lowville, he journeyed south to the other significant town near the Tract, Boonville, arriving there on September 5.

> *. . . This day arrived in Boonville & found myself beset by road and bridge jobbers. The fame of my road having spread over the whole country. I was received with great civilitiy as the grandson of old John Brown who is esteemed in these parts, a greater man even than I think. Frederick the Great. A thousand questions have been asked, a thousand stories told of this honored grandfather for my diversion. Nothing would satisfy them that he was not also the richest man in the Country & that I myself am not* weighed *down in the same manner. Every imposition therefore is legalized according to their morality for a rich man is always fair game when one appears it is what the boys call scrambling & it requires the watchfulness of a weasel.*[39]

A few days later Francis paid a call on a Colonel Mappa, agent for the neighboring Adgate Tract, who received "2400 per annum & his Sons $500 all for a mere bagatelle, he acknowledged to me that he had not sold a lot for the last two years. His sole business then must have been to pay taxes & prevent trespassers on timber!!"

He then returned to Boonville, did some more research on the costs of roads, and offered a man named Prindle 12½ dollars a mile. "He to cut, smooth & clear out between the two rivers (Black and Moose), one rod in width & wait for his money until it was receivable from the Treasury." In this, he was referring to the legislation which appointed him a road commissioner and levied a tax on the landowners through whose property the road passed.

That same day he contracted "with Asa Dibble & Jared Ives to construct two bridges such as described in the contract filed among my papers. One over the Black & the other over the Moose River to be completed in the month of Nov. & paid for when the assessment before referred to become due, the first for three Hundred Dollars, the second for two hundred & fifty. . . .[40]

On September 11, 1816, we find an entry that refers to a woman we have never been able to identify beyond her name, Eliza. Plainly, John Brown Francis cared for her but how much it is hard to say. This is what he wrote:

> *. . . Rec'd letters today from Eliza & Mr. Shearmon. E anticipates a returned to P*[hiladelphia, we assume] *when the old Doctor dies. This information disappoints me tho' I ought to have known before that a City woman was always a City woman. I expected something more from Eliza. What woman accustomed to Society & fond of admiration will ever be satisfied with a Country life. This question has agitated me a thousand times & I tho't Eliza one—but where shall I find one now? In Prov.? Rouchefucault perhaps settles the point when he says the man deceives himself when he flatters himself exempt from the partialities or frailties that characterize certain situations. There are not exceptions. Here me miserable. I could point to one if I had not this standard case before me but that person has never like E been up to the world, she may possibly therefor despise it.*[41]

Francis, like his father, was interested in politics, hardly surprising since he later became one of the most important figures in Rhode Island political history, serving for years in the state legislature and as governor and United States senator. Several people from Canada passed through the area, which set him to thinking about relations between the young United States and the British colony to the north. At that time, many Americans confidently expected that, in due course, Canada would become part of the United States.[42] Young Francis astutely concluded that this would never happen.

. . . Should the Government of England hold out the same parental aid for years their hearts must be truly English & they a powerful people—but whether this is the case or not their interests will never lead them to join our confederation.

As things are situated now it is impossible for us with our whole disposable [military] *force to conquer that country.*[43]

With a cold rain confining him to Boonville for some days, he had time to reflect on one of his favorite subjects, especially as he could find little to read in that small village. "Inquired of Grant the *Taverner* for books, but the bible & psalm books composed his stock & my hand were too unhallowed for their touch . . ."

One gathers that Francis had been accused of being irreligious:

. . . No person has suffered more religious intolerance who so invariably perceived the happiness of mankind vitally connected with Christianism. A casual expression should never been taken for a fixed & serious expression without subsequent & considerable corroboration. To say that I have much faith in the miracles & mysteries of religion is what I do not mean but that the system is an excellent one whether of divine or human origin is enough for me & whenever my expressions are construed otherwise is is done . . .

In this light I view all the missions to India. I entirely accord with Mr. Jefferson in the belief that it is of no consequence whether our neighbour worships one God or twenty Gods. It neither picks our pockets nor breaks our legs.

Is he an honest man? for an honest man's the noble work of God—This is all we have a right to enquire into . . .[44]

Francis, as we saw earlier, cared a great deal about receiving letters from his family and friends. When he did not receive an answer to his letters to his mother and Moses Brown Ives, a cousin, he grew concerned. Yet "When a man suspects his mother tis time for him to give over life. My case is not yet, thank God so deplorable."[45]

He muses in his diary whether he should stay on the Brown's Tract or make his life in Rhode Island. Although he does not say so directly, one infers that a lot depends on Eliza.

. . . But I have hopes—hopes of such a nature that I hardly dare avow them to myself.

I will not long remain in this state of doubt. As soon as I can get home I will & then see whether the plan that occupies the chief place in my heart is altogether illusory.[46]

Although it is only mid-September, Francis records that Boonville had a severe frost and that the temperature is usually lower on the slopes of the Brown's Tract. Plainly, if there is severe frost by mid-September, and frost is common in June, that allows of a very short growing season.

That day also saw Ives and Dibble beginning their work on the bridges. "God speed them."[47]

And again, Francis muses on the choice between the Tract and Rhode Island.

. . . From some cause or other could not sleep last night—never recollect to have been so restless in health. It was Black River or Providence river—a struggle between a life of activity & enterprise with influence & its concomitant cares & a life in a smaller sphere of action the world forgetting by the world forgot. But however the first might preponderate as a simple case of itself yet the impossibility of removing myself from my mother is always the stumbling block. With this & one other chose [French word for "thing"] *hors du combat Black River has the decided preference . . .*[48]

The other thing we assume was Eliza.

For days, Francis had been waiting at Boonville for Smith the surveyor. On September 21, he finally arrived. The following day, Francis and Smith set off to the east, accompanied by a chainman, a marksman (to provide game for the table, we assume) and a dozen volunteers. "20 pounds of hard bread besides one loaf of soft, 15 pounds of pork, three pounds of sugar, one pound of chocolate, ½ pound of tea, raw onions, fireworks, axe, 3 qts whiskey & blankets compose our packs."

The chocolate had been provided by Mrs. Post, "hearing of my distress for that article." The whiskey cost a dollar a gallon and Francis described the maple sugar as "always miserable stuff."[49]

When they reached the river, presumably the Black, they found a marvelous scene.

. . . At the river found an assemblage of men, women & children drawn together from the fame of our bridge. We crossed in a boat. Ives & Dibble hard at work building pier which looks as well as & could wish. There were several young lasses bedecked in their Sunday clothes & surrounded by lovers. They were not driven from their embracements *by our approach. The girls sat in the laps of their swains, on the wilderness side of the roaring flood in the true style of romance until I called on them to bring us over. Perhaps they had better be at meeting but this is questi Vescata. My only complaint is the publicity of courtship.*[50]

On September 23, Francis recalled the terrible hurricane that struck coastal New England the year before. "God preserve them from such another." And he reported that two of his men were indisposed.

. . . The remedy applied to one was memorable to me. His complaint of violent pain in the back—for this he was laid on his belly & one of the men danced on his back!! It is not less singular that he found relief from the barbarous prescription.

Then Francis goes on to describe how they struck a route for the road.

. . . To straighten our course or rather to get a good one thro' this gulph Smith has gone ahead of me. I am at the Banks of a stream large enough for a mill. Prindle is back of me, Grant of him and Boem at the compass. Smith screeching first & all of us in succession—a curious way of finding a route thro' the wilderness. One of which I lay claim to the invention—for Heaven knows as little ingenuity as there may be in it patents *have been obtained for less.*

It came on to rain, but the surveying party found shelter in their old chanty near the Moose River.

. . . The earth was on fire for a considerable distance around. We had made this fire the last day of August. It had not however consumed the back of our chanty which was infinitely valuable to us in a rain when the trees would no longer peal [to provide bark for shelter]. *The pumpies* [an insect] *bite so damnable that I can sit in no comfort—chanty on the banks of Moose river.*

The Moose River, Francis records, is not as wide there as at their crossing on the Black River. That measured 13 rods, about 215 feet.

. . . Boem has set fire to an old dead tree which burns most majestically. The blaze reaching 80 or one hundred feet & the whole surrounding wilderness illuminated. We have fears for our chanty but fear will hardly keep our eyes open. There is nothing like fatigue.[51]

Francis agreed with Prindle for him to cut a road between the rivers of "12½ Dollars the mile—one rod wide to be done immediately." The next night they had to abandon their chanty and sleep on the banks of the Moose, "fire raging on all sides . . . Homes may be made in many places hereabouts & water enough obtained to carry all the cotton spindles in R. I. Spruce timber of first quality. . . ."[52]

His last night on the surveying job was rather spectacular:

. . . The night a very severe one & having no axe were unable to procure wood enough to make us comfortable. Occupied one of Gay's camps—a miserable place. The fire had burned the ground two or three feet lower than the chanty—it was literally in a cellar & I spent some hours of the night anathematisating & not in prayer of thanksgiving.

But after the most severe trial of this campaign I have to thank God for the preservation of my health when the severe fatigue overpower'd hardier frames—& for my safe return to the Settlement.

The expedition and the diary ended simultaneously, with Francis making the final entries on the inside of the back cover. His last words were: "Walked in Joys road nine miles examining it & dissatisfied."

On one cover of the diary, he wrote a memo that, of 72,200 acres he had examined on the John Brown's Tract, "57,800 are saleable and 22,400 acres poor." Of the "saleable" land, Francis termed "14,600 acres first rate or excellent land" and "37,200 second best or good land." And on another cover, he recorded that he had

. . . Agreed with the two Dodges to make a road from the Boonville village road to Black River for 30 Dr the mile—to be cut smoothed & cleared out one rod on each side of this rod in width before winter sets in & to be clashed one road on each side of this rod during the winter.[53]

All during these months we learn almost nothing about Charles Frederick Herreshoff. There are no letters, and his nephew scarcely mentioned him in his diary, all of which was written when he was separated from Herreshoff, either off the Tract or in the wilderness surveying. For that entire summer we have only the three letters earlier mentioned: a rather gloomy one from Herreshoff to his daughter Anne, his long, desperately hopeful letter to Brown & Ives and their friendly but firm rejection.

The year 1817 saw the beginning of construction of the Erie Canal from Albany west to Oswego on Lake Ontario. That canal, which followed the course of the Mohawk River forty or more miles south of the Tract, and the later Black River Canal that went north-south a dozen miles to the west of the Tract, were often viewed as saviours, transportation links that would encourage settlement of John Brown's land. One can understand such hopes, but the reality was that the canals diverted the course of settlement to the west, where there was better land at a competitive cost.

That year both John Brown Francis and Charles Frederick Herreshoff returned to the Tract in June, Francis continuing his work on the roads and Herreshoff beginning his latest attempt to wrest prosperity from a grudging nature, iron manufacture.

Francis arrived first, taking a week to get from Providence to Boonville. He made his first entry on June 20 at the Middle Settlement.

. . . The weather has been bad all the way—intolerably so between Albany & Utica. There was a frost throughout the cold region on the 15th & a very severe one which killed the potatoes & crops on the 16th.

On the Tract the loss not been more severe. The English grain (oats and rye) is backward but never looked more promising. The Potatoes just coming up. It has rained plentifully since my arrival on the Tract & almost every day or night in greater or less quantities since I left home . . .

There is less calculation to be made on the weather in this mountain climate

than in R. I. I rode the last two hours in a soaking rain & was exposed in addition to this misery, to the perils of falling trees. The wind raged & the crash of trees with the rolling thunder had quite enough of the grand & terrific in it.

Herreshoff arrived on June 23, and the next day "Smith appear, engaged him to work on the road with a gang of five or eight – to have 2 Doll's a day & be allowed three doll's a week for boarding the men." That was, we assume, per man.[54]

Francis' diary entry for June 26 describes graphically, and concisely, the route between Boonville and the Tract.

. . . With Mr. H, two women, a hunter, & Nicholas Vincent, three pack horses & two cows – in all five souls & mine. Beasts proceeded to the Tract road beyond Moose River – horribly bad. 11 hours going 20 miles & half way in the rain.

The following day he recorded that "All well on the Tract. . . Went to the n[orth] branch to be bit by mosquitoes for we caught no fish." And a couple of days later, he described a Sunday expedition:

. . . Blustering weather. Set off on an expedition to the fourth Lake, prepared to pass the night out, but relinquished the undertaking at the mill. White having taken our boat. We could not have gone had it been there, the wind being too high & ahead with occasional showers.

Mr. H. remarked that the high winds were unknown here as far back as 1811.

Francis also recorded the painful death of Captain Gould, whose misfortunes in love had earlier been reported by Herreshoff. A runaway returned "confirms the death of poor Captain Gould by a kick in the testicles from an ox. The boys take care of Grammy by their father's dying request."[55]

This seemed to be the social season on the Tract, for Francis recorded that "Mrs. Vincent has a tea party this afternoon. Six smart women, one only unmarried compose the party."

The following day, Francis recorded that the water on the lakes "has not settled three inches this season – this is a remarkable case & unfortunate for Mr. H. who is anxious to examine the beach for black sand (for indications of iron)."

. . . Another tea party this afternoon. All the women on the Tract present making of eight precious souls. Pound cake, preserved currants etc. for the entertainment!![56]

We can assume that there were not many families on the Tract. But there were still a number of sheep, for "George Grave from Russia comes to purchase Mr. H.'s wool, taked most of it on shares. He to have one half of the cloth. Mr. H had previously sold common wool for 50 cts. & half, & three quarters blood for 75 cts." Per pound, we imagine.

There was a Fourth of July celebration on the Tract. Such celebrations must have had a particular significance in those days, for there were still many who were alive on that first Fourth of July. The event was much as it would be today.

> *... The same heat continues. All hands disposed to spend the day in frolick. Go with them to the mills where they play ball all day & I look on, exposed to a baking sun.*[57]

The next day Francis finally met William Constable, proprietor of the great tract to the west, where, in Constable Hall, his family lived until recently. "Has the manners of a man who has seen good company."[58]

For the next few days we find little items about progress on the bridges. Then, another example of the difficulties that were forever arising between the proprietors of the Brown's Tract and the men they hired.

> *... Buem returns & says he has made fifty three rod (about 875 feet) of log way on the other side of Moose River. He swears that he will do nothing more to the hundred dollars job. Not one of the men who have taken jobs are satisfied with us or we with them. So impracticable it is to deal with the vagabonds in this quarter without imposition.*

Francis may have been glad to leave for the Tract, which he did the next day in "flattering weather," with "five pounds of powder & seven of sugar in a good pair of saddle bags. . . ." But if the weather started off good, it did not long remain that way, for Francis had to ride nine miles while the "rain poured in torrents." He was 'Wet thro' thro' & no whiskey or spirits of any sort." When he arrived, he found Herreshoff "blowing rocks for iron ore." The rye on the Hill was, he wrote, "looking charmingly. The grass also—pretty well at the middle settlement."

On the 13th of July, he recorded this encouraging report:

> *... A fine day—walk on the hill to see the grain. The oats & rye of a monstrous growth. Wheat has not come up well, but is notwithstanding very strong & healthy. Potatoes backward but thrifty. The promise of a great crop from all these—buck wheat too."*

The next day, however, he reported "a slight frost here, no mischief done, . . ."[59]

A few days later, Francis met Joy on the road he was building through No. 1. "Had a little sparring with the Major & left him in very ill blood. He has cheated me out of 85 dollars in the most barefaced manner. I threatened him with prosecution for burning my barn — called him a cheat & left him.

Until now there had been no indication that he was thinking of leaving, but then he "Received a letter from Eliza. I had almost made up my mind for a trip to Niagara yesterday but circumstances seem not to admit of it.

"Now I think of departing for Providence by the first stage." Which is exactly what he did, leaving Boonville the next afternoon. He noted that he had "been entrusted with three packages of money for Albany this afternoon, one from an entire stranger."

The road from Utica to Albany was "excessively rough" and "So dusty we could scarely breathe for the last twenty miles." The entire trip to Providence took him 10 days.

On the flyleaf of this diary for 1817, Francis jotted some interesting notes. For the road built through No. 1 by Major Joy, he gave him for the "Whole cost of his work $679.37½." Some other costs were: chopping at $6 an acre, and clearing from $13 to $15. Men were paid a dollar or 75¢ a day and one man, Sam Rowland, with his oxen, received just one dollar a day for 11 days.[60]

During these weeks, we know little of Herreshoff's activities, although it is probably safe to assume that he devoted himself with characteristic energy to seeking iron ore. We do know that he, three times during the summer, drew on Brown & Ives for $350, $300, and $300.[61]

The first Herreshoff letter we have for 1817, although we know from references in it that it was not the only one, was sent to his daughter Anne on September 5.

> *. . . I was determined not to let Mamma's birthday pass over without writing to you. . . . I received your third letter. . . last night. I can assure you that I appreciate your kind attention. I cannot help thinking that of all my children you think of me most and with most affection when absent, nor can I help entertaining the same feelings.*

One cannot help wondering why Herreshoff did not write directly to his wife Sally on her birthday. He wrote also of his son Charles Frederick.

> *. . . Our little Pip's birthday was with us also a most delightful one. I took my first trip on that day (July 26) in my new ship to the lakes, as I mentioned in my last, and my ship's crew wishing me during our passage to give her a name, I named her in honour of our little ship carpenter, the good ship Frederic, which was received with 3 cheers over a glass of grog. We returned the next day with a rich cargo.*

The letter continues, in contrast to some earlier ones, in a sometimes optimistic vein.

> . . . *We are now indeed all over end in business & shall be for some time, every day indeed brings his trouble, but in the main things go very prosperously. The forge is raised without incident, two gangs of carpenters are busy at it, one at the outworks & the other on the machinery inside, and the calculation is that it will be ready to go into operation by the 1st of November. We shall have blacksmiths, masons & coalmakers in a few days to add to the liveliness of the scene. My time is divided between that, the farming* [illegible] *& especially mining. We keep, you may tell Cousin John, the old Rock now thundering from morning to night, like a Volcano, nor does he produce mere empty sounds, but begins to throw out valuable matter. There is no more doubt but what we have two sources of the most valuable ore, and both inexhaustible.*

Herreshoff then discussed the progress he had made in farming. "We have had an uncommon show of warm weather this summer, upon the whole a fine growing season both for grass and grain, but a most horrid spell of bad hay weather; for three weeks it rained almost every day; you have no doubt heard of the great damage the freshets have made in many places, much grain also has been spoiled in this very neighborhood by the long continuance of wet sultry weather; we have luckily escaped all hurt, except the damage of some hay; I have however all my barns full & with oats, straw I shall have fodder enough for twice as much stock as I have. We are rather behind in our business on account of this delay and am driven to harvesting before we have finished hay making. My large rye field of 20 acres presents the finest show I ever saw of the kind, our best reapers find it a hard task to reap half an acre a day. I have 125 good loads of hay in safety and about 20 acres out."

Then Herreshoff launched into a discussion of Anne's penmanship, recommending that she practice more often. But he says something about his own penmanship as well.

> . . . *You may well observe that as to writing an apology of some sort would not be a bad apendia to my own letter. The iron bar, the drill, the hammer and sledge which I handle now with great earnest almost all day long, except while holding my pipe, are my apology; indeed my hands are so stiff, bruised and battered, that I can hardly hold my pen.* [We should note that nonetheless his handwriting is perfectly legible a century and two-thirds later.] *The slow progress of all my work here has tried my patience very much this season, when I think how fast winter is approaching and how much there is to be done yet before we are*

buried under snow, I almost despair of performing. It would however be a terrible mortification to me if I should not succeed making iron this winter, I could hardly live through it, hardly eat my Christmas dinner with you.[62]

Plainly, Herreshoff was planning to spend the long, bitter winter alone. How driven he must have been and what a strain this must have been for his family—and for him.

Even though Brown & Ives turned down his request for $5,000, Herreshoff was not reluctant to write drafts on them for smaller amounts, even though there is reason to believe, from the drift of their commmunications, that he was not authorized to do so. Indeed, Brown & Ives was itself in financial difficulty from over-extending credit to textile firms that bought the products of their spinning mills. In a letter notifying them that he had drawn on them for $400, Herreshoff wrote:

> *. . . My forge is in considerable forwardness, and will probably be ready to work about 1st November. Our ores are now beyond all doubt inexhaustible and of the richest quality.* [How tragically mistaken he was.] *It remains only to ascertain whether those same ores will yield a good iron here, as they do in other countries. There is indeed every possible prospect not only of a successful experiment, but of an opportunity for the most lucrative business on an extensive scale. The season has been a favourable one; my crop of english grain is extraordinary, both as to quantity and quality.*[63]

About now, we have to begin to wonder whether Herreshoff was beginning to succumb to a very human failing: to believe that something will succeed because one so very much wants it to, to make the wish color the facts. Dreams are essential to every great enterprise, but a dream falsely based usually becomes, as did this one, a terrible nightmare.

Six weeks later, on November 6, 1817, Herreshoff again drew on Brown & Ives, this time for $900. "My forge being so far completed that I dismissed the master workman and most of the other hands; I took the liberty to pass the following drafts upon your house. . . ."[64]

Again, about three weeks later, a draft for $300 is accompanied by another optimistic note. "I was confident of the richness of the ore, but the quality of the iron which it produced by far exceeds what I suffered myself to hope for."[65]

We know little of what happened on the John Brown's Tract during the winter, other than that Herreshoff wrote at least two more drafts on Brown & Ives, totaling $700. In the notice of the second draft, Herreshoff wrote: "Our season for these six weeks past has been inclement and snowy, almost beyond example. This has not slackt our exertions, but has rendered our progress difficult and slow. The gloomy days are however wearing fast away."[66]

On April 3, 1818, Herreshoff wrote two heartfelt letters, a short one to his wife and a long one to Brown & Ives.

> *... Could I give you an exact account of my past vicissitudes and troubles, you would not blame me for wishing my existence to be forgot by all my friends, till I could give a more agreeable account of myself. Nor have I by any means enjoyed my usual health. I enjoy however the pleasing reflection that I have been successful beyond expection in my undertaking in all the material points. If I can only retain one half it will be a solid foundation for a fortune to our children. I am now hurrying away as fast as I can and must hurry to close this on account of an intolerable tooth ache. We have yet about 2 feet of snow, but it begins to be very watery. Remember me to the dear children. I hope soon to be with you, and remain unaltered....* [torn][67]

In his long letter to Brown & Ives, he again tried to convince them that his labors over the winter had set the stage for a great success.

> *... I am now preparing for my return, after an absence of ten arduous months, at the close of which however I have reason to be thankful for signal success in all the essential branches of my pursuit....*
>
> *I would have returned four months ago, could I have been satisfied with my belief, grounded on appearances however strong, that my ore was surely as inexhaustible as it is excellent; without which the combination of so many favorable circmstances would in the end prove but a source of regret. Instead of suspending therefore, I pursued the mining business with redoubled vigour through the whole of this severe season and have by that means exposed to full view that Nature in forming this body of ore, has worked on a vast and magnificent scale. Thousands of tons are now as it were in plain sight.*

Herreshoff conceded that, although "the iron is much extolled, as new things often are," this is "most likely beyond reality."

> *... There is no need however of the wonderful. The truth is, it is without defect, and answers every purpose of the best imported iron, with the addition of perfect uniformity, no shade of variety being discoverable in the ore. These qualities ensure an extensive and permanent market. It is the opinion of the merchants in Utica that more than 500 tons would find a ready sale in that direction only which does not appear extravagant, considering that throughout this extensive country, North & West of Albany there cannot be a ton of bar iron made for common purposes, for want of good ore. The price of foreign ore has never been less than 130$ a ton in Utica and I can confidently assert that I will sell below that price with a profit of one hundred pCt, on the materials & labour. — We have ascer-*

tained the practicality of conveying the iron from the forge 13 miles westward by water, and within 12 miles only of the Utica turnpike, avoiding thereby all the bad road. The question is merely whether it may not require something like 100$ to remove some impediments in our little river.

Finally, Herreshoff explained to Brown and Ives why he had gone over the credit limit set by them.

. . . My effort, it is true, has not only been an irksome but also an expensive one, and I must appeal to your generosity on somewhat transgressing the limits of my credit. But the consequence resulting from it are such, that I cannot feel the least apprehension but that you will fully and heartily approve of my conduct. The great and solid value of the thing stands now beyond all doubt. Indeed it is an object, which to part with, One hundred thousand D^rs could be no temptation to a man with the means and inclination to pursue the business on a moderatley large scale, say for 400 to 500 tons annually. Nor did I intend to run the risk of your displeasure in this respect. Had I failed, whatever the consequences might have been, I would not have overstepped the limits.[68]

When, shortly thereafter, Herreshoff returned to Rhode Island, he again wrote to Brown & Ives, asking for a loan. He would need, he said, to buy coal and ore (until he could supply his own), build a dwelling for the workmen, a coal house and a depot at the head of river navigation for the outgoing iron.

. . . I pray for a credit to the extent of $3000—in case of absolute necessity. By the end of the year I will have made iron enough to cover the whole expenditure of the year, with a stock on hand, already paid for, to work 5 months longer. Arrived at that point I shall want no more assistance except from above.[69]

About two weeks later, on May 27, 1818, Brown & Ives sent its reply. Although it did not entirely shut the door, it was hardly encouraging.

. . . It appears that we have already paid & accepted a larger sum, than was contemplated & agreed upon when the mortgage was executed. It is very inconvenient going further in supply of funds for carrying on your Iron Manufactory, as we are hiring large sums of money for our own business & are paying 12 pCt p annum on very heavy Debts, therefore we should be doing an injustice to ourselves to proceed in this question, & more especially considering the great uncertainty of being reimbursed by a security on the Estate. However sanguine you may feel of having a substantial basis to meet these advances, you must recollect it depends on contingencys. Deprived of your personal *exertions, the Estate would at once degenerate, & leave a deficiency for what has already been done by us.*

After these discouraging words, however, Brown & Ives did hold open a possibility.

... We hope your family Friends, who are interested in your future prosperity would join and give you a proportionable aid. If they decline on the inability or in consequence of hiring for you the additional Funds, you may require, & yet are disposed in securing the advance, we have to propose that we ourselves will agree to hire, or supply the amt if either Mr James Brown, Mr Mason or the Female branches of the Family will undertake & engage to us in a written stipulation to make us safe by a collateral security. This last proposition, considering our own private Money engagements, must be rec^d by you as proceeding from motives of friendship, & we should say your influence might prevail with some branches of the Family & without this cooperation, you ought to excuse our declining.[70]

It would be unfair to fault Brown & ives for not being enthusiastic, for Herreshoff had had an unfortunate business career. And they did hold open a possibility of helping, should he get the backing of his family. Although we do not know to what extent, that backing was forthcoming, for by June 30, Herreshoff was back on the Tract. John Brown Francis was supposed to join him in early September, but on September 1, the day after he left Providence, he contracted a fever and was confined to bed for 25 days in Brookfield, Massachusetts, 30 or so miles northwest of Providence.

Thus, Herreshoff labored on alone. Things did not go well, as we see in this letter addressed to his wife Sally on her birthday, September 5. On this letter, his wife made the simple but melancholy notation: "The last letter I ever received. Dated Sept. 5th, 1818." Because of this special significance, we will quote the entire letter.

... My Dear Wife:

I had secretly determined not to write to you till I could give you the pleasing information that my forge was in full operation. But though I cannot give you such good news yet, I will not let this day pass by without some token of remembrance. I should at least have answered your letter so full of pleasing information, was it not so much against my inclination to write in an unhappy mood. How true what some celebrated author says, that the best human conjectures are but weak.

When I arrived here on the last day of June, I found myself very unexpectedly farther remote from the accomplishment of my plan than on parting. From a misunderstanding of my orders my overseer had set the rock blowers to work in the mine three weeks before my return. I found to my surprise that things had taken such a turn that I could not proceed without danger that the expense of getting the ore would be far exceed my calculations, nor did I see any prospect of arriving at a certainty for the future. I therefore determined upon a bold and tedious, but decisive manoeuvre, the result of which must either realize all my hopes to the fullest, or at once prove them to be out of my reach under present circumstances. I calculated it would take me about three months to accomplish that object; I have already entered the third withough having gained any great degree of certainty. The appearances, however, keep increasing in my favor, in my own judgment.

Everybody that sees this piece of Herculean work exclaims what a grand affair it would be if I succeeded, but, to tell the truth, not one single soul has the smallest belief in a favorable issue. That however operates rather as a spur than a discouragement upon me. I am still full of faith, or else infatuation, that I shall come off triumphantly in a short time.

Like all the rest of the world we have had a most glorious season, fine weather all the time, even during haying, when generally we are here most favored with copious showers. I have made one hundred tons of hay, and left grass unmowed. We might this summer have raised as good corn as any of our neighbors, if any had been planted. Of all the fine weather, however, I enjoyed but little else than the satisfaction that the storms did not interrupt my work in the quarry; there I have spent all my hours from morning till night, Sundays not excepted.

Once however I have been out as far as Trenton, 18 miles beyond Boonville, to stand my trial in the suit of the villain Joy, before Referees under rule of the supreme court. Though it lasted a part of two days, it remained undecided, and an argument of the lawyers on both sides is to take place this very day in Utica, which will bring the business to a close. It will make a difference of about 900 dollars to me whether I gain or lose the case, but I shall feel horribly mortified to have that ungrateful monster triumph over me. So far the case stands almost entirely in my favor.

Our daughter Anna I suppose is so absorbed by her studies that she never thought of me. How different last year; how grateful I felt then for her frequent letters. I love her more I imagine than I was ever conscious of before.

Sunday 27th September

I have let several opportunities go by to send out the above. I was constantly in hopes that by waiting a few days longer I might be able to say something rather more decisive in regards to my iron prospects. I can at last tell you that all is well. I am now only waiting for my blowers who stand ready to repair hither at my call, but are at present 120 miles from here. The moment they arrive I shall set the hammer in motion, not to rest again very soon I hope.

I have also gained a victory over old Joy, to his great grief. Several letter addressed to John Francis have arrived at Boonville; he had not made his appearance there last Thursday. Our summer is over; the nights turn frosty and the woods pale, I keep however no fire yet in my room. You shall soon hear from me again. Give my love to our dear children and believe me

Affectionately yours
C. F. Herreshoff[71]

One can only wonder how his beloved Sally reacted to this letter, all the more moving because of its restraint. Unhappy he plainly was, but he did his considerable best to keep self pity out of the letter.

For nearly the next three months we have a journal that Herreshoff kept. One suspects that his moods followed the news he recorded, sometimes good often not so good. For instance, on September 8, he wrote: "Great probability of having come to a body of good ore." But the next day he said: "The great appearance of yesterday, vanished today."[72] And on Friday, the 18th, Herreshoff recorded: "hopeless for the present." By the 19th, he noted "Things approximating to the certainty of a favorable issue," but added, rather more skeptically, "Like Christmas always coming." On Monday the 28th, he had all hands – his crew was usually four to six men – in the quarry working "to keep the water out."

On October 1, John Brown Francis, not entirely recovered from his ailment, resumed his journey to the Tract. Meanwhile, Herreshoff wrote that same day: "Found some very pure ore on the west side, and great appearance of its being a large and solid body – of red rock!" But the next day he wrote, "Every blast discouraging." The entry on October 3 was even more solemn: "All hopes blasted, at least for the present, . . ." And he recorded more bad news: "Letter from my daughter Anna . . . with the intelligence of J. Francis who left Prov. 31 Aug. being taking seriously sick at Brookfield Mass." Herreshoff, of course, had no way of knowing that his nephew, with whom he shared a mutual affection, had recovered and was on his way. Also that day he lists some goods that arrived at the Tract. It is interesting to note that coffee cost 37½ a pound and that he was using Dupont gunpowder at $9 a keg.

All during this period when Herreshoff could spare the men from the quarry, he had them digging potatoes, a product of the earth that cost a lot less and provided more value than the ore he was able to dig out.

On October 6, he noted that the dam was finished. On the 10th he recorded the rather equivocal notation that several blasts were "not quite discouraging. We concluded to make a few more experimental blasts for a day or two." But later in that same entry, Herreshoff said: "Everything is gloomy & desperate as possible." That same day, the 10th, John Brown Francis arrived in Boonville.

Up and down, up and down went the mood of poor Charles Frederick Herreshoff. It was a bit up on October 11, but a reader gets the impression that he was grasping for straws:

> . . . *Felt lowspirited in the morning and told Griff they might all depart to morrow. Going to the quarry however, I found upon examination some little glance*

of hope and determined once more to make a few blasts to morrow. Returning again to the quarry I had some new thoughths [sic] *on the appearance of things and made some little discoveries, which gave my ideas a very different turn from what they have been these ten days past. God grant that they may be realized.*

And on the 13th, Herreshoff wrote: "Find rays of new hope."

John Brown Francis, on October 11, reported in his journal that "Eliza's second daughter born in September."[73] Plainly, his lady love lost was still on his mind. He arrived at the Herreshoff Manor about six o'clock in the evening of the 14th, having spent seven hours on horseback making the 24-mile trip from Boonville.

The difficulty of the journey was attested to the next day by Nicholas Brown, Francis' uncle, who surprised them by arriving on the Tract the next day. "N Brown Jun'r surprised us by his presence this Even'g. He had no conception of the distance or state of the road or not a bribe would have got him here."

Although Herreshoff and Francis were surprised to see Cousin Nicholas, he had ample reason for visiting: family feeling, curiosity and, a factor not inconsiderable with a Yankee businessman, the fact that Herreshoff owed his firm, Brown & Ives, a lot of money. He could hardly fail to be interested.

There was a lot to be interested in. Herreshoff not only demonstrated perseverance, but a considerable technical ingenuity, as we see in Francis' journal for October 16:

. . . Mr H invention for cleaning ore a very ingenious one — a cylinder the size of a beer barrel is coated with a thousand magnets. It is put in motion (a very slow one) by a water power — as it turns, the ore is attracted by the magnet and then drops off. The ore falls on the cylinder thro' a hopper. This operation must be repeated twice as some of the ore is not separated the first time. The cylinder is free from the ore by a brush. Mr. H thinks with six cylinders revolving under the other he could clean two thousand pounds in a day.

The reputation of Herreshoff's invention must have spread, for many years later, Francis was addressed on the subject by men involved in a patent dispute. They were trying to prove that Herreshoff's device predated one patented later.[74]

That same day Francis also entered a social note: "Dine on venison, take tea with Mr Brown — pies such as would do credit to R.I." The following day he noted that "Mr H's sheep reduced to a flock of less than 100."

Winter arrived as, on October 19, Francis recorded that ice was a quarter of an inch thick. More important, however, is the fact that Herreshoff was not content with just one experiment to separate ore from the earth.

. . . Mr. H tried an experiment yesterday to clean the ore by throwing it in the flume at the mill. The current floated the light stone and earth some distance whilst the heavy ore sunk directly.

Herreshoff, in his diary for October 18, says of the experiment that it "promised to answer a great purpose."

Francis also discussed the commercial prospects of Herreshoff's iron manufactory. Although some of the figures in his journal do not appear to add up, he wrote that Herreshoff said he could sell iron for $140 a ton while producing it at a cost that would produce a profit of $82 a ton, with the capacity for making two tons a week. Thus, Francis entered exuberantly in his journal: "164 Dr a week!"

. . . There can be no fluctuation in the demands for iron. It must be eternally an article of the first necessity — hence the saying that ironmongers never become bankrupt. Their goods never go out of fashion.

If the ore is found in plenty *& of the same quality that has received such universal praise, nothing can prevent Mr H's success and he richly deserves it.*

Francis correctly perceived that the quantity and quality of iron ore was the key to the success of Herreshoff's dream or, as it unhappily turned out, the key to the failure of his dream. But that grim knowledge was yet to come.

On October 20 he noted: "My anxiety to see iron made here is the cause of my detention. Heaven knows how anxious I am to see home." Two days later he recorded that the "earth is cover'd with snow" and that he stayed indoors, "The walking being intolerably bad & the air too chilly for comfort." He wrote sympathetically of Morgan the hunter, who came in seeking relief from the cold because the weather was "too eternal" for his thin breeches. "The poor devil must have passed a miserable night. The life of a hunter has no attractions for me save what it partakes of independency."

On October 23 he recorded that it was cold and wintry, with snow on the ground all day.

. . . go to the forge & witness for the first time the manufacture of iron. Passed a very tedious day burning on one side & freezing on the other — but a coup-the *technical name for the iron that may be made (as corruption as I suppose of lump) was taken out just before night & put under the trip hammer. The iron of the same quality with all that has been made — its weight about 84 pounds.*

Mr H says 3 hours is long enough for a blast that 3 coups may be formed in a day — but double that time was consumed in the formation of this.

In his diary for the day, Herreshoff recorded that they "worked very slowly and cautiously."

On October 25, John Brown Francis made his last entries from the Brown's Tract during the life of his uncle Charles Frederick. He wrote highly of the iron produced. "Swedes iron is probably inferior. This is saying enough in its praises." And he reported of the workers that "They never saw ore work more kindly."

. . . Mr H is more confident than ever today that the ore such as he is in search of (so pure as not to need washing) is within a weeks drilling which may God in his mercy grant . . . They will make 40 tons of iron which Mr H hopes to see before he sees Rhode Island.

The forge is a substantial building fast by & is pronounced by judges to be remarkably well contrived.

I regret its vicinity to my mill on acc't of fire. There is said to be water for eight forges — or in fact double that number.

The following day John Brown Francis began the long trip home, stopping for a couple of weeks at the home of Stephen Smith in the nearby town of Russia. Smith, of course, was the surveyor who had long worked on the John Brown's tract. With him, as recorded in Herreshoff's diary, Francis carried letters from his uncle to his daughter Anna, to Brown & Ives, and some friends.

We can infer from his letter to Anna that she felt neglected, for Herreshoff wrote: "You are wrong if you ever let the idea slip into your mind that I could under any circumstances forget you, or which is rather the real meaning, gross indifference towards you, nothing can alienate my heart from you my dearest Anna as long as you remain good." Then he apologizes for what we take to be his neglect in writing. "I will not pretend to say however that any events or feelings form a just cause for depriving our absent friends of the satisfaction of hearing from us."

Herreshoff then wrote of her cousins, John Brown Francis and Nicholas Brown:

. . . I have received two letters from you. From the suspense in which I was left after the one which acquainted me with our cousin John's sickness at Deerfield, I was not relieved until I heard of his arrival in Utica. He arrived here the 14th inst and takes his departure to morrow morning. You may judge what an agreeable relaxation from my gloomy solitude these few days have been, and you

may also judge with what regret I see them passed away. Your cousin has been much benefited by our pure air and temperate diet, and looks now as well as ever. You will no doubt have heard before this that your cousin Nicholas Brown also paid us a visit and spent a day with us. The shortness of his stay you must not consider a proof that he was not over and above pleased; I believe he does not generally love to stay long in one place, except Providence.

As usual, in his rare letters, he tried to provide parental counsel.

. . . I am disappointed at your saying you were not sorry for having quitted your school, being you, as I imagined, much pleased with it, and in a good turn of improvement. If anything has turned up to disgust you with your school, let it not deter you from pursuing your studies, schools are of little use without private application, they ought only to be considered by young people as intended to teach them how to teach themselves.

The Herreshoff went on to say that he did not have much more to say! ". . . I can give you no news of anybody but myself, and when I tell you that I am well, it is nothing new."[75]

Francis stopped for a couple of days in Albany and visited the state comptroller on November 2, presumably to discuss taxes. The Brown family, like taxpayers in all times and all places, believed the taxes were too high. The comptroller "Thinks that the acc't may be settled & promises to send it to Prov as soon as it has been examined."

Francis, in his journal, discussed the Erie Canal, which, rather than bringing development to the Tract as hoped, was to divert settlers right past it.

. . . Albany is a place of perpetual bustle—the main street has all the air *of a city—shops without number & supplied on an extensive scale.*
But the spirit of the inhabitants now depressed. Prospects are s'd to be not the most flattering. This Canal which is to enrich so many may they apprehend impoverish them. The western country & NYK city will enjoy the highest benefits.

Francis left Albany on the evening of November 2 and, traveling on horseback, arrived in Providence on November 6, 1818. That was his last visit to the Tract before the death of Charles Frederick Herreshoff.

Herreshoff, saddened by his nephew's departure, nonetheless struggled on, and on October 30 "Discovered a vein of Peru ore, which has the strongest and most regular appearance of any yet found." The next day brought a letter from his wife.

Not until November 10 was there anything of note, but then, Herreshoff wrote of the "Discovery of a new vein in the new quarry from appearance by far the most important discovery yet made." On November 16, he recorded that

Mr Hoyt agreed to move to Moose river to keep a public house immediately, on the following conditions: 50 acres of land the old clearing included near Moose River and 50 acres more of his own choosing in the neighborhood to be given to him. I further promise to furnish him with a pair of cattle next spring....

On November 18 it was snowing all day, and Herreshoff reported the good news that "Mrs Keth had a son born last night." But then, three days later, he wrote: "Mrs Keth's infant died this evening at 8 ' Ocl." And on November 23: Mrs Keth's infant we buried in the afternoon on the mile farm."

From the quarries, the news was the same: sometimes good, sometimes not so good. For a few days Herreshoff was troubled with a toothache he described on the day of the funeral as "violent."

On November 24 he reported "rich ore," yet, by the 28th, he was saying of one of the quarries, "determined to give it up for the present." And on the 30th, he wrote, "nothing decisive or very encouraging," That was the final entry in the journal.

Certainly, the letter sent by Brown & Ives on December 5 could have done very little to encourage him.

... The amount of bills drawn upon us & of which we have been advised, since you were last in Providence, is Eighteen Hundred & twelve Dlls. The Guarantee sent from New York by Mr. Meirs [Meier] *is for* Fifteen Hundred dollars. *You being in the interior, far from the busy Cities, cannot be aware of the extreme distress amongst Commercial People for Money, which is certainly greater than has been known for many years. The inconvenience to us, of continuing these advances is much more serious that* [sic] *you can possibly be aware of. Our own want & the demands of other friends at this time of peculiar difficulty in raising funds induces us to beg you not to draw any further Sum upon us until again authorized by us.*[76]

However courteously put, the message was simple: No more money. But while that letter was en route to the John Brown's Tract, Herreshoff had drawn on B & I for another $300. This occasioned another letter from Nicholas Brown's firm.

... We beg leave to refer you to our letter of the 5 inst: which advised that we then had notice of your bills on us, to the amount of 1812 Dlls & that we had a guarantee for $1500 only, the one sent us from NYK by Mr. Miers. This day yours of the 8th has been rec^d by which we are informed that you drew on us that day to the order of A Vanstandwood [VanSantvoord], *for $300 at 60 days*

date. You will perceive by our letter, our great anxiety that you should desist drawing until further notice from us. The times are critical, Money scarce & confidence in a great measure destroyed among trading people. You will please recollect, you did not ask any advance of us, subsequent to your last visit, to this place, without giving satisfactory security. Mr Mier's we readily rec^d^ for the $1500 & we thought it was understood that Genl. Mason & Mr. Francis would assist you by giving a guarantee for the same amo^t^. This was our impression but we may have been mistaken. If so you will put us right by stating what the agreement actually was.[77]

We must assume that Herreshoff did not return to Rhode Island, but spent the winter of 1818-19 on the Tract, for he did not reply to the above until April of 1819. Surely, if he had been in Rhode Island, he would have visited Brown & Ives to discuss these pressing financial matters. This, of course, means that he did not see his family during the last year of his life. We can only imagine what a terrible strain it must have been on him and on his family. Especially since we assume that, during his last year, Herreshoff wrote even less frequently that in previous years. Thus, he and his family were cut off not only by distance, but by long periods of silence that must have seemed ominous to them. As to Herreshoff's state of mind, again we can only speculate, but the tone of the few letters we have, and his tragic end, permit of only one conclusion: a great and growing melancholy with no family or friends present to help him combat the gloom.

Since we have so few letters from Herreshoff's last year, it seems right to quote from them at length. First is that reply to Brown & Ives.

. . . *What you have pleased to say in your fav. of 17th Decbr. is perfectly correct, as regards the spirit of our arrangement last spring. I beg leave however to put you in mind of a circumstance, which makes a material difference as to my subsequent proceedings. On the morning of my departure from Providence I called on you with Mr Francis and proposed to you his guarantee for $1500 – and that of Mr C Meier for another $1500 – both of which you expressed yourself satisfied with. I never enquired of Mr Francis whether he had executed the requisite writing to that effect, taking it for granted. I now can but presume that he imagined you would call on him for it when the occasion required it. I will not pretend to any right, but I may say that I was not censurable for calculating upon a credit for $3000. I could have stopt short where you bid me to, had I been but a couple of months ago as far advanced in my business, as I am this moment, and probably could yet, had I not been so unfortunate as to lose my friend VanSantvoord; which cuts me of*[f] *from all further accommodation, and may likely distress me for the past, for it may yet require some months before I can realise something of consequence: I am in arrears to him for about $900 – I am now compelled to draw upon you, and most earnestly beg you not to view it as in defiance of your* *injunction, but as a step reserved for the last necessity. My forgemen going home to Vermont, in order to settle their affairs and to return in one month to establish themselves here. I have dismissed for that space of time, all my workmen, and am of course obliged to pay them most of their arrears, — not less than* [at this point the letter is blank]. *I have in consequence drawn this day upon your house $400 — fav. A Camp (who closes the business of the firm of Vansantvoord & Co.) — 60 days* [on account] *payable in NYork and $150 — 3 months after sight fav. Sheldon Fuller.*

I will not tire you with the particulars of the present state of my affairs, but Mr. Francis will shortly receive an ample detail.[78]

His elegant language and courtesy cannot hide the fact that Herreshoff was desperate. This desperation is more explicit in his letter of "ample detail" to John Brown Francis, which, however, he did not send until June 1819, more than two months after his letter to Brown & Ives.

Addressing his nephew as "My dear friend," he said that Francis has been "long ago sufficiently aware of the cause of my obstinate silence; I thought it indeed worse than useless to make any communication of my vicissitudes, until things had come to a perfect crisis; . . . ."

He reported that his forgemen, the Fullers, had not yet returned from Vermont; "They found some difficulty in collecting their debts." Plainly, as Brown & Ives wrote, the nation was suffering severe credit problems everywhere. He wrote that he had operated the forge during the winter "but . . . not in the right way, unless the ore can go straight to the fire from the mine, without magnetism or baptism (washing), the thing will never become an object of the magnitude" he had long hoped for. Evidently, the project depended on his finding ore of such quality that it did not have to be separated from the earth.

. . . I have done an immense deal of work since you left this; much more than all that was done before; I have had from 8 to 10 hands in the quarry at the time. One great point was my aim, for which I have been striving at all hazard: That whatever might be of my fate, I might feel sure that I had carried the business to such a stage, that it could not possibly be abandoned, but would be continued for the benefit of my friends concerned in my affairs and that of my family — But reflecting on all the circumstances I feel satisfied that nothing can make it sure, but a full perfect experiment — I have not succeeded in my pursuit, till after the eleventh hour; I have not the least reason to hope that I shall be able to carry it through unless some very unexpected aid should come to my relief, from whence I do not know; but you may rely upon it that if I fail, it will be like a man, in the last trench.

Herreshoff then asked Francis to notify Brown & Ives that he had written his last draft on them, one of $350, "which makes up the credit of 3000 Drs. overrunning rather a few Drs.

> *. . . But there is now an end of it on all sides. VanSantvoord you will have no doubt heard is broke and has moved off—If he had remained sound, I doubt not but that every thing would have gone well here.*

Added to his problems was the collapse of the Moose River Bridge. "I do not know what more to say than that it has been a subject of considerable distress, and that for 200$ a better one can be built, the loss of which is only owing to its miserable construction."

And Herreshoff ends with these sad words:

> *. . . Do not communicate to my family the contents of this letter till you hear again, which must be very soon; expect the worst, if it does not happen—tant mieux (so much the better)!*[79]

After that, a long silence. We do not know what was happening with Herreshoff's project on the Tract, but we must assume there was little good news, or he would have communicated it.

That year, 1819, saw the death of both of John Brown's surviving sons-in-law, James B. Mason, as well as Herreshoff. Mason, who briefly played a role in family attempts to develop the Tract, died suddenly on August 31. He was only 44. Although he entered the Brown family rather less than admired, he made a distinguished record for himself. For ten years he was a member of the Rhode Island House of Representatives, serving as Speaker in 1812 and 1813. He was also active in military affairs, and during "the alarm created by rumors of British invasion of Rhode Island during the War of 1812, was elected Major General of the militia of the state, and was reelected from 1814 to 1817. In October, 1814, he was elected Representative to the Congress of the United States, and was reelected, without opposition, in 1816. He was a trustee of Brown University and a member of the Cincinnati."[80]

Why James Mason ended his involvement in the Tract, after his vigorous efforts in the early years after John Brown's death, we cannot know. Maybe he saw that such efforts were a waste of time, or perhaps his life simply led him in other directions, for he was deeply engaged in business, political, and military affairs. But, to the best of our knowledge, the Mason branch of the Brown family was never again a significant factor on the Tract.

Shortly after Mason's funeral, Sarah Brown, John Brown's widow, turned over Townships No. 1, No. 2, and No. 3 to her daughter Abby Francis, her grandson John Brown Francis, and her other daughter Sarah Herreshoff.[81]

Just a few weeks earlier Herreshoff had written a despondent letter to John Brown Francis.

> . . . *The Br. Tr.* [Brown Tract] *account I shall approve with all possible measures in my power, if I should live to see Providence again, and if I should not I hope you will do it; you know that certain letters are here in my hands; written at that time by individuals here, which will have some weight. There are also statements of a few accounts with some of my workmen, sealed and directed to you, with remarks; thinking that in case of any accident happening to me, every one would be eager to help himself, and of more than his due. I have received yours of the 6th inst which gave me the first advice of Mr M.* [James B. Mason] *death, which of course I could not but anticipate. I have been for some time in the habit of burning your letters as soon as read, and I believe every body ought to do so with the letters of friends, when they contain any thing that the writer would not wish every body to see; we are in general too careless in that respect. I have no time now to give you a particular account of any thing; Gardner Vincent is this moment moving of*[f] *with his family; Browns wife has come in to take care of the house for a little while. Nicholas Vincent went away last spring. Remember me to the few you know I wish to be remembered. . . .*[82]

We do not know what Herreshoff was referring to in mentioning the "Br. Tr. account," but it is evident from the letter that he was preoccupied with the notion that he might not live much longer. Since, over the years, he frequently spoke of his good health, only one conclusion is possible.

A couple of weeks later, Herreshoff wrote to his beloved daughter Anna what is believed to be his last letter. She wrote on it: "The last letter I ever received from my beloved father." From what he wrote, it is evident that Anna, then only 17, volunteered to come live with him on the Tract. Although one must assume that his spirits were low indeed, there was no self pity in the letter. Rather, it was a lovely and affectionate letter, and only in the last sentence can we see, after the fact, that he had little confidence that he would see his family again. Since as far as we know these are the final words of Charles Frederick Herreshoff, we shall quote the entire letter.

> *My Dear Daughter Anna*
>
> . . . *And would you really leave so many dear friends, give up all you pleasures and comforts, to go into the wilderness to be a comfort to your poor old father? Heaven bless you. Surely I am better off yet than the poor wretch of a king who*

cried in the agony of despair: God help me, my own children have forsaken me!

I have yet what a crown can not buy: a heart that remains true to me through all the vicissitudes of life. Remain where you are, my dear child; make the best of your present time, such opportunities for improvement you will never have again. Enjoy the innocent pleasures of your age; the days in which you shall find no pleasure will come without your seeking. [Here the words "This is verified," have been added, years afterward presumably, in a woman's small, fine hand.] *I understand your sister Agnes is now with you. She learns with such ease whatever she is interested in, that it must give you pleasure to assist her in her studies. Her chief aim I hope will be to deserve the love of her friends by an amiable conduct. Be kind to her, my dear Anna, that she may be inclined to take advice from you; let those little explosions of a quick temper never make you for a moment forget that she is your sister, your own blood; nay, to speak the truth, they ought to remind you of it.*

Winter is again approaching, and you are not one of those, I know, who hail his grim visage. I never thought much of the heart of young people who prefer winter on account of parties, balls, etc. They ought to be sent to Siberia, without benefit of muffs or tippitts. The sociable shade of a tree is to me as far before your sociable fireside, as the sun is before the moon. People who have lost their hearts and are out of their heads, I believe always love the fireside and the moon, and they should be excused.

The season with us has been the finest I ever witnessed here; we raised no large crops of any kinds, but what we raised was remarkably good, as rye, wheat, corn, peas, and potatoes. Though we had much heat, yet we never suffered in the least from drought, which has been very harmful in some places of our neighborhood; neither have we been visited by hailstorms, tornadoes, floods, nor earthquakes, and of mosquitoes and flies we had no more than our usual crop. In fact, the whole season from May until now has been like one fine summer day, nor have the rude winds yet encroached upon it. Even today one would think it was mid-summer, walking through the woods, if it were not for the showers of pale and tumbling leaves that drop at every breath of the breeze. They are the tears of a parting friend, mingled with smiles, as if saying: we shall meet again! That we too may meet again, my dear daughter, is the ardent wish of

Your ever affectionate father,

C. F. Herreshoff[83]

What a lovely letter, and how often it must have been read in future years by Anna, who never married, and perhaps by other members of the family.

We do not know precisely what happened in those final two months of Herreshoff's life, but there can be little doubt that he encouraged his workmen, hoping to strike the rich vein of iron ore that could have made a success of his vision. Although we have no direct evidence of it, the story was passed down though generations that, instead of producing iron at a cost that would provide a handsome profit, it instead cost him a dollar a pound for the little he succeeded in making.

What we do know is that settlers were beginning to drift away from the Tract and that Herreshoff saw little chance of financial assistance from anyone. Perhaps we can assume that even his own family was reluctant to advance any more money, believing, like good Yankees, that it is wrong to throw good money after bad.

Anyway, winter settled in, the approach of Christmas, with family and friends so distant, could hardly raise his spirits, and then, finally, the quarry, his last forlorn hope, was flooded. On Sunday, December 19, life must have seemed insupportable. He picked up his pistol and ended the life that often, in his love letters to Sarah Brown, he said would forever be spent at the side of his beloved Sally.

Given the tone of his letters, his family, especially John Brown Francis, who got bleak reports that Herreshoff denied to others, may not have been entirely surprised. The family learned of his death in a roundabout fashion from a letter dated December 21 at Herkimer Village, some considerable distance south of the Tract. It was written to Dr. William Bowen of Providence by a man name Simeon Ford. Considering the appalling state of the roads in Herkimer County, the news traveled very fast, but then, bad news often does.

Ford wrote:

> *. . . A Man from the tract of land in the extreme north part of this county known by the name of "*John Browns tract*" called on me this afternoon with the extreme unwelcome information that Mr. Harrisoff (I do not know that I spell the name right never having seen it written) who married one of the daughters of the late Mr. John Brown of Providence put an end to his life by discharging the contents of a pistol through his heart on Sunday at his place—The Messenger was in pursuit of a Coroner to hold an Inquest on the body and called on me for directions—one has gone from this Village—the distance is about 50 miles—the jury will most of them be taken from Russia and have to travel about 25 or so miles there not being a sufficient number of persons on the tract to form a Jury—We gave to the Coroner in charge to have the body intered in a decent & proper Manner with as decent a coffin as could be procured thinking the friends might wish to remove the same which they can do if they choose—I communicate this to you as the only person in Providence with whom I have the honor of a particular acquaintance that you may communicate the same to the friends of the deceased—I was unable to learn anything particularly as to circumstances the Messenger appearing to be a man not very intelligent. . . .*[84]

It was more than a week before the unhappy news reached the family. Some time later, Abby Francis wrote this note:

> . . . *On the Eveg of the 30th of Decr 1819 we recd the melancholy intelligence of my brother in law Mr Herreshoffs death – The following morng I took Ann & Sarah w*[it]*h me & James drove us to Pt Pl* [Point Pleasant] *in my old carriage. After tea Sister discovered fm the appearance of Anne that something painful had occurred when, Alas! I was compelled to say that two days more only were wanted to make a fortnight since the fatal deed terminated the life of a friend who from my first acquaintance had been so interestg to me – The f*[irs]*t letters f*[ro]*m my Son informs me that a Wm Post was soon expected f*[ro]*m Boon Ville who had assisted at the funeral of our friend, I remained w*[it]*h the afflicted family untill Thursday #5# of Jany 1820 – The boys go to Mr Bates in Bristol.*
>
> *I found Mr Post on the Eveg of his departure – he appears to be a worthy Man & I hope his pecuniary loss will eventually be made up to him – it was at Boon Ville that the remains of Mr H. were deposited.*[85]

Among the family papers there is a handwritten copy of the notice that appeared in the "R. I. American of Dec 31, 1819:"

> . . . *In Herkimer Co NY on the 19 inst, Charles F. Herreshoff Esquire, of Bristol R. I. aged 50 years. A native of Prussia, he received his education in the German Universities, and was highly esteemed for his unblemished integrity, and for his accomplishments as a gentleman and a scholar.*[86]

There is an odd postscript to this melancholy tale. It has long been the accepted story that on Sunday, December 19, workmen came to the Manor and told Herreshoff that the quarry was flooding. Then, the story goes, Herreshoff went to the quarry, saw that the rising waters had extinguished his last hope, returned to the Manor to obtain the pistol, and put an end to his anguished life.

But, an account of Herreshoff's last days, that appeared in the 1860 edition of J. H. French's Gazetteer of the State of New York, gives a new dimension to the story, one we have encountered nowhere else. According to French, a respected historian, this is what happened:

> . . . *It is said that the day before his death he made preparations for going to Providence, and gave particular orders for his men to go out the next morning after he left and fill up a large hole that had been dug for ore. They went out to perform their labor; but one of them went down to see if any tools had been left, and at the bottom he found Harrisoff* [sic] *who had secreted himself there, intending to be buried. The next day he accomplished his object by a pistol shot.*[87]

What is there finally to say about Charles Frederick Herreshoff? By now, the reader will have reached his own conclusions, perhaps coinciding with the authors' that he was a man of intelligence, sensitivity, eloquence, devotion and integrity. So determined was he to overcome his disastrous business losses and establish financial security for his family, that he undertook in a fashion that can truly be called obsessive, the monumental task that finally broke even his great spirit.

We believe, too, that the conventional assessment of this fine man was ultimately incorrect. Not in recording that "He was a man of polished address, highly educated, an accomplished linguist in seven languages, and a good musician," for he was all those things. We think the conventional judgement that he was too fine a gentleman for such a daunting task is wrong. "His education and tastes were illy adapted to frontier life, and were not conducive to success in the pursuits in which he was engaged."[88]

On the contrary, Herreshoff demonstrated great technical inventiveness, he plainly inspired the devotion of his workmen, he constructed functional saw and grist mills and a forge, he raised crops in an inhospitable soil and he, over a period of years, proved that he had physical and mental stamina. No, the cause for his failure was not in Herreshoff, but in what he attempted. He had done all that any man could do, but nature was unyielding. Faced by nature's implacability, Herreshoff, given his earlier failures and ill fortune, simply could not return to his beloved family and admit this ultimate failure. It was as he said at the beginning: "I will settle the tract or settle myself."

10

The Third Generation

. . . or go on paying [taxes] until all the rest of our substance is swallowed up by this great Black River leviathan.

John Brown Francis, 1830

The country will remain for some time unsettled, in consequence of the rich lands which encircle the whole . . . region not being fully occupied, and of the facilities given to westward travelling, where land is as cheap and far more productive.

Lardner Vanuxem, 1842[1]

IF THE STORY of the John Brown's Tract were fiction, the sad death of Charles Frederick Herreshoff would be the place to end. But, as we all know, life is far less tidy than fiction, and the story of the Tract was not to end for another three decades. For all of that time the leading role was played by John Brown Francis, son of the man who, quite inadvertently, began the story. For much of that time, a significant role was played by his cousin, John Brown Herreshoff, son of the man who seemed hounded for his entire short life by ill fortune.

Although, as we have seen, Francis was the most realistic and skeptical of anyone in the three generations that comprise our cast, even he fell under the spell of the Tract. For some years he believed, like his grandfather and his uncle, that the Tract could be successfully developed. Only gradually did he come to realize what was immediately apparent to the geologist Lardner Vanuxem, that nature and the circumstance of history (the ready availability of far better land) had predestined failure.

For a time, Francis even believed that the dream of his uncle to manufacture iron in what is now the Old Forge area could be realized, but after a time he shifted his emphasis from Township No. 7 to Township No. 4, which did linger on for a couple of decades after a hopeful start, and which still appears on road maps of the region.

However, before we look at the final efforts to develop the John Brown's Tract, we must pause for a moment for John Brown Francis to perform a melancholy family duty. As Francis wrote, probably sometime in July 1820, "Aunt H slipped this into my hand as I was getting into the chaise desiring me to read it on the way."

. . . As you are going in the neighbourhood of Boonville or if you do not go, I wish you would order a plain grave-Stone to be placed with this inscription. "To the Memory of C. F. Herreshoff died Dec 19th 1819 aged 50 – born at Minden, Westphalia in Europe."

Some time hence perhaps there may be a monument erected elsewhere –

NB: I will furnish Cash to pay for this grave stone if there should be nothing there to pay it with – and I hope it will be done before the 19th of Dec. 1820.[2]

Herreshoff's tragic death at age fifty would place his birth as 1769, not as earlier chronicles recorded as 1763.

In July Francis journeyed up to the Tract, and appointed Charles Dayan of Lowville, a businessman and politician long prominent in the region, to be agent for his aunt Sarah and himself to sell lands in Townships No. 2 and 3 that straddled the Herkimer and Lewis County line.[3]

Francis evidently spent most of the summer on the Tract, for he was at No. 7, presumably staying in Herreshoff Manor, when, on September 30, he wrote a long, interesting and wise letter to his cousin John Brown Herreshoff, who was then only 15. Francis himself was only 29.

The letter began with words reminiscent of the younger Herreshoff's father, for Francis explained that he had intended to write earlier "but the desire of first seeing affairs in a less melancholy train than I found them in and of having it in my power to cheer you all with more agreeable expectations from this territory has hitherto restrained me." He continued in optimistic terms as, it seems, every episode in this narrative begins.

. . . I think it can now be unhesitatingly stated that affairs are in a train for a settlement and you may safely anticipate by the time you are of age that your mothers interest here will be worth your attention. Before then she may possibly be so fortunate as to have disencumbered herself of this land but such will not probably be the case, and you may therefore calculate at a future day to be called to some of the duties which now occupy me.

Francis then suggested some of the things that the young Herreshoff should study. Foremost among them he put "mensuration," or surveying, "the first study which will be indispensable in your case and which boys seldom attend to. . . ."

. . . There are many other studies in college which will be particularly useful to you such as chemistry, geology and mineralogy the latter was a very favorite study of your Father's whose memory must always be dear to you and which from this cause alone will be interesting to you. Indeed there is no study which will come amiss nor no situation in which intellectual cultivations is more desirable than in the life to which you are probably destined. I mean to that of the country gentleman whose resources must be within himself perhaps too there is no life more consonant with reason and true enjoyment. You must disregard the vulgar idea, so prevalent in New England that you cannot cultivate land without being a drudge yourself and that the most labourious man is the best farmer – in other words that agriculture is an occupation only for hewers of wood and drawers of water. At the same time you should be minutely versed in all that appurtaining to the business of a farmer or you will forever be at the mercy of those whom you employ.

John Brown Francis then went on in these philosophical terms about the place in society of the gentleman farmer.

. . . It is unfortunate that in our country almost everyone who receives a liberal education feels himself degraded by rustic employment and thinks there is no other resource than to apply himself to one of the learned professions – two of which are already filled to repletion. Indeed in the interior of this state it is said that there are more lawyers than cases & more doctors than patients. Upon the whole I see no other avocation for you but the primitive, and as I believe the most independent and happiest one.

Commerce you cannot think of as long as your mother owns fifty thousand acres of land it will be madness to dream of enterprises on the sea. Leave these to capitalists and adventurers who have nothing to lose and unless you have a decided disrelish for agriculture prepare yourself now in your youth for "just as the twig is bent the trees inclined." The situation of farmers in this state is more elevated than with us. Here the husbandman is really the lord of the soil. The agricultural interest is predominant if there is any one profession or body of men more influential than another, it is that of the large landholder and there are not a few of this description and in this neighborhood too. Even the King himself Jos Bonaparte is engaged in the same pursuit which may hereafter engross your care. Bear in mind I beseech you that these proprietors are not of ignoromi *that they are all well informed men and that their children will receive the best education as would not choose to rank below them then you will aim at their attainments; & of course reach their level.*

From every consideration then you are impelled to a diligent attention to your studies: to know the true use and value of time. Lord Chesterfield tells his son that whatever knowledge he does not solidly lay the foundation of before he is eighteen he will never be master of whilst he breathes.

The older cousin closed by urging the younger to "assiduous application" and bid him "never forget that you have a mother and sisters who will expect and have a right to expect a great deal from you."[4]

Wise as Francis was in discussing young Herreshoff's future, it was predicated on a false premise: that the family's vast landholdings were valuable.

After spending at least three months on the Tract, in mid-October 1820, Francis prepared to leave. As his grandfather before him, he had no choice but to rely, in his absence, on a local man. He chose Silas Thomas and, like John Brown, left him detailed instructions. Francis ordered that the saw and grist mills be kept in good repair, that Thomas was entitled to compensation for any sawing or grinding he did, but that he should not ask for cash from three settlers expected next spring: Humphrey, Lewis, and Perry. "As the settlers will generally be destitute of money I shall expect that you will saw on share or in any customary way which may accomodate you and them."

He also gave instructions as to the terms for selling land:

. . . I shall expect also that you will point out the land to the men who may come here after I am gone: representing its advantages etc and offering land to those who will move on next Spring at this rate viz — To every many with a family who will take up eighty acres you may offer twenty acres as a bounty. Deed after three years if the person has resided on the lot during the whole term. The remaining sixty acres at two dollars the acre payable in seven years with interest after two years. No man who takes less than eighty acres is to be entitled to a bounty.

Then, in a burst of confidence, he informed Thomas that "The cleared land near this house [Herreshoff Manor] I have reserved for the PASTOR with the two acres we talk of from Herreshoff & Meiers land a very pleasant residence may be obtained."

Francis wrote that he expected Thomas to build a house and reside for another season on the Mill farm, and he declared that he would give him one two-acre lot in the village [actually, *proposed* village would be more accurate], and sell him the other for $10, with the deed to be given "as soon as you have built the house which you contemplated."

. . . Another lot I have promised White. It is nearly opposite yours & he is to pay the same price which you pay in Martin [marten, an animal similar to the sable that bears fine fur] *skins. A deed to be given when he moves on with his family & builds a house and improves the land or as soon after as he delivers the Martin skins.*

After giving Thomas some other instructions as to crops and cows, he said "it is my express desire that you write to me at all times during my absence when there is anything worth communicating."[5] In this, Francis had about the same luck as his grandfather. Thomas evidently seldom thought there was anything worth communicating.

In a couple of days, Francis wrote to Thomas from Boonville. Now, he was so optimistic about selling land that he instructed Thomas not to offer a bounty.

. . . The news by the Fullers [the forgemen] *was very cheering and I have agreed with them to be here early in the Spring and to take the forge. If the water at the ore bed should subside they will agree with you to cart forty of fifty tons to the mills. You will therefore inform them of the situation of the bed by letter directed to Russie iron works. It would be a great thing to get ore this winter and you ought so to represent to them in your letter. We shall now have no want of settlers. There will be a throng next season and I would not have you offer any more land as bounty. Two dollars will be low enough. . . .*[6]

The next day Francis entered into an agreement with Robert Prichart of Boonville to buy the Gould farm, "lot No 11 in the 4th range of lots in the Township No. 7." These were the terms:

. . . provided the said Prichart removes to said lot before the fifteenth day of May next with his family and resides thereon three years in succession with his family improving the same during the said term according to the rules of good husbandry: that is to say: ploughing, manuring and seeding the old fields to grass also by transplanting the nursery on said farms and keeping the trees from the cattle also by clearing wild land on said lot, also by fencing the said lot into suitable fields also by repairing the old barn and finishing the new barn and keeping the said farm buildings and all appertaining to said premises in good order. Then with all *these requisitions faithfully performed and not otherwise the said Francis at the expiration of the said three years from the 15th day of May next promises to convey to said Prichart forty acres of land from some part of the said lot where the said Francis may choose.*

And the said Prichart on his part promises to remove to said farm with all his family before the said 15th of May & to pay to said Francis for the remaining part of said lot at the rate of two dollars the acre in ten years from the signing of this contract with interest annually after three years, . . .[7]

Another letter followed the next day, in which Francis discussed the road at Middle Settlement.

. . . Pray drive the business as much as possible for it is extremely important that the road should be a tolerable one at least & I hope you will set the Mill at work as soon as possible. It ought to be in motion all winter and if you undertake to get ore for the Fullers you will be obliged to employ a sawyer. A great quantity of lumber will be wanted. That coal heap ought also to be fired. I shall let the Fullers have it as well as the other coal heaps if there are any of which I have not heard.

Then Francis said that he had reconsidered his decision on not offering any bounty land.

. . . I wrote you that I should give no more bounty land but I had not time to express myself fully on that head. I leave this in some measure at your discretion. If you think that a number of settlers might be engaged this autumn if a bounty were offered who would not otherwise engage you may offer the bounty of twenty acres and if conversing with the Welsh or the Yankees you find that by writing or sending any one off, as I sent Prichart to publish to his countrymen the advantages attending a settlement on our Tract I hope you will not fail to do it. By the first Welshman you see [quite a number had moved into the general area] *you should send information of this kind and Sweet ought to let Justin know that the forge is to go into operation. Every body ought to know it. And the consequence would be a crowd of settlers in the Spring.*

They all tell me here that the moment I am gone things will be dead—nothing will be done until my return. But you must show them that it is not so [at this point he penned extra large letters] *And try to keep up the current which has been sent towards us by Heaven.*

Francis then reported on a trip to High Falls, now Lyons Falls, a few miles north of Boonville.

. . . The distance from the High Falls or a little above the Falls where they have built a bridge, is precisely eight miles from the line (boundary) of our Tract & this part of our line cannot be more than three miles from the middle settlement. I tell them I am ready to cut a road to the Tract line as soon as they will open one to the Falls where there will be in the course of a few years a considerable manufacturing establishment. [In this he was correct.] *From the High Falls to the long falls the river is boatable and from the latter place a canal is talked of to Indian river—thus in the course of a few years, a water conveyance will be opened from a place eight miles from my land to the St Lawrence and by this route our iron might be taken north.*

The soon-to-be absentee landholder then urged Thomas to try to find settlers who would pay for their land in stock. "Take cows as many as offered at a certain price," and he mentioned that one potential buyer had offered cows at $25 a head. And he urged that land be planted early in the spring.[8]

By the end of the month Francis was back in Providence. In a short note to Thomas, he discussed the road he planned to build to the east from the mills. "What part of it thro(ugh) my land must be made without money. Any person who will undertake it for land at 1½ Dollars per acre and will become settlers may have the job but they must be good settlers. Men I mean able to support themselves."

Speaking of the forge, Francis wrote: "I hope you have taken care to inform the Fullers of the situation of the ore bed but I am afraid there is no digging this season.

. . . Don't let those Welshmen get faint-hearted nor any one else but tell them all what indeed is very true that prospects are very flattering.[9]

In mid-November 1820, Francis responded to two letters from Thomas. He agreed on the need to buy a pair of horses. He said he would also send him money to build the road to the east, and to purchase provisions "which I shall expect you will yourself convey to the Tract and I shall depend on you for keeping the road open . . . You will also inform me how great a quantity of provisions will probably be wanted by the road jobbers how many dollars will supply them whilst making the road from the mills to the east road."[10] Although it may well be that road to the east was built, we have encountered no account of it.

Of the winter of 1820-21, there is nothing to report from the Tract, but on March 5, 1821, occurred the untimely death at the age of only 54 of Abby Brown Francis, daughter of John Brown, wife of John Francis, and mother of John Brown Francis. The latter was not yet 30 when his beloved mother died. She died leaving no last will and testament. This created a title cloud on Township No. 1 for a later owner, Mr. Lyon de Camp, which was cleared only in November 1931 by Julia Ann Herreshoff, the great-great-granddaughter of John Brown and great-granddaughter of Charles Frederick Herreshoff.

Almost immediately, Francis moved from Providence to Spring Green Farm in Warwick, where he lived in a rural setting for the rest of his life. At about the same time, he was elected to the Rhode Island General

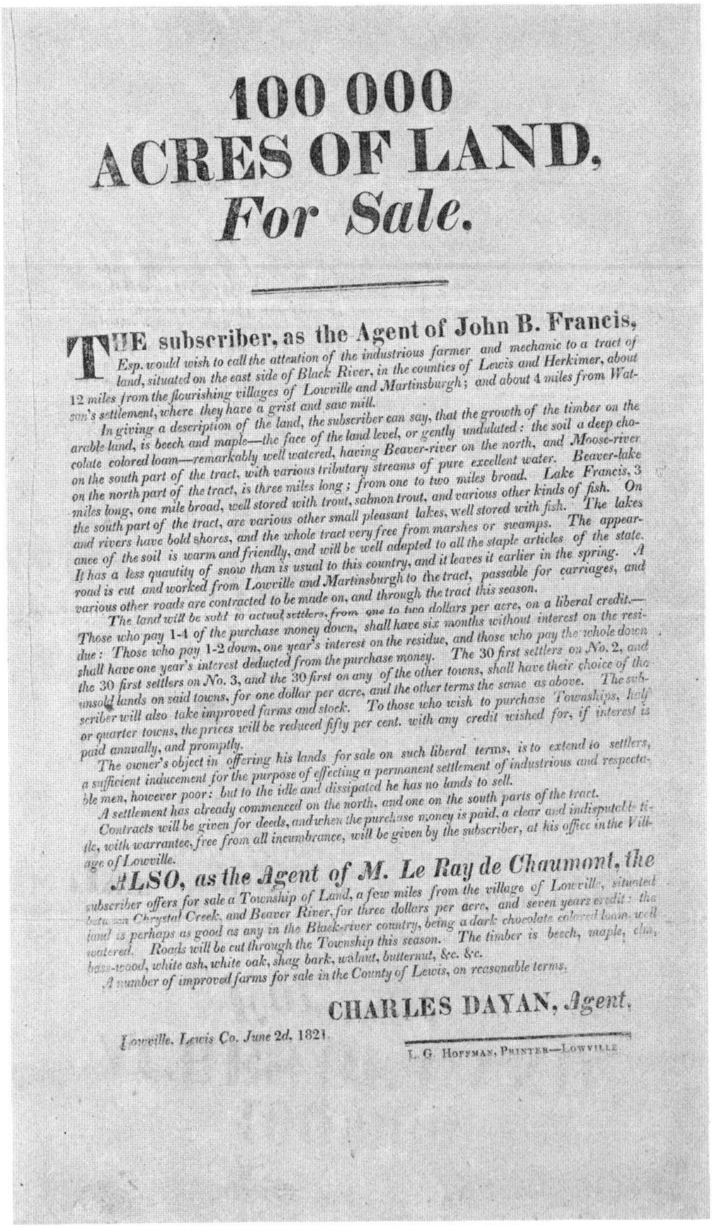

100 000 ACRES OF LAND, *For Sale.*

THE subscriber, as the Agent of John B. Francis,
Esp. would wish to call the attention of the industrious farmer and mechanic to a tract of
land, situated on the east side of Black River, in the counties of Lewis and Herkimer, about
12 miles from the flourishing villages of Lowville and Martinsburgh; and about 4 miles from Wat-
son's settlement, where they have a grist and saw mill.
In giving a description of the land, the subscriber can say, that the growth of the timber on the
arable land, is beech and maple—the face of the land level, or gently undulated: the soil a deep cho-
colate colored loam—remarkably well watered, having Beaver-river on the north, and Moose-river
on the south part of the tract, with various tributary streams of pure excellent water. Beaver-lake
on the north part of the tract, is three miles long; from one to two miles broad. Lake Francis, 3
miles long, one mile broad, well stored with trout, salmon trout, and various other kinds of fish. On
the south part of the tract, are various other small pleasant lakes, well stored with fish. The lakes
and rivers have bold shores, and the whole tract very free from marshes or swamps. The appear-
ance of the soil is warm and friendly, and will be well adapted to all the staple articles of the state.
It has a less quautity of snow than is usual to this country, and it leaves it earlier in the spring. A
road is cut and worked from Lowville and Martinsburgh to the tract, passable for carriages, and
various other roads are contracted to be made on, and through the tract this season.
The land will be sold to actual settlers, from one to two dollars per acre, on a liberal credit.—
Those who pay 1-4 of the purchase money down, shall have six months without interest on the resi-
due: Those who pay 1-2 down, one year's interest on the residue, and those who pay the whole down
shall have one year's interest deducted from the purchase money. The 30 first settlers on No. 2, and
the 30 first settlers on No. 3, and the 30 first on any of the other towns, shall have their choice of the
unsold lands on said towns, for one dollar per acre, and the other terms the same as above. The sub-
scriber will also take improved farms and stock. To those who wish to purchase Townships, half
or quarter towns, the prices will be reduced fifty per cent. with any credit wished for, if interest is
paid annually, and promptly.
The owner's object in offering his lands for sale on such liberal terms, is to extend to settlers,
a sufficient inducement for the purpose of effecting a permanent settlement of industrious and respecta-
ble men, however poor: but to the idle and dissipated he has no lands to sell.
A settlement has already commenced on the north, and one on the south parts of the tract.
Contracts will be given for deeds, and when the purchase money is paid, a clear and indisputable ti-
tle, with warrantee, free from all incumbrance, will be given by the subscriber, at his office in the Vill-
age of Lowville.

ALSO, as the Agent of M. Le Ray de Chaumont, the
subscriber offers for sale a Township of Land, a few miles from the village of Lowville, situated
between Chrystal Creek, and Beaver River, for three dollars per acre, and seven years credit: the
land is perhaps as good as any in the Black-river country, being a dark chocolate colored loam, well
watered. Roads will be cut through the Township this season. The timber is beech, maple, elm,
bass-wood, white ash, white oak, shag bark, walnut, butternut, &c. &c.
A number of improved farms for sale in the County of Lewis, on reasonable terms.

CHARLES DAYAN, *Agent.*

Lowville, Lewis Co. June 2d, 1821.

L. G. HOFFMAN, PRINTER—LOWVILLE

1821 broadside advertising 100,000 acres of Tract land for sale.

Assembly, beginning a political career that saw him in office at the local, state, or national level for 35 years. He held a number of local offices, and served also as a member of the Rhode Island House and Senate, as governor and as United States senator.

On June 2, 1821, Charles Dayan had printed a broadside advertising "100 000 ACRES OF LAND For Sale."

. . . THE subscriber, as the Agent of John B. Francis, Esq. would wish to call to the attention of the industrious farmer and mechanic to a tract of land, situated on the east side of Black River, in the counties of Lewis and Herkimer, about 12 miles from the flourishing villages of Lowville and Martinsburgh; and about 4 miles from Watson's settlement, where they have a grist and saw mill.

In giving a description of the land, the subscriber can say, that the growth of the timber on the arable land, is beech and maple—the face of the land level, or gently undulated: the soil a deep chocolate colored loam—remarkably well watered, having Beaver-river on the north, and Moose-river on the south part of the tract, with various tributary streams of pure excellent water. Beaver-lake on the north part of the tract, is three miles long; from one to two miles broad. Lake Francis, 3 miles long, one mile broad, well stored with trout, salmon trout, and various other small pleasant lakes, well stored with fish. The lakes and rivers have bold shores, and the whole tract very free from marshes or swamps. The appearance of the soil is warm and friendly, and will be well adapted to all the staple articles of the state. It has a less quantity of snow than is usual to this country, and it leaves it earlier in the spring. A road is cut and worked from Lowville and Martinsburgh to the tract, passable for carriages, and various other roads are contracted to be made on, and through the tract this season.

The land will be sold to actual settlers, from one to two dollars per acre, on a liberal credit—Those who pay 1-4 of the purchase money down, shall have six months without interest on the residue: Those who pay 1-2 down, one year's interest on the residue, and those who pay the whole down shall have one year's interest deducted from the purchase money. The 30 first settlers on No. 2, and the 30 first settlers on No. 3, and the 30 first on any of the other towns, shall have their choice of the unsold lands on said towns, for one dollar per acre, and the other terms the same as above. The subscriber will also take improved farms and stock. To those who wish to purchase Townships, half or quarter towns, the prices will be reduced fifty per cent, with any credit wished for, if interest is paid annually, and promptly.

The owner's object in offering his lands for sale on such liberal terms, is to extend to settlers, a sufficient inducement for the purpose of effecting a permanent settlement of industrious and respectable men, however poor: but to the idle and dissipated he has no lands to sell [emphasis added].

A settlement has already commenced on the north, and one on the south parts of the tract.

Contracts will be given for deeds, and when the purchase money is paid, a clear and indisputable title, with warantee, free from all incumbrance, will be given by the subscriber, at his office in the Village of Lowville.[11]

The Tract certainly sounded appealing, but has it not always been thus with land advertisements?

Dayan, also agent for Le Ray de Chaumont, a big French landholder in the vicinity, was a man of considerable prominence. An attorney, he was later elected to the state senate, serving as president pro tem of that body and as acting lieutenant governor. Subsequently, he was elected to a single term in Congress and to the state assembly. There, in company with his friend and neighbor Francis Seger, a member of the senate, he was largely responsible in the 1830's for legislative approval of the Black River Canal, a hugely popular project in the area.[12] The Brown family hoped, as they had with the Erie Canal, that it would stimulate development of the John Brown's Tract. But the Black River Canal, like the Erie, served largely to by-pass the Tract.

Either John Brown Francis lost interest, at least temporarily, in the Tract or his letters have disappeared, for we have only one brief note for all of 1821 and it is not very illuminating. This is the entire note:

. . . I have not had the pleasure of hearing a word from you or of the Settlement since I left there. I do not even know whether you have not all been devoured by the Grass Hoppers. Please to write & inform me how you progress—also whether Mr. Lyon has been out & what he is doing—Remember me to all the settlers & believe me, Yr friend JBF

He added a postscript: "Did you conclude to take the oxen & what cattle can be sold this autumn?"[13]

Francis evidently forgot that he had received a couple of letters from Thomas the previous fall, but he plainly was not thinking about Township No. 7 a great deal. One important bit of information did emerge from the note, however, "Mr Lyon" was almost certainly Caleb Lyon, father of the Lyman R. Lyon who, three decades later, would buy up almost all of the John Brown's Tract.

For whatever reason, Francis' apparent waning interest or, more likely, nature's inhospitality, the ten or so families in the Old Forge area began to drift away. The little school run by Emeline Sperry began to dwindle from its peak enrollment of about 15 children. And Herreshoff's forge no longer served as a favorite plaything of the children, who delighted in turning on the water wheel and watching the huge hammer crush stones. The mills began to fall into disrepair and, within a few years of the death of Charles Frederick Herreshoff, the settlement to which he had devoted all the energies of his last years began to crumble.[14]

John Brown Francis now turned his attention to Township No. 4, Unanimity, but never with the vigor or personal participation that long characterized the family's efforts at No. 7. Never again would Francis spend long months on the Tract. Perhaps other matters, such as his increasingly important political career, took precedence, or he had concluded that, since the long and dedicated labors of his uncle Charles Frederick Herreshoff and himself had achieved so little, any further efforts would be a waste of time, energy, and money.

Whatever the reason, the emphasis shifted from the Old Forge area to the northwest corner of the Tract. For a while, development there showed promise, more with little assistance from the family than was ever shown at No. 7, despited the strenuous and costly efforts of three generations of Browns. Yet, No. 4 also, after a decade or so, began to fade and for the same reason, the inhospitality of nature.

The story of No. 4 lends itself to being told largely in one section, for there is not nearly as much original material available for it as there is for the Old Forge area and the Tract as a whole. Although there are a few family documents and some land records at the Lewis County Clerk's office in Lowville, the chief source is a quaint and curious little pamphlet written in 1863 by W. Hudson Stephens, an attorney who had professional dealings with Orrin Fenton who lived at No. 4 for 36 years, long after everyone else had left. Published in Utica in 1864, it is very rare, with only a few copies known to exist. Fortunately, Donaldson, in his magisterial history of the Adirondacks, includes it as an appendix. It has the charmingly archaic title of: HISTORICAL NOTES OF THE SETTLEMENT ON NO. 4, BROWN'S TRACT, IN WATSON, LEWIS COUNTY, N.Y. WITH NOTICES OF THE EARLY SETTLERS.[15]

According to Stephens, the district first came to notice in 1818 or 1819 when a group of prominent men from Lowville, including Cornelius Low (after whose father the town was named) and Charles Dayan, with Thomas Puffer as guide, went fishing for eight days at Beaver Falls. The first settler in the vicinity, a bit to the east between No. 4 and the Beaver River, was believed to be Ephraim Craft. Then a man named Lippincott lived for one season at No. 4 "in a stockade of upright sticks."

Organized settlement began in 1822, when Francis offered "a farm of one hundred acres to the first ten settlers." That year the offer was taken up by Aaron Barber and Benjamin Bunce. In subsequent years they were followed by William Chandler, Levi Barber, Lorenzo Post, Hezekiah Tiffany, Ives B. Rich, John Gordon, John Rettis and Jabez Carter.

Little is known about any of these pioneers, other than Carter. About him, Stephens provided this brief sketch:

. . . Jabez Carter, settled in February 1825, one hundred and two acres under contract with Herreshoff to remain thereon four years, to clear sixteen acres and build a house and barn, for which was to receive at the expiration of four years a deed of his "inducement." He removed therefrom in December, 1831, but not without giving the settlement the benefit of his varied skill and capacity, he having taught at No. 4, the first school of about thirty-five scholars at fifteen dollars a month, and boarded himself. He engaged in the mercantile business and potash manufacture, and established a still for expressing hemlock, balsam, and tamarac oils, of which he marketed a total of one hundred pounds. He also acted one year as superintendent of the common school, of which he was the teacher, and trusted out as a permanent sinking fund about $300 of his goods and groceries for the general well being of the infant settlement. He still retains, however, the fee of his one hundred and two acres, with its ninety cents yearly tax; though his attention at the age of seventy-three in public affairs is engrossed in the manifold and multiplied duties of Liquor Commissioner of Lewis County, residing at Lowville.

The reference to Herreshoff is probably mistaken, or the date of Carter's arrival, for John Brown Herreshoff did not move to Lowville as agent for the Tract until 1830.

Orrin Fenton, the longest and most notable inhabitant, came to No. 4 in 1826 at the age of 41. A native of Mansfield, Connecticut, he moved out to No. 4 from Lowville with his second wife, Lucy Weller of Westfield, Massachusetts. There they remained for 36 years, until 1862. They had, however, not discovered a way, unknown to other settlers, to make a farm flourish. Rather, they quickly concluded that, since farming did not pay, they had to do something else. They decided on establishing a hotel and, rustic as it was, it prospered as long as they lived there and longer, with Fenton serving as guide to hunters and fishermen.

"When Fenton established a post office at his hotel, it was given the official designation of 'Number Four,' the only instance of the kind on record."[16]

Clearly, the other inhabitants of No. 4 were not prospering, for on December 10, 1827, eight of the settlers, including Fenton, sent this plaintive note to John Brown Francis:

. . . We the subscribers and inhabitants of your humble society on No. 4 send greeting this stipulation viewing our present situation we are constrainted to write a few lines to acquaint you of the situation in this place the prospects that we

anticipated when you was present with us have not realized we understood that some provision was made for the survey of some lots of land in this place and also for some roads but there is not anything of this kind been done nor is there we think any prospects of any thing being done we are afraid the settlement will decrease in this situation we know that something must be done for the growth of this place we are being very urnest in our request to you to solicit you as the power lies wholey on you to in the present situation we write to your with confidence that sumthing will be done to benefit us

Signed in behalf of your humble society

Lorenzo S. Post
Jabez Carter
William S. Chandler
Peter Wakefield
Ives B. Rich
William Stanton
Orrin Fenton
Hezekiah Tiffany[17]

We do not know what response, if any, Francis made to these dispirited men, but most of them stayed, at least for a while, for we find in the Lewis County land records that, over the next few years, Rich, Chandler, Carter, Wakefield and Tiffany received, for a nominal fee, often $1, deeds for their land.[18]

The settlement reached its peak in the mid-1830's. A saw mill had been built and "more than a thousand acres were cleared and fenced off into farms and gardens. A schoolhouse was erected, and more than sixty scholars gathered in. Within ten years after the first clearing was made, some seventy-five settlers were trying their fortunes at No. 4.[19]

Church, as was not uncommon in pioneer society, was apparently the center of life at No. 4, and "in 1842, a religious revival took place, at which Elder —— Blodget and others ministered making sixty converts." Some years earlier the Lowville Baptist Church had established a branch at No. 4.

. . . The Fenton family and some others resided there. Several were baptized and became members of this church. Mrs. Eunice Fenton McGlachlin was baptized May 10, 1835, and died June 28th, 1908. Her brother George Fenton, died January 6th, 1921, aged 101 years, having been a member of this church 77 years. These were the last surviving members of the Number Four branch.[20]

Although the settlement was fairly large, it was surrounded by very wild country. There is, for instance, the famous story of Orrin Fenton and his panther. About 1835, he went out to check on his wolf trap and found that it had been carried away. He followed the trail, first arming himself with a club, and when he came across the tormented animal, it was not a wolf but a huge, and very angry, panther. He quickly thought better of trying to dispatch the beast with his club and hurried back to the settlement for a better weapon, and reinforcements. He returned with his rifle and a neighbor, Isaac Wetmore. It took two shots to kill the panther, which measured nine feet from tip to tip and weighed about 200 pounds.

And, as late as 1863, when Stephens wrote his pamphlet, No. 4 was so remote as to be "Without litigation – almost beyond all public duty or burdens, except the draft (the call of war reaches every abode) these families, without school or ministration, have mingled the duties of the farm and the sports of the field and stream."

The settlement's peak did not last long, and soon thereafter, the discouraged farmers began to drift away. The 1894 report of the New York State Forest Commission explained why:

> *. . . But it would seem as if Nature had designed the Adirondack Plateau for forests and not for farms; and all the patient toils expended on the enterprise at Number Four, all the hopes and fears of these early settlers, added but another chapter to the old, sad story of a Wilderness that will not be tamed by man.*
>
> *The soil was none of the best, the climate was cold, the summers were short, and the winters were long; the markets were distant, and the roads to them through the forest were almost impassable during much of the year. One by one the settlers, growing weary of the undertaking, sold out their improvements or abandoned them, and with their families left the forest hamlet to seek other homes. And now the old dwellings, with two or three exceptions, have disappeared; the school-house and its children are no longer to be seen; the fences are gone, and the once cleared fields have reverted to their original forest state.*[21]

But the settlement at No. 4 was active for a dozen years or so, which, despited the fervent efforts of Charles Frederick Herreshoff and those of his nephew John Brown Francis, was more than was ever accomplished at No. 7. Finally, in 1862, at the age of seventy-eight, even Orrin Fenton and his wife had to leave. When, with W. Hudson Stephens as the attorney, they were closing their sale, they produced, discolored with age, the original deed of 1826, signed by John Brown Francis and his wife Anne, and never recorded.

Returning to our chronological narrative, we find that on June 18, 1822, John Brown Francis married his cousin Anne Carter Brown, daughter of Nicholas Brown, Jr., and granddaughter of Nicholas, eldest brother of

John Brown. For their wedding trip, they journeyed to Albany, Saratoga Springs, Niagara Falls, Montreal and Quebec, accompanied by their cousin Anna Herreshoff, stopping briefly at the John Brown's Tract. Anna wrote a long letter to her sister Agnes describing the trip, but of the Tract, all she reported was that "the warm welcome we received was highly gratifying."[22] She did not indicate where on the Tract they visited.

Plainly, John Brown Francis was not in close touch with developments—if there were any developments—in the Old Forge area. This is clear from a letter he wrote to Silas Thomas in November 1822.

> *. . . I have delayed sending you the hundred dollars which I promised expecting every day first to hear from you acknowledging the receipt of the money which I sent in the summer—but having rec'd a letter from the Capt expressing great anxiety on your score for money I herewith send you C R Staffords order for one hundred dollars on Mess Dunham & Auchincloss of New York—I shall not send you any more money until I hear from you. I beg you to write me particulary* [sic] *respecting my concerns & whether you wish to come down here the latter end of feb'y. Furs would sell as well here as in any part of the U. S.*
>
> *What good would be answered by yr coming? Are those horses worth anything? Are they not too old? Are they good for anything? What plan have you for the Spring! How is the settlement to get on? What do you hear of Lyon or of Dayan?*
>
> *I have neither heard from them or anyone else in your quarter; & am utterly ignorant what you are all about.*
>
> *The Capt said something of an offer from Wilcox to furnish sheep. If you see Wilcox inform me of his terms & tell me what he has done. Do you think that he would be concerned with Lyon or that Lyon would bring aught to pass? I am strongly inclined to sell a few thousand acres to some enterprising man.*
>
> *There was one in Lowville of the name of Stickney.*
>
> *All the information you can furnish write me immediately. . . .*[23]

The reader will perhaps share with the authors a sense of *deja vu*, for previous absentee landlords John Brown and James B. Mason found themselves in a similar predicament. They simply did not know what, if anything, was happening.

During 1822, Francis took an action that was to significantly influence his life. He became secretary of the Rhode Island Society for the Encouragement of Domestic Industry, an association of many of the leading men of the state dedicated to promoting the interests of agriculture and industry. This association with so many prominent men obviously helped his rapid advance in public life.

After the letter to Thomas, seven months passed until July 1823 before we have any more information, this time in a letter from Charles Dayan.

We infer that the silence has been on the part of Francis. "I again wish to approach you on the subject of the agency and in doing so ask your pardon for troubling you on a subject of which (I presume from your silence on my former communications) you are already weary or disgusted, that I have been to [sic] sanguine for your wishes I think probably but not for your interest, if you have an interest for the settlement of your lands—"

Dayan then said that two men from Harrisburg, a town next to Lowville, had examined that Tract and wished to exchange their developed farms for Tract lands

> *... now under my present authority I can do nothing with these men I have reason to believe that if those men go on others will follow (but here again I may be to [sic] sanguine) I give you the facts draw your own inferences; we have four men on the tract that are making considerable improvements and others have spoken for land there—I hope therefore that you will answer me one way or the other, if you have reason to withhold the promised authority I have nothing to say, but if the only fault is that I am too sanguine I will endeavor to be more moderate—that part of my former letter and that one that remains yet unanswered which spoke of the commission probably gave you offence, but it was intended to show you that your interest and my determination influenced me and not my individual interest—But if it is your wish to displace me but say the word and it is done*
>
> *Your settlement advances slowly but I hope what is done will be done permanently the inhabitants now on are sober industrious and good members of society they are much pleased there, and according to the common course of things will soon draw on their friends who as I understand are only waiting the see the productions which I have many reasons to believe will be good*
>
> *There is no prospect here of selling any large quantity of land Gen Martin tells me that he has no wish to purchase but at other times he says he will go over but it('s) only to fish—It is true that I have been mistaken as to the rapidity of settlement but that that mistake or my visionary exertions and chimeras has retarded it I shall not believe and I think you yourself wished me to keep the iron hot... The reputation of the tract is now increasing good (as better reports are brought from it daily) and people are induced to say that it is probably that a settlement can be made this is more than they used to say the land which is now taken is by gift and I have acted under the authority of Mr Beach if that is not right or revoked I ought to know it from you—*[24]

Francis had had enough empty optimism, for it had long brought financial distress to the Brown family. We get the impression, although he did not say it directly for some time, that Francis would be happy to dump his lands if only he could find a buyer.

For a moment, there seemed as if there might be such a buyer. An Elisha Smith wrote to Francis that he had visited the Black River area and had talked with Caleb Lyon about

> *the* Brown *tract of which I was informed by him that you are part owner & that he has an agency under you. Although attempts to settle this tract have heretofore as I understand been unsuccessful, and the tract is in bad repute yet I am induced to believe that a settlement may be made on the tract by exchanging for improved farms. I however can only be satisfied as to this on viewing the tract. I have been engaged in selling a tract in the Western part of Pennsylvania which we have principally exchanged for farms in this section of the state of New York which was the only means of selling the tract.*

Smith said that he would be in Providence in two or three weeks, and would like to see Francis. "I found Mr. Lyon a friendly, intelligent man and well calculated to settle a new country . . . If I should undertake a settlement on your tract I should be glad to have Mr Lyon have an interest in the tract for I consider him endowed with first rate talent, and perseverance to effect an object of this land. . . . ;"[25]

The exchange of improved land, as we saw earlier, was a common practice. A farmer and his family would go to wild lands, clear and farm them, and then exchange them for a large piece of undeveloped land. With each exchange, the farmer's property would grow appreciably in size until he finally decided to settle down.

This letter from Elisha Smith was typical of what would happen time and again for the next quarter century or so. Someone would express interest, Francis would respond, but eventually nothing would come of it, until finally, Caleb Lyon's son purchased the Tract.

Virtually nothing was heard of the Tract for more than a year, but then in December 1824, a mortgage was drawn up in which Francis, for $796, sold a parcel at No. 7, one that included buildings, machinery, and water rights. Although the lot was described, its size was not specified, but plainly it was the acreage that included the forge and mills built or put into good repair by Charles Frederick Herreshoff. The purchaser was Justus Goodwin of West Brunswick, Herkimer County. But since that parcel apparently ended up in other hands, we must assume that Goodwin left before long.

The year 1825 was an auspicious one for upstate New York. The entire length of the Erie Canal was opened. The joyous news was carried from Buffalo to New York in just eighty minutes by a succession of cannon shots. Once, there was a conviction that the opening of the canal would greatly benefit the Tract, but just the contrary was true. "The Erie Canal, completed in 1825, provided an easy route to the West. Land agents in Albany were no longer able to turn settlers north."[26]

That year, 1825, also saw Providence grow to a town of 16,000, although it was possible still to address a letter solely with the person's name. And that year, on February 25, saw the death of Sarah, widow of John Brown, at the age of eighty-six, having survived her husband by twenty-two years. She left her house, the great mansion that is now the centerpiece of the Rhode Island Historical Society, to son James, and the furniture to daughter Sarah.

Other that those few items, the year 1825 slipped by with no news from the John Brown's Tract. Were it not for one letter, 1826 would also have passed similarly unnoticed. The letter was from an E. Varney of the Herkimer County town of Russia. It begins rather amusingly:

I take the liberty of addressing you on a subject which may prove of more importance to you than to myself (to wit) will you have the goodness to inform me what No. of acres of land you own in a tract of land known and distinguished by the name of Browns tract—please to give me the No of the Township, the No of acres in Each township, and if you wish to dispose of your lands, viz said tract inform me what your price would be for the whole quantity—

Varney said he was enquiring on behalf of some men who wanted to establish settlements

in that section of this state—and as the drift of emigration continues to be to the far west, some of our enterprising citizens would be willing if possible the western emigration by holding out some inducements to them nearer home,—if you should think proper to answer the above I will correspond with you farther on this subject[27]

In July 1827, James Brown, then sixty-five, journeyed to Niagara Falls, with a brief stop at Albany. Although we know he had a letter of introduction to Governor Clinton, we do not know whether they met.[28] If so, we can only presume the subject was the familiar one: the taxes on the Tract were too high.

Taxes were the subject of a postscript John Brown Francis added to his wife's letter to Anna Herreshoff:

. . . Perhaps it is best for your Mother to express to me her views in relation to Township No. 3. Whether she is willing to sell should an opportunity offer at a very very *low rate. I am afraid we must all be driven to this alternative by* taxes—*They will hereafter be heavy—more and more so. Ask her to write on the reception of this to* Boonville. *We hope to reach Albany by 2 oclk on Tuesday Morng, and the Black River on Thursday the 16th—*[29]

We assume that the Francises tarried in the area for a while, for on August 27, they agreed to convey 10 acres to Dayan for $100. Since he was so prominent a man in the area, they probably hoped that his presence on the Tract would served as an inducement.[30]

In 1828, John Brown Herreshoff, eldest child of Charles Frederick, was admitted to the bar. "After leaving college (Brown '25), he pursued the study of the law, in the office of the late Hon. Samuel W. Bridgham, and was admitted to the bar as a practitioner . . . but never engaged in practice."[31]

That same year saw the incorporation of the Black River Canal, with Charles Dayan and Francis Seger as instrumental figures. And on April 23, a third child, Anne Brown Francis, was born to John Brown Francis and Anne Carter Brown. Sadly, however, the mother died just a few days later, on May 1.[32]

About a week later, his Aunt Eliza Francis Fisher wrote to his Aunt Sarah Herreshoff, suggesting that John Brown Francis and his two surviving children visit her in Philadelphia. "He shall be as retired as possible, see no one but those he may be disposed to admit. If he remains at Spring Green, every thing there is calculated to remind him of his dreadful loss . . ."[33]

Francis was so affected that he dropped out of politics for a time, declining his reelection to the General Assembly in 1829 because of his "domestic affliction."[34] During this time, his Brown University classmate, William Marcy, was, along with Martin Van Buren, the future president, a leader of the Albany Regency, a group of political leaders that dominated the state. For some years Francis and Marcy corresponded on a variety of matters, and Francis did not hesitate to mention his concerns, one of which was the effort in the New York State Legislature to build the Black River Canal that Francis mistakenly hoped would help attract settlers to the family lands just to the east.[35] At one time their terms as governor overlapped.

In 1829, Charles Frederick Herreshoff, son of the man whose death is the major tragedy of this book, made his first trip to the Tract. He wrote from Troy, New York, to his brother John that he had planned to spend the summer on the Tract, but that now he was able to spend only a week or two there. He noted that in nearly two months, he had spent less than one dollar, except for meals.[36]

In 1830, John Brown Herreshoff began an annual series of stays just

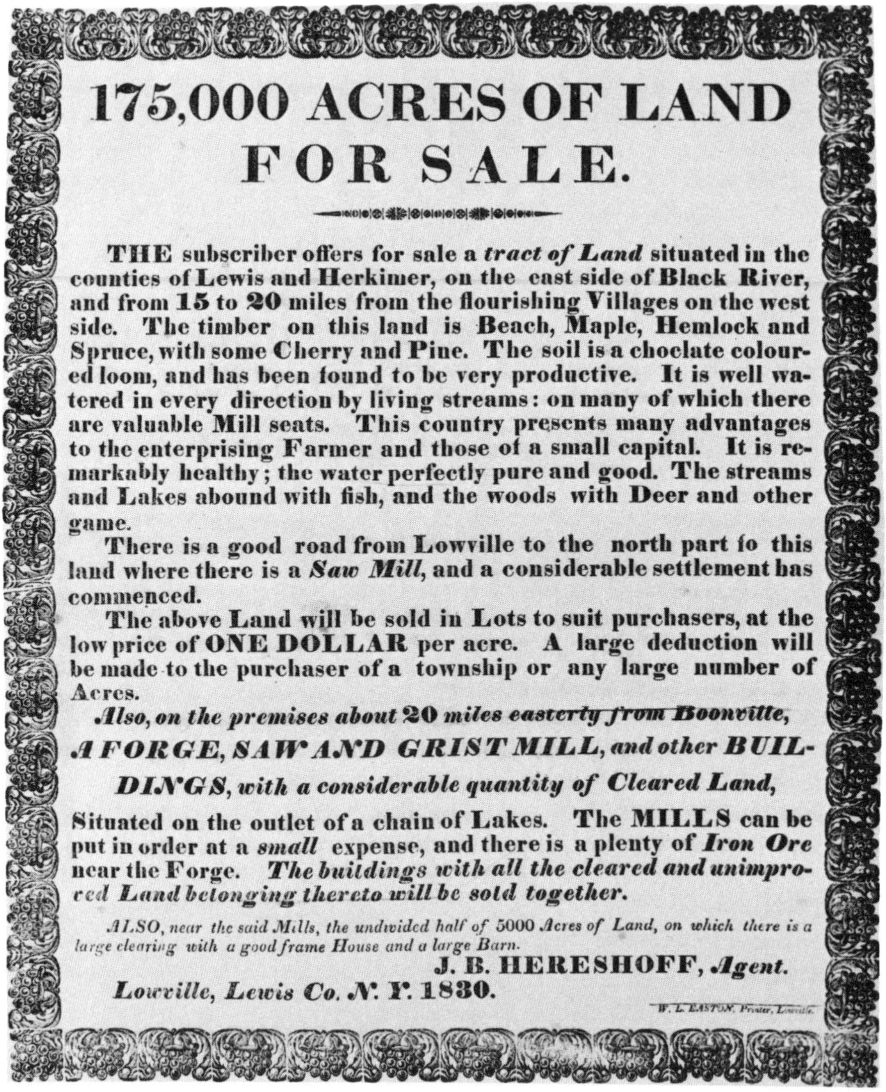

175,000 ACRES OF LAND FOR SALE.

THE subscriber offers for sale a ***tract of Land*** situated in the counties of **Lewis** and **Herkimer**, on the east side of **Black River**, and from **15** to **20** miles from the flourishing Villages on the west side. The timber on this land is Beach, Maple, Hemlock and Spruce, with some Cherry and Pine. The soil is a choclate coloured loom, and has been found to be very productive. It is well watered in every direction by living streams: on many of which there are valuable Mill seats. This country presents many advantages to the enterprising Farmer and those of a small capital. It is remarkably healthy; the water perfectly pure and good. The streams and Lakes abound with fish, and the woods with Deer and other game.

There is a good road from Lowville to the north part fo this land where there is a ***Saw Mill***, and a considerable settlement has commenced.

The above Land will be sold in Lots to suit purchasers, at the low price of **ONE DOLLAR** per acre. A large deduction will be made to the purchaser of a township or any large number of Acres.

Also, on the premises about 20 miles ~~easterly from Boonville~~,

A FORGE, SAW AND GRIST MILL, and other BUILDINGS, with a considerable quantity of Cleared Land,

Situated on the outlet of a chain of Lakes. The **MILLS** can be put in order at a ***small*** expense, and there is a plenty of ***Iron Ore*** near the Forge. ***The buildings with all the cleared and unimproved Land belonging thereto will be sold together.***

ALSO, near the said Mills, the undivided half of 5000 Acres of Land, on which there is a large clearing with a good frame House and a large Barn.

J. B. HERESHOFF, *Agent.*

Lowville, Lewis Co. N. Y. 1830.

W. L. EASTON, Printer, Lowville.

1830 broadside offering 175,000 acres of Tract land for sale with John Brown Herreshoff as agent.

west of the Tract in Lowville. He spent several months a year there through most of the decade, acting as family agent for the lands, but he had little better luck than non-family agents.

One can only speculate why young Herreshoff spent so much of so many years in the small village of Lowville, which necessarily afforded a far different life than that of the small, but relatively sophisticated, city of Providence or the rustic, bayside house at Point Pleasant in Bristol. It might be well to remember that the Tract was in remote country, despite its nearness to Utica and Albany. The great Northwest of the United States was well explored before any white man climbed Mt. Marcy, the highest peak in the Adirondacks, and the source of the Columbia River was known 60 years before the source of the Hudson was discovered.[37] It was still pioneering country, little changed since before the Revolution.

Lowville's only claim to culture was Lowville Academy, with its few students and teachers. One can only wonder at John's perseverance, for he sold very little land. Perhaps he simply enjoyed life on the frontier. Unfortunately, his surviving letters home do not tell us as much about his daily life or life in Lowville or on the Tract as we would like to know, but then, how was he to know he was writing for posterity. He just thought he was writing home, and since he was home much of each year, he had ample opportunity to tell his family and friends about his life in the north country.

One of John's early transaction involved himself. His mother, Sarah, sold to John 5,000 acres in Township No. 3 for $3,000. Presumably, John simply wanted some land where he was spending a good part of each year.[38]

A couple of weeks later, in May 1830, Brown and Ives authorized young Herreshoff as their agent to sell up to one-half the 4,960 acres in No. 7 that they had obtained from his father as security for loans. They said that the price and conditions of sale should be determined by John Brown Francis "in relation to those parts of 'Brown Tract' which you may be authorized to sell for him, or for other members of your family."[39]

The first letter we have of the young Herreshoff was written to his sister Anna from Lowville, dated May 22. He reported tht, even that late in the spring, ice formed overnight to the thickness of window glass. And Herreshoff described the unusual sight at Little Falls, "an arched stone bridge over which boats pass into the village." When finally he reached Lowville by stage "after another pounding," he "took up my quarters at Major Wells."

. . . I am much pleased with him and his family. The people of the Village that I have seen have been very polite. Mr Dayan said he would renew the promise which he had written me of doing all in his power etc I have taken a walk out to the settlement on No 4 which I will tell you more about hereafter when I shall know whether you have been able to decipher this scrawl. It grieved me soarly that Ma should "take to heart" so much my leaving. Tell her that if like the Roman matron she considers her children as her jewels she must set the more value on those that remain with her In the meantime her absent son will never forget that there is nothing like a Mothers love[40]

One can understand why Sarah Herreshoff felt pangs at her son's going to the Tract, for it was the Tract, after all, that had claimed her husband's life.

Faithful correspondent to her brother as she was to her father, Anna promptly replied. Much of the letter is an affectionate lecture as to attending church, watching his health and being alert for the "favourable moment which if suffered to pass unheeded may never return . . ." But, inevitably she writes of their father.

. . . You have probably seen many persons who knew our Father, & you must experience many painful feelings—here I ever look back with regret, but I will not allow myself to refer to this subject—Only I trust my dear brother will be more happy & fortunate than the parent he so much resembles—

To Anna's letter, John Brown Francis added a postscript, reporting that John Beach had resigned as agent, "being overwhelmed by his misfortunes. The road is open for you then as to No. 4. I hope there is no prospect of difficulty with Dayan and in fact that he may prove serviceable to you. But make no contract of a nature which will bind you for a series of years."

Francis then reported that it had also been cold in Rhode Island. "Within a week the beans have been killed by frost, but not at SG [Spring Green]—very wet too as well as cold. I mention this that you may not be discouraged at the frost on BT [Brown's Tract] of which I daresay there has been a quantity."[41]

Toward the end of June 1830, despite saying that "few things are as irksome to me as writing," Herreshoff wrote to his sister a very long and interesting letter. Among the things he described is a curious invention employed by a man named Post, of Boonville, who operated a small dairy. He "shew me the operation of churning performed by a dog—a specimen of this age of invention and labour saving machinery."

Herreshoff also responded to Anna's discussion of religion in terms very similar to those of John Brown Francis we read earlier. A skepticism about the forms (as opposed to the substance) of religion seemed characteristic of the family.

... You ask for a particular account of the inhabitants of Lowville. I am not yet so particularly acquainted as to describe them to you individually but to take them in the mass I should call them an honest sober industrious and religious set of people. How are they disposed with regard to religion you ask – they are in-disposed *as they were at Bristol last winter for they would stultify reason and Deify fanaticism... Deliver me from all such preachers who endeavour to "light up the unhallowed torch of Fanaticism" among the credulous and ignorant. Is Reason the best and noblest gift of God to be discarded when we are told to seek in the paths of Religion for his attributes and goodness? Because forsooth we cannot with our moral vision take in the immensity of creation we must put out what little light we have and receive with implicit obedience the obsessions of the man who may happen to hold the bible over us. I do not cavil at the forms of Religion as you seem to think it is only when I see the form without the substance that I think it useless.*

A fine burst of New England rationalism, perhaps still pertinent today, when there seems to be a revival of religious fundamentalism.

After young Herreshoff simmered down, he gave a brief account of his visit to No. 7, to the Old Forge area and to the Fulton Chain. On the way, he visited the home of Caleb Lyon. He and a chance companion "arrived at Mr. Lyons about 4 ock in the aft After tea I set down to a game of whist the last thing I expected to encounter in this woods...."

He was accompanied on his trip into the Tract by Francis Seger, Lyon's son-in-law.

... We first crossed the Moose river with our horses and waggon upon a raft the bridge being down. The party in all consisted of six. After he had crossed the river Mr S mounted the one horse waggon and drove on shouting and singing like a schoolboy just escaped from the thraldom of a country pedagogue. The rain continued for two or three hours when it cleared off quite pleasant My sensations were quite different from what I experienced when going out to No 4 alone through the wood & in the rain with no great coat or umbrella This time I went supplied with both and was perfectly guarded from the rain. This is certainly the worst road that I was ever on alltogether too bad for wheels. We were obliged to lead the horse most of the way. After several misshaps we reached the house on the tract about 9 in the eve having been more than 12 hours travelling 20 miles. The next morning our party was reinforced by one of the hunters and taking a boat at the Forge we proceeded up the lakes where we chantee'd out – as it is called four nights. We spent two days and nights at Lake No 4 which was as far as we went and is the largest and handsomest of those that we saw We went fishing

near the Island of Elba where David the hunter told me you staid all night when you was in this country I do not recollect ever hearing you mention it Having been our 4 days three of the party and myself returned to the clearing which I explored with a Mr Howard. Mr Seger having met with rather better luck fishing than I in the [illegible] *determined to stay sometime longer so the next day* [illegible] *us came off and left him. We were rather more fortunate coming out We left the tract at 5 ock in the morn and arrived at Mr Lyons at 4 in the aft. The appearance of things on the tract was rather better than I anticipated from the accounts I had received of it. The Gould place which Hunter Johnson now occupies is a very pretty place. He told me that last year he got about 150 bushels of apples from the trees round his house After walking out over this vilest of roads I plunged into the Moose and was greatly refreshed by the luxury of bathing and which I suppose greatly assisted me to set up* [playing whist] *until 12 ock.*[42]

Another long letter, despite his assertion that it was "irksome" to write, came from the pen of young Herreshoff, this time to his mother. In it he repeated what he said he had already written to John Brown Francis, that he and his mother should sent to Herreshoff the power of attorney to sell family lands.

. . . I proposed having some advertisements struck off and circulated about the country. The land has lain dormant so long that people seem to have forgotten that there is such a place, or it is only remembered to be excoriated. Among the endless stories about it there is one of a judge who threatened to banish a criminal to John Brown's tract, which so frightened the poor fellow that he cleared out and has not been heard of since.

From this, and the previous letter, one draws the clear inference that the settlement at No. 7 to which John Herreshoff's father devoted the last years of his life, indeed his life itself, had been abandoned by settlers, its only residents hunters who lived in houses left behind.

He then outlined his plans:

. . . I wrote [to John Brown Francis] *that I had given up the idea of associating myself with any one in the management of the land. The maxim of everyone for himself, is carried to such an extreme in this country that I know of no one that I should be willing to trust with a sixpence. The effect of my being with Mr Dayan would be his getting all the good settlers to go upon LeRoy's tract and all the poor devils would be* banished *to ours. He already has given me one instance of this kind of finesse. But we are great cronies. He says he liked Herreshoff for his dutch qualities. Notwithstanding the god of wealth or whatever it is called is so much worshipped here I like the people very well. For a village of this kind there is very little scandal afloat — everyone minds his own business. They do not enquire how their neighbours live.*

The son then addressed one of his mother's concerns:

... *You say you wish I might not set foot on Browns tract until there is a road and some appearance of civilization. I am happy to inform you that there is both. The road from Lowville to No 4 is very good and they are now making it better. It can be traveled in about four hours with a horse and waggon. The settlement is a very thriving one and the inhabitants very civil. Mr Fenton at whose house I staid is a first rate farmer. He is a justice of the peace and the best man in the town of—Francisville I believe I shall name it. Every morning at breakfast (tell Ann) he gave a long grace or blessing Among other marks of improvement they have a school of twenty three scholars which is doing pretty well for ten or twelve families adding to these several that are grown up and some married. The prospect of effecting a sale or settlement is not very good at present It must be the work of time, and it will require what Burke calls the perseverence of Holland the creativity of France and the unwearied industry of English enterprise. It is by taking a deliberate view of the difficulties that beset us that we are enabled to cope with them, and I hope one day to reap from our wilderness a harvest of independence.*

Aware of how much Sarah Herreshoff missed him, he hastened to reassure her:

... *Do not be alarmed at the suggestion. It does not follow of course that I must make this my fixed abode It is to be sure painful to be separated from ones friends—but circumstances greatly mitigate this calamity. How much better is it for instance to seek a small but sure livelihood in our western wilds than to be driven, as so many of our young men are, by a rash emulation to toil and die under a meridian sun.*

Herreshoff closed by returning to the subject of No. 4:

... *The wheat crops promise to be very heavy as do rye and potatoes. Fruit has been mostly cut off by the frost I brought some spears of rye from No 4 seven feet long and hung them up in the Majors barroom—The natives were 'astonished' Mr. Bostwick was quite incredulous about it coming from over the river.*[43]

Later in the summer, Francis forwarded to his cousin Herreshoff a copy of a letter from Simeon Adams of Otsego County. Adams wrote that he had visited No. 7 and found the mills out of repair, much of the equipment having been stolen. But he thought he saw the prospect of a "comfortable living."

... *Now Sir providing you will give me the privilege to go on & make repairs on the Saw Mill & give me the privilege of sowing a quantity of grain so that I can make a living by it I will go on & do the best I can & providing you will do what is fair on the subject I have no kind of doubt but what there will 7 or 8 families move on with me.*

The Third Generation

Francis suggested that Herreshoff try to learn something of Adams' character.

. . . If your information is of a favorable description you may answer the letter saying that you are the Agent & that the Mills etc are for sale. At present I do not think favorably of his offer. The effect of his going on might be to embarrass the sale hereafter and I am extremely desirous of selling my interest in No 7. I want to be rid of it entirely so that I may forget all the trouble that has grown out of it for thirty years past. Besides all this, its intrinsic value must be retrograding.

But not so with No 4 or either of the other Townships perhaps. 4 will sustain itself.

Taxes were another important consideration, Francis wrote, requiring that they adopt one of three alternatives: "either to sell out for the most we can get to pay them, to abandon and not redeem them, or go on paying until all the rest of our substance is swallowed up by this great Black River Leviathan."

He suggested that Herreshoff try to "swear down the valuation" by appearing before the board of assessors. "This is a business too important to be neglected or overlooked and I solicit your zealous attention to it."

. . . I assent to any arrangements you may conclude between the Settlers on 4: and also that the price shall be one dollar the acre on such credit as is usual or will tend most to the furtherance of the settlement.

You may venture to advertise the whole Tract excepting Township No 6 (belonging to the Mason branch of the family) and 2500 acres belonging to Caspar Meier. I ardently hope you will be able to effect something with No 7. Feel your way with Seger and pull every other string—Your commissions on the Townships shall be very handsome if you can accomplish the sale soon.

Then Francis ruefully recalls the terms of the inheritance left by John Brown:

. . . Originally there were said to be 23180 acres in No 7 which was valued in my Grandfathers will at $29180!! This was a part only of a Moon shine inheritance giving me the appearance of wealth but in reality fastening poverty upon me. But at the time our Grandfather tho't he gave his Granson 120,000 Dollars when he devised to him four Townships. Into what errors the wisest of us (and he did not lack wisdom) are involved.

Francis reported on how much of No. 7 he still owned, having sold to Meier and Herreshoff 5,000 acres, conveyed another 5,000 acres to Brown and Ives, about 200 to Major Joy, 160 to Wilcox and 40 acres to "one Coome." That left him, he figured, about 13,000 acres "and I wish you would so represent to the assessors. I would readily take $7,000 for Forge Mills and all provided I could be rid of the property entirely. But Lyon was never authorized to sell for 5000 Dr."[44]

In his reply a month later, Herreshoff said that Francis had misunderstood him, that the taxes on the Lewis County portion of the Tract were low because the land was assessed at only 16¢ an acre.

Speaking of No. 4, Herreshoff wrote that "Some of the settlers are somewhat discouraged and disappointed that more have not come in—but they are an industrious lot and appear to be doing well and the Settlement is considered the best one on that side of the [Black] river."

> ... *A grist mill on the tract would be a great thing. The settlers being very desirous of having one some arrangement might be made with them to put one up. One of them told me that if I would give 50 acres of land to a miller that they would advance enough in addition to carry the project into effect.*

Herreshoff also said that more roads were needed to get at the land, and he was contemplating one to the northeast part of No. 3 for about $20 a mile.

> ... *I am not in favour of feeding the Leviathan as you term it without a fair prospect of getting some remuneration. I am aware that too much bread has already been cast upon the water and none of it returned to us. I have had some hand bills printed though I have not much faith in the utility of it. Similar ones are stuck up all over the country and I am told that land can be bought in Jefferson country for one dollar per acre.... As to my future plans I hardly know what to say on the subject—I think my best course would be to clear a small farm and fix myself on the land.*

And Herreshoff closed by reporting that "Dayan has been nominated by our County convention a candidate for Congress and will probably succeed."[45]

A few days later—it was now almost the autumnal equinox—John wrote an amusing and charming letter to his brother Charles Frederick back in Bristol.

> ... *I am about sending a packet to Cousin J* [John Brown Francis] *and though I would address a few lines to you though I might say as a French woman did that I begin because I have nothing to do and end because I have nothing to say. I am writing on the crown of my hat by the side of a fire which might be an excuse for bad writing if I ever wrote well. Wood is so plenty in this country that we keep a fire some times when there is no need of one but a good fire has been very comfortable for about half the time this summer.*

John reported to his brother that "the frosts that we have had for several days proclaims the approach of winter." Summer was not yet quite over and already he was writing about the approach of winter. So short was the growing season that year that the corn had been injured by frost, although the "wheat crops here have been very good." He then discussed the sartorial standards of the north country.

... Mr Watson the owner of Watsons tract boards here at the Majors He is quite an original and affords much amusement to the household He says if this country was as good in every thing as it is in respect to ones dress it would be the finest one he ever knew. He wears a pair of co[r]duroy breeches and an old blue short coat that must have been worn in the revolutionary war. He wore one pair of pantaloons here for nine summers and was in hopes that they would never wear out. There is in fact but one man in the village that pays any attention to his dress—I dress pretty much in Mr Ws style. I have not put on my best bib and tucker since here I've been except once when I was invited to a dinner party when merely to let people know that I had better cloth[e]s I put on my new pantaloons. If you was a gentleman of ton or flourished in the pulpit or at the bar I should write you to send me your old clothes but I suppose you can thump out the remnants of your dandyism at the plough tail.[46]

A couple of weeks later Francis wrote to his cousin, asking him to stop at Herkimer on the way home to check on some deeds, and at Albany to "get a list from the comptroller of the taxes due on all the Townships except No. 6. That part of No 8 in Hamilton or Montgomery County I suspect was sold four years ago and it is not worth redeeming—a greater part of it being water." So remote were portions of the Tract that Francis was not even sure what county part of it was in. And No. 6 was plainly no longer of any interest to Francis, presumably because, though the records are difficult to sort out on this point, obviously No. 6 somewhere during this period was sold for taxes and never redeemed.

Francis wrote that he was somewhat encouraged because of the number of inquiries he had received about the mills and cleared land in No. 7, but that was to be the story for the next twenty years: many inquiries but no sales.

If Francis received inquiries, he also received bills from those who had worked—or said they did—for the family.

... Beaches acct must be exhorbitant But at this distance how can I judge. The settlers must be the best judges of his services as surveyor I was not before aware that anything in the way of surveying had been done. Certainly not to such an extent. You who are on the spot can find out how it is best to manage both with

Sheldon and his Father. [Remember that the elder Sheldon had been in John Brown's employ.] *Their services were never worth much. They have done me more hurt than good and have been pretty well paid for it.*[47]

The year 1831 saw the first steam train run between Albany and Schenectady. Thus, trains replaced canals as the instrument that was supposed to bring prosperity to the still-remote forests of the Adirondacks. Unhappily, however, the cinder spewed out by steam locomotives had a tendency to start forest fires; consequently, there were lots of imaginative, but wildly impractical, schemes, such as roofing the railroad tracks.[48] These schemes, like most hatched with regard to the north country, came to nothing.

In April 1831, John Brown Herreshoff returned to Lowville, armed this time with his mother's power of attorney.[49] The family was getting increasingly eager to rid itself of the John Brown's Tract. He gave a vivid account of "pretty tedious journey rendered doubly so by bad weather crowded boats and bad roads."

In Albany, Herreshoff attended a session of the legislature. "The carpeted floors lofty cealings [sic] &c gave the two branches of the Legislature a more august appearance that any thing we see in R[hode] I[sland] but most of the speakers that I heard were bungling fellows none of them can hold a light to Messrs Potter & Hazard of our Assembly."

. . . Saturday morning I left for Schenectady in a stage and after dinner got on board a canal boat for Utica which place I reached Sunday forenoon intending to proceed directly on foot but a couple of pedestrians coming from the north besmirched with mud caused me to flinch so I stayed for the evening stage and in the aft attended a Dutch reformed Church a new and elegant building. At 9 ock in the eve I got into a mud waggon to take a nights thumping and a pretty severe way it was of doing penance I can assure you. At 5 in the morning we had come a little over twenty miles to the breakfast house. This is a cold region about Boonville It froze hard enough in the night to improve the walking. During the rest of the day I led the stage over twenty miles on foot after being awake all night and in the evening at Lowville I went out. Though I say it few men can undergo more fatigue than I can I had a good hearty welcome into this country. . . .[50]

On May 1 he wrote that if the foul weather let up, he intended to walk the next day to the settlement at No. 4. In the meantime, he gave an account of a country funeral.

. . . The body of a young man was escorted by a long procession from his house to that of his Father who was comforted by schnapps. It was there laid upon a stand in the yard while the minister prayed and preached which he did standing

on the threshhold of the door sometimes addressing the people in the yard and sometimes turning round that those in the house might hear him After he had finished the lid of the coffin was opened that everyone might [look] *at its contents. A handsome young widow with an entreating little child born in the arms of a brother of the deceased crowded round among the rest She sob*[b]*ed I believe a little but at the grace a more indifferent set of features can hardly be imagined. I watched her as a subject of interest but own to her steellike face could hardly sympathize with her.*

Going to a funeral through the mud of the country on a dark rainy day is rather sombre kind of business.[51]

For some reason, there were no letters from Herreshoff for the next five months. There is, however, one letter to Brown & Ives from a business correspondent regarding their taxes on the Tract, but it provides more confusion that enlightenment. Plainly, the tax records were in an awful mess that, at this remove in time, is impossible to sort out.[52]

Taxes were the main subject of an almost frantic letter from Francis to Herreshoff. He implored him to try to straighten out the tax mess and "above all, if possible, to obtain a diminution in the valuation."

. . . Are not the assessments arranged in Sept and have you done anything to stay the hand of these cormorants?

Do not these taxes admonish us more and more that at some rate or other we must disencumber ourselves of this land — Have you effected anything with Lyon or Wilcox?

At one time you thot the sale on 4 would certainly meet the taxes but from present appearances the taxes will absorb not only lands but all we have besides along with them — Cant you manage to pay the taxes on Nos 3 & 4 for 1830 or make Fenton do it . . .

Would my meeting you at Lowville produce any desirable purpose? I would not encounter the perils *of a journey without a strong motive for my health of late has not been good . . .*

Have you any new settlers — Do you make any sales — What are the prospects?

Cant No 4 be got rid of in a body? See who Watson was in treaty with in NYK — Why will they not buy of us?[53]

It is not much of an overstatement to say that John Brown Francis was approaching desperation. Yet, it would be nearly twenty years before the family would "disencumber" itself of the Tract.

In October, Herreshoff wrote to his mother. He said little about the Tract other than that he crossed it on a tramp of several days in the pouring rain, up toward the St. Lawrence River to the village of Parishville, living on bread and pork, fording streams, although the largest, the

Raquette River, they were carried across by Indians in canoes. At Parishville they found Watson waiting for them. They were supposed to return with him, but

> *his horse became lame and the waggon broke down so that he was in poor condition to help me along so I started off on foot with Mr Fenton and walked to Lowville a distance of eighty miles in two days and a half and on one of them it rained all day. That is the worst of it in this country. There is too much rain. It set in very early this year—with the exception of a few days it rained all last month and it is pouring down at this moment.*[54]

About that same time, Francis was writing to Herreshoff that he had made that same difficult jaunt fourteen or fifteen years earlier. The rest of the letter was, as always, concerned with taxes. While it might have been true that taxes were draining the two branches of the Brown family still interested in the Tract, the Herreshoff and the Francis, certainly Herreshoff's expenses at Lowville were not much of a drain. Happily, an old receipt survives, showing that Herreshoff's room and board for thirty weeks, between April 25 and December 10, 1830, came to a total of $52.50, which meant he paid $1.75 a week for room and meals, a sum that would seldom purchase a sandwich today.

Although there is evidence that Herreshoff spent at least part of 1832 at Lowville, we do not know how long, since the only documentary evidence is dated in October. The year is, however, of some significance, both in Rhode Island and on the Tract. In Rhode Island there were, for some reason, several elections for governor, but none was chosen, setting the stage for John Brown Francis to be elected the following year. And on the Tract there was the arrival of a man who has passed into the lore of the Adirondacks.

He was Nat Foster, son of a Rhode Island man and one of the most legendary hunters and marksmen of his time. It has been said, and disputed, that he was used as a model for James Fenimore Cooper's immortal "Deerslayer." Whether that is so or not, Nat became a legendary figure in his own right for, among other things, the slaying of the Indian Drid. The Drid story has been told so often, in so many places, most notably in Jeptha R. Simm's "Trappers of New York," that it needs only brief retelling here.

We must remember that, in the 1830's, the John Brown's Tract, with its thick forest and numerous lakes, was still a popular hunting ground for the Indians from Canada who, as we saw earlier, eventually gave their name to the Adirondacks. Late in the 19th century, as Charles E. Snyder recorded in his invaluable short history of the Brown's Tract, it was "still remembered by a few old people now living."

. . . Canadian Indians from the north would gradually work their way through the forest, hunting and trapping as they went, taking their furs to the Albany market; and it was not an unfrequent sight for the early settlers at No. 4, to see at times, Indians proudly walking through the forest past the settlement, guns in hand ready for an emergency, while on behind trudged the patient squaws, drawing rude sleds made of birch saplings loaded with furs and camp outfit.[55]

Foster, who leased Herreshoff Manor, apparently did not like any Indians and developed a particular dislike for an Indian, Peter Waters, better known as Drid. According to the story, and it is impossible to know how accurate it is, an enmity developed that made it a question of who would shoot first. The fatal incident was triggered by a fight between the 30-year-old Drid and the 60-year-old Foster, in which the Indian reportedly pulled a knife.

Foster went home, got his rifle, and crossed to a point where he thought Drid's canoe would pass. Drid soon came by in a party of canoes. Expecting trouble, he kept the other canoes between him and the shore, but Foster was too good a marksman. Two bullets ended the quarrel forever. Foster was brought to trial, but acquitted on testimony that Drid had threatened his life. Foster, fearing vengeful relatives of Drid, fled to the wilds of Pennsylvania, where he lived as hunter and trapper until, finally, old age brought him back to the area of the Tract, where he lived out his years with one of his children in Boonville.

In October 1832 Francis wrote a fascinating letter to Herreshoff:

. . . On the other side you have an agreement which Uncle Charles [brother of John and Thomas Willing Francis] *has, as I fear most unwarily, concluded with a Mr. Charles Kahn — I say unwarily not because I am not satisfied with the 18000 Dr but from a fifteen minute conversation with the man and a total absence of all information respecting him I am led to conclude that he is a mere adventurer worth only the rings on his fingers.* [Years earlier, May 16, 1807, he had served as super cargo for Thomas Willing Francis of Philadelphia, uncle of John Brown Francis.]

I have made up my mind not to ratify the contract unless I am better informed of his ability to pay; and I write to you for the purpose of requesting you to aid me in decyphering the mystery as the man I am told is now with you. You need not inform Kahn [sic] *that you have seen his agreement nor that you have heard from me — I do not wish to commit myself in any way situated as things now are — If*

Khan is really a responsible man as Uncle C suppose him to be I consider the sale a great one. But if he proves not to be worth money how am I to manage in a way to escape trouble? You will see Khan and his character will be developed to you. If you are satisfied that he is not a knave & that he means to complete the bargain explain yr views to me as soon as possible—Again if you are of the adverse opinion state yr reasons and then consult Collins [apparently a Lowville attorney] *as to my best way to escape. . . . Only be satisfied that Kahn will pay three thousand Dr in April & I would complete the bargain altho I might doubt of the subsequent payments. Khan was here only twenty minutes & I thot from appearances that he was as little calculated to settle a new country as any man I ever saw. But if he is really worth money that is not my lookout.*

The air of wonderment is apparent as John Brown Francis again reiterated his doubts about the deal.

. . . I do not know what you may think of it but 18000 Dr seems to me a great price for my remaining acres.—I pray you my dear J to exert yourself to the utmost in this business—arouse all your energies and if this affair has a successful issue it will add infinity [sic] *to yr interest—In fact you are nearly as much interested in it as I am—But, to be honest, I am entirely incredulous—I do not believe that anything but trouble will ever grow out of Uncle C's extraordinary agreement.*[56]

The note of urgency is explained by the fact that, under a power of attorney from John Brown Francis and his new wife Elizabeth (daughter of Thomas Willing Francis and thus his first cousin), Uncle Charles had sold the land on September 14, with the deed to be delivered by October 1. Plainly, Charles Francis was as eager to rush the deal as his nephew was to stall it. The deal provided for the sale of 81,000 to 85,000 acres for the $18,000, spread over eight years.[57]

We know, of course, that the deal was never completed, but it would be interesting to know (as, unhappily, we do not) what Herreshoff reported to Francis, and how Francis got out of the deal. Evidently, however, the deal at first seemed to go through, for on November 20, a month and a half after Francis' disbelieving letter to Herreshoff, Charles Dayan wrote to Francis that "I am much pleased that you have disposed of your land, I hope the man you sold to will make it profitable."

Dayan was writing to enclose a deed for one hundred acres, given him by Herreshoff, that he wanted Francis and his wife to execute. We have that deed, but it was not signed by the Francises, so we do not know what happened with that transaction.[58] In any case, Dayan sent a most cordial letter to Francis about a month later from Washington, where he was serving in the House of Representatives. He wrote that President Andrew Jackson's plan to sell land cheaply in the West "will have the effect to drain the old thirteen states of her population and consequently decrease the value of our lands both wild and improved at least 33½ per cent." In that same note he wrote that "John B Herrishoff [sic] is a fine young man – but wants energy. His prospect now is some what better than it has been –"[59]

11

The End of the Dream

If there is really no expectation of a rise in the value of our land, it is ruinous to think of holding on . . . . . .[1]

EIGHTEEN-THIRTY-THREE. An important year for John Brown Francis, for the political stalemate in Rhode Island was broken by his election to the first of five consecutive one-year terms. And that year saw John Brown Herreshoff spend his first winter in the north country. He wrote a long letter to his mother that was concerned largely with his liberal views on religion, and his distaste at sectarian squabbling. He ended by noting that "Last Tuesday new years day I attended a Court at Martinnsburg & swore over the bible (& kissed it) that I would support the Constitution &c as one of the attorneys at law of this county."[2]

Students of language might also note that he used the term "bottom line" in the same way that it is frequently used now, a usage that had appeared to be recent, not at least a century and a half old.

There was not much to read in Lowville, he reported, although a reading room had just been established "but as yet it is supplied with nothing but newspapers though of them there is quite a variety and in these stirring times they contain a great deal that is interesting. There is a set of Shakespeare in the office where I am now writing which I can always take up with pleasure when I have nothing else on hand."

On March 27, his 28th birthday, Herreshoff wrote to his mother a letter that was more philosophic than newsy. "A few years ago at Pt Pl [Point Pleasant] we used to celebrate our birth days by making bonfires or some such childish sport — but as we get older we begin to regard the day with different feelings — with feelings more akin to sorrow than to mirth and when a man has finished half his race, if like me, his sombre views of this life will be better fitted for the dormitory of his own bosom [than] calculated to excite interest in others."

Continuing his letter the next day, Herreshoff asked his mother "to send me the Prov Journal now and then that I may see how Mr F is treated by his opponents." He was referring, of course, to his cousin John Brown Francis.

Finally, he attempted to dissuade his mother from making the arduous trip to visit him.

> *. . . I hardly know what to say of your project of coming into this country with Agnes. It is a long journey for women to undertake alone though the worst-part-of the way would be between Utica and this place if you came there by water. I think you would badly stand the usual conveyance from Utica unless the roads were better than usual. The stage generally travels in the night which makes it still more disagreeable. But apart from the journey this country would offer but few attractions for you & Ag You would have none of the comforts of home at a Country tavern . . . You need not construe this into a disinclination on my part to see you here—but for these & other circumstances that I need not mention I should be very glad to see you all here.*
>
> *But I forget all this time that I intend going to RI this summer which may induce you to pos*[t]*pone your journey unless you wish to see this country more than my humble self.*[3]

Sarah Brown was then nearly 60 years old, and it was indeed an arduous trip, but perhaps before she was too old to make such a journey, she wanted to see where her husband had died and her son was living, and seemed likely to live for some years to come. There is no evidence, however, that she ever made the trip.

In May, Herreshoff wrote a touching account of the death of the ten-year-old grandson of Major Welles, the tavernkeeper. And he wrote his sister Anna that "I smile at Agnes' fears of a getting a backwoods sister. I can assure her that the girls here are not wanting in beauty or manners or education. What fine things philosophy & experience are especially when they teach us to draw good out of evil. For instance my poverty and inaptitude to get along in the world offer for consolation the assurance that I shall never be burdened with the cares of a married man." And he never was.

He closed his letter to Anna, who was so involved in religion, by saying, "In your next let me have more of *State* & less of *Church*."[4]

A couple of weeks later his mother closed a letter, in which she had referred to John Brown Francis as "his Excellency the governor," with these stern words:

... I require of you my dear John an immediate & categorical answers (as my father used to term it) I wish to know if you are coming and how soon, do not think of the postage that is a trifle, but the anxiety we feel is very great when we continue in suspense week after week with the hope you will soon be ready to join us here.[5]

Plainly, John did not rush home, for on July 2, his brother Charles wrote, reporting of President Jackson's visit to Rhode Island. "Shook hands & were introduced to him together with Anna & the governor's lady." And he urged his elder brother to come home.

... Perhaps there is another motive wh[ich] *as it is allied to feelings of a nobler kind would have a grater sway over a mind like yours—I mean the inducement, the duty, of cheering the remnants of a Mothers life! Perhaps it may be but a short term that this privilege is allowed us. I do not think a melancholy mind can find lasting comfort in any created thing but may be soothed & made rather happier. Mother has improved in appearance beyond my expectations but has not acquired much strength. Riding no doubt wd. benefit her—But she shakes her head and says 'I have no John now you know to ride with me'—*[6]

Despite the fears of her children, Sarah Herreshoff was to live for another thirteen years.

In July of 1833, we find the first notice in years of interest in the Brown's Tract by the Mason branch of the family. It appears in a letter from Amasa Mason, brother and executor of James B. Mason, to John Brown Herreshoff.

... Gov. Francis has informed me, with a few days that the Black river Lands of the late Hon^be John Browns tract are taxed upon a valuation much too high, and that there is no relief except by Swearing the Valuation down, and that there should be some Authorized Agent on the ground for that purpose I have never learned that Township N^o Six which I think was given to your Aunt Mason & her heirs has been taxed at anything of Value, but as Gov. Francis seems to think that possibly it may be in future, I hereby authorize you, in Case it Should be Valued in your Opinion too high for the purpose of taxation to Act in behalf of the Heirs of Alice Mason as their Agent & Representative to Swear to, and establish a proper Value to the Land for the purpose of Levying or Assessing a tax thereon if any Should be ordered, and have the goodness to Advise me of your proceedings in the Case, and any information respecting the Situation of Value of the Land & if there is any Sale for it will be thankfully received.[7]

In November John Brown Francis and Elizabeth Francis conveyed their power of attorney to John Brown Herreshoff, who was still living in Lowville.[8] However, some time during the year Herreshoff had visited

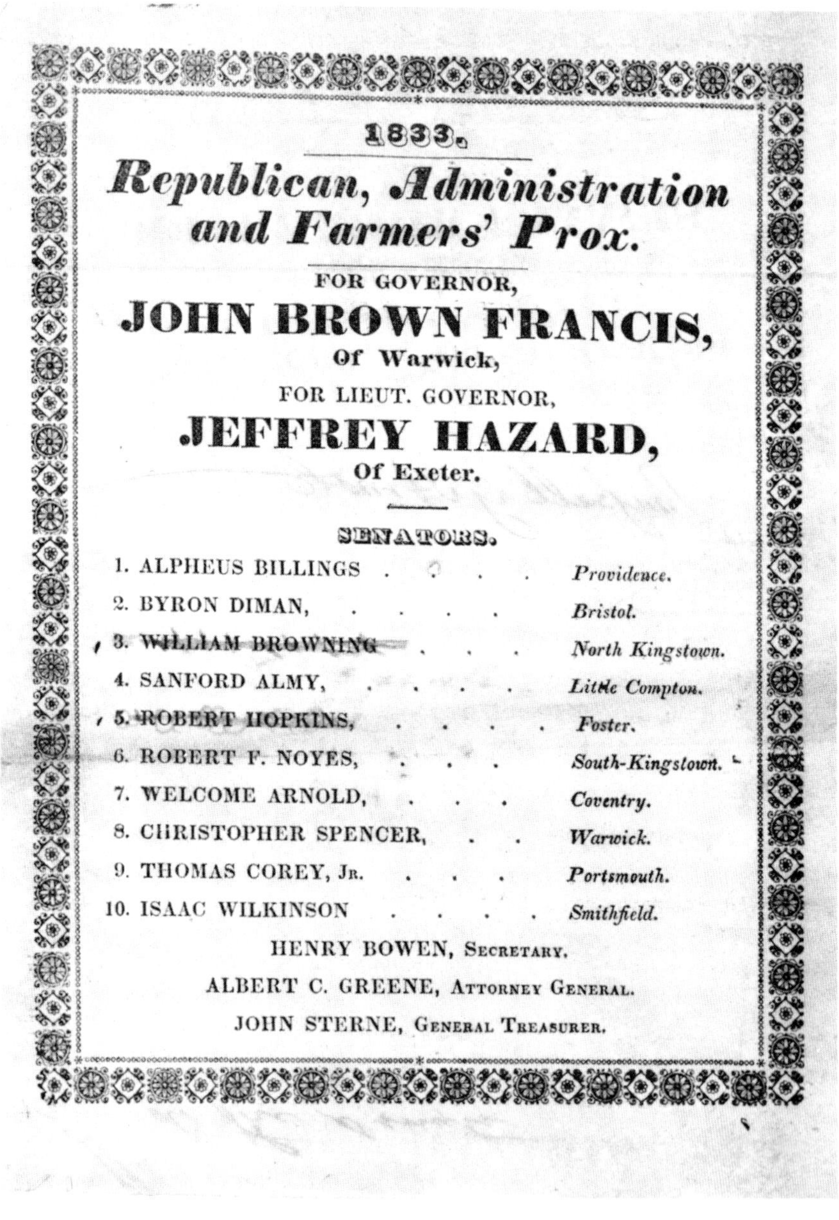

1833.

Republican, Administration and Farmers' Prox.

FOR GOVERNOR,

JOHN BROWN FRANCIS,

Of Warwick,

FOR LIEUT. GOVERNOR,

JEFFREY HAZARD,

Of Exeter.

SENATORS.

1.	ALPHEUS BILLINGS	*Providence.*
2.	BYRON DIMAN,	*Bristol.*
3.	~~WILLIAM BROWNING~~	*North Kingstown.*
4.	SANFORD ALMY,	*Little Compton.*
5.	~~ROBERT HOPKINS,~~	*Foster.*
6.	ROBERT F. NOYES,	*South-Kingstown.*
7.	WELCOME ARNOLD,	*Coventry.*
8.	CHRISTOPHER SPENCER,	*Warwick.*
9.	THOMAS COREY, Jr.	*Portsmouth.*
10.	ISAAC WILKINSON	*Smithfield.*

HENRY BOWEN, SECRETARY.

ALBERT C. GREENE, ATTORNEY GENERAL.

JOHN STERNE, GENERAL TREASURER.

1833 election ballot proposing John Brown Francis for governor.

his family, for on November 27 he wrote to his mother another interesting account of the difficult journey from Bristol to Lowville:

> *. . . The journey from Utica to this place, 53 miles, is at this time past endurance for any delicately nerved person. You are thumped about most unmercifully over rough frozen ground in a waggon without springs although they scarcely raise a trot the whole way. I got along tolerably well by paying for my passage with the privilege of walking which I claimed pretty often though at the further expense of shoe leather, stubbed toes, and muddy breeches.*

In Albany he heard Henry Clay speak. "He is a most admirable speaker and has one of the most melodious voices I ever heard, the lowest tones of which can be heard in a large & crowded room."

Two days after Christmas 1833, Herreshoff wrote to his sister Anna an interesting letter that ranged from social life ("I showed my gallantry by kissing some of the prettiest girls there") to religion: "Surely a man must be excused for keeping aloof from all religious parties where sectarian strifes are only distinguished from those that occur in the political world by an increased rancour & bitterness. . . ."

He closed with some comments on the country "doomed by Nature to sterility & by Fortune to be a curse upon its owners," and he reported that "A few days after my arrival here there came 15 inches of snow & every few days additions are made to it so we shall probably get a bountiful supply of this staple commodity of the Country"[9]

Taxes, taxes and again taxes. The year 1834 saw even more concern about this vexing business as portions of the Tract were sold for taxes. One memo found in family papers notes that "1700 acres NW corner of N° 5 sold to Peter Smith of Schenectady for 29 dols 72 cts." In Township No. 3 in Lewis County "5500 acres NW corner of sold to J W James for 75 dols 17 ct years 27,28,29,30." And in Township No. 1 "4800 acres SW ex 80 a[cres] P^{d}. sold to P Smith for 54 dols 42 cts."[10]

So it was to go for the remaining sixteen years that the Francis and Herreshoff branches owned the Tract. Land would be sold, then redeemed within the allowable two years and John Brown Francis would worry that the taxes would be a fatal drain on the family resources. Somewhere along this time, No. 6, owned by the Mason branch, would be sold and not redeemed, evidently on the theory that it was foolish to throw good money after bad.

Toward the end of February, Herreshoff wrote to his sister Agnes, as he often did, saying that he had little to say, but nonetheless running on for three interesting pages, including a passage, rare in his letters, about the Tract.

. . . I have visited our famous region — where stood formerly (in imagination) the famous city of New Dublin but which region a libellous [sic] *gazeteer says is famous only for the moral names of its Townships which you may have heard are called on some old maps Industry Economy Prudence &c Things had a sombre appearance there with a deep snow on the ground & seemed to call into requisition these cardinal virtues. Though there is plenty of wood & water there what is termed boiling a pot implies the want of other ingredients — I crossed Beaver Lake in a two horse sleigh. The ice which I cut through with considerable labor was about two feet thick. This lake is a beautiful sheet of water about two miles long in sight of the settlement. I have selected a site on its banks for my country house."*

Herreshoff also spoke warmly of the Fentons, the family that persevered at No. 4 for nearly forty years. "I have often been struck with envy admiration at the Industry and Cheerfulness in the Family of Fentons — "

He also included a passage that must have been of particular interest to his sisters and mother. "I believe I have mentioned before the beauties of Lowville I mean corporal & feminine. I hardly know their equals anywhere. I believe it is considered something 'passing strange' that a man of my large estate should not succumb to their charms.[11]

We learn that in March the land deal with Charles Kahn was not quite dead. Associated with Kahn was John A. Siddell, a well-known attorney with good political connections. He was pursuing the on-again, off-again negotiations, and John Brown Francis asked his cousin to check on his reputation. Herreshoff learned from a correspondent that Siddell "is represented as an honourable man and probably worth some property — on one of his city speculations, I am informed that he has or can clear some $5000 or $6000 — but the opinion seems to be that he is not worth the sum which you mention." We must assume it is the $18,000 originally offered by Kahn.

Herreshoff added that "I believe I mentioned to you that he refused (very politely) to let me have the maps &c left with him by Khan [sic]" The younger cousin also asked the governor if the taxes on the Tract had been paid. "If not most of the Tract will be or has been sold this month."[12]

The news that his cousin had been reelected governor 'after a close pull" caused Herreshoff in a letter to his sister Anna to discourse on politics, during which he mentioned that in a recent election, "Thinking my vote might be challenged in the village I made it convenient to vote out on the Tract."

And he noted that "I got a few lines last night from Cousin J in which he mentions a story of some ones taking timber off the Tract. He may rest assured there is not a word of truth in it. Tell him this"

Herreshoff also took note of the birth of the first in another generation of Herreshoffs. "I learnt accidently [sic] of the birth of another JBH. How does the mother? I think it was well enough to name the child after its worthy Uncle but I doubt whether christening every child that comes along with the famous name of Brown serves to improve the breed." He was referring not to another John Brown Herreshoff (that was yet to come) but to James Brown Herreshoff, a son born to his brother Charles Frederick Herreshoff and his wife Julia Ann Lewis, and named after their uncle James. It was Charles Frederick Herreshoff, namesake of the first American Herreshoff, who was responsible for the continuation not only of the family name but of the family, for neither his brother nor his three sisters ever married.

Also, as in so many letters from the north country, there was an account of the weather. "There is one bad habit in the winds of this quarter; they bring storms from every point of the compass, and North West is not, as in RI, a guarantee of fair weather."[13]

On the Fourth of July, Sarah Herreshoff wrote to her son in terms that she had no wasy of knowing were prophetic.

> *. . . F— launched his boat on Tuesday or Wednesday he took his wife & child to Providence after waiting from 6 oclock in the morng untill 3 in the afternoon they set sail the wind died away and thunder and lightning came so that they did not reach Providence untill half past nine just as they were going to bed and yesterday he hurried Julia back they were from Eleven until 4 on the water part of the time with a high wind and then becalmed so that they landed on the west shore, Julia appears quite disgusted with sailing and wished Fred to sell the boat and unless he does he will go on just so thro' life! wasting his time and talents, working hard and gaining nothing. every thing has been neglected on account of this Boat, it is true she is as beautiful as you can imagine a boat to be, and beats all the small craft in the river—*

Any lover of boats is horrified at the thought that Frederick might have sold his boat, for if he had, the entire history of sailboating in America might well have been different.

Again, his mother urged John to come home. ". . . as to pecuniary matters I beg you not to feel any uneasiness on that score but return home where your presence is wanted more than you can imagine. . . ."[14]

Later that month, John Brown Francis received a letter from James Watson, proprietor of the neighboring land, in which he said he understood that Governor Francis was a friend of Governor William Marcy of New York, and asking him to use his influence to further the cause of the Black River Canal.[15]

The End of the Dream

That autumn, in November, John Brown Francis wrote to his Uncle Charles Francis in Philadelphia, urging a prompt end to negotiations under way.

. . . I am desirous of bringing your negociation [sic] *with Mr. Hirst to a close, and, if possible, of effecting a sale of my Black River Land, 'tho' at a sacrifice.*

Did I not, with my large and expensive family, require more income I should not dream of selling the land at a moment so unpropitious as this and confident as I am that the contemplated Canal to Rome, and other cause, may, ere long, greatly enhance its value.

But I am determined on putting Mr H to the test; and if he is really in earnest in his application doubtless he will close with you at the offer which I now propose. I give him until Monday to ponder upon it.

You can offer the Land to him — viz. all my interest, say 80,000 acres or more as the case may be — at Thirteen Thousand Dollars . . . .

Hirst was to be responsible for the back taxes, with the $10,000 after the down payment to be secured by a mortgage on property in Philadelphia.[16]

In December, John Brown Herreshoff, still up in Lowville, received the unhappy news from his sister Agnes of their beloved Uncle James Brown's fatal illness. The news came in a letter that stretched over several days. First she wrote that a number of people he knew were ill. "It is very sickly in our City now . . . ." A few days later she added that "On coming home Wednesday evg — we found Uncle in great pain — he was not willing to have the Dr — but the next m[ornin]g sent for him — he gave him medicine, & in the aft he was relieved — his complaint is inflammation of the bladder . ."

Anna wrote that, although some wished John were there, "I said I do not — the state of things are entirely opposed to all yr feelings — & I had rather suffer alone — I hope Mother will not come — I feel able to stand by myself John — I am not the weak creature I used to be — I have been led step by step till I am willing to leave all things to the wise maker of the universe — It is this dependance that gives us true strength — "

She needed all her strength, for Thomas Poynton Ives, another relative, was also very sick: "you will probably never see him again — " She reported that "these two or three days" Uncle James "has voided clear blood & his strength is all gone."

A few hours later she wrote: "Our poor Uncle is no more, he expired about 8 oclk." James Brown, beloved brother, uncle and friend, was seventy-three. After some small bequests to nieces and nephews, he left one-sixth of his ample estate to his nephew, and executor, John Brown

Francis, and five-sixths, including the great mansion house, to his sister Sarah Herreshoff.[17]

On December 18, Agnes again wrote to her brother that because of James Brown's bequest, valued in total at $90,000, a large sum in those days, "Mother now has enough to be comfortable – we wish you to consult your own judgement with regard to coming." But Agnes did all she could to influence his judgement in this moving passage:

You must so well recollect my dearest John how reluctantly we parted with you, that you may now judge the anxiety we feel for your safe return, come as soon as you can to a helpless family of females who now look to you as their greatest earthly comfort

And she wrote that "We call you the best of us all."[18]

It is difficult to say exactly what effect this appeal had, for although John spent some months each year in Rhode Island, he also spent much of each year in Lowville and on the Tract.

In 1835 Francis Seger, son-in-law to Caleb Lyon and brother-in-law to Lyman R. Lyon, eventual purchaser of most of the John Brown's Tract, was working diligently, as a member of the New York Senate, toward the passage of a Black River Canal Bill, which would certainly foster the prosperity of Lowville and Boonville, the two most important villages on the western edge of the Tract, and, as the two John Browns, Francis and Herreshoff, hoped, the Tract itself.

Albany was also the focus of their concern about that old matter, taxes. On January 3, Herreshoff wrote to his cousin the governor.

. . . I propose trying what can be done with the Legislature towards getting a reduction of the interest on the tax bill & to be there myself at the presenting a petition if it is thought advisable to take that course. You once hinted that you might, – through your acquaintance with Gov. Marcy, get him to use his influence in the matter. He has been Comptroller, & is no doubt well acquainted with the fiscal regulations of the State, & would know whether what we want could be obtained without infringing upon the rules of the office. If you write him it would be well to do it directly as I may be in Albany in the course of a fortnight. I should state the matter to him strongly – It is in fact (what we ask) but a trifling act of justice considering the system of espionage that has been carried on by the Assessors for years . . .[19]

But Francis, an experienced politician, knew that you do not put such things bluntly, but use the code language that politicians understand so well, but which is designed to protect them against charges of what has come to be called "cronyism."

The End of the Dream

A PETITION FOR THE
Black River Canal.

To the Honorable the Senate and Assembly of the State of New York.

The petition of the undersigned citizens of Jefferson, St. Lawrence, Lewis and Oneida counties respectfully sheweth:

That in the year 1825, the executive of this state among other improvements, recommended to the favorable consideration of the Legislature, the construction of the Black River Canal. In pursuance of that recommendation, the Legislature authorised the survey of various routes, and among the rest, that of the Black river. Mr. Geddes, an engineer appointed for that purpose, made the surveys and estimates and reported the same to the next legislature. Since which time the said canal has been, surveyed by Mr. Cruger, by Mr. Hutchinson, and the last year under a law passed in 1834, it was surveyed by Mr Jarvis. Mr. Geddes, Mr. Cruger, Mr. Hutchinson and Mr. Jarvis, have severally acknowledged the feasibility and practicability of the work. At the last session of the Legislature, a bill for the construction of this work passed the Assembly after a full discussion of its merits with great unanimity of sentiment in its favour; and the conclusion now seems to be irresistible that public sentiment calls for its immediate commencement.

The proposed canal commences at Rome, in the county of Oneida, and terminates at the High falls of Black river in the town of West Turin, and is thirty-five miles long. Boonville in the county of Oneida, is the summit on which the waters of the Black river are to be brought by a navigable feeder 11 miles long. From the High falls on the Black river, to Carthage, following the river is a distance of 40 miles; this river for this distance is navigable for steam boats.

This canal would accommodate the inhabitants of the north part of Oneida, the whole of Lewis and terminates at a point in Jefferson county calculated to receive the productions of a great part of Jefferson and St. Lawrence counties. But few countries combine more advantages than the counties bordering on the entire rout of this canal. This fact must be acknowledged by all who have ever visited this part of the State, and examined the fertility of the soil, the superabundance of its timber and iron ore, its water power, and above all the rigid economy, the unwearied industry and the increasing wealth of its citizens. Your petitioners would further represent to your honorable body that in the counties of Lewis, Jefferson and St. Lawrence are immense forests of pine, cherry and other valuable timber, now, comparatively speaking, worth little or nothing in consequence of its distance from the Erie canal. There are also inexhaustible beds of iron ore, both bog and mountain yielding from 50 to 70 lbs. of iron from 100 lbs. of ore, which would be worked should this canal be made. These two items furnish the best evidence of a long continued source of prospective tonnage. Make this canal and this section of the country might emphatically be called the Sweden of America.

Should your honorable body deem it expedient to grant to your petitioners this just and reasonable request, an impetus will be given to the people hitherto unknown, new energies will be created, capital will be sought after and profitably employed, agriculture will be extended, manufactories will be increased, and in fine, the whole resources of the country will be developed in an astonishing degree.

Your petitioners would further represent to your honorable body, that although they possess a healthy climate, a fertile soil, innumerable water powers, inexhaustible beds of ore, extensive forests of valuable timber, with wealth and enterprise sufficient to call them into requisition, yet by being so remote from market, without a water communication they are scarcely worth enjoying. Thus situated we call upon the fostering hand of Government to shield and protect us; we ask it as a matter of right, not doubting but that when the merits of the application shall be fairly tested it will be granted.

While other parts of the state have been signally benefited by internal improvements, our claims have been passed by. While we have for almost 20 years been called upon to contribute our proportion towards the expenses of their construction, we have done it with a cheerfulness which has never admitted a murmur, confidently relying upon the liberality and justice of the State to construct our canal whenever the finances of the State would admit. The time has now arrived as we confidently believe, when the State can construct the Black river Canal without any derangement of its finances. Relying therefore upon the merits of the application and the justice of your honorable body, we are led to believe that the time has at length arrived when the prayer of your petitioners will be heard & answered. We feel and we have a pleasure in the reflection that we are a portion of the State, and as much entitled to the aid and protection of the State as other sections thereof. It cannot be denied when we take into consideration the facility of emigration on the Erie canal and the cheapness of government lands, that unless something is done for us, we must abandon our connections and our homes for some more favored parts of the world. It is a fact which it is useless to attempt any longer to conceal, that the increased facilities of other parts hold out strong inducements for our people to emigrate, and particularly those of them who are apprehensive that the Black river canal will never be made.

It is clearly perceivable that this state of things operates in a two fold manner to injure, and ultimately to ruin us; first, it prevents persons from settling in this part of the State, and secondly it encourages others settled here to leave it. This evil has long been anticipated and it is now seriously felt, and unless your honorable body will stay the evil by holding out some encouragement to its inhabitants, no one can determine when and where it will terminate.

Your petitioners would therefore in order to shield and protect them from those evils which are more than anticipated earnestly but respectfully pray that your honorable body will pass a law authorizing the construction of the Black river canal and the improvement of the navigation of the Black river in continuation thereof, and for such further aid as your honorable body may see fit and proper to grant.

And your petitioners as in duty bound will ever pray.

Petition to the New York Legislature for the Black River Canal.

We found in the family papers a letter from Francis to his Brown University classmate. Since there are so many crossouts and insertions, it must be a draft. But Francis did not ask Marcy for help — that would have been too blatant — but rather asked him to "advise" the bearer of the note, Herreshoff, "as to the course he ought to pursue — whether he can expect what we wish without infringing on the rule of the Comptrollers department . . . that it [their case] is a just one there can be no doubt — We have been most confoundedly fleeced by yr assessors — "

Francis wrote his classmate that he "should not have ventured to trouble" him had not Herreshoff been in Albany "& had I known any other influential individual to whom I might have referred him — but I dare say you will cheerfully put him on the right track and gratify an old friend."[20]

We do not know what assistance, if any, Marcy offered. All we do know is that Francis and Herreshoff continued to pay the taxes, although often late, until the Tract was finally sold. The Masons, however, as we have noted, somewhere during this period, failed to redeem their land sold for taxes, so No. 6 passed out of the family.

Charles Dayan again entered the story in March, with a letter to Francis from Albany. The former Congressman had been elected to the state Assembly on the Black River Canal issue and, with Seger, was instrumental in its eventual approval. He was also interested in again becoming agent for the John Brown's Tract.

> *. . . I am surrounded by land speculators and particularly so while there is a prospect for the passage of the B. R. canal which I think will not pass the Senate this Session. Now Sir to come at once to the point I will take the agency of yr tract in Lewis & Herkimer if it do not interfere with my friend Herrishoff* [sic] *at one half that I can get over 20 cents the acres (if I sell for 30 I am entitled to 5 cents the acres for my pay. There is a prospect that some of it might now be sold. This is the only terms on which I would under any circumstances take it and it only remains with you to say whether you will give it —*

And he scribbled on the side: "If you should comply an immediate power of atty sufficient for me to sell would be desirable that I might do something before I leave Albany — "[21]

It was nearly a month before Francis replied. He explained that Dayan's letter had arrived "when absorbed in *political matters*, from which I have only just escaped. The election has been a very close one (it was indeed; Francis defeated Nehemiah R. Knight by 3,880 to 3,774) but there can be no doubt of my re-election . . . . "

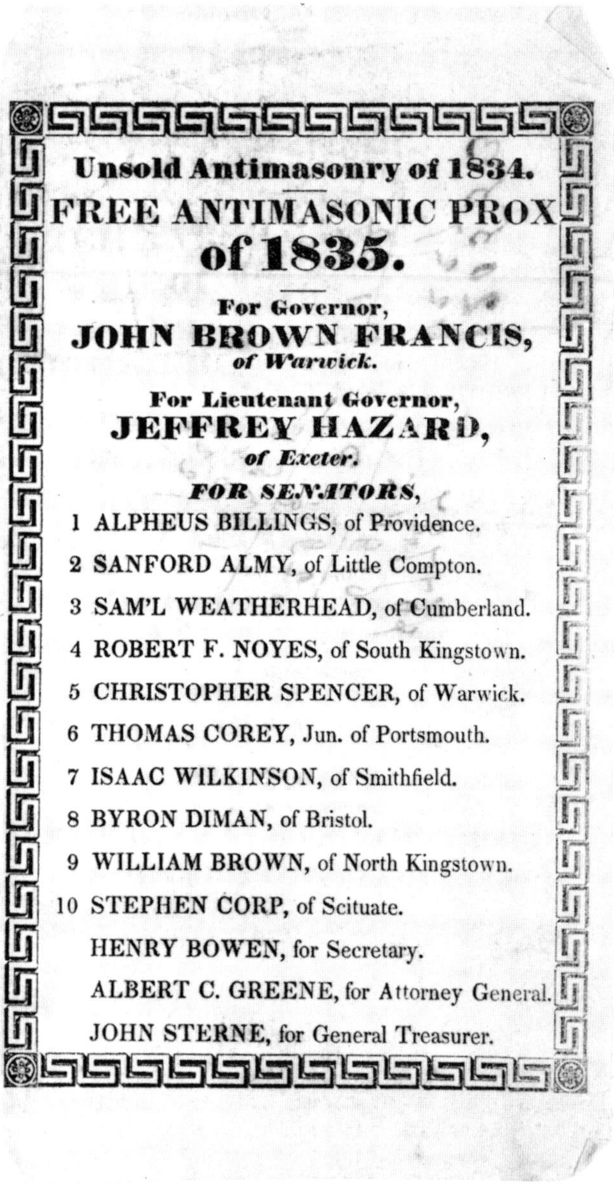

Unsold Antimasonry of 1834.

FREE ANTIMASONIC PROX of 1835.

For Governor,
JOHN BROWN FRANCIS,
of Warwick.

For Lieutenant Governor,
JEFFREY HAZARD,
of Exeter.

FOR SENATORS,

1 ALPHEUS BILLINGS, of Providence.
2 SANFORD ALMY, of Little Compton.
3 SAM'L WEATHERHEAD, of Cumberland.
4 ROBERT F. NOYES, of South Kingstown.
5 CHRISTOPHER SPENCER, of Warwick.
6 THOMAS COREY, Jun. of Portsmouth.
7 ISAAC WILKINSON, of Smithfield.
8 BYRON DIMAN, of Bristol.
9 WILLIAM BROWN, of North Kingstown.
10 STEPHEN CORP, of Scituate.
HENRY BOWEN, for Secretary.
ALBERT C. GREENE, for Attorney General.
JOHN STERNE, for General Treasurer.

1835 election ballot once again proposing John Brown Francis for governor.

This letter, in the elegant hand of a secretary (with one insertion in Francis' hand), continued:

> . . . *Now, as to your offer—you would* not *interfere with Mr. Herreshoff—You propose to take ½ over 20 cts. the acre—you mean at wholesale. How would you retail? Your proposition is not sufficiently definite. Probably when you say ½ over 20 cts. you mean to incur* all *expense including Taxes. Explain your whole plan &* then *I can judge. You speak of being "surrounded with Land Speculators." Pray is the land at last in demand? At what could it be sold under the hammer? I mean my Township. Has the Canal Bill passed?*
>
> *You do not refer to the fate of our Petition, for an exemption from interest on taxes. What has been the fate of the Petition?*
>
> *I propose making you a visit in all next month. Put on paper your ideas of what ought to be our Contract—or rather what you would agree to.*[22]

Dayan quickly responded in his vigorous scrawl. He reported that the committee to which the petition had been referred had reported against it, and he said bluntly, "As to your lands I have nothing to say more than I said in my former communication."

> . . . *First I would of course do nothing without the consent or permission of Mr. Herrishoff—I of course will pay no taxes or assessments—I am not anxious about it any rate. All I wished that if these people of whom I spoke came into the country to purchase lands with a belief that the Canal would be made I might be in a situation to meet them. If you want to sell is one question if you do not that is another—while the Canal question is pending those might be sold in parcels at public or private sale. I know two men who now say they want 20,000 each if they can get it cheap. One of them has agreed to call on me at my house on 7th of May next. The other in the course of the next summer. They are able to pay cash down; and I think will. On this subject however I care but very little.*

A wonderfully brusque letter from one who had approached Francis with the idea of again representing the Tract. Although he did add in rather more cordial terms, "And we are all overjoyed at the result of your election. . . .[23]

That those two men had cash, there is no reason to doubt, but they did not spend it on purchasing land from the Brown family. Again and again, for another fifteen years, prospects would appear and quickly vanish.

In mid-July we have another of those interesting letters from John Brown Herreshoff to his family (this time his mother) about his journey from Bristol to Lowville. In New York City he visited James Watson, proprietor of the neighboring tract.

. . . He was in fine health & spirits & amused me highly with a project of getting a large blackberry party to the Town of Watson this summer. He said he should go to Browns Tract to catch some salmon trout for the occasion & then have about thirty from the villages of Lowville & Martinsburg with the Esquire

From Albany he took the train and "steamed" up to Saratoga Springs, whose hotels he described as "grand almost beyond description." But he ended his long letter with a little postscript scribbled on the envelope: "Your elegant retreat at P[oin]t P[leasan]t is as far superior to Saratoga as Sols meridian splendor to Stygian gloom."[24]

About that time, Francis learned from Richard Peters [son-in-law of financier Thomas Willing and thus John Brown Francis' uncle by marriage], recorder to the United States Supreme Court, that Joseph Bonaparte, brother to Napoleon and former King of Naples and of Spain, had sold his nearby lands for $80,000, and that the purchaser expected to make a $100,000 profit, but then, the purchasers of north country land always expected to make big profits and seldom did. Donaldson gives a different account, writing that Bonaparte in 1836 gave the land to his son and returned to France.[25]

Another would-be purchaser of the year before, William L. Hirst, the Philadelphia lawyer, in mid-1835 drew up a sales agreement for the Francis land at a price of $12,000, $1000 less than Francis had proposed the previous year. Hirst added a postscript to the agreement: "I believe the above embodies an agreement. If not, please add, alter or amend, – and on rect [receipt of] yr reply, I will immediately have it executed. We wish the matter closed as soon as your convenience will permit."[26] Why this sale did not go through, we cannot say. It seems doubtful that, given his eagerness to sell, Francis would have balked at the reduction of $1,000.

In November, Herreshoff wrote another of his good travel letters to his mother, noting that in New York he had met a man named Brown who "thought that he (the Gov) ought of all men to belong to *the gentlemens party*." He reported that the steamboat passage to Albany cost 50¢. Of the canal boat he reported that "The comfort of passing the night on board one of these boats is rather less than that of a steamboat as you are stowed away upon a kind of hanging shelf with hardly room to turn around." So he "jumped out of the boat before sunrise & walked five miles before sunrise keeping ahead of the boat and getting in at a lock."[27]

In December, Governor Francis received an inquiry which, had he been able to respond affirmatively, might have changed the course of the history of the John Brown's Tract. It was from State Senator Francis Seger in Albany.

. . . I have been desired by Mr. Noble Phelps of Turin Lewis Co. to write you for the purpose of ascertaining whether the Forge clearing could be hired at a moderate rent. He proposes to take the property for five years at an annual rent of fifty dollars payable in repairs and highway labor. His design is to establish a dairy and open a public house to accomodate gentlemen who resort there to enjoy the sports of angling. He is an enterprising healthy man and I should think might do well, and perhaps his success would promote your interest better than a large rent, for there is a general impression that no family can live there; his success would at least do away that, and I think many other unjustifiable prejudices that are now entertained in regard to these lands.[28]

Phelps had the right idea, for the Adirondacks, about the time of the Civil War, would begin to prosper, as it still does, as a resort, a natural refuge. It is interesting (and futile) to speculate what might have happened had Phelps been established on No. 7. The forge area, now Old Forge, was to become prosperous indeed, and this book might have been written not on Governor Francis' farm on Narragansett Bay in Rhode Island, but at his resort on the John Brown's Tract. Plainly, the land was not going to succeed as a settlement when, as one inquirer put it, "The present reputation of that country is bad."[29]

Also, in December, John Brown Francis and his aunt Sarah Herreshoff exchanged considerable property in which Francis surrendered his one-sixth claim to the great John Brown mansion house, now the possession of the Rhode Island Historical Society.[30]

At the end of the month Francis received a letter from Seger that explained why the governor had not accepted the proposal for Phelps to establish a resort. The specific pieces of land that Phelps wanted had evidently been sold. Since they were uncertain as to who owned what, it is impossible a century and a half later to sort out the confusion. In our search of the land records, we encountered no such sale, but land was sold for taxes and then redeemed time and time again, so that precise knowledge of ownership is difficult in the extreme to establish. We can only assume that the land Phelps wanted was owned, as Seger suggested, by a J. W. James and/or Mrs. James Sargent, both of New York.

This letter also provides a clue as to why the Hirst deal, which seemed a reasonable one, did not go through, for Seger wrote:

. . . I cannot but deem your determination not to sell at this time, proper. There is certainly a reasonable chance for the passage of the canal bill the ensuing winter—and should our efforts be crowned with success, your entire tract will be brought nearer to a market than Lewis county now is, *where wild lands have been selling from 3 to 6$ the acre.*

The End of the Dream

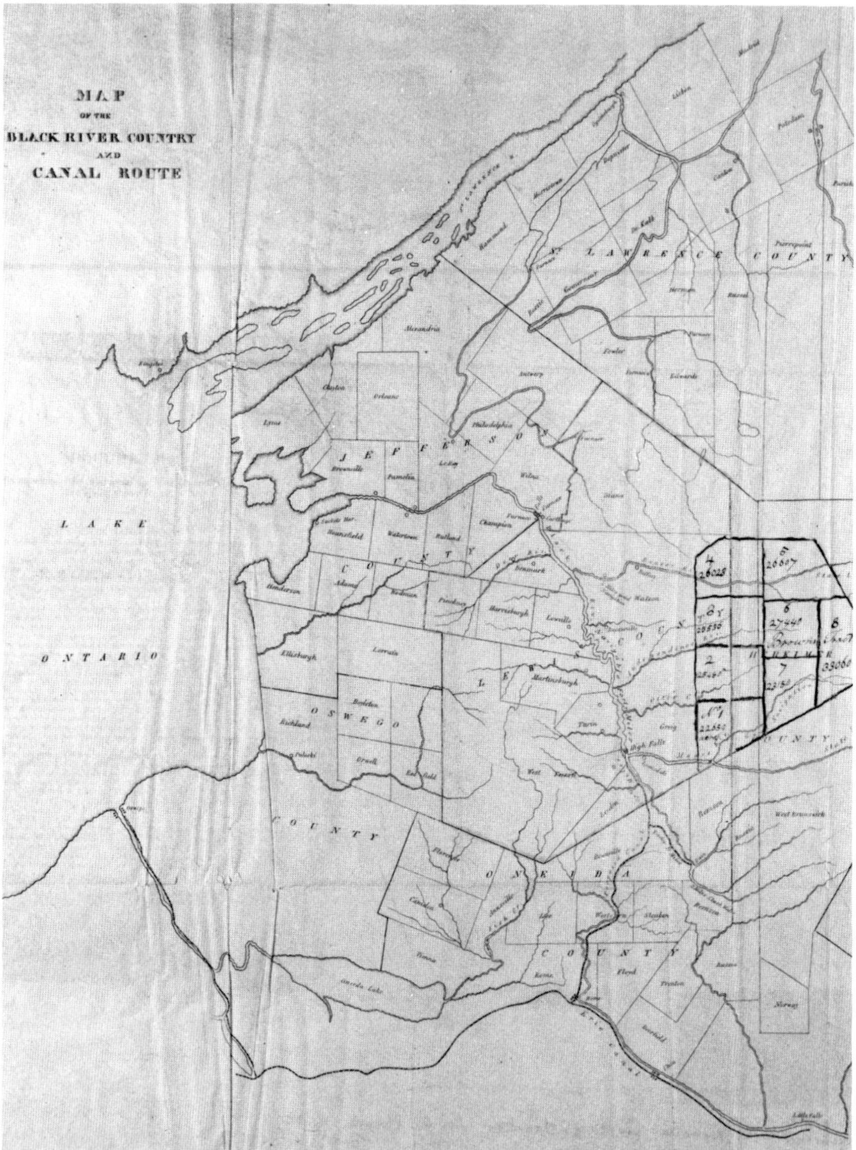

Map of the Black River area and proposed canal route which accompanied the "Memorial for the construction of the Black River Canal." John Brown Francis outlined the Tract in red.

Again, here was the dream that something external was going to make the John Brown's Tract desirable, but even the eventual building of the canal could not change its intrinsic characteristics. The land was not suitable for farming or manufacture, there was plenty of Adirondack timber much closer to population centers, the tide of vacationers was still some decades off, and one site, where there was an immediate potential as a resort, the forge lands sought by Phelps, were apparently no longer the property of Governor Francis.

Seger was pleased that Francis was willing to journey to Albany to help lobby for the Black River Canal bill.

> *. . . I think your assistance may be of essential service, and I should be very much gratified to learn that you would be willing to spend a short time here, at such times as it might be deemed important, of which you could readily be apprised, probably about the time of the opening of navigation.*[31]

Amusingly, on the last day of 1835, a letter was addressed to "Mr John Brown" as owner of the Tract. The inquiry was forwarded from Brown & Ives to Governor Francis.[32]

In 1836 there began a trickle of writing about the Adirondacks, not yet so called, that within a few years would become a flood. The first travel writer was Harriet Martineau, the famous British author. She had visited Saratoga and was not keen on it, so she headed for the storied beauty of Lake George. Her glowing accounts were published in London two years later.[33] But, although the trickle did eventually become a flood, it was decades before much was written about the wild lands of the northwestern Adirondacks.

During the first month of 1836, Governor Francis received a letter that, years after the fact, shows beyond question that Charles Frederick Herreshoff had demonstrated considerable ingenuity in his process for separating iron ore. It is evident that the elder Herreshoff's device was, if not the first of its kind, one of the earliest used in the Adirondacks. Thus was its reputation, for James H. Rogers and Joseph Goulding wanted information on the Herreshoff device for use in a patent dispute in a United States court. They were seeking to prove that the Herreshoff device had predated one for which a patent was claimed.[34]

In March, Governor Francis wrote again to his friend Governor Marcy in support of the Black River Canal bill. We have two very slightly different drafts of the letter, which shed light also on the political situation in Rhode Island, where Francis was not only seeking election, but was supporting the presidential aspirations of Martin Van Buren, the New York politician who was a close associate of Marcy.

. . . I had promised myself the pleasure of a short sojourn at your Capitol pending the discussion of the Black River Canal question: but the nomination of Mr Burgess as the Whig candidate for Governor defeats that plan and obliges me, of course, to stay at home and run the gauntlet with what appetite I may . . . We have, it cannot be denied, a formidable Phalanx to contend with but I am confident of victory; and the result of this election will put at rest all opposition to our VanBuren electors in Nov – but, eventuate as this Spring's election may, you need not entertain a doubt but that we shall go for the Baltimore nominee.

Francis then turned to the purpose of his letter, promoting the Black River Canal. Here he changed roles – if indeed they are much different – from politician to salesman, speaking not only of his own lands, but the state-owned lands immediately to the south of the John Brown's Tract. He spoke glowingly of the soil and the timber.

. . . And I do have no scruples in testifying that for vegetables, oats, rye, & peas there is no better land in the State of NYK and as to climate Mr H who passed many winters on Brown's Tract always avered that he would prefer encountering that climate to ours of N England As a growing country it must likewise become valuable: but the great advantage to the Public from this Canal will result from the inexhaustible store of Lumber Spruce & Hemlock which it will bring to market – All that portion of Land now deemed valueless because covered with evergreen timber will have more value than the Maple & Basswood regions which are considered best for agricultural purposes.[35]

Reading Governor Francis' enthusiastic description of the region, like similar descriptions we have encountered over a forty-year period, one can only wonder why the Tract did not flourish. One can only assume that the three generations of Browns, in entirely human fashion, made a rather more optimistic assessment of the Tract than the facts of an intractable nature warranted.

Governor Marcy did not reply for nearly a month, waiting for something to report. He then wrote that the Senate had just passed the bill by 17-10, and that, since it had passed the House the previous year, he presumed, and in this he was correct, that it would soon pass there as well. And he referred to his classmate's race for reelection. "You have not only my best but my most ardent wishes for success."[36]

The canal was soon authorized and then built and, eventually, abandoned. Its locks can still be seen in the grassy median strip of State Highway 12 between Lowville and Boonville. While it did benefit the region through which it passed, its benefits never spread much to the John Brown's Tract, for in those few miles to the east, the topography so changed that it never, to this day, attracted much population.

That year, 1836, also saw the formation of the Town of Wilmurt, then the largest town in New York, nearly fifty miles from north to south and nearly sixteen from east to west, including all of the Herkimer County portion of John Brown's Tract. It was described in an 1893 history of the county as "rocky and mountainous and a large part of it is unfit for cultivation. In the deep valleys among the mountains are numerous beautiful and picturesque lakes, often connected by streams of pure cold water." This accurately describes what the Tract is not good for, farming, and what it is good for, a natural resort. By 1840, the population of this enormous town, two-thirds the size of Rhode Island, was only 60.[37]

The year 1837 was an important year, not only to the Brown's Tract but to the entire Adirondack region, although it was never to benefit the Brown family. That year, Otis Arnold, a struggling thirty-three-year-old farmer from Boonville, ventured into the Tract seeking a better future for a family that already included six children. In the early spring, he happened upon Herreshoff Manor and here, without any bothersome details of rent or purchase, he established himself. Eventually, John Brown Francis must have learned of his presence, but we have no record of it. He may have been glad to have anyone living on the Tract, in the hopes that one settler would attract others. There have been many accounts of Otis Arnold, for his establishment became what is believed to be the beginning of the hotel business in the Adirondacks, for more than a century now, deservedly one of the most popular resort areas in the nation. These accounts, however, owe as much to the creative imaginations of their authors as to the available facts. This passage by Joseph Grady, however, does keep close to the facts.

. . . A few months after the family had moved into the Manor a fisherman knocked at the door in search of food and lodging. He was received hospitably and accommodated with pancakes, venison and a bed. In the morning he paid the modest reckoning, complimented the hostess on her cookery, and departed—a satisfied patron. That was the beginning of the hotel business in the Adirondacks. Other hungry wayfarers were housed and fed at intervals, hunters, trappers and fishermen, and occasionally a sight-seeing tourist. They were all received with hearty informality and at low rates, and in time the Manor became known as an inn. It was also a tavern, for Otis kept a stock of liquors on hand to be dispensed to thirsty travellers who had not appetite for spring water. Otis did not consider himself to be an innkeeper or taverner in 1837, yet the entertainment which he furnished to the public and for which he received compensation that year heralded the approach of the modern resort hotels which now dot the shores of the principal Adirondack lakes, and his Manor home is properly regarded as the first hotel to have opened its doors within the foothills of the mountains.[38]

The End of the Dream

Over the years Arnold made an addition to the Manor, and his packhorses, to carry supplies from Boonville, became a stable of riding horses, leading to the legend of his eleven daughters riding wildly through the woods and clearings, their long hair streaming behind. Eventually, about 2,000 vacationers a year found their difficult way into the Tract and stayed with the Arnolds in their crude but beautifully situated inn. Yet, although Herreshoff Manor in its fashion had finally become the center of a successful enterprise, it seemed to have had no effect on the Brown family's plans for the Tract. Perhaps the resort business simply did not interest them.

In that year Ebenezer Emmons, the state geologist, began his great survey, in which he used the term Adirondacks to name the area, a name that gradually supplanted the use of John Brown's Tract to designate the entire vast wilderness.

Disturbing news was sent to John Brown Herreshoff by Governor Francis in March.

> *... In a Bill sent me recently the Dep. Comptroller of NYK, it is manifest that I was right in the fears I have so often suggested to you that 1800 acres only in No. 7 remain. All the cleared and best land is gone beyond redemption and probably a good portion of B & I's 5000 acres. There must have been sales since 1830. Did you ever consult the Comptroller's Advertisements?*[39]

In this and other letters there is implicit criticism – it was never directly stated – that Herreshoff could have devoted more attention to tax matters and thus have avoided the loss of lands for non-payment of taxes. Such matters were fearfully confused in those days, however. This could explain how Otis Arnold lived for three decades in Herreshoff Manor paying neither rent nor taxes. Quite possibly, the land belonged to the state or to an absentee landlord who simply never bothered.

In June 1837 there was a mysterious reference in a letter to Governor Francis, from his Uncle Charles Francis, of an offer of $19,000 in cash. In August, Uncle Charles, apparently referring to the same offer, wrote that he had heard from a Mr. Morris that the Governor had declined an offer of 25-30¢ an acre. This is puzzling, since, in a letter to his cousin John in October, he wrote: "If there is really no expectation of a rise in the value of our land, it is ruinous to think of holding on." And he spoke of selling at 20¢ an acre, saying that the land in the area was not worth 50¢ an acre, or half that.[40]

Herreshoff returned to Lowville in October, stopping at the Comptroller's office in Albany, where he was "perplexed most of the forenoon."[41] Another step regarding taxes was taken by an E. Varney, who had Francis' power of attorney. He approached an assessor in Wilmurt, who was also town supervisor, since there were "but five families in that town." He agreed, if not opposed by the other assessors, to cut the valuation of the Tract in half.[42]

A curious letter arrived at the office of Governor Francis in December 1837. It was from a J. W. Parkins, and written from New York. It referred to the proposed purchase of Tract land by Charles Kahn and John Sidell, who was not only a well-known New York attorney, but son-in-law of Commodore Matthew Perry, the famous Rhode Islander who "opened up" Japan. Parkins wrote that Kahn was supposed to turn over that contract—at 10¢ an acre—to him.

> *... very shortly after this period Kahn took his departure from New York, where he transgressed the Laws, since then I have not heard any thing on the subject as to whether or not the land has been sold, except that on my enquiring of Aaron Sargeant, formerly Auctioneer of New York, he said that the only part of that property that was* worth any thing, *was in his possession amounting to about* 2000 acres, *which he had purchased, along with* Mill Seats Water power *and some extensive buildings, erected for the purpose of carrying on an Iron Foundery &c—I need not tell you, Sir, that this Aaron Sergeant is a man whose veracity is so questionable that no credit can be given to what he says. I therefore take the liberty to request to be favoured with a few lines from you, to inform me if the said 85,000 acres of land called "Browns Tract" are still for sale,? and what is the lowest price per acre, ...*[43]

We, of course, can make no judgment as to the veracity of Aaron Sargeant, but this does seem to tie in to something we cited earlier. We noted that Francis Seger said that the property at No. 7, on which Noble Phelps wanted to build a public house, was owned by a J. W. James or a Mrs. James Sargent. Perhaps the names Sargent/Sergeant on what may have been the same piece of property was sheer coincidence or a case of two spellings of the same name in an era that was not as fastidious in these matters as our own. Maybe this Aaron Sergeant did in fact own the best piece of No. 7, land that is still the most valuable in the area. As an auctioneer, Sergeant might well have been aware of the availability of the choicest piece of No. 7.

In any case, Governor Francis quickly responded to Parkins, which elicited another letter.

Governor John Brown Francis (1791-1864) circa 1860.

. . . I merely write this to say that it is usual in such matters, than of purchsing an Estate, particularly of such magnitude as 85,000 *acres of land, for the person selling to mention his price when* Cash *is the medium — and I should expect it to be at a considerable reduction, from that at which it was offered to me; the beginning of 1832 viz* ten cents per acre.

And he refers to the "meretricious conduct" of Sidell and Kahn, about whom, you will remember, Francis said he was worth only the rings on his fingers.[44] It does seem odd that Francis did not say how much he wanted, although he may have been engaged in the bargaining tactic of letting the other person make the first offer.

The year 1838 yielded no significant information about the Tract. Since John Brown Herreshoff had been in Lowville for the previous eight years, and was there in the succeeding two years, we assume that was the case in 1838 as well, but we have no documentary evidence to that effect.

In 1838 Francis' political luck ran out, and he was defeated by William Sprague, 3,894 to 3,504. But this was only a temporary setback in his political career. He later served for years in the state senate and, briefly, the U. S. Senate.

In 1839 we finally get some precise figures as to how much tax was being paid on the Tract. In a note from the Deputy Comptroller, the county and town taxes for 1836 were put at $407.21, and the highway tax at $478.82, for a total of $886.03. For 1837: county and town taxes, $158.84, and highway tax, $530.90, for a total of $689.74.[45] Since the county and town taxes for 1837 were so much lower, it is safe to assume that Varney had indeed succeeded in getting the valuation reduced. Now, $700 a year on so vast an estate hardly seems onerous until you consider that, with little or no income, the entire value of the Tract would be eaten up in 20 or so years.

The life of a farmer in this era was bitterly described by an historian of Hamilton County, which contained a tiny corner of the Tract. But what was written by Ted Aber and Stella King applied to the entire Tract, and to farming anywhere in the Adirondacks.

. . . The very idea of farming was a ruse perpetuated by unknowing land-owners on unknowing people. Not until years later was it realized, thanks to the State geologist, Verplanck Colvin, that moving to higher altitudes was like moving many miles northward. The climate was colder, the growing seasons shorter. Hardship became the inevitable lot of the constant pioneers of the mountain regions. Almost anywhere else in New York State would their agricultural efforts have yielded better rewards.[46]

Indeed, life on the Tract, for the few who stuck it out, was difficult indeed, a constant comfortless struggle against nature, with bare subsistence the lot of most. Somehow, intelligent as the Brown family members were, they never quite understood that.

In September 1840, we have the last letter of John Brown Herreshoff from the north country, leading to the inference that that was the last year he spent any significant period of time near or on the Tract. This last letter does not have anything terribly important, but a couple of tidbits characteristic of the area.

Speaking of the kitchen at Point Pleasant, he wrote, "The work of our kitchen is mere girls play to what Mrs Fenton of Brown Tract does in rearing a large family of children & doing all the cooking & washing spinning weaving milking the cows feed the pigs &c &c."

Later, he wrote:

I have doffed my summer clothes & enjoy a roaring Black River fire. [And at midday, he added] *I have just put down my pen to take a lunch of blackberry pie which nice article and a plenty of blackberries & cream I have had every day since I have been here. I wish I could send you a few quarts out of the 1000 bushels it is said have been brought from the east side of the river...* [which would be along the edge of the Tract][47]

With that letter to one of his sisters—we do not know whether it was to Anna or Agnes, since it was begun "Dear A"—we hear the last of John Brown Herreshoff from northern New York. For eleven years he lived much of the time in the simple society of Lowville and, since his sale of family lands was negligible, something else must have kept him there. Persistence, as we saw with his father, ran in the family, and maybe he lasted all those years in the hope that, sooner or later, things would improve. Or maybe he enjoyed the rugged life of the frontier. But by 1840, he was thirty-five and he may have felt it was time to do something else.

Anyway, his last sale was to his old friend Charles Dayan, who purchased 84.88 acres in the Watson section of No. 4 for $100 a few days after that final letter. He did not get around to recording the deed for more than ten years, about the time that Lyman R. Lyon was purchasing the John Brown's Tract.[48]

About that time, the last decade that the Brown family owned most of the original John Brown's Tract, information is sparse. With John Brown Herreshoff no longer in the area, all we have is some fitful evidence of John Brown Francis' efforts to rid the family of this financial albatross. So this story, as if often the case with life itself, just dwindles away. Indeed, so was the life of one of the major figures, Sarah Brown Herreshoff, owner of a large section of the Tract and wife and mother of two of the principal players. In 1841, Anna Herreshoff, the indefatigable letter writer, wrote from Providence to her family in Bristol. It was a lively letter, filled with family gossip, in which she informed them that Sarah had "very weak eyes—they are swollen, & I fear she will soon be unable to read or sew," a serious loss to a woman who had loved things of the mind her entire life.[49]

Although she was to live for another five years, Sarah must have felt the end drawing nigh, for she wrote this note to John Brown Herreshoff in a hand no longer firm:

... In memory of your honor'd and revered grand-father whose name you bear, and in remembrance of your much loved grand-mother whose kindness and endearments must be well fixed in your mind; and I may add in token of affection for your continual attention to my wants, I do this day request your acceptance of the silver punch-urn which was his, and the two tankards, which were the gift

of my mother to me—I hope you will be able to keep them and let them descent in a straight line this trifling bequest will appear in a Will I hope shortly to make. .[50]

Within the year, John Brown Francis, who had already lost his first wife, Anne Carter Brown, in childbirth, and his second child John in 1826, when he was less than a year old, suffered another grievous loss, that of his first born, Abby, and Mary, daughter of his wife Elizabeth's first marriage. One being eighteen, the other nineteen.

In 1842 Lardner Vanuxem made his famous geological survey. He immediately saw in the region that included John Brown's Tract what its owners never recognized, or refused to admit to themselves. "The country will remain for some time unsettled, in consequence of the rich lands which encircle the whole of the Primary region not being fully occupied, and of the facilities given to westward travelling, where land is as cheap and far more productive." But he also saw what would be the most valuable use of the land. Speaking of the region's lakes, he wrote: "The beauty of their waters, their elevation, and the wild scenery which surrounds them, would not fail to attract visitors."[51] For more than a century now, that region has indeed attracted visitors, but in the last decade of Brown ownership, only a trickle of vacationers came, and the family would wait no longer.

Documenting Vanuxem's views are the population figures for 1842. Whereas sixty years before, the area from Utica to Buffalo was a wilderness, criss-crossed by tribes of roving Indians, now it was home to more than a million people.[52] Yet, except for the few settlers at No. 4 and Arnold's little clan at No. 7, the Tract was virtually empty, with perhaps 50 or 60 people in an area of 328 square miles.

Every now and then Francis received an inquiry, but nothing ever came of them. Taxes, as always, were a concern. The lumber industry was rapidly pushing into the area, making New York State the nation's leading lumber producer, but, probably for market and transportation reasons, lumber never became much of a factor on the Tract. By 1846 Francis was again trying to interest William Hirst in the land, writing to his Philadelphia attorney, Henry D. Gilpin, that "I am so anxious to disincumber myself of wild land. . . ." He again was seeking $13,000 for land that Hirst, some years before, had seemed eager to acquire.[53] But again, nothing came of it.

On August 2, 1846, Sarah Brown Herreshoff died, a month before her seventy-third birthday. She left the great mansion house to her twelve-

Hunting cabin on John Brown's Tract at Third Lake, circa 1869.

year-old grandson James Brown Herreshoff, with the proviso that her son John and her unmarried daughters could live there until 1852, when he turned eighteen.

In January 1847 John Brown Herreshoff received a letter from a David Read of Winooski Falls, Vermont, who wanted to buy 50,000 acres of the Tract. He said that on a recent visit to Albany, he had noticed that most of the Tract had been sold for taxes. He offered to take the 50,000 acres—all of the Tract in Lewis County and the rest in Herkimer—and "give you some compensation therefore, over and above the taxes." He did not specify how much, but since, according to him, nearby land was being sold by the state for 5¢ an acre, and since the back taxes amounted to 3 to 5¢ an acre, plainly it would have been a nominal sum. Even if the taxes were not figured in, 50,000 acres at 5¢ an acre came to only $2,500, hardly a princely sum for so huge a parcel.[54] Thus, it is not surprising that the offer was not taken up.

In 1848 the other John Brown, the one whose "body lies amoulderin' in the grave," came to North Alba on the plain below Lake Placid. His few years' residence in the Adirondacks before his historic raids on "bloody Kansas" have ever since caused confusion between him and our John Brown.

Also in 1848 a railroad from Saratoga Springs across the Adirondacks to Sackets Harbor, traversing the Tract, was supposed to be yet another salvation. But the railroad, like so many Adirondack schemes, turned out to be a financial and operational disaster, and only a few miles of track were ever laid.[55]

That year, in January, Francis received an unusual approach, unusual in that it was from a woman, Mary White of New York, who thought she could sell his land if "Mr H (I am at a loss to spell the name) would also add his tract to your own. . . ." She asked if Francis were interested. Obviously he was, for in just twelve days she was responding to his reply.

> *I'm afraid that the price required for your "land of* promise" *will make it impossible to effect the sale I proposed—Simply because other lands in the same Counties are offered at lower rates, and I learn that the Real estate brokers are full of lots & parcels of land at very low prices, & even for land South of the Black River! I do not wish to undervalue your property but I may as well state frankly what information I derive from those who can have no object to gain in misleading me,* . . .

She also told Francis that "The Maps of the Counties embracing the 'John Brown' tract are almost useless, & I beg that Mr H may send an order to obtain such papers as will enable me to exhibit to some interested persons the exact localities of the property."[56]

Mary White sounded like a very competent woman, but we can only assume that Francis and Herreshoff were still hoping for more money.

A Horatio Tracy of Sackets Harbor wrote Francis in April 1848 that the granting of a charter for the Sackets Harbor & Saratoga Railroad, however "visionary," might cause a surge of interest in the Tract, and suggested that he attempt to sell the land. "I can only say, that a Bumble Bee is always the largest when it is first *hatched*. If I owned I would sell."

Francis quickly responded, for he heard again from Tracy about three weeks after the original letter. Tracy was suggesting a price of 10 to 15¢ an acre, and said "I have started a fever here among our mechanics they want to know your lowest terms. They want to visit it. I think we had better selling without visiting what is your opinion . . . the fever is now raging & this is the time to sell."[57] Tracy was a classic land salesman: try to sell it to people before they've seen it. In any case, the fever must have burned itself out, for yet again, nothing came of the proposal.

The End of the Dream

A very informative letter from a J. H. Van Benthuysen of Glens Falls, New York reached Francis in July. Benthuysen reported that most of the Tract would be sold for taxes in November. He also reported on the results of his study of the Comptroller's records. He said that a fairly small section of Township No. 6 had been conveyed to William Grosvenor, who had married a daughter of James and Alice Brown Mason. And he also confirmed that Aaron Sergeant, the confident auctioneer, did indeed own portions of No. 7. Benthuysen, who referred to a visit with Francis at Spring Green, was eager to make a substantial purchase, and offered to meet with Francis for that purpose at Albany or Spring Green. Again, nothing happened.

Amusing, in a perverse sort of way, is another letter Francis received in July. It was from a Benjamin Cory of Watertown, New York, writing on behalf of a kinsman who was interested in buying some land.

. . . I learn, for I never was on the tract, and never expect to go on it, unless for fishing or hunting, that there are but two families on the tract, a Mr. Arnold and his son, and no one else resides within 15 or 20 miles.

Mr. Coe has two sons about of age, and says he wants to give them a setting out, but it is a country in which I would never have a child of mine go to settle.[58]

That same month at Spring Green, Francis' last surviving child of his first marriage, Anne Brown Francis, was married to Marshall Woods.[59]

Benthuysen wrote again in July, detailing by township, range and lot the land he wanted to buy. Again he urged a prompt response, and said he had already spoken to "a millwright & hands to go along with me to those wilds and commence operations. . . . I have not the least doubt if I am successful in the operations which I propose, the balance of your territory will speedily come into market whereas at the present time there is no earthly inducement for a man to locate himself there . . ."

Crossing in the mail were another letter from Van Benthuysen, his fourth, and a response from Francis, who explained that he had never seen the first. The second arrived just as he was preparing for his daughter's marriage, and the third when he was away visiting a sick friend. In his draft, Francis said he rejected an offer of $18,000 and, recently, an offer of $13,000, but would now sell for $13,000.[60] He also mentioned that Herreshoff might be at Lowville or No. 4, the only hint we've seen that he was back in the region.

Toward the end of the year, Francis and Hirst were still discussing a deal, with Hirst reporting to Francis that he was "startled" at the amount of taxes owed for 1843 and 1844, $1,373.97, with taxes for 1845/46/47 not included. He still believed that "we can strike a bargain, . . ."[61]

In December a New York merchant, Rembrandt Wood, wrote to Francis at the suggestion of Van Benthuysen, who wanted Wood to buy the entire Tract and sell a portion to him. Wood asked how much Francis wanted. "I observe in referring to your letter that you ask Mr. V. B. to make you an *offer* for the lands. It will be of *no use* to repeat this to me. I *never dicker.* I shall *not* offer you *less* than your *price* for the lands. . . ."[62] This no-nonsense businessman was saying: Name your price; I'll either take it or leave it.

Francis replied in January 1849 that he would stop in New York to see Wood on the way to Philadelphia to see an aged relative, perhaps his Uncle Charles Francis. He said that Herreshoff had given him *carte blanche* "touching this wild land in Lewis & Herkimer which I shall be heartily glad to sell."[63] No pretence there that Wood would have to make a generous offer to get the Tract.

That year, 1849, finally saw the opening of the Black River Canal. It may well have benefited the area—although its benefits did not extend to the Brown Tract—but it lost enormous sums of money.[64]

During that year a few offers trickled in, but none proposed much more than paying off the taxes. With state land selling for 5¢ an acre, the John Brown's Tract could hardly be expected to attract offers much higher. So, when Lyman R. Lyon, son of Caleb, offered $18,500 for all the land owned by John Brown Francis and John Brown Herreshoff, it seemed like a good offer. It probably was, for if we assume that the Tract, despite the few private sales and the tax sales, still consisted of about 164,000 acres—an estimate, for no one knew then or knows now exactly how much was subtracted—that comes to a little more than 11¢ an acre. It is irrelevant, although irresistible, to speculate what that land is worth now. Less than fifty years after the sale, Snyder, in his valuable brief study of the Tract in 1896, said it was then worth "about $1,000,000 at least."[65]

John Brown, with characteristic optimism, had valued the land at a dollar an acre and believed, as we noted earlier, that he was settling on his favorite grandchild an estate that would be worth half a million dollars. But his grandsons had learned that virtually no one wanted to buy the land, that no one had been able to develop it, and that taxes, decade after decade, were devouring what little value the land had.

What is it exactly that they had? A lot of land and a lot of trees. But despite all the efforts at development, efforts that claimed the life of Charles

Frederick Herreshoff, by 1850 the Tract had only the Orrin Fenton family, perhaps a few others at No. 4, and the Arnolds at No. 7. According to a gazetteer of the time, the entire town of Wilmurt, which included the Herkimer County portion of the Tract (some 167,000 acres), had "no p.o. [post office], village, store, church, or gristmill in town."[66]

In any case, in 1850, the Brown family finally "disincumbered" itself of its wild lands. After years in which propositions petered out for one reason or another, Francis accepted an offer of $12,500 for his interest and Herreshoff $6,000 for his, and thus, in March and April of 1850, the John Brown's Tract, an empire turned millstone, passed out of the family. Why Lyman R. Lyon bought it is a matter of speculation. Maybe he believed that the railroad would finally turn the land of promise into the land of fulfillment.

Whatever Lyon's reason, on March 20, 1850, John Brown Francis and his wife Elizabeth sold to him for $12,500 all their remaining interest in townships No. 1, No. 2, No. 3, No. 4, No. 7 and No. 8, approximately 95,000 acres. And on April 4, John Brown Herreshoff sold all his family's remaining interest in No. 3, No. 5 and No. 6, approximately 69,000 acres. The total sale amounted to about 164,000 acres.[67] Although the family and Brown & Ives for several years thereafter would receive inquiries about the land, John Brown's Tract no longer belonged to John Brown's descendants. The name became part of the legend of the Adirondacks and, indeed, for some time persisted as the rather vague designation of the whole wild north country. But the land belonged to Lymon R. Lyon, except for two relatively small parcels that he acquired some years later, on March 3, 1856, with Herreshoff's power of attorney, and Francis Seger, his brother-in-law, 590 acres in the Watson section of No. 3 for $600. Seger then sold them to Lyon for $5. And on July 30, 1860, Lyon, again using Herreshoff's power of attorney, sold Seger 1,500 acres in No. 3 for $5.[68]

Who was this new lord of the John Brown's Tract? He came from a family celebrated in the region. His father, Caleb, was a pioneer of the Lowville area. His younger brother, also Caleb, was well-known as a writer, poet and speaker, gifts which clearly helped him in his political career. He was elected to the state Assembly and Senate and, in 1852, to Congress. Later, President Lincoln appointed him territorial governor of Idaho, and he served as secretary of the California Constitutional Convention.

Lyman stayed closer to home. After being educated at the regionally famous Lowville Academy, he was deputy clerk of the Assembly in

Albany. Subsequently, he became president and cashier of the Lewis County Bank, and was "extensively engaged in tanning and in the management of business connected with lands, of which he owned a larger amount than any other resident proprietor in the country."

Lyon also owned the High Falls, in recent decades, the site of substantial lumbering operations, which eventually took his name, as did the nearby community of Lyonsdale. He also became active in steamboat operations on the Black River and, as a member of the state Assembly, was instrumental in having the Black River Canal extended forty-two miles north from Lyons Falls to Carthage. He died in 1869 at the age of sixty-three.[69]

We have attempted, with only limited success, to determine just how much the Brown family gained and lost on the Tract, in an effort to strike some sort of a balance. For both expenditures and income we can make only very rough estimates. We do know that John Brown paid $33,000 for the Tract. Of the sales, many were at a nominal fee, often as low as $1, in the hope that successful farmers would attract others to the tract. As best we can calculate, total family sales (not including sales to each other) came to $33,303.50, just $303.50 more than John Brown paid to obtain the Tract. Not much for more than half a century, although that figure does not include what little the family earned from the sale of crops and timber, a total that certainly must have been negligible, especially compared to what the family paid in taxes over that half century.

An army of accountants could not be sure that they calculated the taxes correctly, but even allowing the modest sum of $500 a year – and surely, given the few tax expenditures we have seen, that is low – the total tax bill was at least $25,000. To this must be added the substantial costs – $25,000 by John Brown alone – of clearing land, constructing roads and bridges, building dwellings, mills, barns, etc., plus all that Charles Frederick Herreshoff spent trying, first, to establish a farming settlement, and then an iron manufacturing industry. Plus, the many thousands of dollars for necessary supplies.

Also, we must add the human cost. The decades of hope turned to anxiety, and even near panic, the months every year for ten years that John Brown Herreshoff spent at Lowville and, the most terrible cost of all, the death of Charles Frederick Herreshoff. The reader can, just as well as the authors, try to strike a balance, but clearly it was a very great deficit. No wonder John Brown Francis was so eager to disincumber himself of the Tract, for John Brown's dream had turned into a nightmare. Ever the optimist, he bought land known to be of questionable quality at the worst

Trout fishing in the Adirondacks as drawn by E. Forbes and engraved by Meeder Chubb for the August 1868 issue of the "American Agriculturist."

possible time, the peak of land speculation fever. John Brown bought high and his descendants had to sell low. Given the nation's growth patterns, it was just too soon to have purchased that land.

What has happened to the John Brown's Tract in all these intervening decades? Not a great deal, for the entire Tract is within the bounds of the Adirondack forest preserve. Portions of it have been bought and sold. Some of it still exists in large parcels, but, given how much the world has changed, the Tract has changed remarkably little.

Should you want to know what it looked like nearly two centuries ago, go visit it now. You will not have to stretch your imagination much. If you glance at a map, you will see that only one substantial road, New York Route 28, crosses the Tract, and that along the southern edge. Erase that road, the cars that traverse it, the flourishing resort community at Old Forge and the smaller communities at Thendara, Eagle Bay and Inlet, plunge into the woods, and you will find it much as John Brown found it in 1799. You will see a place of great beauty and rare tranquility, still much as it was in those years long gone by—John Brown's Tract.

We must end by taking note of a nice coincidence. In 1850 (on February 7), the year that the Brown family finally sold the Tract, was born a son who combined all the important male names of this chronicle: John Brown Francis Herreshoff. In the name of this one child: John Brown, John Francis, John Brown Francis, and Herreshoff were remembered.

Ruins of Herreshoff Manor near Thendara.

Appendices

NOTES

The following abbreviations have been used throughout the notes which follow:

HALB	*Henry A. L. Brown collection*	*OHS*	*Oneida Historical Society*
RIHS	*Rhode Island Historical Society*	*JCB*	*John Carter Brown Library, Brown University*

Chapter 1

1. F. B. Hough, *Gazeteer,* Albany, Andrew Boyd, 1872, p. 367.

2. James B. Hedges, *The Browns of Providence Plantations The Colonial Years,* Cambridge, Mass.; Harvard University Press, 1952, p. 208.

3. There have been many scientific descriptions of the topography, flora and fauna, and climate of the Adirondacks generally and the Brown's Tract particularly. Good solid accounts for the layman can be found in Donaldson, White, Grady and Sylvester. For complete names and titles see bibliography.

4. Although the commonly-accepted story of the source of the name "Adirondacks" has been recounted in many places, a particularly colorful version has been given by Joseph F. Grady in his *The Adirondacks,* Little Falls, N.Y., Journal & Courier Co., 1933, p. 9.

5. William Chapman White, *Adirondack Country,* New York, Alfred A. Knopf, 1967, p. 3.

6. Nathaniel Bartlett Sylvester, *Historical Sketches of Northern New York and the Adirondack Wilderness,* Troy, N.Y., William H. Young, 1877, p. 31.

7. Grady, p. 278.

8. Recollections of Joshua Francis Fisher written in 1864. Arranged by Sophia Cadwalader, privately printed 1929, p. 127.

9. This genealogical tangle was extracted from an even more complex family tree that appeared in *Letters and Papers Relating Chiefly to the Provincial History of Pennsylvania, with Some Notices of the Writers,* Philadelphia, 1855, Privately printed, p. xliii. All nine children married well and *their* family trees contain governors, judges and ranking military officers, both American and British.

10. R. E. Shaw, *Erie Water West: A History of the Erie Canal 1792-1854,* Lexington, Kentucky, University of Kentucky Press, 1966, p. 10; A. Barton Hepburn, *Artificial Waterways of the World,* New York, Macmillan, p. 34.

11. White, p. 56.

12. The authors are deeply indebted to the late Professor James B. Hedges of Brown University whose two-volume history of the Brown family's commercial affairs is justly regarded as a model of economic history, Vol. I, p. 158-161.

13. A full account of the life of Thomas Willing is given by Burton Alva Konkle in his *Thomas Willing and the First Financial System,* Philadelphia, University of Pennsylvania Press, 1937.

14. Hedges, Vol. I, pp. 123, 153.

15. Fisher, Joshua Francis, *Recollections,* p. 138.

16. There are many accounts of this first speculation. Among them are Frank Graham, Jr., *The Adirondack Park: A Political History,* New York, Alfred A. Knopf, 1978, p. 6; David H. Beetle, *Up Old Forge Way,* Utica, Utica Observer-Dispatch, 1948, p. 167; White, p. 60.

17. Graham, p. 6.

Chapter 2

1. John Brown to James Brown, December 24, 1782. HALB.
2. Hedges, Vol II, p. 2 and following.
3. John Brown to James Brown, November 11, 1782. RIHS
4. Charles A. Stewart to John Francis, August 15 and August 22, 1782. HALB.
5. White, p. 66.
6. John Francis to Anne Willing Francis, April 24, 1783. John Francis to Tench Francis, April 26 and April 30, 1783. John Hay Library, Brown University. Anne Willing Francis to John Francis, March 8, 1783. HALB.
7. Anne Willing Francis to John Francis, April 7, 1783. HALB.
8. From diary of John Quincy Adams, cited in Rhode Island History, Rhode Island Historical Society, Vol. II, No. 4, October 1943.
9. Anne Willing Francis to John Francis, April 7, 1783. HALB.
10. Anne Willing Francis to James Brown, September 3, 1783. HALB.
11. Robert Morris, August 13, 1783. Letterbook in HALB.
12. Peter Whiteside, August 13, 1783. Letterbook in HALB.
13. Robert Morris, August 14, 1783. Letterbook in HALB.
14. John Francis to Peter Whiteside, October 24, 1783. Letterbook in HALB.
15. John Francis to Tench Francis, October 24, 1783. Letterbook in HALB.
16. John Francis Diary, August 15, 1783 to April 4, 1784, R.I.H.S., Vault Collection, p. 56.
17. Anne Willing Francis to John Francis, August 31, 1783. HALB.
18. Diary entry for October 3 cited in "In Search of Cahoone, the 1790 Diary of John Francis," edited by Glenn B. Skillin in Old-Time New England: The Bulletin of the Society for the Preservation of New England Antiquities, Vol. LX, No. 2, Fall 1969, pp. 55-71. Boston, 1969.
19. See, for instance, the warm letter written from Sheffield, England on December 12, 1784 by Benjamin Roebuck Jr. HALB.
20. John Francis to Abby Brown, November 5, 1785. Herreshoff Collection, RIHS.
21. Thomas Willing Francis to Abby Brown, July 2, 1786. HALB.
22. White, p. 54.
23. Anne Willing Francis to Abby Brown, January 18, 1787. HALB.
24. John Francis to Abby Brown, February 4, 1787. HALB.
25. Anne Willing Francis to Abby Brown, March 18, 1787. HALB.
26. Anne Willing Francis to John Francis, July 19, 1786. HALB.
27. John Francis Journal 1787. HALB.
28. John Francis to John Brown, October 16, 1787. HALB.
29. John Francis to John Brown, November 11, 1787. HALB.
30. John Francis to Abby Brown, November 13, 1787. HALB.
31. Hedges, Vol. II, pp. 16-20.
32. Rhode Island Historical Society Collections, October 1941, Vol. XXXIV, No. 4, p. 108.
33. Elisa Bowen to Mrs. Abigail Goddard, Jan. 4, 1788. Rhode Island History, Vol. VI, October 1947, No. 4, p. 101. Also following letter.
34. Anna Bowen to Mrs. Abigail Goddard, January 4, 1788. RIHS.
35. James Brown Diary 1788. HALB.
36. Elkanah Watson, *History of the Western Canals*, Albany, D. Steele, 1820, p. 13.
37. Anne Willing Francis to Abby Francis, February 27, 1788. HALB.
38. This leather-bound journal, found among the Brown family papers, was only slightly used by John Francis and in the years after his death it was used front to back and back to front by his frugal Yankee descendants. When, in these notes, we refer to the Brown family papers, we refer not to the original Brown family of Providence but other Browns, including one of the authors, who are descended from the Francis family. One assumes that this tangle

in the Brown and Francis family trees that confuses the layman, including the other author, brings delight, and employment, to genealogists.

39. Anne Willing Francis to Abby Francis, March 18, 1789. HALB.

40. Abigail Adams to her sister Mary Cranch, June 28, 1789. Rhode Island History, October 1942, Vol. I, No. 4, p. 103.

41. Sophia Francis to Sarah Brown, June 29, 1789. HALB.

42. Hedges, Vol. II, p. 25 and following.

43. Anne Willing Francis to Abby Francis, February 3, 1790. HALB.

44. Anne Willing Francis to Abby Francis, April 4, 1790. HALB.

Chapter 3

1. Journal of John Francis, July 20, 1792, John Carter Brown Library, Brown University.

2. Letter from James Brown to Thomas Willing Francis, December 25, 1791 reports that John Brown Francis was born on May 31, the same day Nicholas Brown died. Plainly there was some slight confusion as to the exact dates. However, the *Chad Brown Memorial* gives the date of Nicholas Brown's death as May 29 but concurs with May 31 as John Brown Francis' birthdate.

3. Tench Francis to John Brown, May 22, 1791, HALB; Hedges, Vol. II, p. 187; Diary of James Brown, R.I.H.S.; Letter from John Brown to Moses Brown, August 14, 1791, Rhode Island Historical Society Collections, October 1941, Vol. XXXIV, No. 4, p. 113 and following.

4. Theodore Foster to John Francis, January 6, 1794. HALB.

5. Federal Rhode Island: The Age of the China Trade 1790-1820, Edited by Linda Lotridge Levin, Rhode Island Historical Society, 1978, p. 46.

6. From the introduction by Arthur Einhorn, Lewis County historian, to a 1976 reprint of Franklin B. Hough's classic *A History of Lewis County in the State of New York from the Beginning of its Settlement to the Present Time*, Merrick, N.Y., Richwood Publishing Co. Originally published in 1860 by Munsell & Rowland, Albany. Hough's discussion of land titles begins on p. 21.

7. Watson, pp. 30, 45, 47.

8. John Brown Francis to Anne Francis Woods, date uncertain, believed to be 1863 or 1864. R.I.H.S. Washburn Collection.

9. David Howell to Granville Sharp, November 12, 1791. JCB.

10. John Francis to Abby Francis, June 25, 1792. HALB.

11. Journal of John Francis, July 20, 1792. JCB.

12. Journal, July 21, 1792. JCB.

13. Journal, July 22, 1792. JCB.

14. Journal, July 23, 1792. JCB.

15. Journal, July 25, 1792. JCB.

16. Journal, July 25, 1792. JCB.

17. Journal, July 27, 1792. JCB.

18. Journal, August 3, 1792. JCB.

19. Journal, August 5, 1792. JCB.

20. Journal, August 6, 1792. JCB.

21. Howard Swigget, *The Extraordinary Mr. Morris*, New York, Doubleday, 1952, p. 233.

22. Journal, August 11, 1792. JCB.

23. Journal, August 12, 1792. JCB.

24. Rhode Island Historical Society Collections, October 1941, Vol. XXXIV, No. 4, p. 128.

25. Hedges, Vol. II, p. 28.

26. Anne Willing Francis to Abby Francis, July 12, 1792. HALB.

27. Thomas Mayne Willing to Thomas Willing Francis, July 2, 1792. HALB.

28. Accounts of these transactions can be found in Hough, White and an admirable short account by Charles E. Snyder, *John Brown's Tract*, Herkimer, N.Y., Herkimer County Historical Society Transactions I, 1896, pp. 94-108.

29. Genealogy of the Ward Family, Compiled by Clifford P. Monahon, Providence, Rhode Island Historical Society, 1952.

30. Genealogy of the Greenleaf Family, Compiled by James Edward Greenleaf, Boston, 1896.

31. William Graham Sumner, *The Financier and the Finances of the American Revolution*, Vol. II, New York, Dodd, Mead, & Co., 1891, p. 247.

32. Thomas Mayne Willing to Thomas Willing Francis, January 12, 1793. HALB.

33. Thomas Mayne Willing to Thomas Willing Francis, February 5, 1793. HALB.

34. Thomas Mayne Willing to Thomas Willing Francis, May 4, 1793. HALB.

35. Thomas Mayne Willing to Thomas Willing Francis, May 29, 1793. HALB.

36. Thomas Mayne Willing to Thomas Willing Francis, September 5, 1793. HALB.

37. Thomas Mayne Willing to Thomas Willing Francis, September 17, 1793. HALB.

38. Sophia Francis Harrison to John Francis, September 28, 1793. HALB. A book on the plague, *Bring Out Your Dead* by J. H. Powell was published by the University of Pennsylvania Press in 1949.

39. Anne Willing Francis to Abby Francis, January 25, 1793. HALB.

40. John Francis to James Brown, May 31, 1793. HALB.

41. *Chad Browne Memorial 1638-1888*. Privately printed for the family, Brooklyn, N.Y., Brooklyn Eagle Press, 1888, p. 54.

Chapter 4

1. Hedges, Vol. II, p. 72.

2. Sophia Francis Harrison to Abby Francis, February 11, 1794. HALB.

3. Anne Willing Francis to Abby Francis, May 24, 1794. HALB.

4. Thomas Mayne Willing to Thomas Willing Francis, February 20, 1794. HALB.

5. Thomas Willing Francis to Samuel Blagge, October 11, 1794. HALB.

6. Thomas Willing Francis to Captain James Worseley, November 2, 1794. HALB.

7. Thomas Willing Francis to John Francis, November 11, 1794. HALB.

8. Thomas Willing Francis to Jn. & F. [John and Francis] Baring & Co., November 16, 1794. HALB.

9. Thomas Willing Francis to David Scott & Co., November 16, 1794. HALB.

10. Thomas Willing Francis to Brown & Francis, November 17, 1794. HALB.

11. Thomas Willing Francis to Samuel Blagge, November 18, 1794. HALB.

12. Thomas Willing Francis to Brown, Benson & Ives, November 28, 1794. HALB.

13. Thomas Willing Francis to Captain James Worseley, November 28, 1794. HALB.

14. Thomas Willing Francis to David Scott & Co., December 16, 1794. HALB.

15. There are innumerable accounts of this transaction in Donaldson, Vol. I, p. 94; Snyder, p. 96; *Gazetteer and Business Directory of Lewis County, N.Y. for 1872-3*. Compiled and published by Hamilton Child, Syracuse, N.Y., 1872, p. 10; Hedges, Vol. II, p. 222 and all are in agreement except that Hedges has Constable selling the land directly to Greenleaf. The most detailed account appears in Hough, p. 33. According to Hough, the land was, about this time, sold to several men, among them John Julius Angerstein, a rich London merchant, a couple of other Greenleafs and Aaron Burr. This, of course, was a time of, to use current slang, "wheeling and dealing" and it will probably never be known what happened in those intervening deals.

16. Thomas Willing Francis to Samuel Blagge, January 4, 1795. HALB.

17. A whole series of letters from Thomas Willing Francis shed considerable, but one-sided, light on this matter. Letters in the HALB.

18. John Brown to Thomas Willing Francis, March 22, 1795. HALB.

19. John Brown to Thomas Willing Francis, April 11, 1795. HALB.

20. John Brown to Thomas Willing Francis, April 11, 1795. HALB.

21. John Brown to Thomas Willing Francis, April 11, 1795. HALB.

22. Thomas Willing Francis to William Fairlie, May 4, 1795. HALB.

23. Thomas Willing Francis to David Scott & Co., June 27, 1795. HALB.

24. Sumner, Vol. II, p. 284. Morris' financial problems are also discussed in two other useful books, *Forgotten Patriot: Robert Morris* by Eleanor Young, New York, Macmillan, 1950, and *Robert Morris: Patriot and Financier* by Ellis Paxson Oberholtzer, New York, Macmillan, 1903.

25. See *The Provincial Councillors of Pennsylvania*. . . by Charles P. Keith, Philadelphia, 1883.

26. Sumner, Vol. II, p. 281.

27. Albany, Liber 107 of Mortgages, p. 127. Abstract of Title, July 29, 1795, John Brown's Tract. Courtesy of A. Richard Cohen.

28. Donaldson, Vol. I, p. 94.

29. Donaldson, Vol. I, p. 96.

30. Keith, p. 425.

31. Articles of Agreement: John Francis for Brown and Francis with James Greenleaf. July 30, 1795; Etting papers, misc., mss, Vol. 2, p. 79. John Francis to James Greenleaf. August 14, 1795; Etting papers, misc., mss, Vol. 2, p. 78. Historical Society of Pennsylvania.

32. John Brown to Thomas Willing Francis, June 29, 1798. HALB.

33. There is a long series of letters between John Brown and Thomas Willing Francis that will be cited individually as appropriate. HALB.

34. George A. Hardin, ed. *History of Herkimer County*, Syracuse, N.Y., D. Mason & Co., 1893, p. 451.

35. James Brown to Thomas Willing Francis, November 4, 1795. RIHS.

36. Anne Willing Francis to John Francis, May 30, 1796. HALB.

37. John Brown to Thomas Willing Francis, June 2, 1796. HALB.

38. Child, p. 77.

39. Cahoone, p. 59.

40. The United States Chronicle, November 10, 1796, cited in Cahoone, p. 60.

41. Cahoone, p. 59.

Chapter 5

1. Hardin, p. 451.

2. Hedges, Vol. II, pp. 224-5. Hedges accepted, with little qualification, Donaldson's account.

3. John Brown to Thomas Willing Francis, December 3, 1796. HALB.

4. John Brown to unknown recipient, July 17, 1797. Frederick Peck Papers, RIHS.

5. This reconstruction is based on bits and pieces in letters now in the HALB. Specific letters will be referred to as appropriate. Thomas Willing Francis to James Greenleaf, October 19, 1796. HALB.

6. John Brown to Thomas Willing Francis, December 7, 1796. HALB.

7. John Brown to Thomas Willing Francis, December 16, 1796. HALB.

8. John Brown to unknown recipient, July 17, 1797. Frederick Peck Papers, RIHS.

9. John Brown to Thomas Willing Francis, December 22, 1796. HALB.

10. An interesting account is given in Hedges, Vol. I, p. 83, 1952.

11. John Brown to Thomas Willing Francis, January 11, 1797. HALB.

12. John Brown to Thomas Willing Francis, January 22, 1797. HALB.

13. Robert C. Alberts, *The Golden Voyage: The Life and Times of William Bingham 1752-1804*, Boston, Houghton Mifflin Company, 1969, p. 320.

14. Thomas Willing Francis to John Brown, April 8, 1797. HALB.

15. John Brown to Thomas Willing Francis, April 19, 1797. HALB.

16. Thomas Willing Francis to John Brown, April 20, 1797. HALB.

17. John Brown to Thomas Willing Francis, April 21, 1789. HALB.

Appendices

18. Thomas Willing Francis to Robert Lenox, April 26, 1797. HALB.
19. John Brown to Thomas Willing Francis, April 30, 1797. HALB; James Brown Diary for May 7, 1797. RIHS.
20. Hedges, Vol. II, 1968, p. 73.
21. John Brown to Thomas Willing Francis, December 21, 1797. HALB.
22. Abby Brown to Thomas Willing Francis, May 3, 1797. HALB.

23. Brockholst Levingston to John Brown, May 12, 1797. HALB.
24. John Brown to Thomas Willing Francis, May 9, 1797. HALB.
25. Hough, p. 35. Hough goes into some detail about Burr, whom he terms a "polished scoundrel."
26. Thomas Willing Francis to John Brown, September 26, 1797. HALB.
27. John Brown to Thomas Willing Francis, October 27, 1797; Thomas Willing Francis to John Brown, October 1, 1797. HALB.
28. John Brown to Thomas Willing Francis, October 27, 1797. HALB.
29. James Brown Diary, December 10, 1797, RIHS.
30. Thomas Willing Francis to John Brown, December 11, 1797. HALB.
31. John Brown to Thomas Willing Francis, December 21, 1797. HALB.
32. Donaldson, Vol. I, p. 94.
33. Thomas Willing Francis to Joseph Thomas, February 22, 1798. HALB.
34. Charles Frederick Herreshoff to Sarah Brown, March 29, 1798. RIHS.
35. Thomas Willing Francis to John Brown, March 8, 1798. HALB.
36. John Brown to Thomas Willing Francis, March 21, 1798. HALB.
37. James Brown Almanack. 1798, RIHS.
38. Grady, p. 25.
39. John Brown to Thomas Willing Francis, June 2, 1798. HALB.
40. Indenture date December 29, 1798 in Liber No. 1, pp. 103-107, Lewis County Clerk's Office, Lowville, N.Y.
41. John Brown to Thomas Willing Francis, June 13, 1798. HALB.
42. Thomas Willing Francis to John Brown, June 20, 1798. HALB.
43. Thomas Willing Francis to James Greenleaf, June 20, 1798. HALB.
44. John Brown to Thomas Willing Francis, June 29, 1798. HALB.
45. Thomas Willing Francis to John Brown, July 27, 1798. HALB.
46. James Brown Almanack, 1798. RIHS.
47. John Brown to Thomas Willing Francis, August 25, 1798. HALB.
48. *Chad Browne Memorial*, p. 54.
49. Donaldson, Vol. I, p. 103.
50. *Chad Browne Memorial*, p. 54.
51. Charles Frederick Herreshoff to Sarah Brown, September 1, 1798. RIHS.
52. John Brown to Thomas Willing Francis, September 7, 1798. HALB.
53. Rhode Island Manual, 1917, p. 176.
54. Thomas Willing Francis to John Brown, October 3, 1798. HALB.
55. John Brown to Thomas Willing Francis, October 7, 1798. HALB.
56. John Brown to Thomas Willing Francis, October 19, 1798. HALB.
57. Charles Frederick Herreshoff to Sarah Brown, October 30, 1798. RIHS.
58. James Brown Almanack, 1798. RIHS.
59. Liber No. 1, p. 103, Lewis County Clerk's Office, Lowville, N.Y.
60. Donaldson, Vol. I, p. 97.

Chapter 6

1. J. H. French, *Gazetteer of the State of New York*, 1860, p. 47.
2. Charles Frederick Herreshoff to Sarah Brown, November 27, 1798. RIHS.
3. Charles Frederick Herreshoff to Sarah Brown, December 2, 1798. RIHS.

4. Charles Frederick Herreshoff to Sarah Brown, January 1, 1799. RIHS.
5. Charles Frederick Herreshoff to Sarah Brown, April 17, 1799. RIHS.
6. James Brown to Thomas Willing Francis, February 27, 1799, HALB; Grady, p. 26; letter to Elder John Hammond, Jr. at the Webb Historical Society, Old Forge, N.Y.; John Brown to James Brown, December 23, 1799, HALB.
7. John Brown to Elder John Hammon Sr., March 31, 1799, Webb Historical Society, Old Forge, N.Y.
8. Thomas Willing Francis to Charles Francis, February 22, 1799. HALB.
9. Charles Frederick Herreshoff to Sarah Brown, May 3, 1799. RIHS.
10. Charles Frederick Herreshoff to Sarah Brown, June 7, 1799. RIHS.
11. French, p. 47.
12. James Brown Diary, May 11, 1799. RIHS.
13. John Brown to James Sheldon, May 24, 1799. OHS.
14. Brown to Sheldon, May 26, 1799. OHS.
15. Brown to Sheldon, May 28, 1799. OHS.
16. Brown to Sheldon, May 30, 1799. OHS.
17. Brown to Sheldon, May 30, 1799. OHS.
18. Brown to Sheldon, May 31, 1799. OHS.
19. James Brown Diary, 1798. RIHS.
20. Brown to Sheldon, June 10, 1799. OHS.
21. Brown to Sheldon, June 14, 1799. OHS.
22. Brown to Sheldon, June 15, 1799. OHS.
23. Brown to Sheldon, June 17, 1799. OHS.
24. Brown to Sheldon, June 19, 1799. OHS.
25. Brown to Sheldon, June 25, 26, 27, 1799. OHS.
26. Brown to Sheldon, June 29, 1799. OHS.
27. Brown to Sheldon, June 29, 1799. OHS.
28. Brown to Sheldon, July 10, 1799. OHS.
29. Brown to Sheldon, July 17, 1799. OHS.
30. Brown to Sheldon, August 5, 1799. OHS.
31. Brown to Sheldon, September or October, 1799. OHS.
32. Brown to Sheldon, October 23, 1799. OHS.
33. John Brown to James Brown, December 23, 1799. RIHS.
34. Charles Frederick Herreshoff to Sarah Brown, August 12, 1799. Herreshoff Collection, RIHS.
35. Charles Frederick Herreshoff to Sarah Brown, October 30, 1799. Herreshoff Collection, RIHS.
36. Sampson Mason Genealogy, RIHS; The Biographical Cyclopedia, Providence, National Biographical Publishing Co., 1881.
37. Charles Frederick Herreshoff to Sarah Brown, October 30, 1799; November 11, 1799.
38. Charles Frederick Herreshoff to Sarah Brown, December 10, 1799, Herreshoff Collection, RIHS.
39. James Brown Diary, 1798. RIHS.
40. Rhode Island Manual 1917, pp. 153, 176.
41. John Brown to James Brown, November 27, 1799. RIHS.
42. John Brown to James Brown, December 2, 1799. RIHS.
43. Herreshoff Collection, RIHS.
44. HALB.
45. Frank Hail Brown, September 15, 1952. HALB.

Chapter 7

1. Nathaniel S. Benton, *A History of Herkimer County*. Albany, J. Munsell, 1856, p. 469.
2. Hamilton Child, *Gazetteer and Business Directory of Lewis County, New York*. Syracuse, Syracuse Journal, 1873.
3. Clarence L. Fisher, *History of Lyons Falls*, The Willard Press, Boonville, 1918.
4. Charles P. Keith, *The Provincial Councillors of Pennsylvania. . . .*, Philadelphia, 1883.
5. James Brown Diary, 1798. RIHS.
6. John Brown to James Brown, January 12, 1800. Herreshoff Collection, RIHS.
7. Brown to Sheldon, January 24, 1800. OHS.
8. Brown to Sheldon, February 4, 1800. OHS.
9. Brown to Sheldon, February 9, 1800. OHS.
10. John Brown to James Brown, March 2, 1800. RIHS.
11. Brown to Sheldon, February 9, 1800. OHS.
12. John Brown Francis to Thomas Willing Francis, October 12, 1811. Historical Society of Pennsylvania.
13. John Brown to James Brown, March 15, 1800. RIHS.
14. John Brown to James Brown, March 22, 1800. RIHS.
15. John Brown to James Brown and Abby Francis, April 13, 1800. RIHS.
16. John Brown to James Brown, May 1, 1800. RIHS.
17. Abby Francis Notes 1797-1815. Written in Journal originally begun by John Francis in 1792. RIHS.
18. John Brown to James Brown, May 8, 1800. RIHS.
19. Charles Frederick Herreshoff to Sarah Brown, June 17, 1800. Herreshoff Collection, RIHS.
20. Abby Francis Notes, June 23, 1800. RIHS.
21. The Biographical Cyclopedia, p. 189.
22. Charles Frederick Herreshoff to Sarah Brown, July 21, 1800. Herreshoff Collection, RIHS.
23. Abby Francis Notes, November 18, 1800. RIHS.
24. Charles Frederick Herreshoff to Sarah Brown, July 23, 1800. Herreshoff Collection, RIHS.
25. James Brown Diary, August 18, 1800. RIHS.
26. September 12, 1800. Herreshoff Collection, RIHS.
27. Herreshoff to Sarah Brown, October 1, 1800. Herreshoff Collection, RIHS.
28. Herreshoff to Sarah Brown, October 20, 1800. Herreshoff Collection, RIHS.
29. Herreshoff to Sarah Brown, October 22, 1800. Herreshoff Collection, RIHS.
30. Herreshoff to Sarah Brown, November 5, 1800. Herreshoff Collection, RIHS.
31. Herreshoff to Sarah Brown, November 24, 1800. Herreshoff Collection, RIHS.
32. Sarah Brown to John Brown, November 29, 1800. RIHS.
33. John Brown to James Brown, December 13, 1800. RIHS.
34. Rhode Island Manual 1917, p. 176.
35. Herreshoff to Sarah Brown, February 5, 1801. Herreshoff Collection, RIHS.
36. Herreshoff to Sarah Brown, February 16, 1801. Herreshoff Collection, RIHS.
37. Herreshoff to Sarah Brown, March 4, 1801. Herreshoff Collection, RIHS.
38. James Brown Diary, March 12, 1801. RIHS.
39. John Brown to James Sheldon, March 20, 1801. RIHS.
40. Herreshoff to Sarah Brown, April 8, 1801. Herreshoff Collection, RIHS.
41. Herreshoff to Sarah Brown, May 6, 1801. Herreshoff Collection, RIHS.
42. James Brown Diary, July 2, 1801. RIHS.
43. Herreshoff to Abby Francis, July 15, 1801. Herreshoff Collection, RIHS.
44. Abby Francis to Sarah Herreshoff, July 16, 1801. Herreshoff Collection, RIHS.
45. John Brown to Charles Frederick Herreshoff, September 26, 1801. Herreshoff Collection, RIHS.

46. Brown to Herreshoff, November 2, 1801. Herreshoff Collection, RIHS.

47. Brown to Herreshoff, November 29, 1801. Herreshoff Colletion, RIHS.

48. Abby Francis Notes, RIHS; John Brown to Thomas Willing Francis, HALB. Both November 7, 1801.

49. James Brown Diary. RIHS; Brown & Ives to George Champlin, March 22, 1802. RIHS.

50. Abby Francis Notes. RIHS. John Brown Francis to Anne Francis Woods, 1863/1864? Washburn Collection, RIHS. James Brown Diary; RIHS.

Chapter 8

1. James B. Mason to Amasa Dow. Believed to be in 1807. HALB.

2. The original of John Brown's very long and detailed will is at the Rhode Island Historical Society. A copy is recorded with the Providence Probate Recorder A 3684.

3. William Chapman White, p. 96.

4. Lydia Herrick Pitcher, "A Pioneer's Version of Life in Early Lewis County," North Country Life. Winter 1950, pp. 25-29.

5. Mason to Joseph Shaw, April 22, 1806. HALB.

6. Memorandum of agreement between Mason and Shaw, April 22, 1806. HALB.

7. Mason to Charles Frederick Herreshoff, April 28, 1806. Herreshoff Collection, RIHS.

8. Jeremiah Crosby to James B. Mason, January 16, 1807. HALB.

9. Mason to Amasa Dow, June 7, 1807. HALB.

10. Mason to Dow, July 17, 1807. HALB.

11. Asa Leach to James B. Mason, August 31, 1807. HALB.

12. Alice Brown Mason and James B. Mason to Oliver Ingalls, November 29, 1807. Recorded 1818, Liber 11, page 424. Herkimer County Clerk.

13. Mason to Dow. Sections torn; believed to be 1807. HALB.

14. Sale to John Heath, $200, conveyed May 16, 1808; to Joseph Stedman, $400, conveyed May 16, 1808; to Gershon Plimpton, $1250, conveyed May 17, 1808. Recorded in 1815 in Liber 9, pages 181, 180, 178. Herkimer County Clerk.

15. Promissory notes from Seiger, July 26, 1808; from Leach and Crosby, July 28, 1808. HALB.

16. John Joy Jr. to James B. Mason, December 31, 1808. HALB.

17. Herreshoff Collection, RIHS.

18. J. French to James B. Mason, February 19, 1809. HALB.

19. Receipt, April 20, 1809. HALB.

20. Benjamin Bowen to James B. Mason, March 10, 1810. HALB.

21. Thomas M. Palmer to James B. Mason, May 28, 1810. HALB.

22. Palmer to Mason, August 13, 1810. HALB.

23. John Brown Francis to David Putnam, August 14, 1810. HALB.

24. Thomas Willing Francis to Col. Alexander Haig, September 27, 1810. HALB.

25. Thomas M. Palmer to James B. Mason, November 20, 1810. HALB.

26. Palmer to Mason, November 25, 1810. HALB.

27. Benjamin Bowen to James B. Mason, December 20, 1810. HALB.

28. Palmer to Mason, February 5, 1811. HALB.

29. James Palmer agreement with H. Bagagona and J. Miscobimis, April 6, 1811. HALB.

30. Palmer to Mason, February 6, 1811. HALB.

31. Palmer to Mason, March 8, 1811. HALB.

32. Palmer to Mason, May 5, 1811. HALB.

33. Palmer to Mason, July 27, 1811. HALB.

34. Donaldson, Vol. I, p. 99; New York State *Annual Report of the Forest Commission for the Year 1893*, Vol. I, p. 319; Snyder, p. 99; Grady, p. 58; W. J. Thistlewaite, *The Romance of Old Forge*. Reprinted from the Utica Daily Press, December 8, 1915, p. 31.

Chapter 9

1. Nathaniel Sylvester. *Historical Sketches of Northern New York and the Adirondack Wilderness*, Troy, N.Y., William H. Young, 1877, p. 173.
2. Charles Frederick Herreshoff to Sarah Herreshoff, September 20, 1811. Herreshoff Collection, RIHS.
3. John Brown Francis to Thomas Willing Francis, October 2, 1811. Historical Society of Pennsylvania.
4. John Brown Francis to Charles Frederick Herreshoff, April 20, 1812. Herreshoff Collection, RIHS.
5. Anne Herreshoff to Charles Frederick Herreshoff, August 25, 1812. Herreshoff Collection, RIHS.
6. Herreshoff to Sarah Herreshoff, September 27, 1812. Herreshoff Collection, RIHS.
7. Herreshoff to Sarah Herreshoff, November 19, 1812. Herreshoff Collection, RIHS.
8. Taken from various ledgers. HALB.
9. Ted Aber and Stella King. *The History of Hamilton County*. Lake Pleasant, N.Y. Great Wilderness Books, 1965, p. 24.
10. Horatio Gates Spafford. *A Gazetteer of the State of New York*. Albany, H. C. Southwick, 1813. This was the first New York State gazetteer.
11. William Chapman White, p. 48.
12. Sarah Herreshoff to John Brown Francis, May 14, 1813. Herreshoff Collection, RIHS.
13. James Brown will, September 25, 1813. RIHS.
14. Herreshoff to Anne Herreshoff, May 9, 1814. Herreshoff Collection, RIHS.
15. Herreshoff to daughter Sarah Herreshoff, June 3, 1814. Herreshoff Collection, RIHS.
16. Herreshoff to Sarah Herreshoff, June 14, 1814. Herreshoff Collection, RIHS.
17. Herreshoff to Anne Herreshoff, July 1, 1814. Herreshoff Collection, RIHS.
18. Herreshoff to daughter Sarah Herreshoff, July 29, 1814. Herreshoff Collection, RIHS.
19. Herkimer County Liber 12, page 169; Grady, p. 49.
20. New York State *Annual Report of the Forest Commission for the Year 1893*, Vol. II, p. 307.
21. Henry Stommel and Elizabeth Stommel. *Volcano Weather: The Story of the Year Without a Summer*, Newport, Seven Seas Press, 1983.
22. Herkimer County Liber 9, p. 350. Herkimer County Clerk.
23. Herreshoff to Anne Herreshoff, May 10, 1815. Herreshoff Collection, RIHS.
24. Herreshoff to Anne Herreshoff, June 26, 1815. Herreshoff Collection, RIHS.
25. Herreshoff to daughter Sarah Herreshoff, September 23, 1815. Herreshoff Collection, RIHS.
26. Herreshoff to Anne Herreshoff, October 16, 1815. Herreshoff Collection, RIHS.
27. Herreshoff to Anne Herreshoff, July 25, 1816. Herreshoff Collection, RIHS.
28. Herreshoff to Brown & Ives, August 12, 1816. JCB.
29. Brown & Ives to Herreshoff, November 26, 1816. JCB.
30. John Brown Francis Diary, August 6, 1816. HALB.
31. Francis Diary, August 12, 1816. HALB.
32. Francis Diary, August 16, 1816. HALB.
33. Francis Diary, August 17, 1816. HALB.
34. Francis Diary, August 19, 1816. HALB.
35. Francis Diary, August 22, 1816. HALB.
36. Francis Diary, August 27, 1816. HALB.
37. Francis Diary, August 28, 1816. HALB.

38. Francis Diary, September 1816. HALB.
39. Francis Diary, September 5, 1816. HALB.
40. Francis Diary, September 10, 1816. HALB.
41. John Brown Francis Diary, September 11, 1816. HALB.
42. See *Canada and the U. S. A.* By Richard J. Walton. New York. Parent's Magazine Press, 1972.
43. Francis Diary, September 11, 1816. HALB.
44. Francis Diary, September 14, 1816. HALB.
45. Francis Diary, September 15, 1816. HALB.
46. Francis Diary, September 16, 1816. HALB.
47. Francis Diary, September 17, 1816. HALB.
48. Francis Diary, September 19, 1816. HALB.
49. Francis Diary, September 21, 1816. HALB.
50. Francis Diary, September 22, 1816. HALB.
51. Francis Diary, September 23, 1816. HALB.
52. Francis Diary, September 25, 1816. HALB.
53. Francis Diary, Undated. HALB.
54. Francis Diary, June 24, 1817. HALB.
55. Francis Diary, June 29, 1817. HALB.
56. Francis Diary, July 1, 1817. HALB.
57. Francis Diary, July 4, 1817. HALB.
58. Francis Diary, July 5, 1817. HALB.
59. Francis Diary, July 14, 1817. HALB.
60. Francis Diary, Undated, believed to be July, 1817. HALB.
61. Herreshoff to Brown & Ives, July 1, July 24 and August 25, 1817. JCB.
62. Herreshoff to Anne Herreshoff, September 5, 1817. Herreshoff Collection, RIHS.
63. Herreshoff to Brown & Ives, Sepetember 18, 1817. JCB.
64. Herreshoff to Brown & Ives, November 6, 1817. JCB.
65. Herreshoff to Brown & Ives, November 29, 1817. JCB.
66. Herreshoff to Brown & Ives, November 9, 1818. JCB.
67. Herreshoff to Sarah Brown, April 3, 1818. Herreshoff Collection, RIHS.
68. Herreshoff to Brown & Ives, April 3, 1818. JCB.
69. Herreshoff to Brown & Ives, May 14, 1818. JCB.
70. Brown & Ives to Herreshoff, May 27, 1818. JCB.
71. Donaldson, Vol. I, p. 111. September 5, 1818.
72. Items in Herreshoff diary cited by date. September 8, 1818. HALB.
73. Items in John Brown Francis diary cited by date. October 11, 1818. HALB.
74. Francis diary, October 16, 1818. HALB.
75. Herreshoff to Anne Herreshoff, October 25, 1818. Herreshoff Collection, RIHS.
76. Brown & Ives to Herreshoff, December 5, 1818. JCB.
77. Brown & Ives to Herreshoff, December 17, 1818. JCB.
78. Herreshoff to Brown & Ives, April 22, 1819. JCB.
79. Herreshoff to John Brown Francis, June 24, 1819. HALB.
80. Sampson Mason Genealogy, RIHS. pp. 277-8.
81. Sarah Brown will, November 10, 1819.
82. Herreshoff to John Brown Francis, September 21, 1819. HALB.
83. As quoted in Donaldson, Vol. I, p. 113.
84. Simeon Ford to Doctor William Bowen, December 21, 1819. Herreshoff Collection, RIHS.

85. Abby Francis to James Brown, December 28, 1819. Herreshoff Collection, RIHS.
86. Herreshoff Collection, RIHS.
87. French, John Homer. *Gazetteer of the State of New York*. 1860, p. 349.
88. Isabel Bulkley in *Chad Browne Memorial*, pp. 54-5.

Chapter 10

1. John Brown Francis to John Brown Herreshoff, August 25, 1830, HALB; Lardner Vanuxem, *Geology of New York*, Part III, W. and A. White and J. Visscher, Albany, 1842, p. 256.
2. Sarah Herreshoff to Francis, July 1, 1820. HALB.
3. Francis agreement with Charles Dayan, July 21, 1820. HALB.
4. Francis to Herreshoff, September 30, 1820. HALB.
5. Francis to Silas Thomas, October 17, 1820. HALB.
6. Francis to Thomas, October 20, 1820. HALB.
7. Francis agreement with Robert Prichart, October 21, 1820. HALB.
8. Francis to Thomas, October 22, 1820. HALB.
9. Francis to Thomas, October 31, 1820. HALB.
10. Francis to Thomas, November 17, 1820. HALB.
11. Broadside, HALB.
12. Hough, p. 153.
13. Francis to Thomas, July 20, 1821. HALB.
14. Snyder, p. 102.
15. Donaldson, Vol. II, p. 260.
16. New York State, *Annual Report of the Forest Commission for the Year 1893*, Vol. I, p. 104.
17. Orrin Fenton, Lorenzo S. Post et al to John Brown Francis, December 10, 1827. HALB.
18. Lewis County Clerk, Lowville, N.Y., Deedbooks K/303, L/165, O/45, M/254, M/463.
19. *Forest Commission*, p. 105.
20. Booklet published for the Sesquicentennial of Lowville Baptist Church, unpaged. Copy at Lowville Free Library.
21. *Forest Commission*, p. 105.
22. Anne Herreshoff to Agnes Herreshoff, September 21, 1822. Herreshoff Collection, RIHS.
23. Francis to Thomas, November 25, 1822. HALB.
24. Charles Dayan to Francis, July 7, 1823. HALB.
25. Elisha Smith to Francis, August 20, 1823. HALB.
26. Alvin F. Harlow, *Old Towpaths*, New York & London, D. Appleton & Co. 1926, p. 62; William Chapman White, p. 97.
27. E. Varney to Francis, January 25, 1826. HALB.
28. David Thomas to James Brown, June 29, 1827. HALB.
29. Anne Carter Brown Francis to Anne Herreshoff, August 13, 1827. Herreshoff Collection, RIHS.
30. Francis agreement with Charles Dayan, August 27, 1827. HALB.
31. *Transactions of the Rhode Island Society for the Encouragement of Domestic Industry in the Year 1861*, Providence, 1862.
32. Hough, p. 154; *Chad Browne Memorial*, p. 83.

33. Elizabeth Francis Fisher to Sarah Herreshoff, May 7, 1828. Herreshoff Collection, RIHS.

34. *Chad Browne Memorial*, p. 82.

35. Shaw, Robert E., *Erie Water West, A History of the Erie Canal 1792-1854*. Lexington, Ky., University of Kentucky Press, 1966, p. 305.

36. Charles F. Herreshoff (son) to John Brown Herreshoff, September 21, 1829. Herreshoff Collection, RIHS.

37. William Chapman White, p. 5.

38. Lewis County Clerk, Deedbook M/195.

39. Brown & Ives to John Brown Herreshoff, May 10, 1830. Herreshoff Collection, RIHS.

40. Herreshoff to Anne Herreshoff, May 22, 1830. Herreshoff Collection, RIHS.

41. Anne Herreshoff to Herreshoff, May 31, 1830. Herreshoff Collection, RIHS.

42. Herreshoff to Anne Herreshoff, June 22, 1830. Herreshoff Collection, RIHS.

43. Herreshoff to Sarah Herreshoff, July 17, 1830. Herreshoff Collection, RIHS.

44. Francis to Herreshoff, August 25, 1830. Herreshoff Collection, RIHS.

45. Herreshoff to Francis, September 15, 1830. Herreshoff Collection, RIHS.

46. Herreshoff to Charles Frederick Herreshoff, September 19, 1830. Herreshoff Collection, RIHS.

47. Francis to Herreshoff, October 4, 1830. Herreshoff Collection, RIHS.

48. William Chapman White, p. 98.

49. Sarah Herreshoff agreement, April 11, 1831. Herreshoff Collection, RIHS.

50. Herreshoff to his sisters, April 27, 1831. Herreshoff Collection, RIHS.

51. Herreshoff to an unnamed sister, May 1, 1831. Herreshoff Collection, RIHS.

52. Oliver Pearce to Brown & Ives, September 6, 1831. HALB.

53. Francis to Herreshoff, September 10, 1831. HALB.

54. Herreshoff to Sarah Herreshoff, October 7, 1831. Herreshoff Collection, RIHS.

55. Snyder, p. 104.

56. Francis to Herreshoff, October 8, 1831. HALB.

57. John B. and Elizabeth Francis agreement with Charles Francis, May 23, 1832; Charles Francis agreement with Charles Kahn, September 14, 1832. HALB.

58. Charles Dayan to Francis, November 19, 1832; November 20, 1832. HALB.

59. Charles Dayan to Francis, December 13, 1832. HALB.

Chapter 11

1. Francis to Herreshoff, October 19, 1837. HALB.

2. Herreshoff to Sarah Herreshoff, January 3, 1833. Herreshoff Collection, RIHS.

3. Herreshoff to Sarah Herreshoff, March 27, 1833. Herreshoff Collection, RIHS.

4. Herreshoff to Anne Herreshoff, May 14, 1833. Herreshoff Collection, RIHS.

5. Sarah Herreshoff to Herreshoff, May 31, 1833. Herreshoff Collection, RIHS.

6. Charles Frederick Herreshoff to John Brown Herreshoff, July 2, 1833. Herreshoff Collection, RIHS.

7. Amasa Mason to John Brown Francis, July 30, 1833. Herreshoff Collection, RIHS.

8. John B. and Elizabeth Francis agreement with John Brown Herreshoff, November 7, 1833. HALB.

9. Herreshoff to Anne Herreshoff, December 27, 1833. Herreshoff Collection, RIHS.

10. Undated. Herreshoff Collection, RIHS.

11. Herreshoff to Agnes Herreshoff, February 27, 1834. Herreshoff Collection, RIHS.

12. Herreshoff to Francis, March 17, 1834. Herreshoff Collection, RIHS.
13. Herreshoff to Anne Herreshoff, April 27, 1834. Herreshoff Collection, RIHS.
14. Sarah Herreshoff to Herreshoff, July 4, 1834. Herreshoff Collection, RIHS.
15. James Watson to Francis, July 21, 1834. HALB.
16. Francis to Charles Francis, November 19, 1834. HALB.
17. Anne Herreshoff to Herreshoff, December 8, 1834. Herreshoff Collection, RIHS.
18. Agnes Herreshoff to Herreshoff, December 18, 1834. Herreshoff Collection, RIHS.
19. Herreshoff to Francis, January 3, 1835. HALB.
20. Francis to William L. Marcy, May 1835. HALB.
21. Charles Dayan to Francis, March 17, 1835. HALB.
22. Francis to Dayan, April 16, 1835. HALB.
23. Dayan to Francis, April 23, 1835. HALB.
24. Herreshoff to Sarah Herreshoff, July 12, 1835. Herreshoff Collection, RIHS.
25. Richard Peters to Francis, July 22, 1835. HALB; Donaldson, Vol. I, p. 86.
26. Agreement between William L. Hirst and Francis. HALB.
27. Herreshoff to Sarah Herreshoff, November 15, 1835. Herreshoff Collection, RIHS.
28. Francis Seger to Francis, December 4, 1835. HALB.
29. John E. Hinman to Francis, December 7, 1835. HALB.
30. John Brown Francis agreement with Sarah Herreshoff, December 14, 1835. HALB.
31. Seger to Francis, December 30, 1835. HALB.
32. Cyrus Ela to Francis, December 31, 1835. HALB.
33. William Chapman White, p. 100. This is a good account of the writing about the Adirondacks.
34. James H. Rogers and Joseph Goulding to Francis, January 13, 1836. HALB.
35. Francis to William L. Marcy, March 14, 1836. HALB.
36. William L. Marcy to Francis, April 4, 1836. HALB.
37. George A. Hardin, *History of Herkimer County*, Syracuse, D. Mason & Co., 1893, p. 449.
38. Grady, p. 88. Other accounts: T. B. Thorpe, *A Visit to John Brown's Tract*, Harper's New Monthly Magazine, Vol. 19, June to November. New York, Harpers & Bros., 1859, p. 168; Donaldson, Vol. I, p. 123; Sylvester, p. 175; *Forest Commission*, p. 104.
39. Francis to Herreshoff, March 8, 1837. HALB.
40. Francis to Herreshoff, October 19, 1837; Charles Francis to John Brown Francis, August 1, 1837; Charles Francis to John Brown Francis, June 25, 1837. HALB.
41. Herreshoff to Anne Herreshoff, October 10, 1837. Herreshoff Collection, RIHS.
42. E. Varney to Francis, November 6, 1837. HALB.
43. J. W. Parkins to Francis, December 2, 1837. HALB.
44. J. W. Parkins to Francis, December 26, 1837. HALB.
45. Philip Shelpe to Francis, February 25, 1839. HALB.
46. Aber and King, p. 22.
47. Herreshoff to Anne Herreshoff, September 6, 1840. Herreshoff Collection, RIHS.
48. Lewis County Clerk, January 21, 1851, Liber 7/116.
49. Anne Herreshoff to family of Charles Frederick Herreshoff, January 8, 1841. Herreshoff Collection, RIHS.
50. Sarah Herreshoff to Herreshoff, March 27, 1841. Herreshoff Collection, RIHS
51. Vanuxem, p. 2.
52. *Gazetteer of the State of New York*, Albany, J. Disturnell, 1842, p. 27.
53. Francis to Henry D. Gilpin, January 18, 1846. HALB.

54. David Read to Herreshoff, January 5, 1847. Herreshoff Collection, RIHS.
55. Graham, p. 31; Snyder, p. 107.
56. Mary White to Francis, January 10 and 22, 1848. HALB.
57. Horatio Tracy to Francis, May 5, 1848. HALB.
58. Benjamin Cory to Francis, July 8, 1848. HALB.
59. *Chad Browne Memorial*, p. 105.
60. J. H. Van Benthuysen to Francis, July 25 and August 11 and 17, 1848. HALB.
61. Francis to William L. Hirst, October 20, 1848. HALB.
62. Rembrandt Wood to Francis, December 27, 1848. HALB.
63. Francis to Rembrandt Wood, January 19, 1849. HALB.
64. A. Barton Hepburn, *Artificial Waterways of the World*, New York, The Macmillan Co., 1914, pp. 147, 154.
65. Snyder, p. 107.
66. French, p. 38.
67. The Francis sale was recorded in the Lewis County Clerk's office at Lowville on March 26, 1850 in Liber 6, page 171 and in the Herkimer County Clerk's office in Herkimer on May 2, 1850 in Liber 58, page 157. The Herreshoff sale was recorded in the Lewis County Clerk's office on April 18, 1850 in Liber 6, page 198 and in the Herkimer County Clerk's office on May 4, 1850 in Liber 58, page 155. Abstract of title, John Brown Tract. Courtesy A. Richard Cohen.
68. This first transaction was recorded at the Lewis County Clerk's office on May 14, 1856, Liber 15, page 37. The second on January 30, 1865, Liber 28, p. 69, some years after John Brown Herreshoff's death. Abstract of title, John Brown Tract. Courtesy A. Richard Cohen.
69. Clarence L. Fisher, *History of Lyons Falls*, Boonville, N.Y., The Willard Press, 1918, p. 32.

BIBLIOGRAPHY

Abner, Ted and King, Stella, *The History of Hamilton County*. Lake Pleasant, N.Y.: Great Wilderness Books, 1965.

Alberts, Robert C., *The Golden Voyage, Life and Times of William Bingham 1752-1804*. Boston: Houghton Mifflin Company, 1969.

Allen, Samuel H., *The Federal Ascendency of 1812*. Providence: Narragansett Historical Register. October, 1889, p. 381.

Anderson, Robert, *Destination: Brown's Tract*. North Country Life, Winter 1963, pp. 3-8.

Arnold, James N., *Vital Record of Rhode Island 1636-1850*. Providence: Narragansett Historical Publishing Co., 1892.

Arnold, Samuel Greene, *History of the State of Rhode Island and Providence Plantations*. New York: D. Appleton & Company, 1859.

Balsh, Thomas, *Provincial History of Pennsylvania*. Philadelphia: Crissy & Markley, 1855.

Bayles, Richard M., *History of Providence County, Rhode Island*. New York: W. W. Preston, 1891.

Beetle, David H., *Up Old Forge Way*. Utica: Utica Observer-Dispatch, 1948.

Benton, Nathaniel S., *A History of Herkimer County*. Albany: J. Munsell, 1856.

Brown Family Bible. Providence: Herreshoff Collection, Rhode Island Historical Society.

Brown, Frank Hail, Speech, Dedication of John Brown Francis School, Warwick, R. I., October 15, 1952. Henry A. L. Brown Collection.

Brown, James, *1798 Almanac with holograph entries*. Providence: Rhode Island Historical Society collection.

Brown, James, *Diaries, 1787-1803*. The 1789-1789 diary was published by the Rhode Island Historical Society in Rhode Island History, Vol. VI, No. 4. October, 1947.

Brown, John, *John Brown's last will and Testament*. Recorded December 6, 1803. Providence: Rhode Island Historical Society Library.

Brown, John, *Letters to James Sheldon*. Utica: Oneida County Historical Society.

Brown, John, *Letters 1797-1803*. Providence: Rhode Island Historical Society.

Brown University, *Catalogus senatus Academici*. Providence: Knowles, Anthony & Co., 1856.

Bulkey, Abby Isabel, née Brown, *The Chad Browne Memorial*. Brooklyn, N.Y.: *Brooklyn Daily Eagle*, 1888.

Burt, Nathaniel, *The Perennial Philadelphians*. Boston, Toronto: Little, Brown and Company, 1963.

Carmer, Carl, *The Hudson*. New York, Toronto: Farrar & Rhinehart, 1939.

Carter, Samuel 3rd., *The Boatbuilders of Bristol*. Garden City, N.Y.: Doubleday & Co., Inc., 1970.

Chambers, W. and R., *Chambers Encyclopedia*. London: 1876.

Chesebrough, Caroline L. H., *Letters October-November 1894*. Providence: Brown University.

Child, Hamilton, *Gazetteer and Business Directory of Lewis County, New York*. Syracuse: *Syracuse Journal*, 1873.

Cohen, Linda, *A History of the Fulton Chain*. School paper by a member of the family that owns a substantial interest of the John Brown's Tract. Old Forge: undated.

Cole, G. Glyndon, *New York Life and New Tradition*. Saranac: Volume 17, Number 1, Winter 1963.

Conley, Patrick T., *Rhode Island Profile*. Providence: Rhode Island Historical Society, 1982.

Dayan, Charles. Broadside advertising 100,000 acres of the Brown Tract. 1821.

Donaldson, Alfred L., *A History of the Adirondacks*. 2 vols. New York: The Century Co., 1921.

Drew, Hazel C., *Tales from Little Lewis*. Lyons Falls, N.Y.: Privately printed, 1961.

Family Letters, Letters to and from members of the Brown, Francis, Herreshoff, Mason and Willing families in the possession of Henry A. L. Brown are filed chronologically.

Field, Edward, *Index to the Probate Records of the Municipal Court of the City of Providence, Rhode Island*. Providence: The Providence Press, 1902.

————, *Revolutionary Defences in Rhode Island*. Providence: Preston and Rounds, 1896.

————, *A History of the State of Rhode Island and Providence Plantations at the End of the Century*. Boston and Syracuse: Mason Publishing Co., 1902.

Fisher, Clarence L., *History of Lyons Falls*. Boonville, N.Y.: The Willard Press, 1918.

Fisher, Joshua Francis, *Recollections*. Boston: Merrymount Press, 1929.

Francis, John, *Diary 1783-1784*. Providence: Rhode Island Historical Society.

Francis, John, *Lisbon Journal 1783*. Providence: Rhode Island Historical Society.

Francis, John, *Journal 1787*. Providence: Rhode Island Historical Society.

Francis, John, *Diary 1789*. Henry A. L. Brown.

Francis, John, *English Journal 1792*. Providence: John Carter Brown Library.

Francis, John, *French Journal 1792*. Providence: John Carter Brown Library.

Francis, John Brown, *Brown Tract Diary 1816*. Henry A. L. Brown.

Francis, John Brown, *Brown Tract Diary 1817*. Henry A. L. Brown.

Francis, John Brown, *Brown Tract Diary 1818*. Henry A. L. Brown.

Francis, Thomas Willing, *Letterbook 1802-1807*. Henry A. L. Brown.

French, John Homer, *Gazetteer of the State of New York*. 1860.

Gazetteer of the State of New York. Albany: J. Disturnell, 1842.

Grady, Joseph F., *The Adirondacks*. Little Falls: Press of the Journal & Courier Company, 1933.

Graham, Frank Jr., *The Adirondack Park: A Political History*. New York: Alfred A. Knopf, 1978.

Greene, Welcome A., *The Providence Plantations*. Providence: J. A. & R. A. Reid, 1886.

Greenleaf, James Edward, *Genealogy of the Greenleaf Family*. Boston: Frank Wood, 1896.

Guild, R. A., *Historical Sketch of the Library of Brown University*. Providence: Brown University, 1861.

Haley, John W., *George Washington and Rhode Island*. Providence: Haley & Sykes Co., 1932.

Haley, John W., *The Old Stone Bank History of Rhode Island*. Providence: Providence Institution for Savings, 1939.

Hardin, George A., *History of Herkimer County*. Syracuse: D. Mason & Co., 1893.

Harlow, Alvin F., *Old Towpaths*. New York & London: D. Appleton & Co., 1926.

Hawke, David F., *Paine*. Evanston, San Francisco, London: Harper & Row, 1951.

Hedges, James B., *The Browns of Providence Plantations: Colonial Years*. Cambridge: Harvard University Press, 1952.

Hedges, James B., *The Browns of Providence Plantations: The Nineteenth Century*. Providence: Brown University Press, 1968.

Hepborn, A. Barton, *Artificial Waterways of the World*. New York: The Macmillan Company, 1914.

Herkimer County, History of. New York: F. W. Beers & Co., 1879.

Herreshoff, Charles Frederick, *Brown Tract Journal, September 6-November 30, 1818*. Henry A. L. Brown.

Herreshoff, Charles Frederick, *Letters 1785-1811*. Providence: Herreshoff Collection, Rhode Island Historical Collection.

Herreshoff, Charles Frederick, *Letters, 1807-1819*. Providence: John Carter Brown Library.

Herreshoff, John Brown, *Letters, 1820-1849*. Providence: Rhode Island Historical Society.

Herreshoff, John Brown, agent. Broadside advertising, *175,000 Acres of Land for Sale*. Lowville, N.Y.: W. L. Easton, 1830.

Hough, Franklin B., *A History of Lewis County*. Albany: Munsell & Rowland, 1860.
Johnson, Samuel, *Dictionary of the English Language*. London: 1770.
Kane, Hope F. and Roelker, W. G., *The Founding of the Providence Bank*. Providence: Rhode Island Historical Society Collections, Vol. 34, October No. 4, 1941.
Kauffman, Henry J., *Early American Ironware Cast and Wrought*. New York: Weathervane Books, 1966.
Keith, Charles P., *The Provential Councillors of Pennsylvania*. Philadelphia: 1883.
Kollenberg, Bernard, ed., *Correspondence of Governor Samuel Ward May 1775-March 1776 and Genealogy of the Ward Family*. Compiled by Clifford P. Monahon. Providence: Rhode Island Historical Society, 1952.
Konkle, Burton Alva, *Thomas Willing and the First American Financial System*. Philadelphia: University of Pennsylvania, 1937.
Lippincott's Gazetteer of the World. *A complete Pronouncing Gazetteer or Geographical Dictionary of the World*. Philadelphia: G. B. Lippincott & Co., 1883.
Lowville Academy. *Lowville Academy semi-centennial anniversary*. Lowville: Published by the home committee, 1859.
Malone, Dumas, *Jefferson and the Rights of Man*. Boston: Little, Brown and Co., 1951.
Mason, Alverdo Hayward, *Genealogy of the Sampson Mason Family*. East Braintree: 1902.
Masten, Arthur H., *The Story of Adirondac*. Syracuse: The Adirondack Museum/Syracuse University Press, 1968.
Mohr, Ralph S., *Rhode Island Governors for Three Hundred Years*. Providence: Oxford Press, 1959.
Morse, Jedidiah, *American Geography*. Boston: Thomas & Andrews, 1816.
New York Evening Post, *The Adirondacks in 1843*. *St. Lawrence Plaindealer*, August 24, 1881.
New York, State of. *List of Lands to be Sold in March, 1834 for Arrears of Taxes for the Years 1827, 1828, 1829, and 1830*. Albany, 1833.
New York, State of. *Annual Report of the Forest Commission for the Year 1893*. Albany: James B. Lyon, State Printer, 1894, 2 vols.
New York, State of. *Manual for the use of the Legislature*. Albany: Secretary of State, 1866.
New York, State of. *Message from the Governor to the Senate and Assembly*. Albany: January 5, 1836.
New York, State of. *Message from the Governor Senate No. 1*. Albany: January 7, 1834.
New York, State of. *Rates of toll, Canal Regulations, and Distances on the New York State Canalls*. Albany: 1832.
New York, State of. *Remarks of Mr. Segar, in committee of the whole, on the Black River Canal Bill In Senate*. Albany: March 21, 1837.
Nichols, B., *Atlas of Herkimer County, New York*. New York: J. Jay Stranahan & Beach Nichols, 1863. Reprinted 1977 by Martin Wehle, 46 Settle Road, Churchville, N.Y.
North American Land Company, Plan of association of the. Philadelphia: R. Aitken and son, 1795.
Oberholtzer, Ellis Paxson, *Robert Morris Patriot and Financier*. New York: Macmillan Company, 1903.
O'Brien, Clara V., *God's Country*. Sylvan Beach: North Country Books, 1982.
O'Donnell, Thomas C., *Snubbing Posts*. Boonville: Black River Books, 1949.
Overman, Frederick, *The Manufacture of Iron*. Philadelphia: Henry C. Baird, 1850.
Peale, C. W. Letter to John Francis, August 16, 1788. Private Collection.
Pennsylvania Magazine of History and Biography. *Captain Thomas Willing Francis*. Chapter 16. Page 82, January, 1925 Vol. 49. Philadelphia: Historical Society of Pennsylvania, 1925.
Pitcher, Lydia Herrick, *A Pioneer's Version of Life in Early Lewis County*. North Country Life, Winter 1950, pp. 25-29.

Pope, *The Poem of Eloisa to Abelard*. Philadelphia: Samuel Delap, 1775.
Powell, J. A., *Bring Out Your Dead: The Great Plague of Yellow Fever in Philadelphia in 1793*. New York: Time-Life Books, 1965.
Providence Daily Journal, June 12, 1871. Article about John Brown Francis. Signed only with initial "H". Page 1.
Providence Daily Journal. *The Great Storm September 23, 1815*. Providence: Volume 34, Number 225, September 23, 1863.
Providence National Bank. *The Providence National Bank One Hundred and Fiftieth Anniversary 1791-1941*. Providence, 1941.
Rogers, L. E. & Cheever, J. H., *The Biographical Cyclopeadia of Representative Men of Rhode Island*. Providence: National Biographical Publishing Co., 1881.
Rhode Island, State of. *Census of the Inhabitants of the Colony of Rhode Island and Providence Plantations 1774*. Providence: Secretary of State, John R. Barlett, 1858.
Rhode Island Historical Society Collections. *Point Pleasant William Vassall's Confiscated Estate*. Providence: Rhode Island Historical Society, Volume 17, No. 1, January, 1925.
Rhode Island History. *Mrs. Vice-President Dines with Mr. John Brown and Lady*. Providence: Rhode Island Historical Society, Vol. 1, No. 4, October 1942.
Rhode Island, State of. *Manual with Rules and Orders for the use of the General Assembly of the State of Rhode Island*. J. Fred Parker, Secretary of State, 1917.
Rhode Island Society for the Encouragement of Domestic Industry. *Transactions in the year 1861*. Providence: Knowles, Anthony & Co., 1862.
Roelker, W. G., *John Quinsey Adams Admires Mr. John Brown's House*. Providence: Rhode Island Historical Society, 1943. Rhode Island History Volume 2, October No. 4.
Shaw, Robert E., *Erie Water West, A History of the Erie Canal 1792-1854*. Lexington: University of Kentucky Press, 1966.
Sanderson, Edward, *Rhode Island Merchants in the China Trade*. Federal Rhode Island: The Age of the China Trade 1790-1820, Linda Levin, ed., pp. 38-55. Providence: Rhode Island Historical Society, 1978.
Simister, Florence P., *Rhode Island Exodus*. Rhode Island Yearbook Foundation, Inc., 1971.
Simister, Florence P., *The Fire's Center*. Providence: Rhode Island Bicentennial Foundation, 1979.
Skillin, Glenn B. ed., *In Search of Cahoone, the 1790 Diary of John Francis*. Boston: Old Time New England: The Bulletin of the Society for the Preservation of New England Antiquities, Vol. 60, No. 2, Fall 1969, pp. 55-71.
Sleicher, Charles Albert, *The Adirondacks: American Playground*. New York: Exposition Press, 1960.
Smith, Page, *John Adams*. Garden City: Doubleday & Co., 1962.
Snyder, Charles E., *John Brown's Tract*. Herkimer: Herkimer County Historical Society Transactions, An address delivered December 8, 1896, pp. 94-108.
Spafford, Horatio Gates, *A Gazetteer of the State of New York*. Albany: H. C. Southwick, 1813.
Spafford, Horatio Gates, *A Pocket Guide for the Tourist and Traveller along the Line of the Canals and the Interior Commerce of the State of New York*. New York: T. and J. Swords, 1824.
Stommel, Henry and Stommel, Elizabeth., *Volcano Weather*. Newport: Seven Seas Press, 1983.
Sumner, William Graham., *The Financier of the American Revolution*. 2 vols., New York: Dodd, Mead, and Company, 1891.
Swiggert, Howard., *The Extraordinary Mr. Morris*. Garden City: Doubleday & Co., 1952.

Sylvester, Nathaniel Bartlett, *Historical Sketches of Northern New York and the Adirondack Wilderness*. Troy, N.Y.: William H. Young, 1877.

Taft, Harrison S., *John Brown's House on the Hill*. Providence: Rhode Island Historical Society Collection, Vol. 34 October No. 4, 1941.

Thayer, William Roscoe, *Theodore Roosevelt*. Boston and New York: Houghton Mifflin Company, 1919.

Thistlethwaite, W. J., *The Romance of Old Forge*. Reprinted from the *Utica Daily Press*, December 8, 1915.

Thorpe, T. B., *A Visit to "John Brown's Tract". Harper's New Monthly Magazine*. Vol. 19, June to November. New York: Harper & Brothers, 1859.

Touret, Rosa Anne née Grosvenor, ed., *An American Family in the Nineteenth Century. Grosvenor Genealogy, Letters and Diaries*. Privately printed. Copyright 1973.

United States. Herkimer County, New York State Federal Population Census Schedules 1800-1810-1820. Cambridge, Mass.: Ralph V. Wood Jr., 1965.

Vanuxem, Lardner., *Geology of New-York*. Albany: W. & A. White and J. Visscher, 1842.

Watson, Elkanah., *History of the Rise, Progress and Existing Conditions of the Western Canals in the State of New York*. Albany: D. Steele, 1820.

Watt, Alexander., *Compendium of Practical Arithmetic, adapted to the Commerce of United States*. Philadelphia: T. T. Stiles, 1806.

Webster, Noah., *An American Dictionary of the English Language*. New York: Harper & Brothers, 1852.

White, William Chapman., *Adirondack Country*. Boston: Little, Brown & Co., 1954.

Williams, Ben Ames Jr., *Bank of Boston 200*. Boston: Houghton Mifflin Company, 1984.

Williams, Richard L., *The Haunted Colony. Adirondack Life*. Winter-January/February 1977, pp. 44-46.

Wright, Marion I. and Sullivan, Robert, *The Rhode Island Atlas*. Providence: Rhode Island Publications Society, 1982.

Young, Eleanor, *Forgotten Patriot Robert Morris*. New York: Macmillan Company, 1950.

Illustrations and Credits

Although the majority of the illustrations in *John Brown's Tract* came from either the archives of the Rhode Island Historical Society or the private collection of Henry A. L. Brown, the Society and the authors are deeply grateful to all others who provided material specifically for this volume. In the following list the abbreviated title of each illustration is followed by the delineator's or photographer's name when available, the source, and the page number on which it appears. The Rhode Island Historical Society is abbreviated RIHS and Henry A. L. Brown HB.

Index

John Brown's Tract

*has been published in a first edition
of three thousand copies.
Designed by A. L. Morris
the text was composed in Paladium
and printed by Sherwin/Dodge, Printers,
in Littleton, New Hampshire on Warren Antique Text.
The endleaves were printed on Curtis Tweedweave Text
and the binding in James River Kivar and Holliston Roxite
was executed by New Hampshire Bindery
in Concord, New Hampshire.*

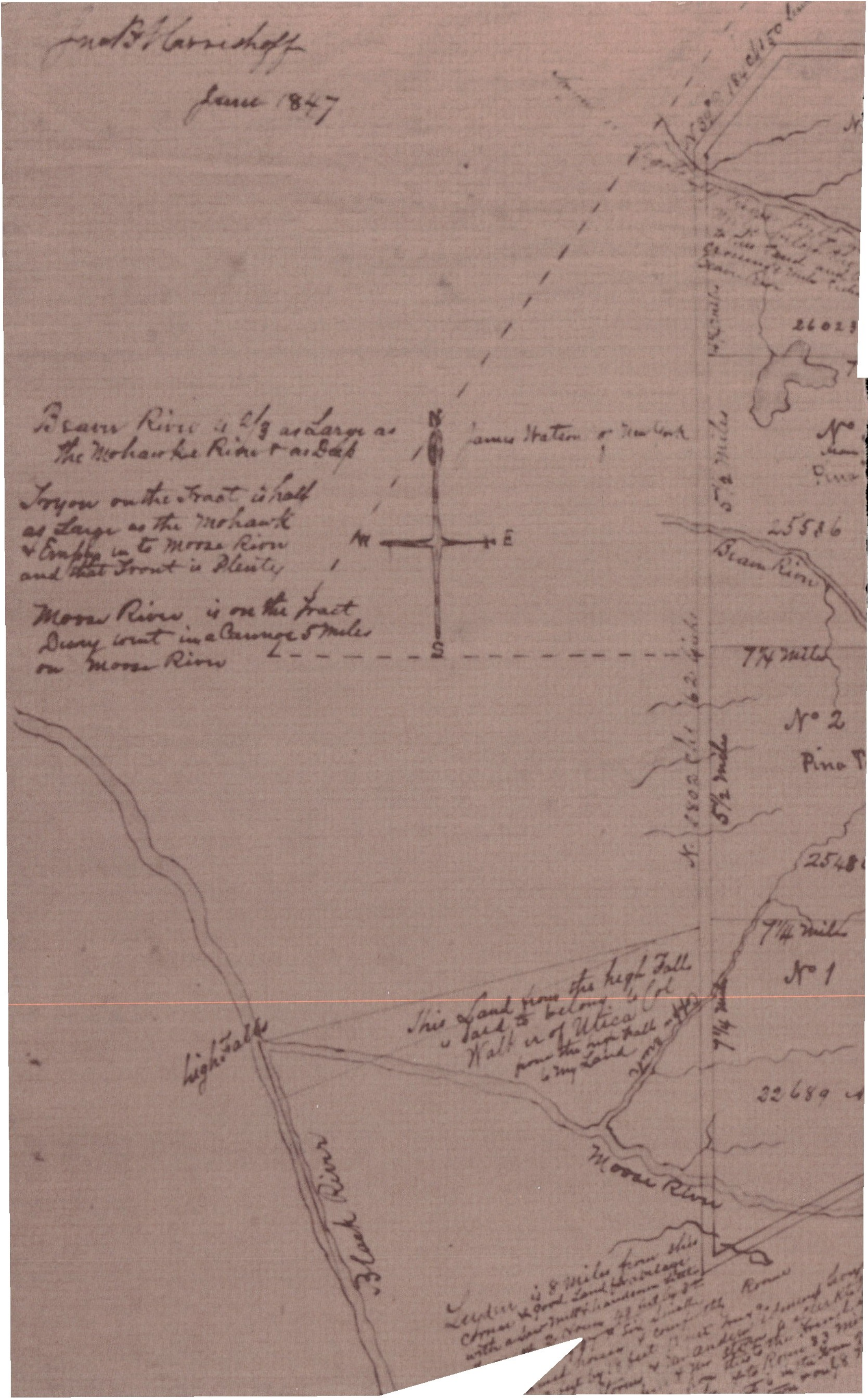
June 1847
Beaver River is 2/3 as Large as the Mohawk River & as Deep
Moose River is on the Tract
on Moose River
James Watson of New York
N
S
E
W
25586
Beaver River
7 1/4 Miles
5 1/2 Miles
No 2
No 1
7 1/4 Miles
22689
This Land from the high Falls to belong to Col Walker of Utica
High Falls
Black River
Moose River